Fraser MacDonald is a lecturer in Human Geography at the University of Edinburgh.

Rachel Hughes is a lecturer in Human Geography at the University of Melbourne.

Klaus Dodds is Professor of Geopolitics at Royal Holloway, University of London.

INTERNATIONAL LIBRARY OF HUMAN GEOGRAPHY

Series ISBN: 978 1 84885 223 5

See www.ibtauris.com/ILHG for a full list of titles

1. *Egypt: An Economic Geography*
Fouad N. Ibrahim and Barbara Ibrahim
978 1 86064 548 8

1. *Egypt: An Economic Geography*
Fouad N. Ibrahim and Barbara Ibrahim
978 1 86064 547 1

2. *The Middle East Water Question: Hydropolitics and the Global Economy*
Tony Allan
978 1 86064 582 2

3. *Cultural Geography: A Critical Dictionary of Key Concepts*
David Atkinson, Peter Jackson, David Sibley and Neil Washbourne (Eds)
978 1 86064 703 1

4. *The Cognition of Geographic Space*
Rob Kitchin Mark Blades
978 1 86064 704 8

4. *The Cognition of Geographic Space*
Rob Kitchin Mark Blades
978 1 86064 705 5

5. *Picturing Place: Photography and the Geographical Imagination*
Joan M. Schwartz and James R. Ryan
978 1 86064 751 2

6. *Pink Ice: Britain and the South Atlantic Empire*
Klaus Dodds
978 1 86064 769 7

7. *Human Capital: Population Economics in the Middle East*
I. Sirageldin (Ed).
978 1 86064 795 6

8. *Culture and Space: Conceiving a New Cultural Geography*
Joel Bonnemaison Introduction by John Agnew
978 1 86064 907 3

8. *Culture and Space: Conceiving a New Cultural Geography*
Joel Bonnemaison Introduction by John Agnew
978 1 86064 908 0

9. *Globalization and Identity: Development and Integration in a Changing World*
Edited by Alan Carling
978 1 85043 848 9

10. *Challenging the NGOs: Women, Religion and Western Dialogues in India*
Tamsin Bradley
978 1 84511 152 6

11. *Traditional Buildings: A Global Survey of Structural Forms and Cultural Functions*
Allen Noble
978 1 84511 305 6

12. *Geography and Vision: Seeing, Imagining and Representing the World*
Denis Cosgrove
978 1 85043 846 5

13. *Muslims on the Map: A National Survey of Social Trends in Britain*
Serena Hussain
978 1 84511 471 8

14. *The World Water Crisis: The Failures of Resource Management*
Stephen Brichieri-Colombi
978 1 84511 753 5

15. *High Places: Cultural Geographies of Mountains, Ice and Science*
Denis Cosgrove and Veronica della Dora (Eds)
978 1 84511 616 3

16. *Observant States: Geopolitics and Visual Culture*
Fraser MacDonald, Rachel Hughes and Klaus Dodds (Eds)
978 1 84511 944 7

Observant States
Geopolitics and Visual Culture

Edited by
Fraser MacDonald, Rachel Hughes
and Klaus Dodds

I.B. TAURIS
LONDON · NEW YORK

Published in 2010 by I.B.Tauris & Co. Ltd
6 Salem Road, London W2 4BU
175 Fifth Avenue, New York NY 10010
www.ibtauris.com

Distributed in the United States and Canada Exclusively by Palgrave Macmillan,
175 Fifth Avenue, New York NY 10010

Selection and editorial matter copyright © 2010 Fraser MacDonald, Rachel Hughes and Klaus Dodds

Individual chapters © 2010 Louise Amoore, Judith Butler, David Campbell, Sean Carter, James Der Derian, Klaus Dodds, Emily Gilbert, Stephen Graham, Rachel Hughes, K. Neil Jenkings, Timothy W. Luke, Fraser MacDonald, Derek P. McCormack, Marcus Power, Alison J. Williams, Trish Winter and Rachel Woodward

The right of Fraser MacDonald, Rachel Hughes and Klaus Dodds to be identified as the editors of this work has been asserted by them in accordance with the Copyright, Designs and Patents Act 1988

ISBN: 978 1 978 84511 9 447 (hb)
      978 1 978 84511 9 454 (pb)

A full CIP record for this book is available from the British Library
A full CIP record is available from the Library of Congress

Library of Congress Catalog Card Number: available

Designed and Typeset by 4word Ltd, Bristol, UK
Printed and bound in India by Thomson Press India Ltd

Contents

Acknowledgements vii
List of Contributors ix

Introduction Envisioning Geopolitics 1
                Fraser MacDonald, Rachel Hughes and Klaus Dodds

Part One **Representation**

Chapter 1 Imaging Terror: Logos, Pathos and Ethos 23
                James Der Derian

Chapter 2 Torture and the Ethics of Photography 41
                Judith Butler

Chapter 3 'Not to be Missed' Weapons of Mass Destruction:
                Displaying the *Enola Gay* 65
                Timothy W. Luke

Chapter 4 Flying the Flag: Pan American Airways and the
                Projection of US Power Across the Interwar Pacific 81
                Alison J. Williams

Part Two **Performance**

Chapter 5 Affectivity and Geopolitical Images 103
                Sean Carter and Derek P. McCormack

Chapter 6	Gameworld Geopolitics and the Genre of the Quest *Rachel Hughes*	123
Chapter 7	'I Used to Keep a Camera in My Top Left-Hand Pocket': The Photographic Practices of British Soldiers *Rachel Woodward, Trish Winter and K. Neil Jenkings*	143
Chapter 8	The Scopic Regime of 'Africa' *David Campbell and Marcus Power*	167

Part Three Observant Practice

Chapter 9	Combat Zones that See: Urban Warfare and US Military Technology *Stephen Graham*	199
Chapter 10	Eye to Eye: Biometrics, the Observer, the Observed and the Body Politic *Emily Gilbert*	225
Chapter 11	Vigilant Visualities: The Watchful Politics of the War on Terror *Louise Amoore*	247
Chapter 12	Perpendicular Sublime: Regarding Rocketry and the Cold War *Fraser MacDonald*	267

Notes 291
Index 299

Acknowledgements

Although not a direct outcome of a conference, this collection has benefited from a session at the 2007 annual meeting of the Association of American Geographers (AAG), organised by Rachel Hughes, Fraser MacDonald and David Campbell. We are grateful to the Political Geography Study Group of the AAG for their sponsorship; to David Campbell and James Sidaway for acting as discussants; and to all the other presenters in that session: Gearóid Ó Tuathail, Scott Kirsch and Joseph Palis, Richard Carter-White and Philip Hatfield.

Some of the essays in this collection were originally published in journals and we are grateful to the publishers for permission to reproduce them here. James Der Derian's chapter was originally published in *Third World Quarterly* (Vol. 26.1). Judith Butler's essay was presented as the *Environment and Planning D: Society and Space* lecture at the AAG in San Francisco on 19 April 2007 and published in that journal (Vol. 25). Louise Amoore's chapter originally appeared in a special issue of *Security Dialogue* (Vol. 38.2), edited by David Campbell and Michael J. Shapiro. Other chapters are, to a greater or lesser extent, revisions of essays previously published: Timothy W. Luke's discussion of the *Enola Gay* first appeared in *Arena Journal*; versions of Stephen Graham's chapter first appeared in David Lyon's *Theorizing Surveillance* (2006) and in *War – Citizenship – Territory*, edited by Deborah Cowan and Emily Gilbert; Fraser MacDonald's chapter is a distillation of a paper published in *Transactions of the Institute of British Geographers* (Vol. 31.1).

Lastly, our thanks to Eleanor Collins for her editorial assistance and to David Stonestreet for supporting the project.

Contributors

Louise Amoore is Reader in the Department of Geography, Durham University, UK.

Judith Butler is Maxine Elliot Professor in the Departments of Rhetoric and Comparative Literature at the University of California, Berkeley, USA.

David Campbell is Professor of Cultural and Political Geography at Durham University, and an Associate Director of the Durham Centre for Advanced Photography Studies, UK.

Sean Carter is a lecturer in the School of Geography at the University of Exeter, UK.

James Der Derian is Professor of International Studies and Political Science at the Watson Institute for International Studies at Brown University, Providence, USA.

Klaus Dodds is Professor of Geopolitics at Royal Holloway, University of London, UK.

Emily Gilbert Director of the Canadian Studies Program and Associate Professor in Geography at the University of Toronto, Canada.

Stephen Graham is Professor of Cities and Society at the School of Architecture, Planning and Landscape, Newcastle University UK.

Rachel Hughes is a lecturer in Human Geography at the University of Melbourne, Australia.

K. Neil Jenkings is a senior researcher at the Institute of Health and Society and at the School of Geography, Politics and Sociology, at Newcastle University, UK.

Timothy W. Luke is University Distinguished Professor of Political Science at Virginia Polytechnic Institute and State University in Blacksburg, Virginia, USA.

Fraser MacDonald is a lecturer in Human Geography at the University of Edinburgh, UK.

Derek P. McCormack is University Lecturer in Human Geography at the School of Geography and Environment, University of Oxford, UK.

Marcus Power is Reader in the Department of Geography, Durham University, UK.

Alison J. Williams is an ESRC academic research fellow at the School of Geography, Politics and Sociology, Newcastle University, UK.

Trish Winter is a senior lecturer in film at the University of Sunderland, UK.

Rachel Woodward is Reader in Critical Geography at the School of Geography, Politics and Sociology, Newcastle University, UK.

Introduction

Envisioning Geopolitics

Fraser MacDonald, Rachel Hughes and Klaus Dodds

Let us start with an example that is, in a disciplinary sense, close to home. The academic geographer Professor Ghazi-Walid Falah at the University of Akron, Ohio, a well-known Palestinian writer on geopolitics, was arrested on 8 July 2006. He had been asked by a passer-by what he – an Arab – was doing taking a photograph of the landscape at the popular Israeli tourist resort of Nahariya, not far from the Lebanese border. Taking photographs is an ordinary activity for geographers as it is for tourists. Indeed, to the extent that geography is sometimes considered a visual discipline, this association ought to apply equally to the fieldwork of our colleagues in Israel and the Occupied Territories. For the Israeli police, and subsequently the Israeli Secret Police, Shin Bet, Ghazi's possession of a camera – or rather his being an Arab in possession of a camera – was grounds for arrest under suspicion of espionage; his detention without trial; and his solitary confinement, interrogation and sleep deprivation (see Falah 2007). Three weeks later, after an international campaign by his colleagues, Ghazi was released without charge, but not before repeated interrogations in which his scholarship was presented to him as evidence that he was 'a terrorist, a spy and [a] hater of Israel'. Without going into the many issues that this case brings to light, there is surely something remarkable that for the Israeli state – not known for its timidity in developing systems of the most far-reaching surveillance – a camera in a tourist destination can be read as the sign of a spy. The sovereign state that is so noted for its propensity to use photographic identification as evidence of citizenship is itself strangely camera-shy. It is no surprise, then, that the motto of Shin Bet should turn out to be: 'the defender who shall not be seen' (in Hebrew: יראה אלו מגן).

The fear of a rival gaze to that of the state is a persistent one. Questions of who is eligible to see or be seen, whose details and behaviour can be visually recorded and reproduced are also, at the same time, matters of mobility and fixity, liberty and incarceration, opportunity and struggle, citizenship and statelessness. It is of tangential interest to note that one response to Israel's surveillance and public relations infrastructure has been 'inverse surveillance' activities: for instance, the Israeli human rights group B'Tselem has overseen the distribution of over 100 video cameras to Palestinians in the West Bank in order to film abuses by Israeli settlers and the military. The resulting footage has the capacity to render visible realities which are known but seldom acknowledged; and to make them visible is, in our present era, to enter them into the calculus of geopolitical negotiation. So when a teenage girl in the West Bank filmed an Israeli soldier shooting baton rounds at close range at a blindfolded Palestinian detainee, the video clip, uploaded onto the internet, could initiate a minor scandal.[1] Notably, however, it was not enough to have merely witnessed such an event first-hand; there must be an accompanying record, a stubborn visual trace such that selected elements of the past can be seen again in the future, perhaps by more credible observers. The early positivist origins of photography are of course evident here, as if this imprint of light on film or pixel bears the mark of irrefutable truth – *yes, this really happened* – what Roland Barthes referred to as 'authentification itself' (Barthes 1981: 5). Not that the status of the photographic image is beyond dispute; on the contrary, as this book will make clear, contesting the authenticity of images is now part and parcel of contemporary statecraft.

If these examples seem rather particular, they plainly transcend both their regional setting and the technological specificity of photography. The Israeli occupation and its resistance are by no means the most obvious instance of conflicts in which questions of visuality are paramount. Indeed, one of the arguments of this book is that geopolitics and visual culture have become co-constitutive. It seems that the conduct of war and peace (if indeed these can be individuated), as well as the competition of state sovereignty through diplomacy, is being transformed by our increasing dependence on the visual to comprehend and represent the world around us. Even the very meaning of 'war' and 'peace' has itself been challenged by the power of visual media. As the very different visibilities of, say, Srebrenica and September 11 make clear, geopolitics has to some extent become a question of how particular episodes become figured in visual culture. For to render an event visible is also, in some sense, to catalogue it for public commemoration. While the photograph has long been the basic semantic unit of modern media, the digital proliferation of images and visual data has opened up entirely new ways for political entities to envision and be envisioned. In one sense to talk of a 'visual culture' we must also acknowledge a 'visual economy', a particular settlement of late capitalism in which the production, transmission and consumption of images has become one of the enabling conditions of everyday life for citizen and state alike (Poole 1997; Campbell 2007; Rose 2008). At the same time, however, the significance of what it means to see – and how this problem is folded into contemporary sovereignty – is a bigger question still.

One possible approach to this topic, albeit not one that is not followed in this collection, might detail the giddying diversity of forms, technologies, genres and practices in which visual culture is folded into geopolitical events. This could show, for instance, how photographic and video technologies have been used by both state and non-state actors to address the symbolic needs of combatants and their supporters; to collect surveillance data and to direct missiles to their targets; to provide reportage on the conduct of war; to contest the legitimacy of that war; and to memorialise both military and civilian casualties. One could conduct a detailed visual exegesis of, say, television news; military-themed video games; embedded photo-journalism; Internet sites such as *You Tube*; the so-called 'martyr' videos; cartographic representations, from Geographical Information Systems (GIS) to the Olympian satellite visions of Google; popular cinema; 'high' art; closed-circuit television (CCTV); bio-surveillance techniques such as retinal scanning; all the way through to relatively mundane and domestic technologies such as Microsoft PowerPoint or mobile camera-phones. The list is endless and some of these topics are considered in the essays that follow; others are already the subject of emerging critical scholarship.[2]

This book, however, makes no such attempt at being comprehensive in its treatment. Rather, it takes as its project the more fundamental aim to think more broadly about the meaning and status of visuality in relation to geopolitical practice. We do this at a time when 'visual studies' is itself a well-established field of study, complete with its own university programmes, nominated chairs and academic journals. And yet it is worth reiterating a point made 30 years ago by John Berger when he wrote of:

a widespread assumption that if one is interested in the visual, one's interest must be limited to a technique of somehow treating the visual. Thus the visual is divided into categories of special interest: painting, photography, real appearances, dreams and so on. And what is forgotten – like all essential questions in a positivist culture – is the meaning and enigma of visibility itself. (Berger 1980: 41)

So rather than simply rehearsing the many modalities of the visual, the book attempts to think critically and creatively about what visuality means, how it is put to work, to what end, and with what technical apparatus. While we are often concerned with images, our interest settles on more slippery questions of how visibility (and sometimes *in*visibility) is achieved. What sort of power does it express or enact? And with what geopolitical consequences? We make no claim that this line of enquiry is entirely original. A few recent essays have outlined the parameters for a more systematic investigation into the relationship between geopolitics and visual culture (MacDonald 2006; Campbell 2007; Hughes 2007; Shapiro and Campbell 2007). We are confident that this book takes the discussion a bit further.

One of the underlying themes of the book is that contemporary geopolitical reasoning often relies on a presentation of visual evidence. Geopolitical truths are established, and geopolitical realities enacted, through a process of visual demonstration. This association between visuality and truth-telling strikes at the epistemological heart of Western modernity: W.J.T. Mitchell reminds us that there is a close association between the idea *of* vision and the idea *as* vision, the very term 'idea' having its etymological roots in the Greek verb 'to see' (Mitchell 1986). In the most mundane of sentences in the English language – 'I see' – there is an alignment of vision (the eye) with the Cartesian *cogito* (the 'I') to signify rationale knowledge (Cosgrove 2003: 249). So to visualise something in this traditional model is to know it, to believe it and, ultimately, to verbalise it. But one does not have to adhere to this conception of the visual – and we prefer a messier, affect-orientated understanding of visuality – in order to think about how the visual domain has come to influence (rather than determine) the practice of statecraft. One might go as far as to argue that staging, imaging, surveillance, simulation, display and so on have become some of the foremost activities of state in a bid to sustain or acquire power through the cogency of the visual. Moreover, in our current era, the state has no monopoly in directing visual action.

Geopolitics and the visual grammar of persuasion

An obvious point of reference is the image-event of September 11. (Why, we might ask, should this be obvious?) We have no interest in affirming this date as a pivot of history. On the other hand, it would be disingenuous to pass over the barbarous sublimity of the attacks, an episode which is original not in terms of its scale, nor in its technics, nor even in the indiscriminate targeting of its victims, but primarily in terms of what we might call its 'graphic design'. To think of September 11 in such terms is not simply to aestheticise it, despite the perhaps understandable confusion that surrounded Karlheinz Stockhausen's controversial remark that the World Trade Center attack was 'the biggest work of art there has ever been'.[3] We do not need to set aside our revulsion at the act in order to note the depth of consideration given to what we might call the 'visual grammar' of display. In using such a phrase we loosely draw on a semiotic tradition that thinks of images, like language, as producing certain sorts of regularities that in turn make certain sorts of statements (see Kress and van Leeuwen 2006). Such statements, while by no means always coherent, nevertheless aim to be persuasive: to mobilise political action through the affect of the visual.

Regardless of the intent behind the attacks, the events of September 11 and its aftermath can be understood as part of the visual grammar of persuasion put to work by different (state and non-state) actors, but which in some sense sit apart from – and in excess of – the ordinary frame of rhetoric. Indeed, the image of these burning monuments would become so securely established as the seemingly unanswerable justification for the wars in Afghanistan and Iraq that, even when other rationales came and went (weapons of mass destruction, WMD; terror and the 'axis of evil'; regime change; 'freedom and democracy'), the visual memory of September 11 remained obligingly fresh. 'History breaks down into images, not into stories', as Walter Benjamin famously put it. And this 'indelible image-trail' persisted, according to the Retort Collective, precisely because in the succeeding weeks it became taboo to replay the footage, as if this 'image-defeat' was itself the scandalous kernel of the event. It seems apposite then that they should refer to September 11 as 'an occurrence in a war of images' (Retort 2005: 25). Nicholas Mirzoeff takes a similar view when he argues that 'images have become weapons in the military-visual economy' (Mirzoeff 2004: 13). But rather than focusing our emphasis on images – an iconology or an iconography – we prefer to think of visuality in its broadest guise. We think of visuality as both indivisible from a wider bodily sensorium and as being inevitably implicated in the world of words. As Jacques Rancière has noted:

> the image is not exclusive to the visible. There is visibility that does not amount to an image; there are images that consist wholly in words. But the commonest regime of the image is one that presents a relationship between the sayable and the visible, a relationship which plays on both the analogy *and* dissemblance between them. (Rancière 2007: 7; original emphasis)

Subsequent episodes in the unhappy aftermath of September 11 reveal quite different modalities of the visual, but which nonetheless cannot be lightly conflated with 'images'. The 'war of images' is more accurately a war of visuality, a contest over what can be seen and, significantly, what must be occluded or veiled.

Veiling and unveiling

Something of all this is evident in the events of 5 February 2003, the day that US Secretary of State Colin Powell appeared before the UN Security Council (UNSC) in a failed bid to get international authorisation for the war on Iraq.[4] On the day before this meeting, UN officials were instructed to cover the copy of Picasso's *Guernica* – with its stark depictions of the carnage from Nazi bombing during the Spanish Civil War – which is usually on display at the entrance to the Security Council.[5] Arguing that a more appropriate backdrop was required for press conferences on the war, UN officials were told by the State Department to cover the art with a blue cloth, which would in turn be covered with flags. The politics of this veiling should be set in a wider context. The Bush administration's previous war in Afghanistan had, among other things, been fought over a certain *un*veiling: the ostensible 'liberation' of Afghan women from the burqa, the removal of which had become a visual shorthand for the anticipated triumph of 'our' (Western) values over 'their' (Islamic) religious fundamentalism. (The burqa was confronting to the West not least because it made it impossible to see the face of the Other, while in no way impeding 'their' looking at 'us'.) 'Veiling', writes the psychoanalytic writer Justin Clemens, 'is simultaneously a political declaration (our way of life against theirs!) and a sexual operation (dividing the polity internally) and, precisely because the veil is torn between division and exclusion, we're never quite happy with its disposition' (Clemens 2004). In this way, the discomfiting politics and 'excessive modesty' of the burqa became one of the symbols of the war on terror, embodying the hopes and ambitions (not to say contradictions) of Western liberalism.

An episode from the heart of American neo-conservatism provides another counter-veiling example to the discarded burqa. In January 2002, just as the first US soldiers were being killed in Operation Enduring Freedom, US Attorney General John Ashcroft ordered that a partially nude female statue in his Justice Department, the *Spirit of Justice*, be veiled with blue curtains. For a Pentecostal Christian, the sight of bare breasts was considered inappropriate for a room in which press conferences were held. A similar disavowal was made by the usually less buttoned-up Italian prime minister, Silvio Berlusconi, who recently hired a painter to clothe an intrusive breast in Giovanni Battista Tiepolo's *The Truth Unveiled by Time*, which hung in his palace press room (Hooper 2008). Journalists alert to Berlusconi's tortuous dance around corruption charges could not help but notice that the political force of the painting – 'naked truth' – was tellingly inverted if the subject was anything other than resplendent. First justice, then truth! The politics of the veil in the halls of state might seem an obscure entry point to our theme, but it is precisely in these seemingly minor adjustments that the elaborate maintenance of the state's self-image can be glimpsed. Drawing a curtain over *Guernica* likewise corresponds with the prevailing optic of the entire Iraq conflict – one in which the immediate confrontation of carnage is displaced by the obdurate force of the flag.

If *Guernica* needed to be covered up for this event, then the dramatic unveiling of other images would take centre stage at the UNSC. The most dominant visual for those present in the chamber was surely the mural painted by the Norwegian artist Per Krogh, an optimistic picture of a phoenix rising from the ashes of World War II, which towers over the circular meeting table. In press coverage of the event, however, Krogh's painting is almost entirely cropped. Though physically dwarfed by the mural, we are given close-ups of Powell and the two screens on which were projected the most famous PowerPoint presentation to date. In the multi-layered operations of this 'slideware' technology, with its sequential revelation, older regimes of display such as photography and cartography are reworked with new persuasive effects. Microsoft PowerPoint has been available for 20 years and the extent of its embeddedness in the communications infrastructure of business, government and education makes it a worthy topic for scholars of the visual. But the fact that it was the primary component of Powell's *casus belli* is a remarkable example, we would argue, of the ways in which the logic of geopolitical reason is now inseparable from its visual representation. The significance of PowerPoint is not just that it helps a presenter make a case, but in some sense this software makes its own case.[6] Powell's staff at the State Department may not have used the marvellously titled 'AutoContent Wizard' to conjure Saddam's WMD, but they nevertheless work within the linear limits of the PowerPoint template. Edward Tufte, a graphic artist and well-known commentator on data presentation, has argued that PowerPoint embodies a particular cognitive style characterised by a

> foreshortening of evidence and thought, low spatial resolution, an intensely hierarchical single-path structure as the model for organizing every type of content, breaking up narratives and data into slides and minimal fragments, rapid temporal sequencing of thin information ... and a smirky commercialism that turns information into a sales pitch. (Tufte 2006: 4)

In addition to Tufte's critique of PowerPoint's formal qualities, there are other aspects to Powell's presentation that, as human geographers, strike us as being particularly noteworthy. Take, for instance, the centrality of remote sensing – satellite surveillance images – offered as evidence of Iraq's apparently elaborate efforts to disguise their WMD programme (see slide opposite). Many of these slides combine a cartographic aerial perspective with the authority of the photograph to produce a document which, in its very form, sanctions its own claims. The 'critical cartography' turn in geography, inaugurated by the late J.B. Harley, would subject these slides to a detailed visual exegesis of the sort that we cannot undertake here (Harley 1989). But for the moment let us note the disjuncture in the slide between the evidential qualities of the different elements of the slide on the one hand and Powell's rather dramatic interpretation on the other. In order to bridge this gap, some simple captions identify each component in the picture even if no evidence is offered to support this naming. Preceding the slide is Powell's assurance that 'every statement I make today is backed up by sources, solid sources. These are not assertions. What we're giving you are facts and conclusions based on solid intelligence' (Powell 2003).

Of this particular slide, Powell tells the audience that 'the two arrows indicate the presence of sure signs that the bunkers are storing chemical munitions ... the truck you ... see is a signature item. It's a decontamination vehicle in case something goes wrong.'[7] A memo from his own staff in the State Department, commenting on a draft of this speech and later quietly

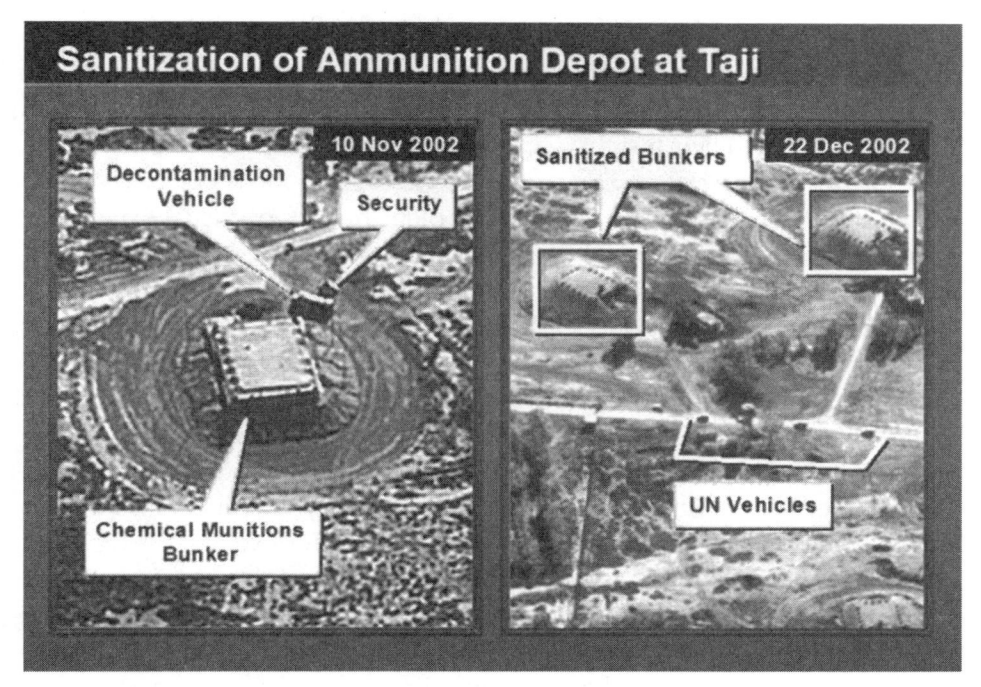

A slide from Colin Powell's PowerPoint presentation to the UN Security Council, 5 February 2003.
Source: US State Department, reproduced with permission

released as an appendix to the Senate Intelligence Committee's report on WMD intelligence,[8] noted:

> decontamination vehicles – cited several times in the text – are water trucks that can have legitimate uses ... Iraq has given UNMOVIC what may be a plausible account for this activity – that this was an exercise involving the movement of conventional explosives; presence of a fire safety truck ... is common in such an event.

What is interesting here is that these slides present no *prima facie* evidence as such. Instead Powell tells the audience *how* to see what his administration desires: implicitly, 'let the arrows stand in as evidence and we can all see the same thing'. If these signs of chemical munitions were indeed sure, then the arrows and captions would be largely superfluous. The arrows exist to veil the unsure sign.

It seems that what we get from Powell are a set of visual instructions – protocols for looking. Here we should mention the pioneering ethnomethodological work of Eric Laurier and Barry Brown, who argue against the idea, so prevalent in the visual studies literature, that sight is the cognitive skill of a lone individual; rather they conceive of vision as the learned outcome of particular communities of practice (Laurier and Brown, In press). Their insight helps us think of Powell's presentation as an attempt to instruct the audience in a particular way of seeing. And in so doing, the PowerPoints also draw on an older history of visual experience in the UNSC chamber. David Stark and Verena Paravel show how Powell builds on Adlai Stevenson's presentation to the UNSC at the height of the Cuban Missile Crisis of 1962 (Stark and Paravel 2008). Stevenson's dramatic revelation of the presence of Soviet missiles in Cuba, as shown on both maps and grainy images from U-2 spy planes, was a humiliation for his counterpart Valerian Zorin and a diplomatic coup for Washington. Where Stevenson used an easel, Powell had PowerPoint to recreate the same persuasive effect – the 'Stevenson moment', as Lawrence Wilkerson, Powell's chief advisor, called it. Stark and Paravel reveal the extent to which the 2003 presentation invokes its successful antecedent. A film of Stevenson's Cuban Missile Crisis presentation was watched by the senior staff at the State Department prior to preparing the PowerPoint. The satellite photographs which were originally transmitted in colour were even shown in black and white to evoke Stevenson's grainy monochromes from the U-2.[9] In this way, then, we want to think of looking itself as a profoundly social act, with diachronic depth and affective potentialities. Powell's performance, together with the blunt captioning and carto-photographic authority of his PowerPoints, evoked the persuasive Stevenson moment with mixed success. While the bid for UN authorisation ultimately failed, many US Senators, including most prominent Democrats, lined up to support Powell. The *Washington Post* felt the evidence was 'irrefutable', while the *New York Times* called it 'the most powerful case to date'. Unlike the materials on Stevenson's easel, however, Powell's file could be globally circulated within seconds – part of what Stark and Paravel call PowerPoint's 'geography of persuasion' – which in turn, of course, opens up the evidence to much wider scrutiny.

Stagecraft and statecraft

What we have been arguing then is that to render certain events more or less visible through the operation of the veil or the screen is to submit them to the calculus of geopolitical negotiation. From the unspeakable horror of corpse mountains at Auschwitz to the personification of suffering in the figure of a nine-year-old girl at My Lai, photography in particular has marked out certain events in the twentieth century as public scandals, which in turn call into question the geopolitical context that produced them. Who can forget the tank-defying protester in Tiananmen Square or, in more recent times, the iconic sadism of Abu Ghraib? In all of these instances, photographs implicitly indict a sovereign state. The role of the state is, of course, to evade such indictments of itself while advancing similar charges against its rivals. A truly successful image in these terms would envision the demise of the sovereign Other. The contrivance of US soldiers to topple the statue of Saddam Hussein outside Baghdad's Palestine Hotel, then home to the world's media, is a case in point. Here the apparently spontaneous uprising of 'the people' – albeit hand-selected people, bussed in by US soldiers – to displace the unyielding figure of Saddam turned into a clumsy bit of White House theatre. Close-up images of 'ordinary Iraqis' jumping on Saddam's head became a live global televisual spectacle, despite the fact that wide-angled photographs of this scene, rarely shown in the mainstream media, revealed the reality of a very sparse gathering. And yet even here, where the stakes could hardly be higher, the choreography of statecraft was marked by inept improvisation rather than by its close scripting. In a strange correlate of the many other veils – the burqa; 'the hooded man' of Abu Ghraib; and the execution hood that Saddam ultimately refused – an American soldier engulfed the statue's head with the Stars and Stripes.[10] *People* magazine went on to describe this rather optimistically as an 'Iwo Jima moment', referring to the iconic photograph of the flag being raised after a key battle on this Pacific island (another version frames New York firefighters holding aloft the flag in the rubble of the World Trade Center). But the making of an icon is surprisingly difficult. Successful stagecraft requires a scene that can tell the right story, can be sufficiently charismatic to be newsworthy and can also efface the conditions of its own production (see Hariman and Lucaites 2007). This last criteria is particularly difficult to achieve, as President George W. Bush's 'Top Gun' performance also revealed.

If this presidential cameo is well known, it is largely because it now seems like a joke in poor taste. On the 1 May 2003, George Bush, clothed in a flight suit, stepped out of a fighter jet to give a speech on board the *USS Abraham Lincoln*, under a banner which read 'Mission Accomplished'. Despite the fact that the Navy aircraft carrier was moored only 39 miles off the San Diego coast – and not, as many believed, in the Persian Gulf – the White House initially insisted that it was too far to travel by helicopter. It certainly required a director's eye to ensure that while the coast could not be visible in the media's camera footage, there would be a flattering evening light to bathe the President as he announced the end of combat operations in Iraq. Much has already been made of this event and its associative play with Tom Cruise in the 1986 movie *Top Gun* (Lukinbeal 2004). Though not without precedent, the fact that a presidential press conference should draw on the tropes of popular cinema in an attempt to project military power is still quite remarkable (see Power and Crampton 2007). But even a little Hollywood magic was not enough to mask the obvious fact that this war was not over: more than 96 per cent of coalition casualties have occurred since 'Mission Accomplished'. Given the indivisibility of the reel and the real, it would not be surprising if the Pentagon hoped that some sort of narrative closure might itself enact a cessation of hostilities.

The flip side of this geopolitical spectacle, and a major component of stagecraft, is the even greater endeavour to pre-empt the 'wrong' images. The logistical effort of the USA in this regard is Herculean, from the control over 'embedded' reporters, to the Defense Department prohibition on picturing even the coffins of US servicemen, to the blocking of Internet sites such as *You Tube* for serving US soldiers, to the campaigns, both propagandist and military,[11] against independent news outlets such as *Al-Jazeera*. At the heart of all this there is a sense of the photographic image as a trickster: while often dismissed as inconsequential, it is at the same time regarded as having an immanent transformative power, iconoclasm and idolatry being invariably entwined. Recalling Donald Rumsfeld's concern that photos of Abu Ghraib might define American nationhood, Judith Butler observes that 'the state operates on the field of perception and more generally, on the field of representability, in order to control affect, and in anticipation of the way that affect informs and galvanizes political opposition to the war'. For Butler, the state defines this field of representability by 'what is cast out and maintained outside the frame', a simultaneous 'jettisoning and presenting'. All of this suggests that scholars of the visual must not only conduct detailed exegetical work on particular images, but also, as importantly, have an analytic attentiveness to the operation of the frame itself and even to its enabling technologies.

When the Islamic Republic of Iran inexpertly used Adobe Photoshop to doctor photographs of their *Shahab* missile testing – cloning an 'exhaust signature' to cover for a missile that failed to launch – it prompted an international chorus of ridicule. One correspondent to the *New York Times* website warned that while the Ahmadinejad regime had long wanted to wipe Israel off the map, 'now they have the Photoshop capability to do it'. Such a visible adjustment of the frame was enough to turn a demonstration of power into an apparent revelation of defeat. It would be wrong to view this as a merely an awkward blunder; so inseparable is geopolitical power from the integrity of its visual representation, that a careless piece of editing can be a more serious breach of Iran's security than a malfunctioning missile. If the primary purpose of the missile is as a monument to power that can be seen, then the malfunction is also at the level of representation. And it is at this scale – we might say, pixel by pixel – that analytical work is necessary.

Representation, performance, observant practice

In our discussion so far we have been dealing largely with the relationship between visuality and what is often called 'practical' geopolitics: with the ways in which visual culture has become part of the apparatus of persuasion. Many of the essays in this collection work with (and indeed across) the commonly made distinction between 'formal', 'practical' and 'popular' geopolitics. In this model, formal geopolitics represents the conceptual labour of traditional geopolitical actors such as academics and think tanks; practical geopolitics is concerned with the operation of foreign policy; and popular geopolitics refers to the expression of geopolitical power through popular culture and everyday life rather than through channels of ruling elites. It is a useful division, first outlined in the work of Gearóid Ó Tuathail, whose 1996 book *Critical Geopolitics: The politics of writing global space* remains an important milestone in thinking about the co-constitution of geopolitics and visual culture. In such pillars of geopolitical thought as Fredrich Ratzel, Nicholas Spykman and Halford Mackinder, Ó Tuathail identified what he saw as an 'ocularcentric' conception of international relations that was grounded in the philosophy of Cartesian perspectivalism. John Agnew makes a similar claim about the centrality of perspective to the geopolitical tradition (Agnew 2006). For Ó Tuathail, the gaze of the geopolitical theorist – configured through a Cartesian binary between an 'in here' mind/self/consciousness and an 'out there' world of objects – is constructed as neutral and disembodied and, by implication, blind to issues of personal subjectivity.[12] In Spykman's famous phrase, 'geopolitics does not argue; it just is'.

It is clear that Ó Tuathail's interest in visuality was primarily as a metaphor for the failure of geopolitical theorists to be aware of their own agency as writers in the scripting of global space. In a review of *Critical Geopolitics*, Michael Heffernan lamented the absence of 'any serious analysis of precisely how specific visual images have been deployed within Western geopolitics' (Heffernan 2000: 348). Ó Tuathail's reply acknowledges the promise of such work at the same time as insisting on the 'graphemetic' character of writing itself (Ó Tuathail 2000: 390). This claim amounts to more than Rancière's line that 'there are images that consist wholly in words'; Ó Tuathail makes the important but relatively neglected point that writing is itself a form of visual culture that institutes particular ways of seeing (see, for instance, Campbell and Power's chapter, Chapter 8). So while the emphasis in this collection is different from Ó Tuathail's original establishment of geopolitics and visuality as relata, it seems to us that both his position, and that of his critics, can be usefully held in productive tension. We differ from Ó Tuathail in that we think of vision first and foremost as a perceptual practice. Where we would go further than Heffernan, as will already be clear, is to insist on a consideration of visuality in general rather than an iconology in particular. We have done this by organising the volume around three key overlapping themes: 'representation', 'performance' and 'observant practice'. These themes are in turn opened up through discussions of quite different geopolitical practices. Given Ó Tuathail's emphasis on 'formal geopolitics', we have instead chosen essays which largely, but not exclusively, attend to popular and practical geopolitics.

Part 1 of *Observant States* is concerned with the power of images and image-making. As we have seen in relation to September 11, the visibility of acts for or against the state becomes the enabling condition for certain forms of geopolitical action. Representation is therefore not just a static 're-presenting', but a process which activates that which it purports to show. The human geographer Nigel Thrift has been scathing of what he sees as the narrow 'representationalist' concern of critical geopolitics: he regards it as having been 'taken in' by representation with our 'mesmerized attention to texts and images' (Thrift 2000: 385, 381). Thrift's call for a greater attentiveness to what he calls 'the little things' is undoubtedly reshaping the object of critical geopolitical enquiry, as is evident in some of the essays in this book. But we hope that this collection will go some way to help dispel the caricature of representation and its critique as being static and lifeless. James Der Derian's chapter, for instance, is concerned with how certain mimetic practices and a particular logic of representation lie at the heart of the war on terror. To the extent that the popular iconography of terror lends itself readily to a glib moralising by both ends of the political spectrum, Der Derian calls for a return to a reinvigorated semiotics. Judith Butler's essay is concerned less with representation per se than with how the 'representability' of the human is permitted, or not, by particular frames which are themselves occluded. Tim Luke addresses the paradoxical invisibility of WMD, narrating two stories about representational practices or what one might call the 'geopolitics of curatorship'. He explores the correspondences between the search for Iraq's missing ordinance and the dilemmas of how to exhibit *Enola Gay*, the delivery vehicle for the world's first atomic bomb. Alison Williams considers how the territorial ambitions of the state have historically been linked with its ability to visualise. She examines the projection of US geopolitical power across the Pacific Ocean through the representational forms and civilian agency of Pan American Airways.

There is a risk, of course, that the tripartite structure of the book might 'flatten' those chapters which speak to all three themes; we must therefore stress the conceptual reciprocity between sections. While in our second part our contributors are still concerned with the power of representation, their emphases falls more heavily on how representational practices – such as film, photography and digital games – enact geopolitical formations. In these essays particular regimes of the visual are conceived in terms of their performativity: various subject positions (citizen, soldier, state) are shown to be constituted through ordinary discursive, affective and gestural improvisations and repetitions (see also Bialasiewicz et al 2007).

The role of affectivity in cinema (and cinema in affectivity) is explored by Sean Carter and Derek McCormack. In their discussion of three contemporary films – *The Thin Red Line* (1998), *Three Kings* (1999) and *United 93* (2006) – they argue that thinking of 'affectivity as non-representational does not necessarily encourage us to attend less to the politics and geopolitics of images'; rather 'it encourages us to ... think differently about what images are ... what images can do within and through contemporary geopolitical cultures'. In her chapter, Rachel Hughes explores the resonance between digital gaming and geopolitical practice, arguing that it is not only war-themed games that support or resist geopolitical power. Tracing the genre of the quest through both the popular action-adventure game Tomb Raider and a variety of contemporary geopolitical situations, she identifies a 'gameworld geopolitics' in which non-state agents undertake the search for talismanic objects.

That representations have discursive geopolitical effects is a key concern of much of the literature on popular geopolitics. Much less common, as Gillian Rose has recently argued, is an awareness of the role of representation in the construction of subject positions (Rose 2008: 3). In this context, the chapter by Rachel Woodward, Trish Winter and Neil Jenkings explores how the figure of the soldier and the practice of soldiering is performed through informal amateur photography. The scale of David Campbell and

Marcus Power's enquiry is wider. Their focus is on 'Africa' as an historically specific suite of imagery – a particularly entrenched 'scopic regime' – that marshals various technologies of observation, reproduction and display into a frame that delimits the 'performance of perceptible places'. Across a range of media from colonial literary pictorialism to contemporary digital gaming, they undertake a theoretically expansive and empirically rich reworking of the term 'scopic regime'.

The final section considers visuality in its most literal and empirical sense, as a situated and embodied practice of looking. If this emphasis seems entirely obvious it is remarkable how little work in visual culture, until recently at least, has been concerned with vision as a practical business. The influence of three quite different writers informs our inclusion of this theme. In the first instance we are mindful of John Berger's analysis that to look at an object or a person is to construct the relationship that exists between things, people and ourselves. 'We only see what we look at', he wrote. 'To look is an act of choice. As a result of this act, what we see is brought within our reach' (Berger 1972: 8). Secondly, Tim Ingold's insistence on the connective rather than discrete character of the human senses raises for us the necessity of more empirical work on vision as an embodied perceptual practice (Ingold 2000; see also Laurier and Brown 2008). Thirdly, there is W.J.T. Mitchell's influential critique of visual culture which declares that 'the supposed "hegemony of the visible" ... is a chimera that has outlived its usefulness' (Mitchell 2005: 349).[13] For all the hyperbole about the proliferation of screens, the viral abundance of images and the 'rule of appearances', we do not believe that we are living in an age that is somehow 'more visual' than before. Rather the challenge for visual studies is to discern how our sensory engagements are distinctively correspondent to particular forms of sociality. This means, among other things, that we need to think more literally about what it means to see and how looking takes place.

We draw these strands together under the rubric of 'observant practice', a term which we hope carries our commitment to thinking of vision as a constantly rehearsed extra-ocular competency (see MacDonald 2006, 2009). Such an emphasis in turn brings to bear distinctive expressions of geopolitical power. In this analysis, the simple act of, say, looking at a flag or refusing to 'see' political violence become constitutive of geopolitical subjectivities. There are, it seems, ways of looking which are compliant and mutinous, appropriate and inappropriate, respectful and scornful, safe and dangerous. Nikita Khrushchev's famous disavowal of Stalin, in his speech to the 20th Congress of the Soviet Communist Party, turned on his characterisation of Uncle Joe as 'sickly suspicious' precisely because 'he could look at a man and say: "Why are your eyes so shifty today?" or "Why are you ... avoiding to look me directly in the eyes?"'. At Potsdam in 1945, US President Truman was reassured by the way that Stalin 'looked him straight in the eye' (Truman 1973: 268). Observant practice is thus the precondition for geopolitics rather than simply the means by which power is apprehended or experienced. The act of looking is an act of the state as well as of the individual, using various visual technologies from the integrated military systems of detection and targeting that Graham describes, to the biometric scanning of civilians at airports that is the subject of Emily Gilbert's chapter. In both these cases the perceptual faculties of individual bodies are increasingly being transferred to machines in order to provide a more comprehensive means for the state to both regulate its own citizens and pre-emptively anticipate external threats. The specific relation between sight and sovereignty is the subject of Louise Amoore's chapter. She asks whether vision has been conceived not only as the primary sense (an ocularcentrism), but also as the *sovereign* sense through which the legitimacy of the state can be secured. She goes on to explore a specific mode of visuality, a 'watchful politics', that has been called into being during the war on terror. Lastly, Fraser MacDonald extends the discussion of observant practice through a story about a schoolboy desire to see one of the emblematic sights of the twentieth century: the ascent of a rocket into space. Such mundane acts of looking, he argues, were part of the ordinary citational practices through which the Cold War took shape. At the heart of this story, as in all the chapters in this book, lies the still under-examined nexus between bodies, senses and states (Manning 2006). This volume, we hope, suggests that it is worth a second glance.

Bibliography

Agnew, John, *Geopolitics: Re-visioning World Politics* (London, 2006).
Amoore, Louise, 'Vigilant visualities: The watchful politics of the war on terror', *Security Dialogue* 38.2 (2007), pp.215–32.
Barthes, Roland, *Camera Lucida* (New York, 1981).
Berger, John, *Ways of Seeing* (London, 1972).
Berger, John, *About Looking* (New York, 1980).
Bialasiewicz, Luiza, Campbell, David, Elden, Stuart, Graham, Stephen D.N. and Williams, Alison J., 'Performing security: The imaginative geographies of current US strategy', *Political Geography* 26 (2007), pp.405–22.

Campbell, David, 'Horrific blindness: Images of death in contemporary media', *Journal for Cultural Research* 8(1) (2004), pp.55–74.
Campbell, David, 'Geopolitics and visuality: Sighting the Darfur conflict', *Political Geography* 26.4 (2007), pp.357–82.
Campbell, David and Shapiro, Michael, 'Guest Editors' Introduction', *Security Dialogue* [Special Issue on 'Securitization, militarization and visual culture in the worlds of post-9/11'] 38.2 (2007), pp.131–7.
Carter, Sean and McCormack, Derek, 'Film, geopolitics and the affective logics of intervention', *Political Geography* 25 (2006), pp.228–45.
Christensen, Christian, 'Uploading dissonance: YouTube and the US occupation of Iraq', *Media, War and Conflict* 1.2 (2008), pp.155–75.
Clemens, Justin, 'The purloined veil: Notes on an image', (a) 4.1 (2004), pp.75–88.
Dodds, Klaus, 'Steve Bell's eye: Cartoons, geopolitics and the visualization of the war on terror', *Security Dialogue* 38.2 (2007), pp.157–77.
Dodds, Klaus, ' "Have you seen any good films lately?" Geopolitics, international relations and film', *Geography Compass* 2:2 (2008), pp.476–94.
Falah, Ghazi, 'The politics of doing geography: 23 days in the hell of Israeli detention', *Environment and Planning D: Society and Space*, 25 (2007), pp.587–93.
Graham, Stephen, *Cities, War and Terrorism: Towards an Urban Geopolitics* (Oxford, 2004).
Griffin, Michael, 'Picturing America's "War on Terrorism" in Afghanistan and Iraq photographic motifs as news frames', *Journalism* 5.4 (2004), pp.381–402.
Hafez, Mohammed M., 'Martyrdom mythology in Iraq: How jihadists frame suicide terrorism in videos and biographies', *Terrorism and Political Violence* 19.1 (2007), pp.95–115.
Hariman, Robert and Lucaites, John Louis, *No Caption Needed: Iconic Photographs, Public Culture, and Liberal Democracy* (Chicago, 2007).
Harley, J.B., 'Deconstructing the map', *Cartographica* 26.2 (1989), pp.1–20.
Heffernan, Michael, 'Balancing visions: Comments on Gearóid Ó Tuathail's *Critical Geopolitics*', *Political Geography* 19 (2000), pp.347–52.
Hooper, John, 'Truth, lies and Berlusconi: Italy's playboy premier accused of nudity cover-up', the *Guardian*, 4 August 2008, http://www.guardian.co.uk/world/2008/aug/04/italy.art (accessed 5 August 2008).
Hughes, Rachel, 'Through the looking blast: Geopolitics and visual culture', *Geography Compass* 1.5 (2007), pp.976–94.
Kitchin, Rob and Dodge, Martin, 'Rethinking maps', *Progress in Human Geography* 31.3 (2007), pp.331–44.
Kress, Gunther and van Leeuwen, Theo, *Reading Images: The Grammar of Visual Design* (London, 2006).
Laurier, Eric and Brown, Barry, 'Cultures of seeing: Pedagogies of the riverbank' (in press), http://www.geos.ed.ac.uk/homes/elaurier/texts/seeing_fish.pdf (accessed 9 September 2008).
Lentricchia, Frank and McAuliffe, Jody, *Crimes of Art + Terror* (Chicago, 2003).
Luke, Tim and Ó Tuathail, Gearóid, 'On videocameralistics: The geopolitics of failed states, the CNN International and (UN) governmentality', *Review of International Political Economy* 4.4 (1997), pp.709–33.

Lukinbeal, Chris, 'The map that precedes the territory', *GeoJournal* 59 (2004), pp.247–51.
MacDonald, Fraser, 'Paul Strand and the Atlanticist Cold War', *History of Photography* 28.4 (2004), pp.356–73.
MacDonald, Fraser, 'Geopolitics and the vision thing: Regarding Britain and America's first nuclear missile', *Transactions of the Institute of British Geographers*, 31.1 (2006), pp.53–71.
MacDonald, Fraser, 'Social and cultural geography: Visuality', in R. Kitchin and N. Thrift (eds), *International Encyclopaedia of Human Geography* (London, 2009).
Manning, Erin, *Politics of Touch: Sense, Movement, Sovereignty* (Minneapolis, 2006).
Mirzoeff, Nicholas, *Watching Babylon: The War in Iraq and Global Visual Culture* (London, 2005).
Mitchell, W.J.T., *Iconology: Image, Text, Ideology*, (Chicago, 1987).
Mitchell, W.J.T., *What Do Pictures Want? The Lives and Loves of Images* (Chicago, 2005).
Ó Tuathail, Gearóid, *Critical geopolitics: The Politics of Writing Global Space* (Minneapolis, 1996).
Ó Tuathail, Gearóid, 'Dis/placing the geo-politics which one cannot not want', *Political Geography* 19 (2000), pp.385–96.
Parks, Lisa, 'Points of departure: The culture of US Airport screening', *Journal of Visual Culture* 6.2 (2007), pp.183–200.
Parks, Lisa, 'Digging into Google Earth: Humanitarian intervention in the digital age', *Geoforum* (in press).
Pickles, John, *A History of Spaces* (London, 2004).
Power, Marcus and Crampton, Andrew, *Cinema and Popular Geo-Politics* (London, 2007).
Rancière, Jacques, *The Future of the Image* (London, 2007).
Retort, *Afflicted Powers: Capital and Spectacle in a New Age of War* (London, 2005).
Rooney, Ben, 'PowerPoint of view', the *Guardian*, 7 February 2003, http://www.guardian.co.uk/technology/2003/feb/07/comment.comment (accessed 16 August 2008).
Rose, Gillian, 'Who cares for which dead and how? British newspaper reporting of the bombings in London, July 2005', *Geoforum* online early: doi:101016/j.geoforum.2008.01.002 (2008).
Ryan, James R., 'Visualising imperial geography: Halford Mackinder and the colonial office visual instruction committee, 1902–1911', *Ecumene* 1.2 (1994), pp.157–76.
Stahl, Roger, 'Have you played the War on Terror?', *Critical Studies in Media Communication* 23.2 (2006), pp.112–30.
Stark, David and Paravel, Verena, 'Powerpoint in public: Digital technologies and the new morphology of demonstration, *Theory, Culture and Society* 25.5 (2008), pp.30–55.
Thrift, Nigel, 'It's the little things', in K. Dodds and D. Atkinson (eds), *Geopolitical Traditions: A Century of Geopolitical Thought*, Routledge (London, 2000), pp.380–7.
Truman, Margaret, *Harry S. Truman* (New York, 1973).
Tufte, Edward, *The Cognitive Style of PowerPoint: Pitching Out Corrupts Within*, second edition (Cheshire, 2006).

Part One

Representation

Chapter 1

Imaging Terror: Logos, Pathos and Ethos

James Der Derian

Introduction: The logos of terror

> Imagination is not a gift usually associated with bureaucracies.
> (The 9/11 Commission Report 2004, p.344)

Two framed artefacts of the second Cold War hang on either side of my desk (Figures 1.1 and 1.2). The first is a simple black and white poster made in 1985, most likely inspired by President Reagan's description of the Afghan *mujahideen* as freedom fighters. Next to a photograph of Reagan is one of a New York City firefighter. The caption underneath asks: 'A firefighter fights fires. A freedomfighter fights _____?'

The second image comes from a 1985 issue of *The Manipulator*, a shortlived, large-format art magazine. On the cover is a Nancy Burston photograph titled 'Warhead 1', a digitised composite of world leaders proportioned according to their country's nuclear weapons, in which the facial features of Reagan (55 per cent of the world's throw-weight) and Brezhnev (45 per cent) dominate the fuzzier visages of Thatcher, Mitterrand and Deng (less than 1 per cent each).[1]

These two images speak volumes, revealing the grammar that underwrites the *logos*, *pathos* and *ethos* of terror. As verb, code and historical method, terrorism has consistently been understood as an act of symbolically intimidating and, if deemed necessary, violently eradicating a personal, political, social, ethnic, religious, ideological or other wisely radically differentiated foe. Yet, as noun, message and catch-all political signifier, the

Figure 1.1 Photograph of 1985 poster advertising 'Reflections on terrorism', an installation by Les LeVeque, New York City.
Source: Author's own photograph

Figure 1.2 Photograph of a 1985 cover of *The Manipulator*, featuring an artwork by Nancy Burston titled 'Warhead 1'.
Source: Author's own photograph

meaning of terrorism has proven more elusive. From Robespierre's endorsement to Burke's condemnation during the French Revolution, from the Jewish Irgun blowing up the King David Hotel to the Palestinian Black September massacre at the Munich Olympics, from bin Laden the Good fighting the Soviet occupiers of Afghanistan to bin Laden the Bad toppling the Twin Towers of New York, terrorism, terrorists and terror itself have morphed into the political pornography of modernity: one knows 'terrorism' with certainty only when, literally, one sees it. But in a blink of the eye, the terrorist can become the freedom fighter and vice versa, for at one time or another nearly everyone, from righteous statesmen who terror-bomb cities to virtuous jihadists who suicide-bomb women and children, seems to have a taste for terror.

Without engaging in nostalgia, one can recognise that the most powerful form of terror mutated at the end of the Cold War. With the decline (if not the total demise) of a logic of deterrence based on a nuclear balance of terror, so too eroded the willingness and capacity to inflict mutually unacceptable harm that had provided a modicum of order if not peace or justice to the bipolar system. In its place a new *imbalance of terror* has emerged, based on a mimetic fear and hatred coupled with an asymmetrical willingness and capacity to destroy the other without the formalities of war (Der Derian 2001). This cannot be reduced, as much as leaders on both sides of the conflict have tried, to merely a post-9/11 phenomenon. It can doctrinally be traced at least as far back to 1998, when the US Defense Policy Guidance shifted from a strategy of *deterring* to *destroying* the enemy (subsequently reiterated in the 2006 Quadrennial Defense Review), and when bin Laden issued his 1998 pseudo-*fatwa*, which decreed Christian and Jewish civilians legitimate targets of the *jihad*.

As in the older, tidier balance of terror, the doctrine of taking civilians hostage and if necessary killing them still held for both sides, but it now operated as a contingent factor of an asymmetrical relationship. Regardless of nomenclature – 'terror' or 'counter-terror' – high numbers of civilians would (and continue to) be killed in the process. It might be small solace to the victims whether they were primary targets as opposed to 'accidental' or 'collateral' victims, especially with casualty rates being terribly skewed in both cases. When one takes into account how war-related fatalities have been reversed in modern times, from 100 years ago, when one civilian was killed per eight soldiers, to the current ratio of eight civilians per soldier killed, then compares the combatant-to-non-combatant casualty figures of 9/11, the Afghan War and the Iraq War, the terror/counter-terror distinction begins to fade even further. Perhaps it is time for a new Burston composite, using the leaders of these three conflicts to proportionally represent the number of civilian casualties.

With weapons systems, war-fighting doctrine and war games often wagging the dog of civilian policy, the narratives as well as the paladins of the Cold War seem destined to an eternal return in US foreign policy. Having mapped this phenomenon before 9/11, I wish to focus on what has changed since then (if anything), and to understand the celerity and alacrity by which our age has now been defined by terrorism (Der Derian 2001). Although the fundamentalist religious and political beliefs of the major combatants have attracted the most attention, I think we need to pay more attention to the multiple media, which transmit powerful images as well as help to trigger highly emotional responses to the terrorist event. Thanks to the immediacy of television, Internet and other networked information technology, we *see* terrorism everywhere in real time, all the time. In turn, terrorism has taken on an iconic, fetishised and, most significantly, a highly *optical* character. After witnessing the televised images of kamikaze planes hitting the World Trade Center, the home videos of bin Laden, the Internet beheading of Nicholas Berg, we were all ready, perhaps too ready, to agree with President Bush: 'Evil now has a face.'

However, somewhere between the Pyrrhic victory of Tora Bora and the disastrous post-war of Iraq, the face of terror began to morph into a new

Burstonian composite. The 'Terrorist' can now easily do double-duty as an airport security profile, featuring the chequered keffiyeh of Arafat, the aquiline nose of Osama bin Laden, the hollowed face of John Walker Lindh, the maniacal grin of Saddam Hussein, the piercing eyes of Abu Musab Zarqawi ('He could direct his men simply by moving his eyes', said Basil Abu Sabha, his Jordanian prison doctor). The historicity, specificity and even the comprehensibility of terrorism have been transmogrified by the new holy and media wars into a single physiognomy of global terror.

Of course, our image of terror did not arrive by itself or on its own. Just as every image comes with an explicit or implicit caption – what Roland Barthes (1977, 1982), the gifted semiologist, referred to as the 'anchorage', which seeks to fix the 'polysemy' of the sign – so too is the war on terror freighted with the narratives of the Cold War. Moreover, the legacy of the Cold War lives on through popular culture, a 'fact' ably noted by a Hollywood actor who knows a thing or two about the morbidity of comebacks. Playing a 'C-fuckin'-I-A agent' doubling as a Gulf War arms dealer, up against FBI straight man (another constant in national security culture) Willem Dafoe, Mickey Rourke colourfully notes, in the easily forgettable 1992 film *White Sands*, how the dead continue to weigh on the living:

> This isn't about sides. This is about confusion. This is about creating enemies when there aren't any. And, man, the whole Goddamn world's falling apart. Peace reigns, freedom reigns, democracy rules. How are we gonna' keep the military-industrial complex chugging forward without clear-cut, pit-faced, scum-sucking evil breathing down our neck? Hmmm? Threatening our very shores. Now my job is to make sure the other side keeps fighting; whatever side – I mean whatever side we're officially not on this year.

Seen in this light, the war on terror is not new, but part of a permanent state of war by which the sovereignty of the most powerful state is reconstituted through the naming of terrorist foe and anti-terrorist friend.

There are lessons to be learned from an earlier interwar – one that is beginning to look too much like our own – in which two media critics, *avant la letter*, first confronted this new matrix of art, politics and terror. Walter Benjamin (1969) took his first measure of film production in his celebrated essay 'The work of art in the age of mechanical reproduction', taking note of how mechanically reproduced art, especially film, could be especially useful to if not generative of Fascism. Quoting the Futurist

Marinetti, he highlights the ease by which an aestheticised politics can mobilize a population for foreign wars without endangering domestic property relations:

> War is beautiful because it establishes man's dominion over the subjugated machinery by means of gas masks, terrifying megaphones, flame throwers and small tanks. War is beautiful because it initiates the dreamt-of metallization of the human body ... War is beautiful because it creates new architecture, like that of the big tanks, the geometrical formation flights, the smoke spirals from burning villages, and many others ... Poets and artists of Futurism! ... remember these principles of an aesthetics of war so that your struggle for a new literature and a new graphic art ... may be illumined by them! (Benjamin 1969, pp.241–2)

The aesthetic of the reproducible image overpowered the aura and authenticity of the original. In *The Arcades Project*, Walter Benjamin (1999) further developed his study of a Rankean realism that hitherto had underwritten much of geopolitical discourse: 'The history that showed things "as they really were" was the strongest narcotic of the century.' He went on to declare that 'history decays into images, not into stories'. Benjamin had a very specific definition in mind for the image, calling it 'that wherein what has been comes together in a flash with the now to form a constellation'; or, as he more simply put it, 'dialectics at a standstill'. The surfeit of images in modernity necessitated a new mode of interpretation and representation: the montage, or 'the art of citing without quotation', in which 'truth is charged to the bursting point with time'. His diagnosis and prescription has once again become valid.

Benjamin's interwar acumen had an equal in Siegfried Kracauer. Observing the immense popularity of Berlin's new picture palaces, Kracauer thought the Berliners had become 'addicted to distraction'. 'To call them movie theaters', he said, 'would be disrespectful'. He referred to them as 'optical fairylands', where 'distraction – which is meaningful only as improvisation, as reflection of the uncontrolled anarchy of the world – is festooned with drapes and forced back into a unity that no longer exists'. In Kracauer's view the picture palaces served as a kind of Hegelian asylum from Weimar disorder, ornate spaces where the alienated Berliner could seek reunification through what he called a 'cult of distraction'. The medium might have changed, but with Fox, CNN and MSNBC the message stays the same: out of chaos, a new order.

The pathos of terror

We 'moderns' might now recognise the increasing power of images over words, but we have been slower to understand the consequences as they have increasingly taken on a pathological character in the war on terror. By now the attack on the World Trade Center towers, guaranteed a visual capture by the 18-minute gap between the air strikes, has been burned into the collective unconscious with looped viewings and repetitious commentary. However, it will probably not be cognitively understood, like all trauma, until we experience a second occurrence. In contrast, there has been limited viewing and even sparser appreciation of the director's commentary on his horror film, the infamous bin Laden tapes.

At first viewing, the bin Laden home videos understandably yielded a fairly uniform and deserved response of outrage in the USA and Europe. However, not just in the Middle East but in parts of the USA with large Arab populations, such as Dearborn, Michigan and Los Angeles, questions were soon raised about their authenticity. The doubts can be understood in Benjamin's terms, of the loss of aura from the original produced by technical reproducibility, but multiplied many times by the convergence of the Age of Terror and Adobe Photoshop, or what I have referred to as the Age of Infoterror.[2] It reflects as well an increasingly global view that Hollywood, Silicon Valley and Washington, DC have joined forces in the war on terror.

For those who might detect a whiff of conspiracy in such claims, a short history of events after 9/11 might be instructive. By early October 2001, White House advisers had already begun a series of meetings with directors, producers and executives from the entertainment industry on how Hollywood might best help the war effort. To be sure, an alliance between the military and the entertainment industry was not entirely new. The mixing of spectacle and war goes back to the beginnings of film, when D.W. Griffith, already famous for his 1915 *Birth of the Nation*, went to work for Lord Beaverbrook's War Office in World War II (Virilio 1983). However, there was some cause for worry with this new overture. My own concern was first triggered at the opening of the innocuous-sounding 'Institute for Creative Technologies' (ICT), which I covered for *Wired* magazine in 1999. The ICT was set up at the University of Southern California (USC) to spearhead a remarkable project: with US$43 million provided by the US Army, it would combine the virtual reality tools of Silicon Valley and the talent of Hollywood film studios to produce state-of-the-art military simulations for future war. On the day of the opening one speaker after another, from the Secretary of the Army to the Governor of California, spoke of 'making the quantum leap to the Army After Next'; 'creating virtual environments for total immersion of participants'; and my favourite, 'engrossing stories stocked with emotional characters who may either be simulated or manned'. Jack Valenti, head of the Motion Picture Association, opened his remarks by correcting a previous speaker: 'Los Angeles is not the "entertainment capital of the world", [pause] Washington, DC, is the entertainment capital of the world. [laughter]'

I expressed my concern at the opening ceremony in the form of a question to Steven Sample, President of USC: Might not the linking up of Hollywood and the Pentagon repeat the World War II experience, when training films were mixed with propaganda films and military simulations became a tool for public dissimulations? Were there any ethical checks and balances to assure that ICT would not produce something like 'Wag the Dog'? President Sample deadpanned a nervous sideway's look and said, 'As Jack is coming up to respond to that ...'. But Sample chose to respond by going back to an earlier observation, that the ICT would develop 'synthetic experiences so compelling that people will react as though they were real – a virtual reality of sensations and sights'. He went on to make a deft analogy to Plato's poor opinion of the poets. Not actually using the word 'mimesis', he suggested as much was going on at the ICT: by performing the classical function of poetry and theatre – artistically and dramatically mimicking reality for a higher purpose – it could not help but arouse anxieties about whose version of reality was the true one. Shadows from the allegory of the cave flickered in the background.

Where Sample applied nuance, Jack Valenti chose pugnacity. Responding to my question, he said: 'I want to illuminate a central truth to the gentleman – everything leaks, in Hollywood, in Washington. There's no way you can keep a secret. You can't fool the people for very long.' He then informed me that I needed to correct my 'Copernican complex'. He contrasted my view to the decision to drop the atomic bomb on the Japanese. Some might have seen that as a 'heartless and terrible thing to do ... but not the 150,000 American boys whose lives would have been lost. This is a lesson in Philosophy 101 that I am giving to you right now.'

I came away with a different lesson. Valenti, like many in power today, is all too ready to drop the bomb on dissident viewpoints. Nonetheless, he was on target in one regard: what separates and elevates war above lesser, 'Copernican', conceits is its intimate relationship to death. The dead body – on the battlefield, in the tomb of the unknown soldier, in the collective memory, even on the movie screen – is what gives war its special status.

This fact can be censored, hidden in a body bag, air-brushed away, but it provides, even in its erasure, the corporal *gravitas* of war. However, everything I witnessed that day at the ICT was dedicated to the disappearance of the body, the aestheticising of violence, the sanitisation of war: in other words, everything we have seen implemented since 9/11.

Barely a week after the terrorist attack, the ICT began to gather top talent from Hollywood to create possible terrorist scenarios that could then be played out in their Marina del Rey virtual reality facilities. Then Karl Rove, White House special adviser, travelled to Beverly Hills to discuss with the top chief executive officers (CEOs) how Hollywood might provide talent and resources for the battle against terrorism. Among those reported as contributing to the virtual war effort were *Die Hard* screenwriter Steven E. De Souza, *Matrix* special effects wizard Paul Debevec, and directors David Fincher (*Fight Club*), Spike Jonze (*Being John Malkovich*) and Randal Kleiser (*Grease*). Fans of Kleiser might wonder why his classic work *Honey I Blew Up the Kid* (about an amateur physicist who turns his son into a giant) went unmentioned in the press releases. Was it proof that the US government might be embarrassed to have hooked up with B-list directors? Or was it part of an infowar campaign to keep the lid on 'Operation Shrink bin Laden Back to Size'? When holy war comes to Hollywood, the truth is hard to come by.

As more bin Laden tapes emerged, there were calls for censorship, heightened threat levels and a cottage industry of media critics. Debates continued to focus on whether the tapes were real or not, was he dead or alive, and then, most ominously, whether he had joined ranks with Saddam Hussein. Gone missing was any attempt to understand why bin Laden continued to command a global audience.

After *Al-Jazeera* broadcast the first videotape, National Security adviser Condoleezza Rice made personal calls to heads of the television networks, asking them to pre-screen and to consider editing Al Qaeda videos for possible coded messages. Secretary of State Powell interpreted the February 2002 audiotape as proof positive that bin Laden had forged an alliance with Saddam Hussein. Yet the most significant and constant message, intended for the aggrieved and dispossessed in Islam, has remained, like Edgar Allan Poe's purloined letter, out in the open, in plain sight and peculiarly unnoticed. Bin Laden was adeptly using networked technology to disseminate a seductive message of prophecy, reciprocity and ultimate victory.

Shortly after the bombing campaign began in Afghanistan and bin Laden delivered his first videotape as a counter air-strike to the USA, he spoke with his guest and camera crew of the many dreams that preceded 9/11: of playing soccer games against US pilots, in which Al Qaeda members become pilots themselves in order to defeat the Americans; of a religious leader who dreamt of carrying a huge plane through the desert; of the wife of a jihadist who saw a plane crashing into a building a week before the event. An unidentified man off-camera interrupts bin Laden, saying that 'Abd Al Rahman saw a vision before the operation, a plane crashed into a tall building, he knew nothing about it'. At this point bin Laden turns to his guest and says: 'I was worried that maybe the secret would be revealed if everyone starts seeing it in their dreams. So I closed the subject.' The Koranic view of dreams as prophecy appeared to be taken so seriously that bin Laden believed operational secrecy was at risk. For bin Laden, prophecy anticipates the inevitable: a violent confrontation with the West. He further states in the video that 'America has been filled with horror from north to south and east to west, and thanks be to God what America is tasting now is only a copy of what we have tasted.'

Prophecy is tied to reciprocity once again in the November audiotape, in which he opens with a florid invocation of 'God, the merciful, the compassionate', who sanctifies Al Qaeda's violence because 'reciprocal treatment is part of justice ... as you kill you will be killed and as you bomb you will be bombed'. With the release of the February tape, most of the media, following Powell's lead, focused on bin Laden's invocation to defend Iraq against the 'crusaders' by copying the 'success' of trench warfare in Tora Bora. Left unnoticed was bin Laden once again calling on religious purity to counter Western technological superiority in not only planes, bombs and soldiers, but also by an infowar: 'We realized from our defence and fighting against the American enemy that, in combat, they mainly depend on psychological warfare.' He adds: 'This is in light of the huge media machine they have.' Bin Laden instructs the jihadist that they will triumph in a 'just war' by fighting 'in the cause of Allah' and 'against the friends of Satan' and by avoiding 'all grave sins, such as consuming alcohol, committing adultery, disobeying parents, and committing perjury'. 'They should', adds bin Laden, 'in particular mention the name of God more before combat.'

Unfortunately, the US intelligence, as well as intellectual community, bound by rational models of decision-making, was slow to comprehend this powerful synergy of prophecy, reciprocity and technology. This mythologically informed terrorism, or *mythoterrorism*, helps explain not only bin Laden's own motivations, but also why his appeal among the aggrieved will probably outlive him and exceed the impact of his own crimes.

Mythoterrorism has similar characteristics to other forms of violence such as wars or revolutions that bind together the deprived, the weak, the resentful, the repressed or just the temporarily disadvantaged. The difference, however, that gives mythoterrorism its spectacular power, as *well* as anticipates its eventual failure, is the targeting of innocent victims in the name of a higher good. Conducted for an imagined collectivity, looking backward to a supposed Golden Age, or predicting a future paradise, mythoterrorism undermines a political order through asymmetrical violence, but is unable to generate public legitimacy for any earthly alternatives. It relies on a perpetual struggle, a jihad or holy war.

The messages of the tapes portray an escalating conflict dating from the Medieval Crusades that can only end in a final conflagration of vengeance against the infidel and of redemption for the *jihadist*. Bin Laden's vision depends not only on the idea of an originary act of injury against Islam, but also on the persistence of reciprocal injustices. From the start, President Bush was quick to fall into this mimetic trap, responding in kind when he vowed at the Washington National Cathedral shortly after the attack 'to rid the world of evil'. By imitating the evangelical rhetoric and practice of with-us-or-against-us, he ignored the counsel and constraint of sympathetic allies that had prior experience with terrorism at home.

The obvious must be re-stated: This is not to claim any moral equivalency between Bush and bin Laden, but rather to identify a mutual pathology in operation, the kind of mimetic relationship that often develops in war and terror. People go to war not only out of rational calculation, but also because of how they see, perceive, picture, imagine and speak of each other: that is, how the construction of difference of other groups, as well as the sameness of their own, takes on irreconcilable conditions of hostility. Neither Bush nor bin Laden is the first to think that mimesis might be mined for political advantage, only to find themselves caught in its own dynamic. From Greek tragedy and Roman gladiatorial spectacles to futurist art and fascist rallies, mimetic violence has regularly overpowered democratic intentions as well as virtuous interventions.

The question, then, is how to break this mimetic encounter of mythoterrorism? Historically, terrorist movements without a mass base quickly weaken and rarely last more than a decade. However, the mimetic struggle between Bush and bin Laden, magnified by the media, fought by advanced technologies of destruction and unchecked by the UN or our allies, has developed a pathologic of its own in which assimilation or extermination become plausible solutions for what appears to be an intractable problem.

As subsequent acts of terror and counter-terror surpassed the immediate effects of the 9/11 attack, as bin Laden morphed into yet another avatar of evil, Saddam Hussein, we faced a pathological form of mimesis that had been medically defined as 'the appearance, often caused by hysteria, of symptoms of a disease not actually present'. Bin Laden's videotapes have inflamed the mimetic condition by linking terrorist attacks in Tunisia, Karachi, Yemen, Kuwait, Bali and even Moscow to an age-old crusade of Islam against the West. In response, the White House's new 'National Strategy to Secure Cyberspace' has called on all Americans to guard against a 'digital disaster' by becoming 'digital citizen soldiers'; the Pentagon's main research arm, DARPA, proposes under the rubric of *'Scientia est potentia'* ('Knowledge is power') data-mining operations to provide 'total information awareness' on citizens and foreigners alike; and a 'Green Scare' of Islam has threatened the body politic as severely as the hysteria of past Red Scares.

Dead or alive, prophet or crackpot, symptom or disease, bin Laden as well as Hussein require a mimetic foe. Without a reciprocal hatred, their prophecies lose their self-fulfilling powers. As is often the case with narcissistic psychopaths, the worst thing we could do is to deprive them of their reflections.

As we know from medical pathology, the auto-immune response can kill as well as cure. The response to the most powerful images after the bin Laden tapes, the Abu Ghraib photos, bears this out. Consider Rumsfeld's first complaint upon the appearance of the Abu Ghraib images:

> In the information age, people are running around with digital cameras and taking these unbelievable photographs and then passing them off, against the law, to the media, to our surprise, when they had not even arrived in the Pentagon. (cited in Dowd 2004)

An escalating war of images ensued. Heinous crimes were revealed, public outrage expressed, official apologies proffered, congressional hearings convened and courts martial put into progress. But something went missing in this mass-mediated picture of pictures. In the rush to moral condemnation and for political expiation, the *meaning* of the images became moot. In the case of the Abu Ghraib photos, once established as 'authentic', they took on a singular significance: a crisis for the Bush administration and the USA's reputation in the world. Numerous reports of earlier instances of dissimulations, group-think acts of self-deception and outright lies by the US government, from claims about Iraqi ties to Al Qaeda, the presence of weapons of mass destruction and the likelihood of a swift post-war transition to peace and democracy, all paled in comparative political effect to the digital images of simulated sex, dominatrix bondage and mock Ku Klux Klan lynching (with electrical wires subbing for the hangman's noose).

Roland Barthes (1982) identifies the source of this power in the image: 'From a phenomenological viewpoint, in the photograph, the power of authentication exceeds the power of representation.' How does the authenticity of the image come to trump the representation of the word? And in the age of Adobe Photoshop, just what does *authentic* mean? This is not to suggest that the photos taken at the Abu Ghraib prison are fake, as proved to be the case with facsimile images published in the *Daily Mirror* tabloid of British soldiers torturing an Iraqi prisoner and the images published by Egyptian newspapers of an American soldier sexually abusing a woman (actually downloaded from an unrelated porn website). It is rather to raise critical questions that the press and academics have been slow to consider, on not just how cultural interpretation, moral judgement and ideological fervour, but also how new technical means of reproduction, real-time transmission and global circulation via the Internet produce profound and potentially uncontrollable truth-effects through the use of photographic and videographic imagery.

As we are exposed to loop-images of prisoner abuse, Islamicist hip-hop videos and brutal snuff films of hostages, at some point (a point rapidly shrinking in duration) between the initial shock produced by the images (they are just too unbelievable) and the banalisation of evil through replication (they have become too familiar), the reality principle itself begins to disappear with a flick of the channel, a click of the mouse. Consider just a few of the 'aberrant' responses to the Abu Ghraib images circulating on the Internet. According to the Associated Press, the editor of one of the Egyptian newspapers in question, Mustafa Bakri, justified publication of the pornographic images of American sexual abuse because 'the kind of pictures on CBS made us believe that any other picture is authentic' (5 May 2004). The *Guardian* quoted the British Liberal Democrat leader, Charles Kennedy, saying that the photos showing British abuse of an Iraqi will lead to renewed violence even if they are fake (7 May 2004). And, as one sample from many blogs, 'SkepticOverlord' likened the fakery to an episode of the CBS-produced television series 'The Agency', in which the CIA staged a porno film to discredit a militant Islamic leader.

It may well be that in the search for authenticity we are witnessing a deeper desire for a lost moral certainty, in which the public representation of reality becomes a function of a collective struggle for ethical superiority, of a kind that initially justified the US intervention into Iraq and that ultimately provides the twisted rationale of the torturer.

The ethos of terror

US foreign policy has always been a struggle of ethics and power, and when politics escalates into war the first casualty is – as isolationist Senator Hiram Johnson famously remarked in 1917 – the truth. With the casualty list growing everyday in the war against terror, a war of images was inevitable. The biggest salvos in this home-grown struggle of morality, truth and power came with Michael Moore's documentary, *Fahrenheit 9/11*.

Promoted in the film trailer as the 'true story that will make your temperature rise', duly attacked by Bill O'Reilly as 'Leni Riefenstahl Third Reich propaganda' and challenged by the right-wing group Citizens United as a violation of federal election laws, *Fahrenheit 9/11*, all about the news, swiftly became the news. Lost in the polarised debate was much of an account of *how* this film succeeds, particularly of Moore's uncanny ability to evince powerful moral and emotional responses from an image-saturated mix of media. Like the Rodney King video (or the Stanley Miller sequel), the looped shot of the twin towers falling, bin Laden's home movies, the Abu Ghraib digital snapshots and the Richard Berg snuff film, *Fahrenheit 9/11* plays to the modern sensibility that our leaders might and often do lie but images cannot.

In the process, irrefutable images damn the guilty by association. Blacked-out names from Bush's National Guard records magically reappear like invisible ink in reverse; the Bush posse morphs into the Cartwright family from the TV series *Bonanza*; and shaking the hands of an Arab becomes proof-positive of calumny and conspiracy. It might be better to celebrate *Fahrenheit 9/11* as an imaginary rather than a documentary.

This is not a criticism. We best remember again the words of Benjamin on realism as 'the strongest narcotic of the century'. He went on to exhort those in the grip of a *faux* realpolitik that 'in times of terror, when everyone is something of a conspirator, everybody will be in a situation where he has to play detective'.

As proof, numerous print reports of earlier instances of dissimulations, group-think acts of self-deception and outright lies by the Bush administration, from claims about Iraqi ties to Al Qaeda, the presence of weapons of mass destruction and the likelihood of a swift post-war transition to peace and democracy, continuously surface, sink and bubble-up from a variety of news-holes. Confusion, not freedom, reigns. But in *Fahrenheit 9/11* the image seized and sustained public attention and demanded a response. Why?

We are back to the power of authentication over representation: what the word can only represent, the picture supposedly proves. The traditional print media have been slow to understand how the Internet, with its real-time transmission and global circulation of images, has force-multiplied this effect and transformed the political as well as media game. Indeed, many of the most ludicrous as well as most disturbing images in Moore's film – such as Bush goofing in the Oval office before he goes primetime to announce the beginning of the Iraq war, or the gun camera shot of an Apache helicopter crew coolly taking out three Iraqis – have long been seen on websites.

However, in an Age of Infoterror one begins to wonder just how profound and lasting these image-effects truly are. The King video incited plenty of righteous anger, but notably failed to indict the perpetrators. Regardless of photographs and videos to the contrary, a French *nonfiction* bestseller arguing that 9/11 was fabricated found a credulous audience. The Abu Ghraib images shocked us, but have yet to cause any heads to roll (or at least not any adorned with stars).

As we were exposed to images of prisoner abuse, Islamicist hip-hop videos and Moore's splice-and-dicing of the war against terror, at some point (a point rapidly shrinking in duration) between the initial shock produced by the images (are they just too unbelievable?) and the banalization of evil through replication (have they become too familiar?), the political significance begins to disappear with a flick of the channel and the click of the mouse. After the aesthetic buzz of the fast edit comes the synaptic crash, triggering a new search for greater visual stimulation and moral satisfaction.

How long before photographic immanence loses its power of authentication and stimulation, we stop believing what we see, and the significance of the image itself is called into question? How many times can the truth take a beating before the public just stops believing *anything* it hears, reads and sees? Not soon enough?

It may well be that the early newspaper ads promoting *Fahrenheit 9/11* – Moore and Bush frolicking hand-in-hand in front of the White House, with 'Controversy ... What Controversy?' underneath – contain a hidden answer to these questions. Bush, bin Laden and Moore have tapped into a great insecurity in which the search for authenticity becomes inseparable from the desire for moral superiority. In their projection (dare I say simulation) of exclusive truths, they each have found their mirror other.

In *The Twilight of the Idols*, Nietzsche exhorts us in our search for meaning to eschew quick moral judgements in favour of a more arduous semiotic investigation:

> Morality is only an interpretation of certain phenomena, more precisely a *mis*interpretation. Moral judgment belongs, as does religious judgment, to a level of ignorance at which even the concept of the real, the distinction between the real and the imaginary, is lacking: so that at such a level 'truth' denotes nothing but things which we today call 'imaginings'. To this extent moral judgment is never to be taken literally: as such it never contains anything but nonsense. But as *semeiotics* it remains of incalculable value: it reveals, to the informed man at least, the most precious realities of cultures and inner worlds, which did not *know* enough to 'understand' themselves. Morality is merely 'sign' language, merely symptomatology; one must already know *what* it is about to derive profit from it. (Nietzsche 1968, p.55)

So what is it about? Here's an historical clue: 'Semiotics', or the study of signs, emerged in the sixteenth century in the arts of war and medicine. It referred to new methods of military manoeuvre based on visual signals, as well as new medical techniques for identifying pathological symptoms in humans. From day one, signs had the power to kill as well as to cure. In the twenty-first century, we need to develop a new semiotics for the images of the war against terror. Otherwise, we will continue treating its most morbid symptoms with morality plays rather than finding a cure for the all-too-real disease of imperial politics.

Epilogue

The war of images continues. Osama bin Laden, who knocked the balance of terror askew, saw fit in an October-surprise election video to give the USA notice that they might kill or capture some terrorists, but the insurgency was now resurgent. Ostensibly directing his remarks to US citizens rather than to the presidential candidates, he provided a civic lesson on the meaning of freedom and security. In case they had found the attacks on the World Trade Center and the Pentagon too subtle, he offered a more explicit explanation for his actions:

> Security is an important pillar of human life. Free people do not relinquish their security. This is contrary to Bush's claim that we hate freedom ... We fought you because we are free and do not accept injustice. We want to restore freedom to our nation. Just as you waste our security, we will waste your security. (cited in BBC News 2004)

After a short digression on the strategic advantage al-Qaeda gained by President Bush 'being preoccupied with the little child's talk about her goat and its butting' (prompting former New York Mayor Giuliani to remark that bin Laden was 'taking his lines from Michael Moore's film'), he ends the video by returning to the security dilemma:

> Your security does not lie in the hands of Kerry, Bush, or al-Qaeda. Your security is in your own hands. Each and every state that does not tamper with our security will have automatically assured its own security. (cited in BBC News 2004)

It took *Saturday Night Live* just two days to subvert not only the medium and the message of bin Laden's videotape, but also the self-image upon which global democracy is supposed to be modelled. In the skit, a news anchor (bearing some resemblance to Tom Brokaw) introduces a clip of an Osama bin Laden impersonator speaking in Arabic with English subtitles:

> Hello. I am Osama bin Laden. And Allah be praised, this is my message to the American people. In a few days, you will hold your election to choose between the ignorant cowboy Bush and the gigolo Kerry. Over the last several months, I have been approached repeatedly by representatives of both candidates, who have asked me if I would please endorse their opponents. But I have refused to do this. First, because frankly, I find this request sort of insulting, which it really is, if you think about it. Especially coming from Bush, who has not shown the least bit of interest in me since he invaded Iraq. And also, because to me, voting is a private matter, and one which I take very seriously. For a time, I feared that I would not be eligible to vote in this election. But recently, praise Allah, I was tracked down by two volunteers from the Kerry campaign. They signed me up, and apparently, I am now registered in Cincinnati. (Saturday Night Live 2004)

It seemed to have worked. Facing the logos, pathos and ethos of terror, the weapon of mass whimsy might be our last resort against a mimetic war of images.

Bibliography

Barthes, Roland, 'Rhetoric of images', in Roland Barthes (ed.), *Image–Music–Text*, translated by Stephen Heath (New York: Hill and Wang, 1977), pp.32–51.

Barthes, Roland, *Camera Lucida: Reflections on Photography* (New York: Hill and Wang, 1982).

BBC News, 'Excerpts: bin Laden video', 29 October 2004, available at: http://news.bbc.co.uk/1/hi/world/middle_east/3966817.stm (accessed).

Benjamin, Walther, 'The work of art in the age of mechanical reproduction', in Hannah Arendt (ed.), *Illuminations* (New York: Schocken, 1969).

Benjamin, Walther, *The Arcades Project*, translated by Howard Eiland and Kevin McLaughlin (Cambridge, MA: Harvard University Press, 1999).

Der Derian, James, *Virtuous War: Mapping the Military-Industrial-Media-Entertainment Network* (Boulder: Westview, 2001).

Dowd, Maureen, 'A world of hurt', *New York Times*, 9 May 2004.

Nietzsche, Friedrich, *Twilight of the Idols*, translated by R.J. Hollingdale (London: Penguin, 1968).

Saturday Night Live, 'Live transcripts', 30 November 2004, available at: http://snltranscripts.jt.org/04/04dnbc.phtml (accessed).

The 9/11 Commission Report (New York: W.W. Norton, 2004).

Virilio, Paul, *Pure War*, translated by M. Polizotti (New York: Semiotext(e), 1983).

Chapter 2

Torture and the Ethics of Photography
Judith Butler

> Photographs state the innocence, the vulnerability of lives heading towards their own destruction, and this link between photography and death haunts all photographs of people. (Susan Sontag, *On Photography*, 1977)

Towards the end of Precarious Life (Butler 2004), I consider the question of what it means to become ethically responsive, to consider and attend to the suffering of others, and, more generally, which frames permit the representability of the human and which do not. This seems important not only to answer the question of whether we might respond effectively to suffering at a distance, but also to formulate a set of precepts that might work to safeguard lives in their fragility and precariousness. I am not asking in this context about the subjective sources of this kind of responsiveness, although I do consider this question in *Giving an Account of Oneself* (2005a). Rather, here I propose to consider the way in which suffering is presented to us and how that presentation affects our responsiveness. In particular, I want to understand how the *frames* that allocate the recognisability of certain figures of the human are themselves linked with broader *norms* that determine questions of humanisation or dehumanisation. My point, which is at this point hardly new, is to suggest that whether and how we respond to the suffering of others, how we formulate moral criticisms, how we articulate political analyses, depend upon a certain field of perceptible reality already being established. This field of perceptible reality is one in which the notion of the recognisable human is formed and maintained over and against what cannot be named or regarded as the human, a figure of the non-human that holds the place of the human in its unrecognisability. At the time that I wrote *Precarious Life*, Abu Ghraib had not yet come to light; I was working then only with the pictures of the shackled and crouched bodies in Guantanamo Bay – not yet knowing the details of torture there – as well as other representational issues of the war: the debates about the war dead in Iraq and the problem of embedded reporting.

Some government officials and representatives of the media claimed that we should not see the war dead, our own or their own, because that would be anti-American; journalists and newspapers were actively denounced for showing coffins of the American war dead shrouded in flags; such images should not be seen because they might arouse certain kinds of sentiments. The mandating of what can be seen – a concern with content – was supplemented by control over the perspective from which the action and destruction of war could be seen at all, which led not only to the institution of 'embedded' reporting, but an unprecedented collaboration between journalists and the Department of Defense. In her text, *Regarding the Pain of Others* (2003), Susan Sontag remarks that this practice of embedded reporting begins earlier with the coverage of the British campaign in the Falklands in 1982 (Sontag 2003: 65), where only two photojournalists were permitted to enter the region and no television broadcasts were allowed. Since that time, journalists have increasingly agreed to comply with the exigencies of embedded reporting in order to secure access to the action itself. But what is the action to which access is then secured through embedded reporting? In the case of the recent and current war, it is action established by the perspective that the Department of Defense orchestrates and permits – so we see something of the performative power of the state to orchestrate and ratify what will be called reality or, more philosophically, the reach and extent of the ontological field.

It will not do to say, as Sontag elsewhere does, that the photograph cannot by itself provide an interpretation, that we need captions and analysis to move beyond the discrete and punctual image. I have no doubt that we need such captions and analyses, but if we say that the photograph is not an interpretation we get in another bind. She writes that, whereas prose and painting can be interpretive, photography is merely selective (Sontag 2003: 6), and later in the same text, she elaborates:

> while a painting, even one that achieves photographic standards of resemblance, is never more than the stating of an interpretation, a photograph is never less than an emanation (light waves reflected by objects) – a material vestige of its subject in a way that no painting can be. (Sontag 2003: 154)

Sontag argued that photographs have the capacity to move us momentarily, but that they do not have the power to build an interpretation. If a photograph becomes effective in informing or moving us politically, it is only because the photograph is received within a context of a relevant political consciousness. For Sontag, photographs render truths in a dissociated moment; they 'flash up' in a Benjaminian sense. As a result, they are always atomic and punctual and discrete. What they appear to lack is narrative coherence that, alone, supplies the needs of the understanding. We can see Sontag the writer here defending her trade over and against the photographers with whom she surrounded herself in the last decades of her life. For our purposes, though, it makes sense to know that the mandated photograph, the one that complies with state department requirements, is building an interpretation. We can even say that the political consciousness that moves the photographer to accept those restrictions and yield the compliant photograph is embedded in the frame itself. We do not have to have a caption or a narrative at work to understand that a political background is being explicitly formulated and renewed through the frame. In this sense, the frame takes part in the active interpretation of the war compelled by the state; it is not just a visual image awaiting its interpretation; it is itself interpreting, actively, even forcibly.

As a visual interpretation, it can only be conducted within certain kinds of lines and so within certain kinds of frames; unless, of course, the mandatory framing becomes part of the story, unless there is a way to photograph the frame itself. At that point the photograph that yields its frame to interpretation is one that opens the restrictions on interpreting reality to critical scrutiny. It exposes and thematises the mechanism of restriction, and it constitutes a disobedient act of seeing. Rarely, if ever, does this operation of mandatory and dramaturgical 'framing' itself become part of what is seen, much less what is told. Whenever and wherever the photograph yields up its own forcible frame to visual scrutiny and interpretation, it opens up the restrictions on interpreting reality to critical scrutiny. What this means is that we come to interpret that interpretation that has been imposed upon us.

So there is, it seems to me, in recent war photography a significant departure from the conventions of war photojournalism that were at work 30 and 40 years ago, where the photographer or camera person would attempt to enter the action through certain angles and modes of access that sought to expose the war in ways that no government had planned. Currently, the state operates on the field of perception and, more generally, the field of representability, in order to control affect and in anticipation of the way that affect informs and galvanises political opposition to the war. I refer to a field of 'representability' rather than 'representation' because this field is structured by state permission; as a result, we cannot understand this field of representability simply by examining its explicit contents, since it is constituted fundamentally by what is cast out and maintained outside the frame within which representations appear. We can think of the frame, then, as active, as jettisoning and presenting, and as doing both at once, in silence, without a visible sign of its operation and yet effectively.

The operation of the frame, where state power exercises its forcible dramaturgy, is not precisely representable or, when it is, it risks becoming insurrectionary, and becomes subject to state punishment and control. Prior to the events and actions that are represented within the frame, there is an active, if unmarked, delimitation of the field itself, and so a set of contents and perspectives that are not shown, never shown, impermissible to show. They constitute the anathematised background of what is represented, one that can only be approached through thematising the delimitating function itself, one that allows for an exposure of the forcible dramaturgy of the state and the collaboration with it by those who deliver the visual news of the war through complying with permissible perspectives. That delimitation is part of an operation of power that does not appear as *a figure* of oppression. We might image the state as dramaturgic and so secure our understanding of this operation of state power through an available figure. But it is essential to the continuing operation of this power not to be seen. Rather, it is precisely a nonfigurable operation of power that works to delimit the domain of representability itself. That it is nonfigurable does not mean it cannot be shown. But what is shown when it comes into view is the staging apparatus itself, the maps that exclude certain regions, the directives of the army, the positioning of the cameras, the communication of the punishments that lay in wait if protocol is breached.

But when one does see the framing of the frame, what is it that is going on? I would suggest that this is not just a problem internal to the life of the media, but one in which certain larger norms, often racialising and civilisational, are able to instate their structuring effect on what for the time being is called 'reality'.

Before the publication of the photos from Abu Ghraib, I sought to relate three different terms in my efforts to understand the visual dimension of war as it relates to the question of whose lives are grievable and whose are not: in the first instance, there are *norms* – explicit or tacit – that govern which human lives count as human and as living and which do not; these norms also determine when and where a life can be said to be lost, and that loss registered as the violent loss of life; in this way, I sought to relate the norms that govern when and where a life counts as human to the question of when and where such a life is grievable and, correlatively, when and where the loss of life remains ungrievable and unrepresentable. Those broader social and political norms that establish the lives that will be considered human, considered a life, and so considered as grievable precisely in those terms, operate in many ways, but one way they operate is through frames that govern the perceptible, frames that effect a delimiting function, bringing into focus an image on the condition that some portion of the visual field is ruled out. What this means, theoretically, is that the image that is represented signifies its admissibility into the domain of representability; that same image thus signifies the delimiting function of the frame even as, or precisely because, it does not represent it.

In the public discourse on Camp Delta in Guantanamo, the treatment of Arabs in the USA (both Arab-Americans and those in the USA as visitors or permanent residents), the suspension of civil liberties, certain norms are operative in establishing who is human and entitled to human rights and who is not, whose life, if extinguished, is publicly grievable and whose life may leave no public trace to grieve. These norms are, as it were, enacted precisely through specific frames, visual and narrative, that presuppose decisions about what will be unframed and what will be left outside the frame. If norms and frames constitute the first two hinges for my analysis, the last term of these three is human suffering itself, and there I am worried slightly about the privileging of the human, the anthropomorphism it implies, but I am willing to take that risk for now; it does not mean to imply a lack of respect or regard for the suffering of sentient beings who are not human. It is meant only to identify a difficulty that happens whenever the human is invoked, since not all humans are included in the invocation as it currently travels, and continuing presumptions about civilisation support which humans we regard as entitled to legal protection and which humans we abandon to a domain unprotected by any law.

We might have thought that the US personnel in Abu Ghraib or Guantanamo were bound to engage in humane treatment by virtue of international accords governing prisoners of war. Very few people at Abu Ghraib even knew about those accords. Moreover, once we grasp that the Geneva Convention, originally instituted in 1949, is only applicable to citizens of those countries *already recognised* as nation-states and that those engaged in conflicts on behalf of emergent nations or outside of the state structure – as non-citizens – are not covered by its terms, it follows that the

Geneva Accord does not extend its protection universally. Or, rather, it maintains a parochial version of universality that only extends to those humans *already recognised* as citizens of existing nation-states. Moreover, the language of the accord makes numerous civilisational and racial presumptions, and it will turn out that racial norms frame the human and also exclude those we must still insist on calling 'human' from within its purview. Do I need to make plain in what I consider the human to consist? For our purposes, I propose that we consider the way it works as a differential norm. Let us think of the human as a value and a morphology that is allocated and retracted, aggrandised, personified, degraded and disavowed, elevated and affirmed. It continues to produce the nearly impossible paradox of a human who is no human, or a norm of the human that effaces the human as it is otherwise known. Wherever there is the human, there is the inhuman: when we proclaim some group of beings who have not been considered to be human, we admit that humanness is a shifting prerogative. Some humans take their humanness for granted and others struggle to gain access to the term. The term 'human' is constantly producing a doubling that exposes the ideality and coercive character of the norm: some humans qualify as human; some humans do not, and when I use the term in the second of these utterances, I do nothing more than assert a discursive life for a human who is not the same as the norm that determines what and who will count as a human life, and what and who will not.

When Donna Haraway asks, 'have we ever yet become human?', she is at once positing a 'we' that is outside the norm of the human and questioning whether the human is ever something that can be fully accomplished. I would suggest that this norm is not something that we must seek to embody, but a differential of power that we must learn to read, to assess culturally and politically and to oppose in the differential way it works. And yet, we also need the term, to assert it precisely where it cannot be asserted, and to do this in the name of opposing the differential of power by which it operates and inciting ethical responsiveness to suffering, as a way of working against the forces of neutralisation or erasure that separate us from knowing and responding to the suffering that is caused in our names.

If, as the philosopher Emmanuel Levinas claims, it is the *face* of the other that demands from us an ethical response, then it would seem that the norms that allocate who is human and who is not arrive in visual form. These norms work to *give face* and *efface*. Accordingly, our capacity to respond with outrage, with opposition and with critique will depend in part on how the differential norm of the human is communicated through visual and discursive frames. There are ways of framing that will bring the human in its frailty and precariousness into view, allow us to stand for the value and dignity of human life, to react with outrage when lives are degraded or eviscerated without regard for their value as lives. And then there are frames that foreclose responsiveness, to be understood as the negative action of existing frames, so that no alternative frames can exist; for them to exist and to permit another kind of content would perhaps communicate a suffering that might lead to an alteration of our political assessment of the current war. For photographs to communicate in this way, they must have a transitive function. They do not merely portray or represent, but they relay affect. In times of war, this transitive affectivity of the photograph may well overwhelm and numb us, but it may also incite and motivate.

In her book *On Photography* in 1977, Sontag argued that the photographic image no longer has the power to enrage, to incite, that the visual representation of suffering has become cliched, that we have become bombarded by sensationalist photography and that, as a result, our capacity for ethical responsiveness has become diminished. In her next book, *Regarding the Pain of Others* (2003), she is more ambivalent about the status of the photograph, since she concedes that it can and must represent human suffering, teach us how to register human loss and devastation across global distances, establish through the visual frame a proximity to suffering that keeps us alert to the human cost of war, famine and destruction in places that are far from us both geographically and culturally. For photographs to accuse and possibly invoke a moral response, they must shock. And shock is something other than aestheticising, conforming to a rote formula, or preparing for a consumer demand.

But she still believes that the photograph is fatally linked to the momentary. Over and against this predicament of the photograph, the pathos of narrative 'does not wear out' (Sontag 2003: 83). She writes, 'narratives can make us understand: photographs do something else. They haunt us.' Of course, we must ask whether narratives do not haunt us as well and whether photographs, in their status as visual representations, do not also make us understand? And is it not the case that the power of the photograph to excite and enrage us is bound up with the very interpretation of reality it delivers? If we claim that only words can offer us that interpretive understanding, have we created a needless divide between photography, understood to convey affect, and prose, understood to convey understanding? What psychological theory would support such a view, and is it actually right?

For Sontag, the matter is more complicated, since before we can even say that the photograph can both affect us emotionally and establish an interpretative understanding, we have to make sure that the photograph still has the power to affect us at all. Sometimes it seems to bespeak our numbness, and other times it seems to establish our prurience and tendency to respond to sensationalism. It would seem that if Sontag were right in her earlier thesis that the photograph no longer has the power to excite and enrage us, then Mr Rumsfeld's response to the photos depicting the torture in the Abu Ghraib prison would not have made sense. When, for instance, Rumsfeld claimed that to show all the photos would allow the photos of torture and humiliation and rape to *define us* as Americans, he attributed an enormous power to photography to construct national identity itself. This seems also to be what one of the more reactionary pundits on US television, a Mr O Reilly, meant – when he proclaimed that to show these photos would constitute Anti-American actions. It would seem that I should show the photos with this essay, but I confess to being worried about how they circulate, a point I will return to later. For now, though, let me recapitulate the argument so that we know where we are heading.

The question for me is the following: How do the *norms* that govern which lives will be regarded as human lives, and which will not, enter into the *frames* through which discourse and visual representation proceed, and how do these in turn delimit and orchestrate or foreclose ethical responsiveness to suffering. I am not suggesting that these norms and frames determine our response, which would make our responses into behaviourist effects of a monstrously powerful visual culture. I am suggesting only that the way these norms enter into frames and into larger circuits of communicability are vigorously contested precisely in an effort to regulate affect, outrage and response.

When some of the Abu Ghraib photos were released, what was the public response, and what has happened to that response over the course of the last years? The problem is not to establish that the public viewing of the photographs led to a significant decline in popular support for the war. I think that surely the photographs did play a role and that methodologists of public opinion have views on how to regard this 'factor'. My concern is rather different. I want to suggest that the photographs do not necessarily numb our senses nor do they necessarily determine a particular response. They are shown again and again, and this history of their differing framing and reception structures, without determining the kinds of public interpretations of torture that we have. In particular, I want to consider how the norms governing the 'human' are relayed and abrogated through the communication of these photos, and that the response of First World viewers is critically involved in the 'trace' of the human. This 'trace' is not the same as the full restitution of the humanity of the victim, however desirable that surely is, but the public condition under which we feel outrage and construct political views that incorporate that outrage. In a sense, my reflections are a further effort to come to terms with the problems that preoccupied Sontag towards the end of her life,[1] even though I differ from her on the relationship between photography and interpretation.

Indeed, I have found Susan Sontag's last publications to be good company as I consider what they are and what they do, and these include both her *Regarding the Pain of Others*, published two years ago, and 'Regarding the torture of others' that was released on the Internet and published in *The New York Times* (Sontag 2004) after the release of these photographs. As you know, the photographs taken within the Abu Ghraib prison showed brutality, humiliation, rape, murder, and in that sense they were clear representational evidence of war crimes. They have functioned in many ways, including as evidence in legal proceedings against those who are pictured as engaging in acts of torture and humiliation. They have also become iconic for the way that the US government, in alliance with Britain, has spurned the Geneva Conventions, particularly the protocols governing the fair treatment of prisoners of war. The photographs showed instances of abuse and torture, but it quickly became clear within the months of April and May of 2004 that there was a pattern among them and that, as the Red Cross contended for many months before the scandal broke, there was a systematic mistreatment of prisoners in Iraq, paralleling a systematic mistreatment at Guantanamo.[2] Only later did it become clear that the protocols devised for Guantanamo were explicitly used by the personnel at Abu Ghraib, and that both sets of protocols were indifferent to the Geneva Accords. Whether governmental officials called what is depicted in the photos 'abuse' or 'torture' suggests that the relation to international law is already at work. They did not dispute that the photographs are real, that they recorded something that did happen. Establishing the referentiality of the photographs was, however, not enough. The photos are not only shown, but named; both the way that they are shown, the way they are framed and the words used to describe what is shown work together to produce an interpretive matrix for what is seen.

But before we consider the conditions under which they are published and the form in which they are made public, let us consider the way the frame works to establish a relation between the photographer, the camera and the scene. The photos depict or represent a scene, the visual image that is preserved within the photographic frame. But the frame also belongs to a camera that is situated spatially in the field of vision, thus not shown within the image, but the technological precondition of an image that indicates that camera through indirect reference. Although the camera is outside the frame, it is clearly 'in' the scene as its constitutive outside. When the photographing of these tortures became the topic for public debate, the scene of the photograph was extended. It is not just the spatial location and social scenario in the prison itself, but the entire social sphere in which the photograph is shown, seen, censored, publicised, discussed and debated. So we might say that the scene of the photograph has changed through time. Let's notice a few things about this larger scene, one in which visual evidence and discursive interpretation play off against one another. There was 'news' because there were photos, the photos lay claim to a representational status, and the photos have travelled beyond the original place where they were taken, the place depicted in the photos themselves. On the one hand, they are referential; on the other hand, they change their meaning depending on the context in which they are shown and the purpose for which they are invoked. They are representing events as they actually were, and so the photos refer and the photo functions as incontestable evidence and proof of torture. The photos are published within newspapers, but the newspapers also make selections: some photos are shown, and others are not. To this day, *Newsweek* maintains possession of numerous photos that it refused to publish on the grounds that the publication would not be 'useful'. Useful for what? Clearly, they mean, 'useful to the war effort' – surely they do not mean 'useful for individuals who require free access to information about the current war in order to establish lines of accountability and to form political viewpoints on the war in question'. In restricting what we may see, do the government and the media then also limit the kinds of evidence that a public has at its disposal in order to make judgements about the wisdom and course of the current war? If, as Sontag claims, the contemporary notion of atrocity requires photographic evidence, then the only way to establish that torture or atrocity has taken place is through photographic evidence, at which point the evidence constitutes the phenomenon. Put another way, the photograph builds the act of torture in its evidentiary form.

In the USA, the prurient interests in the photographs themselves seemed to pre-empt a fair amount of political response. Lynndie England, with the leash around the man's head, can be front and centre in *The New York Times*, and yet some papers relegated that photo to the inside of the newspaper, selecting those that are most incendiary or those that are least incendiary. And yet, within military court proceedings, the photo is considered evidence from within a frame of potential or actual legal proceedings; it is already framed within the discourse of law and of truth. The photo presupposes a photographer, and that person is never shown in the frame. The question of guilt has been juridically restricted to those who committed such actions or who were responsible for those who did commit those actions. And these prosecutions have been limited to the most well-publicised cases.

One question that is not often asked is, who were the people who took these photos, and what can we infer from their occluded spatial relation to the image itself? Did they take them to expose abuse or to gloat in the spirit of US triumphalism? Is the taking of the photo a way to participate in the event and, if so, in what way? It would seem that the photos were taken by those who were recording the event, producing, as the *Guardian* called it, a pornography of the event, but at some point one person, aware of an ongoing investigation, or perhaps a set of persons, realised that there was something wrong with the actions depicted or became fearful of an impending investigation. It may be that the photographers were ambivalent at the time they took the photos or grew ambivalent with time; it may be that they feasted on the sadistic scene in some way that would demand at least a psychological account. I do not dispute the importance of psychology to understanding what goes on here, but psychology should not be used to reduce the torture to exclusively individual acts of pathology. We're in a group scene with these photographs, so we need something more actively approximating a psychology of group behaviour or, better yet, an account of how the norms of war in this instance neutralise morally significant relationships to violence and to humanity. We're also in a specific political situation, so any effort to reduce these acts to individual psychologies alone would return us to a familiar consideration of the individual, along with the concept of personality as the causal matrix for the understanding of events. Understanding the structural and spatial dynamics of the photograph can offer an alternative point of departure for our understanding of these events.

The photographer is recording a visual image of the scene and so approaching the scene through a frame before which those who engaged in torture and its triumphal aftermath also stood and posed. The relation between the photographer and the photographed takes place by virtue of the frame. The frame permits, orchestrates and mediates that relation. And though the photographers at Abu Ghraib had no Defense Department authorisation for the pictures they took, perhaps their perspective can also be rightly considered a form of embedded reporting. After all, the perspective on the so-called enemy was not idiosyncratic, but shared; so widely shared, it seems, that there was hardly a thought that something might be amiss here. Can we see these photographers not only as reiterating and confirming a certain practice of decimating Islamic cultural practice and norms, but as conforming to – and articulating – the widely shared social norms of the war?

So what are the *norms* according to which security personnel, actively recruited from private firms contracted to supervise US domestic prisons, and US soldiers acted as they did? And what are the norms that reside in the active framing by the camera, since these are what forms the basis of the cultural and political text at issue here? If the photograph does not only depict the event, but build and augment the event, if the photograph can be said to reiterate and continue the event, then the photograph does not, strictly speaking, postdate the event, but becomes crucial to its production, its legibility, its illegibility and its very status as reality. Perhaps the camera promises a festive cruelty: 'Oh, good, the camera's here: let's begin the torture so that the photograph might capture and commemorate our act!' If so, the photograph is already at work prompting, framing and orchestrating the act, even as the photograph captures the act at the moment of its accomplishment.

The task, in a way, is to understand the operation of a norm that circumscribes reality that works through the action of the frame itself; we have yet to understand this frame, these frames, where they come from and what kind of action they perform. So if there is more than one photographer and we cannot lay claim to a clear motivation of these photographers from the photos that are available, we are left to read the scene in another way. We can say with some confidence that the photographer is catching the event, but when we say that the photographer is recording the event, an implied audience becomes an issue. It may be that he or she is recording the event to show to those who are perpetrating the torture, so that they may enjoy the reflection of their actions on the digital camera and disseminate that particular accomplishment quickly, as digital technology allows. The photos may also be a kind of evidence, conceived as proof that just punishment was administered. Photographing is a kind of action that is not always anterior to the event, not always posterior to the event. The photograph is a kind of promise that the event will continue, is that very continuation of the event, producing an equivocation at the level of the temporality of the event; did those actions happen then;

do they continue to happen? Does the photograph continue the event in the present?

It would seem that photographing the scene can be a way of contributing to the scene, providing a visual reflection and documentation for it, giving it the status of history in some sense. Does the photograph or, indeed, the photographer, contribute to the scene? Act upon the scene? Intervene upon the scene? Photography has a relation to intervention, but photographing is not the same as intervening. There are the photos of bodies bound together, of individuals killed, of forced fellatio or dehumanising degradation, and they were taken unobstructed. The field of vision is clear. No one is seen lunging in front of the camera to intercept the view. No one is shackling the photographer and throwing him or her in the bin. This is torture in plain view, in front of the camera, even for the camera. After all, it is centred action, and the torturers regularly turn towards the camera to make sure their own faces are shown, even as the faces of those they torture are mainly shrouded. The camera itself is ungagged, unbound, and so occupies and references the safety zone that surrounds and supports the persecutors in this scene. And we do not know how much of this torture is actually done for the camera, to 'show' what the USA can do, as a sign of military triumphalism, sadistic control, the ability to effect a nearly complete degradation of the putative enemy, an effort to win the clash of civilisations and subject the ostensible barbarians to our civilising mission which, we can see, has rid itself so beautifully of its own barbarism. To the extent that the photograph communicates the scene, potentially, to newspapers and media sources, and the torture is, in some sense, *for* the photograph, it is, from the start, meant to be communicated; its own perspective is in plain view, and the cameraman or woman is referenced by the smiles that the torturers offer him or her: as if to say, thank you for taking my picture, thank you for memorialising my triumph. And then there is the question of whether the photographs were shown to those who might be tortured, as a warning and a threat. It is clear that the photographs were used to blackmail those depicted there with the threat that their families would see their humiliation and shame, especially sexual shame.

The photograph depicts; it has a representational and referential function. But it seems there are at least two questions that are raised by this referential function: one is, *what does the referential function do besides refer?* What other functions does it serve? What other effects does it produce? And the second, one that I will deal with below, has to do with the range of what is represented. If the photo represents reality, which reality is it that is represented? And how does the frame circumscribe what will be called reality in this instance?

So we are seeing what is true – in the sense that *this really happened*, and yet the truth of what we see has already been selected for us – *and in that way we do not know precisely where the happening begins and ends*; we see, nevertheless, this true event in the newspaper or on the television or on the Internet, and editorial decisions are being made; they are also being contested; they are also the topic of newspaper articles on editorial decisions, on self-censorship and on the political biases of various instruments of media. And so, what is it that we see? A name must be given to what we see, and at this point a debate ensues: is it poor treatment, is it torture? If it is poor treatment, then it is lamentable, but it does not defy international law and put the USA in direct violation of the Geneva Accord, a situation that could bring the USA before the World Court or the International Criminal Court. If it had been poor treatment, then we could have said that we are 'sorry' for the poor treatment, admit to a moral failure, avert the legal question of non-compliance with international law and of crimes against humanity and get on with the business of war, where the 'business of war' is understood to be something other than this moral failure, illegal torture, where the business of war is understood to be something other than the practice of torture, where the business of war is somehow understood to be morally and politically justified in this instance.

Whether or not this occupation which is supposed to postdate a war, but which continues to be a war, is legal has, of course, not been actively addressed by the US administration or its willing allies, and we can see, I believe, a recourse to extralegal grounds for legitimating this war from the beginning (a refusal to honour either congressional or UN inquiries into the legitimacy of military action), something which has strong implications, as we will see, for how the war is now conducted and whether war crimes can and will be prosecuted. The photographs might be said, then, to depict the extralegality of the war itself.

Do these images, then, refer not only to the continuing extralegality of the war, but to the practice of photography and its relation to violence? Consider the photograph in relation to other photographs that were taken by the same digital cameras. Sontag tells us that photographs cannot narrate, and that narrative alone satisfies the needs of the understanding. But they produce specific kinds of *sequences* in their digital forms; they constitute their own forms of seriality that reflect upon a certain structure of ordinary life under conditions of violently imposed occupation. Some of these digital cameras had files that include pictures of dead Iraqis, Iraqis being killed, murdered, raped and forced into sexual relations, and these are interspersed with photos of the local bazaar, friends smiling and eating, soldiers saluting the flag, views of the street and the neighbourhood, Americans making love in apparently consensual terms a soldier randomly shooting a camel in the head. So in these instances, it would seem that the photos are part of a record of everyday life and that everyday life has to be understood in this context as consisting in a certain sequential interchangeability of such images. According to this view, it would not be triumphalism that motivates the photograph, but something more closely approximating the mundanity of brutality, what Hannah Arendt called the banality of evil and which we might call the 'digitalisation of evil' (though *not* the evil of digitality). The camera is, as it were, in the photo, in many of these instances, since the soldiers are not 'caught' holding the leash tied to the neck of a bound and named man on the floor. They look directly into the camera and wait for the camera to record them in their activity. This activity is not morally alarming; it is quotidian; it only becomes morally alarming after seeing and hearing how people outside the frame react to the image once it is communicated. So when the photo is taken, it seems, it is part of the scene, helping to make the scene possible, orchestrating its pose, but not operated as a tool of investigative journalism or the exposure of human rights abuse. The intention of the photographer does not finally matter, though, since the photos become evidence, even indirectly accusing the one who furnishes them with failing to intervene in a crime against humanity. Although it now turns out that some of the photographers were involved in the torture itself, offering humiliating props and engaging in sexual humiliation.

The action of the camera itself is either oddly compliant, recording, as it were, without comment and raising no alarm, or it works as an incitement to orchestrate the scene, but also to extend the scene in time, to keep the scene going, again and again, promising a further visual consumption of the sadistic pleasure after the event. Indeed, the camera does not exactly delineate the event in time and space, although it does do that, and the time and space can be duly chronicled and recorded. At the same time, it allows the event to continue to happen, and I would suggest that, because of the photo, the event has not stopped happening.

It is difficult to understand this proliferation of images, but it seems to coincide with a proliferation of acts, a frenzy of photography. There is not only a certain pleasure involved in the scenes of torture, something we must consider, but a pleasure or perhaps a compulsion involved in the taking of the photographs itself. Why else would there be so many? Joanna

Bourke, an historian at Birkbeck, who published a book about the history of rape, wrote an article in the *Guardian* on 7 May 2004 entitled 'Torture as pornography'. Some of what she says seems clearly right to me, though I am not sure she can, with the use of 'pornography' as her explanatory category, explain the role of the photograph as actor in the scene. She does write, shrewdly, that there is exultation in the photographer, though we do not get images of the photographer, so it is an inference she makes by considering the photographs, their number, the circumstance of their taking. Although I'm prepared to believe that her attribution of pleasure to the photographer is true, I am not sure on what basis I ground my belief. She writes:

> The people taking the photographs exult in the genitals of their victims. There is no moral confusion here: the photographers don't even seem aware that they are recording a war crime. There is no suggestion that they are documenting anything particularly morally skewed. For the person behind the camera, the aesthetic of pornography protects them from blame. (Bourke 2004)

So perhaps I am odd, but as I understand it, the problem with the photos is *not* that someone is exulting in another person's genitals. Let us assume that we all do that on occasion and that there is nothing particularly objectionable in that exultation, and that it might even be precisely what is needed to make for a good day or a good night. What is clearly objectionable is coercion and force, as well as the exploitation of sexual acts in the service of shaming and debasing another human being. The distinction is crucial, of course, since the first finds sexual exchange to be a problem, and the second finds the coercive nature of sexual acts to be a problem. This equivocation was compounded when Mr Bush emerged from the senate chambers after viewing some of these photographs. When asked for his response, he said, 'it is disgusting', leaving unclear whether the homosexual acts of sodomy and fellatio he witnessed were disgusting, or the physically coercive and psychologically debasing conditions and effects of the torture itself. Indeed, if it is homosexual acts that are 'disgusting' to him, then he misses the point about torture, allowing his sexual revulsion and moralism to take the place of an ethical objection to torture. If the torture is disgusting, why did he use that word, rather than *wrong* or *objectionable*, or *criminal*? The word 'disgusting' keeps the equivocation in tact and so leaves two issues questionably intertwined: homosexual acts, on the one hand, and physical and sexual torture, on the other.

In some ways, the faulting of these photographs as pornography seems to commit a similar category mistake. Bourke's conjectures on the psychology of the photographer are interesting, and there is doubtless some mix of cruelty and pleasure that we need to think about. But how would we go about deciding the issue? Do we not need to ask why we are prepared to believe such things in order to approach the question of photography and torture critically? How would the photographer's awareness that he or she is recording a war crime appear within the terms of the photograph itself? It is one thing to affirm that some of what is recorded is rape and torture, and another to say that the means of representation is pornographic. My fear is that the old slippage between pornography and rape reappears here in unexamined form. In case you do not remember it, the view was that pornography motivates or incites rape, that it is causally linked with rape (those who watch it end up doing what they watch) and that what happens at the level of the body, in rape, happens at the level of representation, in pornography.

I think it is true that there seems to be *no* sense that the photographs, at the time that they are taken, are intervening as an instrument of moral inquiry, political exposure, legal investigation. The soldiers and security personnel photographed are clearly at ease with the camera, playing to it, and though I have suggested that there might be triumphalism, Bourke claims that the photographs themselves act as 'trophies, memorialising agreeable actions' (Bourke 2004). She further argues that the abuse is performed for the camera, and it is this thesis, one that I tentatively share, that leads her to a conclusion with which I disagree. Her argument is that the abuse is performed by the camera, and this leads her to the conclusion that the images are pornographic, producing pleasure in the sight of suffering for the photographer and, I presume, for the consumer of these images. What emerges in the midst of this thoughtful argument is a presumption that pornography is fundamentally defined by visual pleasure taken in the seeing of human and animal suffering and torture. At this point, if the pleasure is in the seeing, and the pleasure is taken in the suffering depicted, the torture is the effect of the camera, and the camera or, rather, its pornographic gaze, is the cause of the scene of suffering itself; in effect, the camera becomes the torturer. Sometimes Bourke refers to the 'perpetrators in these photographs', but other times it seems that the photograph and the photographer are the perpetrators. Both may be true in some significant sense. But the ethical problem becomes more difficult when, at the end of her provocative article, she writes that 'these pornographic images have stripped bare what little force remained in the humanitarian rhetoric concerning the war' (Bourke 2004). I gather she means that these images give the lie to humanitarian justifications for the war. That may well be true for some. But she does not exactly say why this is true. Here it seems that the problem is not what the images are of – namely, torture, rape, humiliation and murder – but the so-called pornography of the image itself, where pornography is defined as the pleasure taken in seeing human degradation, in the eroticisation of human degradation.

This definition of pornography evacuates the photographs of the specific brutality of the photographic scene. There are examples of women torturing men, of men and women both forcing Iraqi women – Muslim women – to bare their breasts, and Iraqi men – Muslim men – to perform homosexual acts or to masturbate. The torturer knows that this will cause the tortured one shame; the photograph enhances the shame, provides a reflection of the act for the one who is forced to do it; threatens to circulate the act as public knowledge and so as public shame. The US soldiers exploit the Muslim prohibition against nudity, homosexuality and masturbation in order to tear down the cultural fabric that keeps the integrity of these persons intact. But the US soldiers have their own erotic shame and fear, one that is mixed with aggression in some very distinct ways. Why, for instance, in both the first and second Gulf War were missiles launched against Iraq on which American soldiers had written, 'up your ass'. In this scenario, the bombing, maiming and killing of Iraqis is figured through sodomy, one that is supposed to inflict the ostensible shame of sodomy on those who are being bombed. But what does it inadvertently say about the bombers, those who ejaculate those missiles? After all, it takes two to commit an act of sodomy, as I understand it, which suggests that the US soldiers secure their place in the fantasised scene of sodomy in the active and penetrating position, a position that makes them no less homosexual for being on top. That the homosexual act is figured as murder, though, suggests that it is fully taken up by an aggressive circuit that exploits the shame of sexuality and converts its pleasure into a more raw version of sadism. That the US prison guards continue this fantasy by coercing their prisoners into acts of sodomy suggests that homosexuality is equated with the decimation of personhood. Paradoxically, this may be a place where the Islamic taboo against homosexual acts works in perfect concert with homophobia within the US military. The scene of torture that coerced homosexual acts, and seeks to decimate personhood through that coercion, presumes that for both torturer and tortured, homosexuality is the destruction of one's being. The problem, of course, is that the US soldiers seek to externalise this truth by coercing others to perform these acts, but the witnesses, the photographers, and those who orchestrate the scene of torture, are all party to the pleasure, exhibiting the very pleasure that they also degrade, acting the top to externalise penetration and yet demanding to see it again and again. A frenzy of the visible. A sadistic frenzy of the visible.

Obviously, Bourke is right to say that some of that kind of pleasure is at work in these photos and in these scenes, but we make an error if we insist that the 'pornography' of the photo is to blame. After all, part of what has to be explained is the excitation of the photo, the proliferation of the imagery, the relation between the acts depicted and the means through which the depiction takes place. And there does seem to be a frenzy and excitement, surely also a sexualisation of the act of seeing and photographing that is distinct, though acting in tandem with the sexualisation of the scene depicted. It is not, however, the practice of eroticised seeing that is the problem here, but the moral indifference of the photograph coupled with its investment in the continuation and reiteration of the scene as a visual icon. But let us not, with this important point, say that it is the technology of the camera or the pornographic gaze that is finally to blame for these actions. The torture may well have been incited by the presence of the camera, continued in anticipation of the camera, but this does not establish as its cause either the camera or 'pornography' – which, after all, has many non-violent versions and several genres that are clearly 'vanilla' at best and whose worst crimes seem to be the failure to supply an innovative plot.

There is an important question raised by all of this about the relationship between the camera and ethical responsiveness. It seems clear that these images were circulated, enjoyed, consumed and communicated without there being any accompanying sense of moral outrage. How this particular banalisation of evil took place, and why the photo did not alarm, or alarmed only too late, or became alarming only to those who were outside the scenes of war and imprisonment, are doubtless crucial to ask. One might expect that the photo would, at once, alert us to the abominable human suffering in the scene, and yet the photo has no magical moral agency of this kind. In the same way, it is not the same as the torturer, even if it functions as an incitement to brutality. The photos have functioned in at least three ways since their publication: as the incitement to brutality, as the testimony to the radical unacceptability of torture, and as documentary work displayed in a few museums in this country, including a gallery in Pittsburgh and the International Center for Photography in New York City (along with a more recent exposition in Venice and the travelling Botero exposition[3] as well). The photo has clearly travelled outside the original scene, left the hands of the photographer, or turned against the photographer him or herself, even perhaps vanquished his or her pleasure. It gave rise to a different gaze than the one that would ask for more, and so we probably need to accept that the photograph neither tortures nor redeems, but can be instrumentalised in radically different directions, depending on how it is discursively framed and through what media presentation the matter of its reality is presented.

One reality we see in these photos is the reality of rules being ignored or broken. So the photograph functions, in part, as a way of registering a certain lawlessness. Recent news reports have confirmed that the rules governing treatment of prisoners in Guantanamo were used as a model for the treatment of prisoners in Iraq. In fact, it seems, the treatment of prisoners in Guantanamo were better. But what do we make of the connection? In the first instance, the USA claimed not to be bound by the Geneva Convention, and in the second instance it is clear that the USA, though legally bound to the Geneva Convention, defies the standards of treatment stipulated by that convention. These prisoners are not humans according to the norms established by the convention, and somehow that legal move in which the USA claimed that the prisoners at Camp Delta were not entitled to protection under the Geneva Convention is one that institutes the expectation, registers the expectation, that these prisoners are less than human. They are considered enemies of the state, but they are also not conceptualisable in terms of the civilisational and racial norms by which the human is constituted. In this sense, their status as less than human is not only presupposed by the torture, but reinstituted by the torture. And here we have to see – as Theodor Adorno cautioned us to see – that violence in the name of civilisation reveals its own barbarism, even as it 'justifies' its own violence by presuming the barbaric subhumanity of the other against whom violence is waged.

The critique of the frame is, of course, beset by the problem that the presumptive viewer is 'outside' the frame, over 'here' in a First World context, and those who are depicted remain nameless and unknown. In this way, the critique I have been following stays on this side of the visual divide, offering a First World critique of First World visual consumption, or offering a First World ethic and politic that would demand an outraged and informed response on the part of those whose government perpetrates or permits such torture. The problem is, of course, compounded by the fact that the publication of the most extensive set of photographs (more than 1000) by *Salon* in February and March of 2006 is constrained by international law to protect the privacy of persons who have been the victims of war crimes. It may well be that the materials received and published by *Salon* are the same as those which had been the subject of legal battles with the Department of Defense, but even if there are some images missing, the number is extensive. The files, leaked from the Criminal Investigation Command of the US Army, included 1325 images and 93 videos. These images do not represent the sum total of torture and, as reporter Joan Walsh pointed out in 2006, 'this set of images from Abu Ghraib is only one snapshot of systematic tactics the United States has used in four-plus years of the global war on terror'.[4]

Salon investigated the 'captions' that the US Army used to identify the various scenes of torture, and they apparently included misspellings of names and unclear accounts of time and place that had to be reconstructed. The 'reality' of the events was not immediately clear on the basis of the imagery alone, and the 'timeline' had to be retrospectively figured out in order to understand the evolution and systematic character of the torture itself. The question of reconstructing or indeed restituting the 'humanity' of the victims is made all the more difficult by the fact that faces, when not already shrouded as part of the act of torture, had to be deliberately obscured to protect the privacy of the victims. What we are left with are photos of people who are for the most part faceless and nameless. But can we nevertheless say that the obscured face and the absent name function as the visual trace – even if it is a lacuna within the visible field – by which the humanity of the victim is marked? This would mean that the humans are not restored to a visual or corporeal or socially recognisable identity, but that their occlusion and erasure become the continuing sign and mark of their suffering and their humanity. The point is not to substitute one set of idealised norms for understanding the 'human' with another, but to grasp those instances in which the norm destroys its instance, when human life exceeds the norm of the human. So the names of the victims are not included in the captions, but the names of the perpetrators are. Do we lament this lack of names? Yes and no. They are, and are not, ours to know. We might think that our norms of humanisation require the name and the face, but perhaps the 'face' functions here precisely through its shroud and the means by which it is subsequently obscured. The face and name are not 'ours' to know, and perhaps affirming this limit is a way of affirming the humanity that has escaped the visual control of the photograph. To expose the victim further would be to reiterate the crime, so the task would seem to be a full documentation of the acts of the torturer as well as a full documentation of those who responsibility exposed the scandal – but all this without intensifying the 'exposure' of the victim, either through discursive or visual means.

When the photos were shown in New York as part of a show curated by Brian Wallis, the photographers were not credited for the pictures; the news organisations that first agreed to publish them were. Importantly, it was the publication of the photos that brings them into the public domain as objects of scrutiny. The photographer is given no credit for this; indeed, the photographer, though not photographed, is part of the scene that is published, and so a certain complicity is exposed. In this sense, the exhibition of the photographs with caption and commentary on the history of their publication and reception becomes a way of exposing and countering the closed circuit of triumphalist and sadistic exchange that formed the original scene of the photograph itself. The scene of that photograph now becomes the object, and we are not so much directed by the frame as directed towards it with a renewed critical capacity.

And though we feel shock at these photographs, it is not the shock that finally informs us. Sontag, in her last chapter of *Regarding the Pain of Others*, seeks to counter her earlier critique of photography. In an emotional, nearly exasperated outcry, one that seems quite different from her usual, measured rationalism, Sontag remarks, 'Let the atrocious images haunt us.' We see the photograph and cannot let go of the image that is transitively relayed to us. Sontag does not think the image alone can educate us, and she opposes the naivete and innocence of those who continue to be shocked again and again by the images of atrocity. Surely, we should have learned something. But she will not stand for coldness either. She writes that the photograph can be an 'invitation' 'to pay attention, reflect ... examine the rationalizations for mass suffering offered by established powers' (Sontag 2003: 117). And it is my sense that the curated exhibition of the Abu Ghraib photos did precisely that. But what is most interesting to me about the increasing outrage and exasperation she expressed not only in this last book, but in her articles on 9/11 and yet another called 'Regarding the torture of others' referring explicitly to Abu Ghraib, is that it continues to be directed against the photograph not only for making her feel outrage, but for failing to show her how to transform that affect into effective political action. She allows that she has in the past turned against the photograph with moralistic denunciation precisely because it enrages without directing the rage, and so excites our moral sentiments at the same time that it confirms our political paralysis. Even this frustration frustrates her, since it remains a guilty and narcissistic preoccupation with what one can do, a First World intellectual, and so fails again to attend to the suffering of others. Even at the end of that consideration, it is a museum piece by Jeff Wall that allows her to formulate this problem of responding to the pain of others, and so, we might surmise, a certain consolidation of the museum world as the one within which she is most likely to find room for reflection and deliberation. A modernist to the end, no doubt, Sontag nevertheless poses a question that I will pose again here, which is the question of whether the tortured can and do look back, and what do they see when they look at us? She was faulted for saying that the photographs in Abu Ghraib were photographs of 'us' and some critics suggested that this was again a kind of self-preoccupation that occluded the suffering of others.

But perhaps she was merely saying that, in seeing the photos, we see ourselves seeing, that we are those photographers to the extent that we share those norms that provide those frames in which those lives are rendered destitute and abject, sometimes clearly beaten to death. In Sontag's view, the dead are profoundly uninterested in us – they do not seek our gaze. This rebuff to our visual consumerism that comes from the shrouded head, the averted glance, the glazed eyes; this indifference to us performs an autocritique of the role of the photograph within media consumption. Although we might want to see, the photograph tells us clearly that the dead do not care whether we see. For Sontag, this is the ethical force of the photograph, to mirror back the final narcissism of our desire to see and to refuse satisfaction to that narcissistic demand.

She may be right, but perhaps it is also our inability to see what we see that is also of critical concern. To learn to see the frame that blinds us to what we see is no easy matter. And if there is a critical role for visual culture during times of war it is precisely to thematise the forcible frame, the one that conducts the dehumanising norm. The restriction we are asked to live with not only imposes constraints on what 'can' be heard, read, seen, felt and known. It is this numbing of the senses that we witness in the photograph, the decimation of the capacity to feel outrage in the face of human suffering, the belief that any suffering one inflicts is justified by the suffering that one has undergone or others have undergone. It is not that some stray people in the military or in security contracts failed to see, to feel, to maintain a moral perception of other persons as persons. This 'not seeing' in the midst of seeing, this not-seeing that is the condition of seeing, has become the visual norm, and it is that norm that is a national norm, one that we read in the photographic frame as it conducts this fateful disavowal.

Bibliography

Butler, J., *Precarious Life: The Powers of Mourning and Violence* (London: Verso, 2004).
Butler, J., *Giving an Account of Oneself* (New York: Fordham University Press, 2005a).
Butler, J., 'Photography, war, outrage', *PMLA* 120 (2005b), pp.318–20.
Salon, 'The Abu Ghraib files', 14 March 2006.
Sontag, S., *On Photography* (New York: Farrar, Strauss and Giroux, 1977).
Sontag, S., *Regarding the Pain of Others* (New York: Farrar, Strauss and Giroux, 2003).
Sontag, S., 'Regarding the torture of others', *The New York Times*, 23 May 2004, available at: http://www.nytimes.com/2004/05/23/magazine/23PRISONS.html (accessed 5 November 2008).

Chapter 3

'Not to be Missed' Weapons of Mass Destruction: Displaying the *Enola Gay*

Timothy W. Luke

On 18 March 2003, US President George W. Bush launched Operation Iraqi Freedom (OIF) with a series of intensely orchestrated assaults into Iraq by small military units mustered from an array of international forces – a 'coalition of the willing' pulled together haphazardly from around the world. By 1 May 2003, President Bush was staging surreal media events on US Navy ships steaming home from OIF actions and his administration was touting 'Mission Accomplished'. The USA has subsequently bungled the occupation of Iraq and mired the dwindling coalition in a bottomless bog of anti-American insurgencies, Islamic resistances, sectarian struggles and ethnic cleansings (Allawi 2007).

One of the main pretexts for war in Iraq advanced by the USA and its global coalition was the fragmentary, but nonetheless worrisome, evidence that suggested 'weapons of mass destruction' (WMD) existed in Iraq. Most significantly, OIF sought to uncover caches of weaponised nuclear explosive devices – weapons using fission and/or fusion technologies, as well as mere dirty radiological materials. Saddam Hussein's aspirations to weaponise Iraq's small civilian nuclear power programmes, and thereby lead a more formidable military nuclear power, had been carefully watched in the West since the 1970s. Between the 1970s and 2003, many Western and Soviet-bloc entities had sold a mix of unusually advanced scientific and technological devices to Baghdad. The pre-emptive Israeli air strike on Iraq's Osirak nuclear reactor and industrial complex in 1981 gave additional credibility to the perceived threat of Saddam's nuclear weapons aspirations.

The conventional war then ongoing between Iraq and Iran only underscored the apparent importance of WMD assets in Baghdad. Indeed, the use of chemical agents by Saddam against the Iranians (and domestic targets in Iraqi Kurdistan) 'proved' to many around the world how truly rogue the Baghdad Ba'athist government could be. Saddam's aggressive campaign of SCUD missile strikes against Israel, Saudi Arabia and other sites during the first Gulf War also demonstrated to the world Iraq's capacity to deploy a WMD-capable delivery system with first-, second- and even third-strike capabilities.

While the USA fixated on detecting and tracking Iraq's elusive nuclear assets from 1991 to 2003, America's first nuclear attack vehicle, the B-29 bomber *Enola Gay*, remained a WMD not easily found at home. Following its return from the Pacific theatre of war, the bomber had been stored at Davis-Monthan Army Airfield in Arizona, then Park Ridge in Illinois, then Pyote Air Force Base in Texas. By July 1961, the plane was parked out on the tarmac of Andrews Air Force Base in Maryland. Worried about its deterioration, the Smithsonian Institution took the *Enola Gay* apart in the late 1960s and moved the pieces inside its Paul E. Garber Museum facility at Suitland, Maryland. Restoration work on the *Enola Gay* began behind closed doors in December 1984 as a seven-year undertaking. Major technical difficulties in the restoration work, as well as a lack of guaranteed Smithsonian funding for the project, extended the duration of restoration to well over a decade. The forward portions of the aircraft's fuselage and other iconic components were brought out of the shop in May 1995 for a controversial showing at the National Air and Space Museum. The entire aircraft remained 'missing in (in)action' until its nose-to-tail restoration was complete and it was put on display at the Smithsonian's new Udvar-Hazy Center in Northern Virginia during December 2003.

In this chapter, I juxtapose the search for hidden WMD in Iraq with the exhibition of the historical US WMD vehicle, the *Enola Gay*. The USA was obsessed with, and anxious about, Iraq's missing WMD. It envisaged secretive development of strategic WMD in Iraq that mirrored the covert germination of its own Manhattan Project and nuclear bomber planning in the 1940s. What the USA condemned in Iraq in 2003 was thus what it celebrated about itself in the same year with the display of the *Enola Gay*.

Inspecting the evidence

Iraq began its nuclear power programme with the construction of a Russian research reactor near Baghdad between 1959 and 1968. The pace of the programme quickened in 1975 after France agreed to build a nuclear power station without International Atomic Energy Agency (IAEA) oversight at Osirak. With additional equipment sourced from German, Italian, Russian, Brazilian, Dutch, Austrian, Spanish, Chinese and American firms, Iraq assembled the industrial infrastructure capable of robust WMD production over the period 1975–90. In part to counteract the rising power of Iran and with a view to recycling Iraq's large reserves of petrodollars, the West cooperated with Baghdad in its nuclear ventures, even after the Israeli air strikes on Osirak crippled Iraq's military nuclear ambitions. Indeed, Osirak remained at the core of Saddam's efforts to reconfigure Iraq as a nuclear power. Saddam and the West wanted such aspirations to be noted in Tehran, but they were also noted in Tel Aviv. As Smithsonian curators busily restored the *Enola Gay* in Washington in a celebration of nuclear weaponry, and as the Reagan and George H.W. Bush administrations looked on benignly, US and other NATO members' high-tech companies actively helped Iraq create WMD factories for biological, chemical and nuclear devices.

The harsh peace terms imposed on Iraq by the USA after the first Gulf War included a UN-led effort to disclose, dismantle and destroy Iraq's various WMD research, development, production and strategic systems. To most neutral observers this initiative appeared successful when Baghdad agreed to WMD inspections in April 1991. During inspections, however, Saddam continued to intimate that he possessed further, well-concealed WMD and that his government stood ready to use them. This blustering took place amidst a jointly enforced aerial policing of Northern and Southern Iraqi 'no-fly zones' by American and British military aircraft, as well as a relatively stringent embargo on industrial, military, scientific and technological goods. All the same, the belief that Iraq had WMD, could readily deploy them and might use them against the USA and its allies became an enduring policy thematic in Washington from 1993 to 2003.

The United Nations Special Commission on Iraq (UNSCOM), founded in 1990 to inspect Iraqi weapons facilities after 1991, discovered credible evidence of biological and chemical agents being weaponised as late as 1995–96. The evidence for nuclear weapons was more ambiguous. UN weapons inspectors were pulled out of the country in 1998, and they did not re-enter Iraq until 2002, a situation that heightened Washington's anxieties over Baghdad successfully developing and deploying some sort of WMD system. President George W. Bush claimed that Saddam Hussein had expelled the inspectors, but back-channel communications from the Clinton White House had in fact asked the Secretary General to pull his inspectors out prior to the joint American and British air strikes on Iraqi military and scientific sites in December 1998. UNSCOM inspectors had asserted that 90–95 per cent of all Iraqi WMD had been destroyed prior to 1998, but other US, British and NATO analysts speculated that Iraq was again reassembling its WMD industries from 1998 to 2002.

When UN inspectors returned in 2002, they found a few chemical and biological weapons and extremely limited delivery capability. Moreover, much of the Iraqi stockpile of biological and chemical agents had become inert, inactive or ineffective. Nevertheless, stories of clandestine efforts to remove nuclear materials continued to circulate in Washington during and after the 2003 invasion. Many of these tales were entangled with Washington and London's justifications for war and the subsequent occupation of Iraq. Despite this, they continued to be given credence. When the *Enola Gay* was put out on display after years out of the public eye, the exhibition was promoted as a 'not to be missed' experience. Iraqi WMD systems were at the same time so threatening in Washington that they too were 'not to be missed' by the coalition of the willing. Iraq's weapons continued to be regarded as 'gone missing' in the context of UN searches, assuring Washington, though somewhat counter-intuitively, that they 'had not [yet] been missed'. Washington's obsession with hidden Iraqi WMD had become the pretext that compelled the nation to go to war against Baghdad. For its part, the exhibited *Enola Gay* potentially revealed the USA's own obsessive compulsion to hide its original, and subsequent, WMD systems.

There were many factors that combined to create anxiety in Washington about WMD during the 1990s and 2000s: the challenge of neutralising the thermonuclear assets of the former USSR (especially in Kazakhstan and Ukraine); the brazen nuclear weapon aspirations of the Democratic Peoples Republic of Korea; the open testing of Pakistani and Indian nuclear weapons; and unusual bombing attacks by new terrorists at home and abroad. Especially worrying were those mysterious nuclear WMD that Baghdad might or might not have in its military inventory. Throughout the 1990s, the USA resolved that WMD were 'not to be missed' in Iraq. Though they did not exist, the Bush Administration could not believe that they were not there.

Missing WMD

American anxieties about WMD practices in Baghdad during the 1990s reverberated in events unfolding at home in Washington. One of the USA's major national museum complexes, the Smithsonian Institution, became embroiled in an intense and bitter controversy over America's own 'not to be missed' history of the weaponising of nuclear energy in the form of a major exhibit planned for the National Air and Space Museum. The display was to be about the secret development of the atomic bomb by the USA during the 1940s and the creation of an operational strategic bombing capability with B-29 Superfortresses. The exhibit was tied to the decades-long restoration of the world's first and most famous B-29 nuclear strategic bomber, the *Enola Gay*. It soon became evident, however, that there was a great deal missing from Washington's own story about the origins of American WMD. When the National Air and Space Museum opened this hotly-contested exhibit in 1995, most of the *Enola Gay* and virtually all signs of its 'Little Boy' fission bomb were, like much of Saddam Hussein's alleged WMD laboratories, missing. The exhibit, having excised almost all artefacts and voices from 'Ground Zero' in Hiroshima and Nagasaki, arguably erased the shocking destruction of these atomic bombings on 6 and 9 August 1945. Instead, the USA elected to celebrate 'the greatest generation' of American airmen from World War II in an exhibition timed to coincide with the 40th anniversary year of V-J Day. By the time the display opened, its biggest investments were in touting the beauty of B-29 'strategic flight' rather than recovering the brutality of the Manhattan Project as a successfully 'hidden' and strategic 'atomic fight'. The blind nationalistic arrogance, selective historical memory and delusional strategic obsession put on display on the Mall in 1995 harked back to the cultural struggles that characterised the conduct of World War II. Nor are these sentiments easily disentangled from White House and Pentagon dealings with Saddam Hussein between 1993 and 2003.

In 2003, nearly a decade after the first Washington exhibit and as US military inspectors frantically combed Iraq for credible evidence of missing Iraqi WMD, the USA again staged a performance of air power. Promoting as 'not to be missed' those American WMD hidden during World War II and the Cold War, the Smithsonian opened the long-awaited Udvar-Hazy Center of the National Air and Space Museum Annex at Dulles International Airport. Parked among scores of other aircraft in a vast new display hall was the fully restored *Enola Gay* B-29 bomber. The *Enola Gay* was celebrated, once again, not as a WMD delivery system kept hidden from the USA's friends, enemies and citizens for decades, but rather as an extraordinary technological achievement in manned flight. As a supremely beautiful airplane, its meaning was declared to be that of a global aeronautical icon, rather than a secret American WMD delivery vehicle much sought after by the Imperial Japanese Army's and Navy's Military Intelligence Offices, the KGB or even MI-5. Washington's anxieties about Baghdad having and hiding WMD provide an additional explanatory frame for the *Enola Gay* controversies of the preceding decade, controversies that throw into stark relief the hiding of the USA's own WMD systems even after 1945 and 1989.

In 1995, at a national and then global level, an ideological, cultural and aesthetic conflict emerged over the display of parts of the *Enola Gay* at the National Air and Space Museum in Washington, DC (Luke 2002). The emblematic components of this one aircraft being put out on display at this location was meant to anchor an historical exhibition that would also erase all that could not be allowed on display (Nobile 1995). Most importantly, the curators of the 1995 exhibition had wanted the display to examine the motives, implementation and, most importantly, the after-effects of the atomic bombing of Hiroshima during its 50th anniversary year. In an August 1994 Washington Post op-ed piece, The National Air and Space Museum's Director, Martin Harwit, had asserted:

> This is our responsibility, as a national museum in a democracy predicated on an informed citizenry. We have found no way to exhibit the *Enola Gay* and satisfy everyone. But a comprehensive and thoughtful discussion can help us learn from history. And this is what we aim to offer our visitors. (cited in Nobile 1995: xxxiii)

The culture wars of the 1990s, however, turned this worthy educational goal into ideological grist for innumerable polemics. In the media, pro-nuclear and anti-nuclear groups sniped back and forth for weeks about the merits and demerits of having dropped the 'Little Boy' U-238 atomic weapon on Hiroshima on 6 August 1945.

Part of the furore of 1995 can be attributed to the Smithsonian's failure to show the whole aircraft on the Mall. In their planning for the memorialisation of the 50th anniversary of the atomic bombings of Japan, the National Air and Space Museum ran a sophisticated 1993–94 programme that anticipated a comprehensive exhibition centred on the on-going renovation of the *Enola Gay*. The restoration could not be completed by 1995, and the entire airplane was simply too large to fit inside the museum on the National Mall. The Smithsonian hoped to direct any public criticism of this situation by sharing its plans with interested stakeholder groups and inviting them to vet the exhibit (Nobile 1995).

Intense protests began immediately after curators circulated their proposal among historians, military experts and World War II servicemen. Most importantly, the Air Force Association (an organisation for retired and active personnel of the US Air Force) and the American Legion (a national veteran's association) launched a lobbying campaign in the local Washington media and the US Congress against the exhibition. They intended to pressure the Smithsonian to alter what they saw as 'revisionist' representations of the atomic bombings of Hiroshima and Nagasaki planned for the 1995 commemoration. For many, the unique role of this one aircraft in human history demanded that far greater reverence be shown to it. For these groups, dragging together a few parts of the fuselage, a propeller, a vertical stabiliser and some wheels or instruments was tantamount to heresy. Such curatorial practice, as they saw it, reduced the *Enola Gay* to an infamous hulk worthy only of being shown in a smattering of leftover fragments.

At the same time, the 'bits and pieces' visibility of this 1940s American WMD system lent an aura of credibility to the discoveries of UN weapons inspectors in Iraq. The assorted WMD components being dug up in Iraq throughout the 1990s led many in Washington to believe that a whole WMD system must surely exist somewhere: in Iraq's desert or mountains, or underneath one of Saddam's many palaces. This suspicion also fed intense anti-Japanese sentiments held by many US World War II veterans, still proud of Tokyo's ignominious capitulation in 1945. Such sentiments in part responded to Japan's deep-seated anger over being bombed in 1945 with real WMD. In greater part, however, claims about justified intervention functioned as the basis for a rhetorical warm-up in the divisive 1996 US presidential campaign: the campaign pitted a World War II veteran against a Vietnam War-era draft evader (Luke 2002).

Missing in plain sight

Many celebrated the early closure of the Air and Space Museum's ill-fated 1995 show on World War II and its atomic bombings. Subsequently, they forgot about the Smithsonian's plans to totally restore and install the *Enola Gay* at a new suburban display site in Northern Virginia. It was known that someday the entire aircraft would be seen, but that was to be seven, eight or ten years into the future. On 15 December 2003, however, that future event came to pass. As part of the 100th anniversary of the Wright brothers' first powered flights at Kitty Hawk, North Carolina, the Steven F. Udvar-Hazy Center or the 'Dulles (International Airport) Annex' of the National Air and Space Museum was inaugurated. The facility opened to crushing crowds during a week-long gala celebration of 100 years of manned flight. Every day visitors lined up in their mini-vans, pick-up trucks and Eurosport sedans for miles outside the facility's gates, hoping to gain admission to its bigger and better air and space displays.

This new museum building had been in planning for decades, but it became a material reality only after Steven F. Udvar-Hazy donated US$65 million to the Smithsonian to help construct the facility. Steven Udvar-Hazy is a first-generation Hungarian immigrant who earned his millions in the aircraft-leasing business. He reportedly funded the facility 'to pay back America for its opportunities and pass on his love of aviation to future generations' (Trescott 2003: A1). Nearly $300 million will eventually be spent on the facility, with the Smithsonian, the Federal government, the Commonwealth of Virginia and other donors all assisting to cover costs (Branigin 2001: 133). Even so, Udvar-Hazy personally contributed some 20 per cent of the building's construction price. The facility is over 980 feet long and it features a ten-storey-high exhibit hall, along with 255,000 square feet of exhibit space on four different levels of display (Trescott 2003: A20). Its 20 one-arced steel ceiling trusses also allow some planes to hang suspended as if in flight. Most planes are clustered together on the floor in thematic zones: pre-1920 Aviation, Commercial Aviation, World War II Aviation, General Aviation, Business Aviation, Korea and Vietnam, Sport Aviation, Cold War Aviation, etc. (Triplett 2003: 58–63).

What had been visible on the Mall only in pieces or pictures could be given close and whole examination in this far more spacious situation. Thousands of square yards of vast new hangar space heralded the Smithsonian's entry into the twenty-first century. The museum purposely styled itself as a national institution: in its first catalogue, the Air and Space Museum proudly referred to the Udvar-Hazy Center as 'America's Hangar' (Smithsonian Institution 2003). In the wake of its opening, however, questions must be asked as to what the Smithsonian is doing at this site and what 'America's Hangar' means for contemporary views on WMD systems. As an exhibition space, the Center could not be more monumental. There is, however, a great irony at work here: the Center's vast space is so packed full with aircraft and artefacts that the display arguably occludes as much or more than it reveals.

Critics of the 1995 display of the *Enola Gay* on the Mall were upset by various things. Some were upset by the downplaying of the Hiroshima bombing, claiming that Japan's atomic bomb victims had been ignored. Others were upset that only fragments of the airplane were put on display and that the accompanying nationalist prose was so subdued. Yet, for all its faults, the 1995 display carried far more information and offered far greater insights than the restored plane does now, being displayed within the 'World War II Aviation' cluster in America's Hangar. It is now difficult to find this rather large airplane in the Udvar-Hazy Center's 40 million cubic feet of space. There, parked in an immense space and cheek-by-jowl with so many other striking aeronautical artefacts and memorabilia, its symbolic power and historical significance dissipates among the site's other attractions.

As shreds of atomic dogma on the Mall in 1995, the *Enola Gay* pieces could be approached as iconic markers of the titanic events of 1945 put into one corner of the museum. As a whole ship in 2003, the *Enola Gay* bomber has become just one more airplane amidst hundreds for the edification of the Annex's visitors. In this awesomely large space, the *Enola Gay* is nested among many other significant 'historic firsts'. One can walk about in the Udvar-Hazy Center in a daze, seeing the first aeronautical type of a wide variety of aircraft from all around the world, with many individual planes often also touted as being the last surviving unit. In this context, the *Enola Gay* truly becomes just another 'first to' example in a seemingly endless series of other path-breaking aircraft. That the *Enola Gay* was the delivery system for the world's first nuclear strategic bombing is not ignored, but neither is it noted as special, significant or sacred in all the many ways that those who flew it, or suffered as a result of it, might have hoped. American teenagers' lives are already marked by two World Trade Center bombings, as well as their continuous televisual afterlife. By contrast, the atomic bombing of Hiroshima is long ago, far away and rarely shown on TV. As such, it is significantly removed from the experience of many of the Center's audience.

Not much has changed between 1995 and 2008 for the *Enola Gay*. It remains hidden, only now out in plain sight. It rests almost nose-to-nose with an iconic German plane from the 1930s – a tri-motor Junkers Ju52/3m. Nearby is a prototype of the Boeing 707 jetliner, the Boeing 367-80. Entering the huge display hall, the visitor approaches the *Enola Gay* only by first passing the alien-looking Lockheed SR-71 'Blackbird' spy plane, whose black titanium skin rivets attention. The visitor's eye is then drawn to the even more unbelievable sight of the Space Shuttle Enterprise in its own side hall, the James S. McDonnell Space Hangar. Approaching the *Enola Gay*, it is impossible to ignore an Air France Concorde and the slick silver presence of the *Clipper Flying Cloud*, a rare Boeing 307 Stratoliner – one of only ten fully pressurised airliners first flown in 1938. This congested situation is set to worsen, since only 10 per cent of the National Air and Space Museum's inventory of aircraft can be put on display on the Mall. While another 10 per cent may be out on loan at any one time, the Udvar-Hazy Center's 82 restored aircraft and 61 spacecraft will be joined by another 118 types in the coming years.

Visually impressive as the cluster of planes contained within the 'World War II Aviation' section are, they are not given a curatorial rendering that explains how nuclear bombs, jet bombers and ballistic missiles were combined into an integrated system – a new form of war machine or WMD – during 1944–5. The curators instead have placed such important information at the other end of the hall, where the 'Korea and Vietnam' and 'Cold War Aviation' clusters of aircraft lie. Even here, however, horrendously destructive systems of Cold War nuclear WMD get glossed over in dry, factual captions about this or that jet's air speed, manufacture date, engine specifications and numbers produced.

The idea that Saddam might have had secret WMD sites that the USA needed to discover – with or without UN support – tacitly acknowledges Washington's own nuclear subterfuges in the post-war period. Perhaps only the nation that produced the *Enola Gay* and used nuclear weapons in war could be so dogged in its search for WMD systems in Iraq. The Manhattan Project spent over $2 billion (in equivalent 1940s dollars) on a vast new industrial and military infrastructure, including three new secret cities in Oak Ridge, Tennessee, Los Alamos, New Mexico and Hanford, Washington. In 1991, as UNSCOM combed nooks and crannies in Iraq, Congress oddly also celebrated its own secret WMD programme of the 1940s by chartering a new display facility and artefact repository, the National Atomic Museum. The facility was based on an earlier museum that had been open since 1969 in Albuquerque, New Mexico. The museum subsequently became the nation's only official site to deal with the issue of American nuclear WMD systems during the first Gulf War.

Strangely, the *Enola Gay* is not at the National Atomic Museum and neither is the Nagasaki bomber, *Bockscar*. Instead another B-29, *The Duke of Albuquerque*, is on display, along with a B-52B that dropped the last American H-Bomb in an airburst test in 1962. In a curatorial move that underscored the versatility of WMD in adaptations to various modern delivery vehicles, however, the National Atomic Museum features a 1960s era Navy TA-7C Corsair II and Air Force F-105D, which are both nuclear-capable fighter bombers. These are the same jet fighter-bomber technologies that Saddam Hussein acquired from the USSR in the 1980s. Soon to be renamed and rebuilt as the National Museum of Nuclear Science and History, the National Atomic Museum only reinforces the sense that no nation seeking nuclear WMD would admit openly to this goal, disclose freely how it was pursuing WMD or willingly reveal what its true WMD capabilities might be. The secrecy celebrated here is one that sees nuclear states working diligently 'not to miss' any WMD developments elsewhere, but also working to ensure that their own nuclear assets 'always must be missed' by others.

The concentrated attention given to the pieces and parts from the *Enola Gay* in 1995 permitted a far greater political consideration of the aircraft's importance in history than its current showing at the Air and Space Museum's Dulles annex. Here the empty immensity of an awesome interior, and the bucolic isolation of the site itself, fosters inattention to the unique significance of this single airplane in human history. Put out on the floor with scores of other commercial and military types from the 1900s to the 1990s, the *Enola Gay* is merely another bug on a pin in a glass box of iron butterflies. Visually, the display context reduces the *Enola Gay* to just one more machinic specimen of an extinct, albeit exotic, species of old-fashioned World War II aircraft. Dwarfed by the supersonic Concorde airliner next to it, overshadowed by the racy sport planes with contemporary corporate logos suspended above it and overexposed against equally iconic World War II aircraft, the extraordinary singularity of the *Enola Gay* is not easily grasped. One bomb from this one airplane killed around 60,000 people in a few seconds and probably 90,000 more over the following decades. Visitors routinely pass by the *Enola Gay*, or stop only for two or three minutes, on their over-simulated pilgrimage through the museum's crowded paths and corridors. The Center cannot serve effectively as a site of terrible existential revelation about nuclear bombings because it too is caught up in the dense machinic celebration of aeronautical engines, airframes, electronics and controls.

The Victorian logic of solidly planted museum vitrines has not so much been transcended as translated into the building-sized scale of a glassed-in 'non-place'. The whole Helmuth, Obata and Kassabaum-designed Udvar-Hazy edifice is a truly massive steel, glass and concrete vitrine. As a structure that seeks 'to meet the special needs of a large collection of aircraft and spacecraft – along with millions of visitors – but still fit the ambience of an airport' (Smithsonian Institution 2003: 6), the Helmuth Obata & Kassabaum design team has succeeded. The space of America's Hangar basically reproduces the non-place aura of a Dulles, Baltimore-Washington International or Reagan National airport rather than the sombre significance of the National Air and Space Museum on the Mall in DC. Visitors to the Annex must alternately descend and ascend within its structures to see all of its aircraft. This transit is very much like going from parking lot, to check-in, to the gate, to the plane, to the seat, to deplane, to the baggage claim at any major airport. The building is experienced as a huge glass conduit which the visitor enters with a glassy stare to gaze at various specimens of aircraft types. The museum intends to tap into 'the spirit' of soaring through the air. Not surprisingly, given this concentration on flight, the Udvar-Hazy building also looks like a huge dirigible hangar from the 1930s. It has a 164-foot tall control tower-like observation pod over it – the Donald D. Engen Observation Tower – a dedicated space for visitors' observation of incoming and outgoing commercial airline flights at Dulles International Airport. In this space one might always be looking, but it is easy to truly not see anything at all.

To discuss the death, destruction or disaster made possible by air combat, air travel or airliners in this structure would detract from the showing of aircraft as splendid specimens of engineering perfection. The celebration of the flight of seemingly cumbersome machines is also the secret of the original Air and Space Museum on the Mall in downtown DC, where the visitor is mesmerised by smaller, older airplanes suspended as if in flight. Visitors are also able to enter into the archetypal glass exhibition case at the DC museum; because the whole structure is a single massive glass case, visitors are bid to violate older museum practices by walking around inside the display. In contrast, the Udvar-Hazy Center dissipates the destructive energy of technics, terror and tourism with its own special whiteout of information overload. The captioning of each airframe's technical flight specifications eclipses the various airplanes' missions, and the visitor moves on, believing they have 'seen it all up close and personal', to ogle the next specimen, be it the Concorde, or the P-47 or the amazing Stratoliner. Within this context, the B-29 Superfortress, the world's first atomic bomb delivery vehicle, is just another great airplane.

The *Enola Gay* is, however, the first airplane to appear in the Udvar-Hazy Center's catalogue, and several photos depict how it was moved, reassembled and restored. The catalogue also judiciously notes how the 1995 show of the *Enola Gay* 'became the center of an exhibition controversy', but the bland copy on the plane itself only outlines its machinic specifications, shows photos of it sitting in Maryland being restored and then factually records its wartime mission:

On August 6 1945, this Martin-built B-29-45-MO dropped the first atomic weapon used in combat on Hiroshima, Japan. Three days later, *Bockscar* (on display at the US Air Force Museum near Dayton, Ohio) dropped a second atomic bomb on Nagasaki, Japan. *Enola Gay* flew as the advance weather reconnaissance aircraft that day. A third B-29, *The Great Artiste*, flew as an observation aircraft on both missions. (Smithsonian Institution 2003: 13)

There is no further discussion of what happened on the ground in Hiroshima and Nagasaki on 6 and 9 August 1945 after the three B-29s flew their WMD missions over Japan. Colonel Paul Tibbets was on hand at the Udvar-Hazy Center's 11 December 2003 dedication day to recall his exploits as pilot and commander of the *Enola Gay* on 6 August 1945, but as an Associated Press account of dedication ceremonies noted:

> Museum officials avoided the controversy that grounded a 1995 exhibit of the *Enola Gay* [by] discuss[ing] the effects of the bomb dropped by the B-29 bomber. Japanese survivors say they want the exhibit to focus more on the damage from the atom bomb. (Roanoke Times, 12 December 2003: A12)

The tepid text in the catalogue about the *Enola Gay* upset many peace activists, historians, public intellectuals, veterans and aviation writers, as well as citizens in Japan and the USA, and all for different reasons. An international petition that called for the museum to detail more information about the bombing and less about the bomber was ignored by the Smithsonian (Trescott 2003: A20).

In his speech, Director of the Air and Space Museum, General John R. 'Jack' Dailey, kept to an exclusively technological script on the *Enola Gay* as a B-29 bomber aircraft, noting that the plane is in the Udvar-Hazy Center's collection because 'we could not find a better B-29 that had better technology' (Dailey in Trescott 2003: A20). By taking this approach, Dailey believes the *Enola Gay* exhibit will leave 'the interpretation of how it was used to the visitor' (Dailey in Triplett 2003: 58–63). Such null observations echo the 1995 exhibit's depoliticised wall captions:

> Something more than an airplane, [the *Enola Gay*] seems almost larger than life; as much an icon, now, as an airplane. After all this time, it still evokes intense emotions from gratitude to grief, its polished surface reflecting the myriad feelings and meanings and memories we bring before it. (Smithsonian 1995)

In 2008, the vapid etiquette of quietist reflection only helps render the *Enola Gay* an even less visible, if not missing, WMD.

Conclusion

Whether in the form of the Tripartite Axis Pact, the Soviet Bloc, the Red Chinese or the 'Axis of Evil', nuclear anxieties are now the most credible correlates for war amongst the American public. Support for the invasion of Iraq in 2003 was neither high nor intense, but the Rice-Rove-Rumsfeld spin on Iraq's WMD brought enough supporters to Congress and to public forums that the invasion was made possible. As each passing day brought more US deaths, civilian deaths and Arab animosity, and as WMD remained missing along with any demonstrable capability to construct them, OIF has become more and more a macabre fraud. Displaying the restored *Enola Gay* six months after Iraq began to sour is a pathetic sign of the ineptitude and foolishness of the George W. Bush White House. Had Bush attempted to displace his government's failure to find WMD onto the past successes of Franklin D. Roosevelt's White House during World War II, he may not have needed to scramble so much to justify the misadventures of Iraq. In the end, the only 'not to be missed' WMD in 2003 was the display of the *Enola Gay* at the Smithsonian.

OIF has brought neither stability nor enduring freedom to Iraq. The Smithsonian Institution gave the US public ready and open access to the meticulous restoration of the *Enola Gay* in December 2003, but reduced the weapon, the delivery system and the events of 1945 to yet another 'missing WMD'. In 1995, many thought that exhibiting the whole *Enola Gay* might bring nuclear weapons issues back on to the agenda for active deliberation in the twenty-first century. Unfortunately, this 'deliberation' came only in the form of Operation Desert Fox in 1998, Operation Enduring Freedom in 2001 and OIF in 2003. Displaying the *Enola Gay* – a real but outdated WMD – has only hidden the horrors of nuclear WMD systems deeper in the past century of the last millennium. That past grows dimmer each day that US military forces or intelligence agencies search Afghanistan, Iraq, Libya or North Korea for the WMD that are allegedly so avidly sought by their rouge regimes.

Saddam Hussein obviously knew very well something was different about 6 August 1945. The credible threat of a successful US bombing was always the image that rose above and beyond the *Enola Gay* aircraft itself. When Colonel Paul Tibbets and his crew so intrepidly flew this B-29

Superfortress from the city of Hiroshima into the annals of history, they also brought back with them a new nuclear standard for national power. In the post-1945 period, designer uranium, plutonium and hydrogen isotopes are the assets that any strong state must consider adopting as a sign of their sovereignty. Displaying the *Enola Gay* at the Udvar-Hazy Center, however, hides Hiroshima by separating the bomb from the bomber and both from the many ill effects of the bombing. Until the atomic bomb is connected with nuclear bombing on the ground and the strategic bomber in the air, the meaning of Hiroshima as a 'WMD event' will continue to go missing for the US public at its national museums.

This curatorial situation arguably weakens rather than strengthens the USA, since its own past and present strategic deceptions and denials are what embolden other states to fabricate atomic bombs. These states include Iran, Iraq, India, Israel, Pakistan and North Korea, as well as Russia, France, China and Great Britain. Just as the USA did during World War II and the Cold War, these states hide their own WMD experiments. All WMD experiments – be they the Manhattan Project of the USA, French *force de frappe* tests in Polynesia, British bomb tests in Australia, clandestine Israeli warhead tests, Soviet bomb tests in Kazakhstan, Chinese weapons tests in Lop Nur, Pakistani bombs in the Ras Koh Hills or Indian warheads in the Pokhran Range – spawn delusions of national invincibility that no nation can easily control and that neighbours rightly fear. It took nearly 50 years to publicly display the missing Hiroshima bomber as the new 'not to be missed' *Enola Gay*, and even then only spare mention of its atomic bombing mission was made. The interplay between the curatorial, military and political actions of the USA during the most recent Iraq war should continue to spell unease for all global publics regarding WMD. They will remain missing as long as they are credible strategic forces. The re-imagining of a World War II propeller-driven B-29 bomber as a beautiful and iconic airplane, over-riding any account of it as a deliverer of atomic doom, played a telling role in the hiding of real WMD.

Bibliography

Allawi, Ali A., *The Occupation of Iraq: Winning the War, Losing the Peace* (New Haven: Yale University Press, 2007).

Alperovitz, Gar., *The Decision to Use the Atomic Bomb and the Architecture of an American Myth* (New York: Knopf, 1995).

Berg, Scott W., 'Winged Migration', *Washington Post Weekend*, 12 December 2003, pp.33–6.

Branigin, William, 'Project prepares for take off: Contract awarded to begin work on air and space annex', *Washington Post*, 11 April 2001, p.B3.

Luke, Timothy W., *Museum Politics: Powerplays at the Exhibition* (Minneapolis: University of Minnesota Press, 2002).

Nobile, Philip (ed.), *Judgment at the Smithsonian: Smithsonian Script by the Curators at the National Air and Space Museum* (New York: Marlowe and Company, 1995).

Roanoke Times, 'Mouths agape as a new air, space museum dedicated', 12 December 2003, p.A12.

Sell, Shawn, 'Travel: 10 great things to take you on a flight into history', *USA Today*, 12 December 2003, p.5D.

Smithsonian Institution, *America's Hangar: Steven F. Udvar-Hazy Center* (Washington, DC: Smithsonian National Air and Space Museum, 2003).

Trescott, Jacqueline, 'Smithsonian's new aviation museum at Dulles gets off to a flying start', *Washington Post*, 12 December 2003, pp.A1, 20.

Triplett, William, 'A century of flight: Hold everything', *Smithsonian* 34.9 (December 2003), pp.58–63.

Chapter 4

Flying the Flag: Pan American Airways and the Projection of US Power Across the Interwar Pacific

Alison J. Williams

Introduction

On 22 November 1935 approximately 25,000 people gathered around San Francisco Bay to witness the inauguration of the world's first trans-Pacific commercial air route (*San Francisco Chronicle* 1935; Bender and Selig 1982; Gandt 1991; Krupnick 2000).[1] They watched enraptured as Captain Ed Musik piloted the Pan American Airways' (Pan Am) M-130 *China Clipper* out across the bay. The lumbering flying boat, with its four huge engines, accelerated into take off and climbed into the sky and out of view over the horizon. Musik and his nine-man crew flew the plane more than 7000 miles across the Pacific over six days, stopping off at the company's purpose-built facilities at Pearl Harbor, Hawaii; Midway Island; Wake Island; and Guam (*San Francisco Chronicle* 1935). The *China Clipper* finally landed in Manila Bay, in the Philippines, on 29 November, to a euphoric reception from a flotilla of vessels, a crowd of over 300,000 and an official welcome from the country's president (Krupnick 2000: 158).

In the mid-1930s commercial aviation was, for the most part, the preserve of the rich and famous. The aircraft flown by Pan Am across the Pacific were designed with the opulence of ocean liners in mind. Passengers could expect meals on china plates with stainless steel cutlery served at tables by stewards, and sleeping facilities similar to those found aboard the Orient Express. They could expect the same standard of accommodation and service at the mid-Pacific stop-over points constructed by Pan Am. In the early years of aviation, less than a century ago, aircraft were marvels to be gazed upon in wonderment, machines that could escape the pull of gravity and ascend into the skies. Breaking these earthly bonds has, since the time of Daedalus and Icarus, held an abiding fascination for humans (Wohl 2005). However, it was not until the interwar period that the spectacle of flight was widely popularised through the adventures of long-distance aerial pioneers, the antics of barnstormers and flying circuses, and the development of commercial air services making long-distance travel fast and charismatic (Corn 1983; Courtwright 2005; Wohl 2005). My interest in this chapter, however, is less on the romance of Pan Am's trans-Pacific route, but on how its development and operation helped to project US power across the Pacific. Using contemporary writings on the 'projection of power', this chapter examines the ways US power was enacted by the diverse agencies and activities of Pan Am's Pacific flights.

Technogeopolitics and the projection of power

The canon of classic geopolitics is peppered with references to transport technologies and how they might affect the geopolitical realities of a state (Mahan 1890; Mackinder 1904, 1919; Spykman 1970; see also Atkinson 1995). It is only recently, however, that attempts have been made to consider this relationship critically. David Butler's concept of technogeopolitics posits a recursive relationship between geopolitics and technology. He sees the need for a 'method for analysing geopolitical events that [is] ... strongly influenced by technological factors' (Butler 2001: 636). Indeed, while Halford Mackinder (1904) and his associates may have made reference to trains, planes and ships in their geopolitical writings, little consideration has been given to how these entities act upon, and are influenced by, geopolitics. A critical geopolitical approach provides the most profitable way of engaging with this relationship, for it encourages us to examine not only the role and place of such technologies within the high-level practical geopolitical planning and strategising, as undertaken by governments, but also to consider the popular geopolitical processes associated with ways of seeing and envisioning geopolitical space created by and through transport technologies. While the perceived compression of space and time by transport technologies has been well documented, and Butler (2001) has identified the existence of a mutually constituted relationship between geopolitics and technology, much less emphasis has been given to the ways in which transport technologies are implicated in the movement of power across space. It is in this context that this chapter considers the projection of power, a metaphor that simultaneously invokes visuality and geopolitics.

The idea of power projection is commonplace in much of the strategic studies and international relations literature, and yet there are relatively few instances where the term is given much theoretical consideration. For instance, the US Department of *Defense Dictionary of Military Terms* (2008) defines power projection as

> the ability of a nation to apply all or some of its elements of national power – political, economic, informational, or military – to rapidly and effectively deploy and sustain forces in and from multiple dispersed locations to respond to crises, to contribute to deterrence and to enhance regional stability.

This definition illustrates the spatial imperative within power projection, even in normative understandings of the term. It does little, however, to explain the manner in which power projection produces specific understandings of space that privilege one state's control over it. Significantly, traditional renderings of power projection usually refer to the deployment of resources beyond the territorial boundaries of a state. However, power projection can also occur within a state's own boundaries; therefore, this chapter examines how Pan Am's trans-Pacific route projected US power both within and beyond US sovereign territory.

One of the more suggestive uses of the term 'power projection' can be found in Philip's Steinberg's analysis of how oceanic space is constructed as a military force-field; a space 'in which battles are waged but also a space across which power is projected' (Steinberg 2001). Steinberg notes that his use of this terminology originated in work by Edward Said, who wrote that 'the idea of overseas rule – jumping beyond adjacent territories to very distant lands ... – has a lot to do with projections, whether in fiction or geography or art' (Said 1993: xxv). For further theoretical elaboration we might turn to John Allen (2003: 33), who explores how various Western theorists conceptualise the movement of power across space. Max Weber, for instance, conceives power as centred in one organisation or level of bureaucracy from which it is transmitted, extended or distributed outwards. In the military arena this form of transmission is more usually conceptualised as dominance. Michael Mann's description of the exercise of military power is often held up as illustrating the ways in which dominance works. He argues:

military power is socio-spatially dual: a concentrated core in which positive coerced controls can be exercised surrounded by an extensive penumbra in which terrorised populations will not normally step beyond certain niceties of compliance but whose behaviour cannot be positively controlled. (Mann 1986: 26)

Thus, according to Mann, dominance refers to the ability to control a population from a distance. This is subtly yet significantly different from power projection because power projection is primarily concerned with controlling space. This may, secondarily, afford control over a population. This chapter shows how power projection over the Pacific Ocean with its scattered island communities then generated, through popular geopolitical constructions, a widespread perception of an American Pacific. Crucially, as John Allen (2003) points out, power projection must be recognised in order to function. Recognition can be achieved through the sublime spectatorship of flight or, as we shall see, through more mundane representational forms such as postage stamps. By these unremarkable means, geopolitical power is made intelligible to public audiences.

Allen's discussion of 'stretching' power also has merit when analysing transport technologies in geopolitical constructions of space (Allen 2003). It is a stronger conceptualisation than more recent notions of 'flows' and 'lines' of power: the projection of power across a space does not occur through a simple flow of power from one node on a network to another; it is less tangible, less linear than this spatial vocabulary affords. 'Stretching' offers a stronger geopolitical imagery of power as highly mobile, but nevertheless tied to the centre and projected outwards. A regular and well-established aviation network was central to the elasticity of US power in the Pacific, as was the widespread public recognition of this power acquired through popularising the very ideal of aviation. The story that follows thus speaks to the parallel and indivisible workings of technogeopolitics and popular geopolitics. It is a narrative about the projection of power that slips easily from details of aerial survey flights and international airport construction to popular media and postage stamps.

The USA in the Pacific

The USA became engaged in the Pacific as early as the 1790s, when the first US whaling ships (based in New England) began rounding Cape Horn in search of the lucrative sperm whale grounds in the eastern Pacific (Boggs

1938; Philbrick 2001). During the nineteenth century, 'US merchantmen, whalers, and surveying and mapping expeditions ... and guano operators' increased US knowledge of, and interest in, the Pacific (Boggs 1938: 177; see also Johnson 1962; Philbrick 2004). In 1898 the USA was victorious in a war with Spain, fought ostensibly over colonial possessions in the Caribbean. However, as part of the peace treaty that ended the conflict, the USA gained the territories of Guam and the Philippines in the western Pacific. In the same year, the USA formally annexed Hawaii as a US Territory (Wiens 1962). Thus, by the beginning of the twentieth century, the USA found itself with a 'formal [Pacific] empire' and a need to re-orient its foreign and security policies to take account of these new possessions (Ferguson 2004: 8; Linn 1997; Killingray and Omissi 1999). Legislative developments, such as the Open Door Policy (1904), made Sino-American trading easier and suggest that the USA was quick to understand the potential of its new-found position (Brogan 1990: 450–1). While geo-economic policies such as the Open Door are evidence of a desire to expand US power across the Pacific, it was not until after World War I that the USA seriously considered its geopolitical and geostrategic position across the region. This was facilitated in no small part by the changing imperial composition of the Pacific. Most significant was Germany's loss of its possessions in the region to Japan, a move codified by the League of Nations, which gave the Japanese a mandate over the Caroline and Marshall group of islands in the western Pacific. For the USA, this provided a very real threat to the security of its western Pacific territories, because the mandates provided a forward staging post from which the Japanese military could, should it wish, cut the USA's supply line to both Guam and the Philippines.

The Washington Naval Treaty (1922)

Concerns within the US administration over Japan's desires in the western Pacific were somewhat mollified by its involvement in international arms limitation talks after the end of the war, which were championed by the USA. The Washington Naval Treaty of 1922 was just one outcome of this anti-war fervour, but, in terms of the Pacific, it was undoubtedly the most significant. Among the provisions of the treaty was one restricting the construction and further development of US military facilities. Article XIX, which dealt with the future militarisation of the Pacific, set out the following restrictions:

> The United States, the British Empire, and Japan agree that the status quo at the time of the signing of the present Treaty, with regard to fortifications and naval bases, shall be maintained in their respective territories and possessions specified hereunder. (Washington Treaty, Article XIX)

The territories listed for the USA were:

> The insular possessions which the United States now holds or may hereafter acquire in the Pacific Ocean, except (a) those adjacent to the coast of the United States, Alaska and the Panama Canal Zone, not including the Aleutian Islands, and (b) the Hawaiian Islands. (Washington Treaty, Article XIX)

The US government therefore agreed to keep its bases in the Philippines and Guam at their 1922 levels until the treaty expired and perhaps more importantly agreed not to build any new military bases west of Hawaii (which might act to counter Japan's growing presence in the western Pacific), thus leaving Guam and the Philippines in a weakened position (Washington Treaty, Article XXIII). Although the administration was in favour of this, the US Navy was sorely aggrieved by it and sought to find new ways to maintain and extend its sphere of influence in the region (Roskill 1968: 95; Miller 1991: 11; Baer 1994: 93).

Pacific Aviation Firsts

The restrictions on militarising the Pacific did not stop aviation enthusiasts, and even the US military, attempting to cross the ocean by plane and providing the first overt imagery of US aviation power across the region. The first aircraft to traverse the Pacific successfully were three US Army 'Douglas World Cruisers' that embarked on a round-the-world flight in 1924 (Glines 2001). Although crossing via the shortest over-water route – from the Aleutians across the Bering Straits – this flight proved that there were aircraft capable of crossing this ocean frontier. A year later, US Navy Commander John Rodger attempted unsuccessfully to become the first to fly the 2400 miles from California to Hawaii, but in 1927 the US Army claimed the honour of being the first to successfully accomplish this feat (Messimer 1981). Indeed, the US–Hawaii flight gripped aviation enthusiasts with a zeal that for many was fatal. Ernie Smith and Emory Bronte became the first civilians to conquer this route on 14 July 1927 (Scheppler 1988). However, only a month later 13 crews were killed or injured during the ill-fated Dole Air Race – a competition with $35,000 prize money for successful completion of the same route (Suchon 2003). It would be a further seven years before the indomitable Amelia Earhart successfully completed the first solo flight between the USA and Hawaii (Rich 1996).

The Dole race all too visibly illustrated the limitations and dangers of transoceanic crossings. However, the desire to cross the Pacific by aircraft was not dulled by these tragedies and in 1928 an Australian, Charles Kingsford-Smith, headed a four-man team that flew the first true trans-Pacific flight (Kingsford-Smith and Ulm 1928; Mackersey 1999). Stopping en route in Hawaii and Fiji, Kingsford-Smith piloted his plane, the Southern Cross, from California to Brisbane (Kingsford-Smith and Ulm 1928: 139–96). Kingsford-Smith's flight was important for two reasons. Firstly, it proved that an air route across the Pacific was achievable, and secondly, it proved the overwhelming need to hold sovereignty over islands that would act as air-base stop-over points along the route. Whilst Clyde 'Upside-down' Pangborn, proved that the Pacific could be flown non-stop in 1931, a commercial air route across the region would require a number of island stop-over points (Cleveland 1978: 154–78). Pangborn's plane had been so heavily modified for the flight it could not have carried any of the cargo or passengers that would make his chosen route commercially viable.

Pan American Airways

It was not until Pan Am's scheduled trans-Pacific service began in late 1935 that the Pacific was truly 'bridged' by aircraft, and US power was more securely projected over the vast expanse of the world's largest ocean (Sayre 1935). This was a considerable achievement for a company that began life as a one-aircraft firm operating the US government's airmail route from Key West in Florida to Havana, Cuba (Steele 2000). The company was shrouded in geopolitical intrigues from the outset. Three Army aviators originally incorporated Pan Am in order to bid for the Havana airmail route and prevent a German-owned company from gaining it (Jackson 1980). After a succession of buy-outs and changes in management, Juan Trippe, a Harvard graduate and World War I aviator, acquired control of the company and began to put into action his plan to make Pan Am the biggest airline in the US. Central to his ambitions were the US Foreign Air Mail routes, owned and subsidised by the US Post Office Department. While Trippe consolidated Pan Am's place in the Caribbean, through successful bids for a number of these routes, his attentions increasingly turned to developing the, as yet unclaimed, prestigious trans-oceanic routes. The highly desirable trans-Atlantic route was soon put on hold by a reciprocity clause, in an agreement between the UK and US, that prevented Pan Am inaugurating such a route until British Imperial Airways was in a position to do the same. Unfortunately for Pan Am, Imperial was not. However, this meant that the trans-Pacific route took centre stage, and all eyes turned to watch the development of this highly risky route.

Planning for the trans-Pacific route can be traced back to 1930, when the famous trans-Atlantic aviator Charles Lindbergh, acting in his capacity as technical advisor to Pan Am, undertook a survey flight of a northern Pacific route via Alaska and the Bering Straits to Kamchatka and the East Asian seaboard (Leuterwitz 1932; Lindbergh 1935). Climatic and political concerns led Pan Am to veto this route. They recognised that a route across central Pacific would be more likely to succeed despite the large over-water distances involved. One of the greatest problems encountered by Lindbergh in 1930 was the Soviet Union's reluctance to grant landing rights in Kamchatka and Japan's reluctance to allow access to its territory (Bender and Altschul 1982: 226). This highlighted the need (as illustrated by Kingsford-Smith in his 1928 flight) to have access to desirable airport locations, and led Pan Am to identify a string of US sovereign islands upon which the company could build the facilities and accommodations for servicing its planes and passengers en route across the Pacific. The identification of these locations and the development of facilities on them would indelibly mark these islands as US territories.

While Pan Am was ostensibly a commercial enterprise seeking to open up East Asian markets to the USA through aerial transportation and its airmail business, the company also had a relationship with the US government that was much more concerned with practical geopolitical matters. Ever since the restrictions placed upon the US military by the 1922 Washington Naval Treaty, the US Navy had sought ways to circumvent them and find other ways to project US power across the Pacific. The growing militarism within Japan, illustrated by its invasion of Manchuria in 1931 and its subsequent withdrawal from the League of Nations in 1933, led to a growing instability in relations (Iriye 1987: 7–8; Nimmo 2003: 137–46). In this deteriorating political climate, the closeness of Japan's mandated territories to the USA's western Pacific outposts served to further increase US military concerns about security across the region.

Into this potentially perilous situation came Trippe and Pan Am with their plans for a Pacific route. In this route the US Navy saw a way of circumventing the treaty's restrictions, for although the construction of military bases was prohibited under the treaty, the construction of commercial aviation facilities was not. As Gandt notes:

> The growing belligerence of Japan following WWI has begun to raise an alarm in both the States Department and in the navy. Having appropriated the Micronesian chain of islands in the western Pacific, Japan then dropped a curtain of secrecy around them, developing harbours and airfields in defiance of the postwar treaties. Intelligence gatherers in the navy feared that the islands were being developed not only as a protective fence guarding the gates of Japan, but also as a staging base for a possible eastward assault on US interests in the central Pacific ... The State Department [thus] found it desirable ... to establish a US presence in the middle and western Pacific, directly beneath the noses of the Japanese. That presence would be legitimised in the form of a commercial airline. (Gandt 1991: 74)

Through Pan Am's enterprise, the US military gained a number of aviation facilities throughout the mid-Pacific. More generally, the operation of the route demonstrated that the Americans enjoyed 'effective occupation' in the western Pacific. In order to be 'effective', this 'occupation' had to be witnessed, not only on the ground as a material presence (bases, flags, surveys) but also by the US public and by America's allies and foes internationally. Pan Am would thus achieve what the US military, hamstrung by the Washington Naval Treaty, was unable to: the material, logistical and symbolic projection of US power across the Pacific. This success was made possible through a disparate suite of practices, ranging from surveys of the route, through the memoirs of Pan Am employees who built the island air bases along the route, to the high theatre of the inaugural flight's departure from San Francisco and its arrival in Manila.

'Some Handy Little Islands in the Pacific'

In October 1934, Trippe (1934) wrote to the Secretary of the US Navy, Claude Swanson, to seek authorisation for Pan Am to use the Navy's facilities at Alameda (a US Navy seaplane base in San Francisco Bay) and at Pearl Harbor, Hawaii (the US Navy's main base in the eastern Pacific). This request was granted. In addition to this, on 12 March 1935 the Navy issued Pan Am with permits to construct and operate airport facilities on the islands of Midway, Wake and Guam (Swanson 1935a–c). These islands were all incontestably US sovereign territory and had been identified by Trippe himself while poring over US Hydrographic Office charts (Bender and Altshul 1982: 230). Once the route had been chosen on paper (Figure 4.1), Pan Am needed to build facilities at each stopover point, then test the route's feasibility through a series of survey flights. These survey flights were crucial to the projection of power across the Pacific. While US ships had long traversed the Pacific, they were slow and inconspicuous modes of transportation. By contrast the speed of the aircraft and the regularity of their passage made them eye-catching symbols of US power. The sheer novelty of aviation meant there was a growing popular interest in planes and their pilots. Moreover, places once considered remote could now be reached with speed and ease, which in turn changed the popular geographical imaginary of US territory.

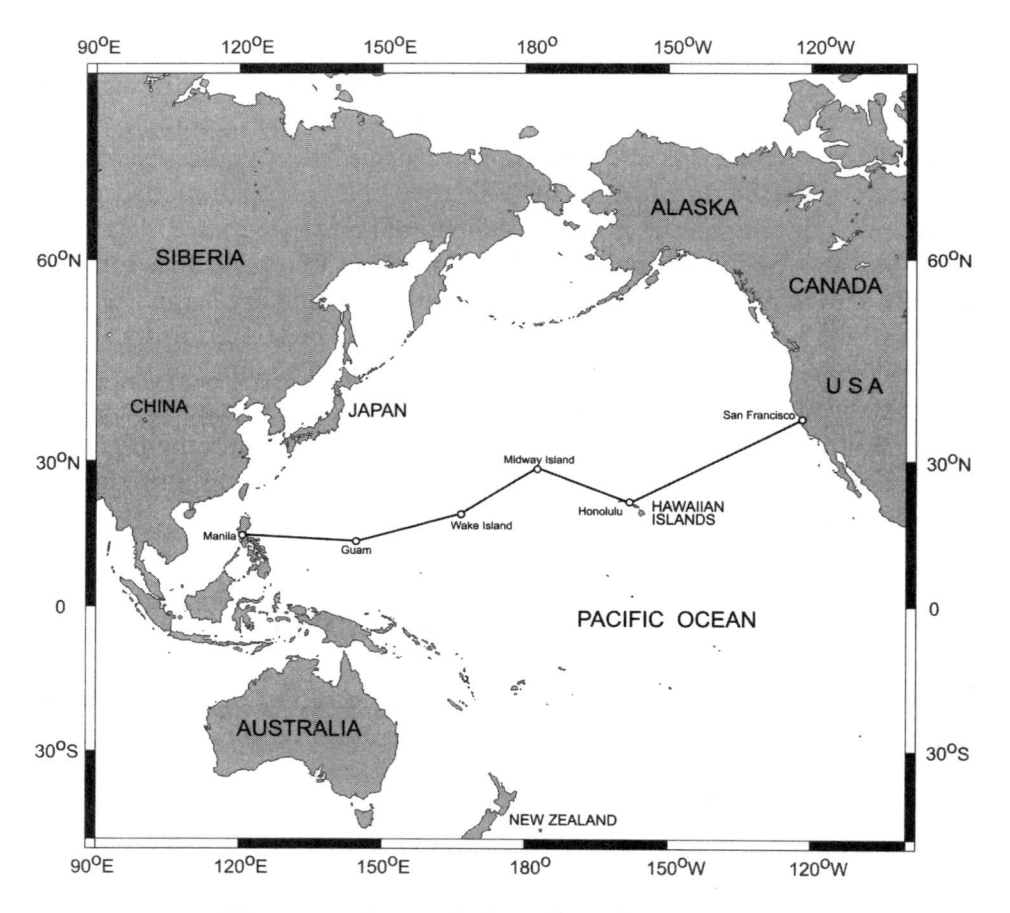

Figure 4.1 Pan Am's Central Pacific route, 1935.
Map drawn by John Garner, University of Hull

Less than two weeks after Pan Am received its permits for Midway, Wake and Guam, the *SS North Haven*, a freighter chartered by the company, left San Francisco bound for Hawaii, and then onwards to each of the islands upon which Pan Am would construct its airports (Grooch 1936; Voortmeyer and Nickisher 2005). Even this trans-Pacific voyage garnered press attention. The *Honolulu Advertiser* listed the *North Haven*'s cargo, illustrating the impact that airport construction would have on these islands:

> A quarter million gallons of gasoline, pump tanks and filters; sectional houses for complete permanent colonies at Midway and Wake and for an operating base at Guam: diesel power plants for radio, lighting, pumping and refrigeration; stoves, ovens and kitchen gear; food for six months after landing, tools and seeds for permanent gardens; launches, lighter and dock floats; radio transmitters, masts and meteorological instruments; house wiring, beacon lights and medical stores and septic tanks and plumbing. (*Honolulu Advertiser* 1935a)

Blueprints had been drawn up for each of the island airports, based on Hydrographic Office charts and maps taken from Navy survey expeditions to the mid-Pacific islands (Anonymous 1935a–c). Specialised plans identified the precise locations on each island where Pan Am's facilities would be constructed. These included offices and living quarters for the radio operators, airport manager and other Pan Am staff, as well as aircraft-servicing facilities, hotel accommodation for trans-Pacific passengers and storage facilities for food, fuel and other goods. These plans provided a less-than-subtle re-imagining of the islands, altering their status from far-flung specks in the vast Pacific, to 'civilised', developed, Americanised places within a network of other similar places, owned and controlled by the US. Recognition of this new status involved a projection of USA power over them and the oceanic space surrounding them. As with the internal frontier in the nineteenth century, the Pacific frontier of the twentieth century was to be 'civilised' and 'pacified'.

The *North Haven* undertook two trans-Pacific voyages, supplying firstly the materials to construct the initial bases at Midway, Wake and Guam, and secondly the prefabricated hotels for Midway and Wake and the furniture to dress them. The building of these facilities was recorded by a number of Pan Am employees, whose memoirs were important in generating public awareness of Pan Am's presence across the region. Among them was William S. Grooch, who was Pan Am's Executive Officer on both *North*

Haven voyages. He wrote about his experiences in three books. The first of these, *Skyway to Asia*, was published in 1936. It detailed the development of the route from the first *North Haven* expedition to the inaugural flight and provides an insight not only into the construction of facilities, but also into media interest in the route. Grooch's description of his arrival at Wake Island leave the reader in little doubt of the desolate and isolated nature of the places upon which Pan Am built its facilities:

> Our charts showed Wake Island to be shaped like a horse-shoe with a lagoon in the center. It is entirely surrounded by a wide reef. The waters around the island are so deep that a ship cannot anchor ... The islands appeared to be covered with scrub trees, brush and jumbled masses of rocks. (Grooch 136: 89–90)

Although the Pacific Cable Company maintained a small cable station on Midway, Wake was seemingly uninhabited and wild. It would be the job of Pan Am to tame this group of islands and make them habitable. Grooch describes how this was achieved by blasting the coral in the lagoons to provide safe ship-landing facilities at the islands, by building unloading docks that enabled the *North Haven*'s cargo to be shipped ashore and by constructing airport buildings. Grooch's writing style creates the impression of Pan Am's employees as rugged adventurers, tasked with the job of civilising these islands.

Stamping Pan Am's mark

One of the most notable vehicles for public interest in Pan Am's route was the issue of souvenir airmail first-day covers. The collection of these covers was a popular hobby during the interwar period, an enthusiasm that extended even to President Roosevelt himself (Weirather 2007). The geopolitics of the postage stamp is highly significant, as Pauliina Raento and others have outlined (see Brunn 2002; Cusack 2005; Jeffrey 2006; Raento 2006; Raento and Brunn 2008). The US Post Office issued three airmail stamps to coincide with the inaugural Pan Am trans-Pacific flight. They showed an aircraft, the *China Clipper*, 'flying out of a sunburst, bracketed by the shields of the United States and the Philippines' (Weirather 2007: 307).

The importance of these souvenirs to the successful projection of US power across the Pacific can be found in the care taken by Pan Am and the US Post Office to ensure stamp collectors supported the venture. The first official first-day cover featuring Pan Am commemorated the first survey

Figure 4.2 The first-day cover marking Pan Am's inaugural trans-Pacific flight, 22 November 1935.
Source: Author's collection

flight from Alameda to Hawaii in April 1935. This flight was actually postponed because not enough notice of the flight date had been given for stamp collectors to post their covers to Alameda. As Krupnick comments:

> It is now hard to imagine how important the concerns and wishes of flight cover collectors were both to Pan Am and to the Post Office Department. First, there were a lot of cover collectors in the 1930s. Secondly, and much more importantly, they increased the general public's awareness of airmail in general and specifically the Pacific airmail service. (Krupnick 2007: 307)

This interest in first-day covers can be seen in the sheer numbers that were produced during the development and inauguration of the route. Pan Am created their own first-day covers to celebrate many of the significant moments in the development of the route, including the *North Haven* voyages and all of the survey flights. These covers were stamped with cachets of the flights, some professionally composed, others apparently created by Pan Am's island employees using carved wood blocks (Krupnick 2000: 36). Such covers were prized by philatelists and air enthusiasts alike and spread beyond the immediate environs of the company. The most significant official first-day cover was that issued to commemorate the inaugural flight (see Figure 4.2). Thousands were produced and taken aboard the *China*

Clipper to the Philippines and back (Krupnick 2000: 589). Indeed, the route initially operated solely to carry airmail to East Asia, and it was the US Postmaster General, James Farley, who gave the official launch speech at the inauguration ceremony (Krupnick 2000: 150). Seemingly insignificant, these everyday objects were despatched around the world in Pan Am's aircraft, by Pan Am employees and the general public, undoubtedly contributing to the stability of Pan Am's achievement. More than this, airmail stamps such as these continue to be a form of representation that also authorise the aerial movement of letters and thus, in a very direct way, enact the power they purport to represent.

Flying the Central Pacific route

The aircraft that Pan Am flew on its trans-Pacific route also provided a significant visual representation of the projection of US power in this endeavour. In 1931, Pan Am wrote to several of the USA's leading aircraft manufacturers requesting them to submit plans for 'a high speed, multi-motored flying boat having a cruising range of 2500 miles against 30-mile headwinds and providing accommodation for a crew of four together with at least 300 pounds of airmail' (Pan-American Airways 1944: 3).

The desired range of 2500 miles would provide these aircraft with the ability to fly non-stop from San Francisco to Honolulu, the longest section of Pan Am's intended route. By the end of the following year, two companies – Martin and Sikorsky – had submitted bids. The *New York Times* reported that Pan Am accepted both of these and work began to construct the prototypes of the Sikorsky S-42 and the Martin M-130 (*New York Times* 1932). The first S-42 was delivered to Pan Am on 1 August 1934 and immediately began flying on its South American routes (Allen 2000: 49). In early 1935 the plane was transferred to the West Coast to undertake several survey flights in preparation for the establishment of the trans-Pacific route. These flights had been on hold until the construction of the airport facilities at Midway, Wake and Guam had advanced sufficiently so that an arriving aircraft could be guided to these locations, using Pan Am's revolutionary radio direction-finding equipment, and serviced ready for the return journey.

The first survey flight left San Francisco on 16 April 1935 and flew to Honolulu and back; the visual representation of what the *Honolulu Advertiser* (1935b) called 'America's bid for air supremacy of the Pacific'. Two months later the second flight travelled to Midway and back, followed by flights to Wake in August and Guam in October (Krupnick 2000: 89). By

November 1935, Pan Am's S-42 had not only proved the feasibility of the trans-Pacific route, but had generated a great deal of interest through media coverage and Pan Am's own advertising. The headline of the *Honolulu Star-Bulletin* of 17 April 1935 read 'Hawaii is linked to coast by air', and was accompanied by a photograph of the S-42 arriving in Pearl Harbor after the first survey flight (Krupnick 2000: 111). The involvement of journalists and photographers in recording these events did more than simply represent Pan Am's route development; these journalists were engaged in developing and sustaining a popular sense that Pan Am was bringing Hawaii closer to the US mainland, a distance now expressed as flying time. Not only did this represent a strengthening of the ties that would lead to union, it rendered the intervening space and, by extension, the wider Pacific Ocean as US territory.

The main aims of these survey flights were two-fold: firstly, to test the aircraft and crews; and secondly, to map the route. Pan Am's radio direction finding equipment allowed its *Clipper* pilots to 'home in' on a signal and follow it to their island destinations. However, the survey flights provided much-needed knowledge for the company's navigators who were tasked with preparing aerial charts and mapping the direction that planes should take and the distances between destinations. These navigation procedures were similar to those used aboard ships. Indeed, the *Clippers* were fitted with a hatch in the roof of the cockpit so that the navigator could use the stars as navigational aids. The survey flights thus not only proved the air-worthiness of the aircraft and crew, but also facilitated the aerial mapping of the Pacific.

Conclusions

The inaugural flight of the *China Clipper* on 22 November 1935 was the pinnacle of Pan Am's achievement in developing and operating a trans-Pacific commercial air route that projected US power across the region. The flight itself was a public spectacle and elicited a range of responses that went beyond merely looking with admiration:

> The Governor of California proclaimed 22 November Pan American Airways day. A state-wide committee was formed to assist at the birth of America's first transoceanic airline. An international broadcast was arranged to include speakers from Alameda, Honolulu and the Philippines. The world was invited to listen in. (Grooch 1936: 185)

While the Pan Am flights were central to the projection of US power across the Pacific, this chapter has sought to highlight the range of practices, activities and documents that contributed to this projection. The fanfare of the inaugural flight may have offered the ultimate representation of Pan Am's primacy in the region, but it was through the surveying and preparation of the route that Pan Am truly made the Pacific a US space. For the six years following the *China Clipper's* first flight, Pan Am consolidated its position as the premier commercial aviation company in the Pacific. As well as the continued operation of the Central Pacific route, a second trans-Pacific route from San Francisco to New Zealand was developed and inaugurated. Both these routes generated ongoing popular interest and media coverage, continuing to sustain Pan Am's cultural as well as aerial dominance. However, the true significance of these routes was not truly understood until 7 December 1941, when the Imperial Japanese Navy launched a pre-emptive air strike against the US Navy's facilities at Pearl Harbor, Hawaii. In the following few days the Philippines and Wake were also overrun by the Japanese. The name Midway would become famous as the site of one of the most significant naval battles of the modern era. Yet, for Americans, these islands were not unknown far-flung outposts of the US military, they were recognised as American soil, home to the airports of Pan Am's Central Pacific air route.

Bibliography

Allen, John, 'Spatial assemblages of power', in D. Massey, J. Allen and P. Sarre (eds), *Human Geography Today* (Cambridge: Polity Press, 1999), pp.194–218.

Allen, John, *Lost Geographies of Power* (Oxford: Blackwell, 2003).

Allen, Roy, *The Pan Am Clipper: The History of Pan American's Flying-Boats 1931–1946* (London: Barnes and Noble, 2000).

Anonymous, *Pan Am Blueprint for Construction at Guam*, Record Group 28, Contract Files, FAM 14, Box 5 (US National Archives and Record Administration, Washington, DC, 1935a).

Anonymous, *Pan Am Blueprint for Construction at Midway*, Record Group 28, Contract Files, FAM 14, Box 5 (US National Archives and Record Administration, Washington, DC, 1935b).

Anonymous, *Pan Am Blueprint for Wake*, Record Group 28, Contract Files, FAM 14, Box 5 (US National Archives and Record Administration, Washington, DC, 1935c).

Atkinson, David, 'Geopolitics, cartography and geographical knowledge: envisioning Africa from fascist Italy', in M. Bell, R.A. Butlin and M.J. Heffernan (eds), *Geography and Imperialism, 1820–1940* (Manchester: Manchester University Press, 1995), pp.265–97.

Baer, George, *One Hundred Years of Sea Power: The US Navy, 1890–1990* (Stanford: Stanford University Press, 1994).
Bender, Marylin and Altschul, Selig, *The Chosen Instrument: Pam Am, Juan Trippe, the rise and fall of an American Entrepreneur* (New York: Simon and Schuster, 1982).
Boggs, Samuel Whittemore, 'American contributions to geographical knowledge of the Central Pacific', *The Geographical Review* XXVIII/2 (1938), pp.177–92.
Brogan, Hugh, *The Penguin History of the United States* (London: Penguin, 1990).
Brunn, Stanley D., 'Stamps as iconography: Celebrating the independence of new European and Central Asian states', *Geojournal* 52 (2002), pp.315–23.
Butler, David, 'Technogeopolitics and the struggle for control of world air routes, 1910–28', *Political Geography* 20 (2001), pp.635–58.
Cleveland, C.M., *Upside-Down Pangborn: King of the Barnstormers* (Glendale: Aviation Book Company, 1978).
Corn, Joseph, *The Winged Gospel: America's Romance with Aviation* (Oxford: Oxford University Press, 1983).
Courtwright, David, *Sky as Frontier: Adventure, Aviation, and Empire* (College Station: Texas A and M University Press, 2005).
Cusack, Igor, 'Tiny transmitters of nationalist and colonial ideology: The postage stamps of Portugal and its empire', *Nations and Nationalism*, 11 (2005), pp.591–612.
Dicken, Peter, *Global Shift* (London: Paul Chapman Publishing, 1998).
Ferguson, Niall, *Colossus: The Rise and Fall of the American Empire* (London: Penguin, 2004).
Gandt, Robert L., *China Clipper: The Age of the Great Flying Boats* (Annapolis: US Naval Institute Press, 1991).
Glines, Carroll V., *Around the World in 175 Days: The First Round-the-World Flight* (Washington, DC: Smithsonian, 2001).
Grooch, William S., *Skyway to Asia* (New York: Longmans, Green and Company, 1936).
Harvey, David, *The Condition of Postmodernity* (Oxford: Blackwell, 1989).
Honolulu Advertiser, 'History of Pan American pioneering in Pacific's commerce is recounted', 17 April (1935a).
Honolulu Advertiser, 'Thousands see flight's start at Golden Gate', 17 April (1935b).
Iriye, A., *The Origins of the Second World War in Asia and the Pacific* (London: Longman, 1987).
Jackson, Ronald W., *China Clipper* (New York: Everest House, 1980).
Jeffrey, Keith, 'Crown, communication and the colonial post: Stamps, the monarchy and the British Empire', *The Journal of Imperial and Commonwealth History* 34 (2006), pp.45–70.
Johnson, Robert E., *Thence Round Cape Horn: The Story of United States Naval Forces on Pacific Station, 1818–1923* (Annapolis: US Naval Institute Press, 1963).
Killingray, David and Omissi, David, *Guardians of Empire: The Armed Forces of the Colonial Powers, c. 1700–1964* (Manchester: Manchester University Press, 1999).
Kingsford-Smith, C.E. and Ulm, C.T.P., *The Great Trans-Pacific Flight* (London: Hutchinson, 1928).
Krupnick, Jon E., *Pan American's Pacific Pioneers: The Rest of the Story* (Montana: Pictorial Histories Publication Company, 2000).

Leuterwitz, H.C., *Lindbergh's Washington DC–Tokyo Flight*, Pan American Airways Archives, Miami University Library, Box 47/5 (1932).
Lindbergh, Anne Morrow, *North to the Orient* (New York: Harcourt Brace and Company, 1935).
Linn, Brian McAllister, *Guardians of Empire: The US Army and the Pacific, 1902–1940* (Chapel Hill: University of North Carolina Press, 1997).
Mackersey, Ian, *Smithy: The Life of Sir Charles Kingsford-Smith* (London: Little, Brown and Company, 1999).
Mackinder, Halford J., 'The geographical pivot of history', *The Geographical Journal*, 23/4 (1904), pp.421–37.
Mackinder, Halford J., *Democratic Ideals and Reality* (Harmondsworth: Penguin, 1919).
Mahan, Alfred T., *The Influence of Sea Power upon History* (London, Little Brown and Company, 1890).
Mann, Michael, *The Sources of Social Power: Vol. I – A History of Power from the Beginning to AD 1760* (Cambridge: Cambridge University Press, 1986).
Messimer, Dwight R., *No Margin for Error: The US Navy's Trans-Pacific Flight of 1925* (Annapolis: US Naval Institute Press, 1981).
Miller, Edward S., *War Plan Orange: The US Strategy to Defeat Japan, 1897–1945* (Annapolis: US Naval Institute Press, 1991).
New York Times, Huge Ocean Planes Ordered by Air Line, 1 December 1932.
Nimmo, W.F., *Stars and Stripes Across the Pacific: The United States, Japan, and the Asia–Pacific region, 1895–1945* (London: Praeger Publishers, 2003).
Ocala Morning Banner, Some Handy Little Islands in the Pacific, 28 August 1935.
Oxford English Dictionary, 'Projection', http://dictionary.oed.com/cgi/entry/50189697?single=1&query_type=word&queryword=projection&first=1&max_to_show=10 (accessed 3 March 2008).
Pan American Airways, *Trans-Pacific Survey Flight 1935*, Nos 1–4, Pan American Airways Archives, Miami University Library, Box 249/7 (1935).
Pan American Airways, *History of the Transpacific Air Services to and through Hawaii*, Pan American Archives, Miami University Library, Box 369/4 (1944).
Philbrick, Nathanial, *In the Heart of the Sea* (London: Viking, 2001).
Philbrick, Nathanial, *Sea of Glory: The Epic South Seas Expedition 1838–1842* (London: Harper, 2004).
Raento, Paulina, 'Communicating geopolitics through postage stamps: The case of Finland', *Geopolitics* 11 (2006), pp.601–29.
Raento, Paulina and Brunn, Stanley D., 'Picturing a Nation:' Finland on postage stamps, 1917–2000', *National Identities* 10 (2008), pp.49–75.
Rich, Doris, *Amelia Earhart: A Biography* (Washington, DC: Smithsonian, 1996).
Roskill, Stephen, *Naval Policy between the Wars* (New York: Walker, 1968).
Said, Edward, *Cultural and Imperialism* (London: Vintage, 1993).
San Francisco Chronicle, Giant China Clipper Hops for Manila, 23 November 1935.
Sayre, Daniel, *Pacific Bridgement, Pan American Airways Supplement 1*, Pan Am Archives, Miami University Library, Box 249/10 (1935).
Scheppler, Robert H., *Pacific Air Race* (Washington, DC: Smithsonian, 1988).
Spykman, Nicholas, *America's Strategy in World Politics* (London: Shoestring Press, 1970).

Steele, John R., *The Early Years*, www.panam.org (accessed 6 October 2000).
Steinberg, Philip, *The Social Construction of the Ocean* (Cambridge: Cambridge University Press, 2001).
Suchon, Josh, *Hawaii Race: Air Tragedy*, http://findarticles.com/p/articles/mi_qn4176/is_20030605/ai_n14547300/?tag=content;col1 (accessed 24 November 2003).
Swanson, Claude, *Revocable Permit for Sand Island*, Pan Am Archives: Miami University Library, Box 21/6 (1935a).
Swanson, Claude, *Revocable Permit for Sumay, Guam*, Pan Am Archives: Miami University Library, Box 21/6 (1935b).
Swanson, Claude, *Revocable Permit for Wake Island*, Pan Am Archives: Miami University Library, Box 21/6 (1935c).
Trippe, Juan, *Letter to Claude Swanson*, Pan Am Archives: Miami University Library, Box 192/15 (1934).
US Department of Defense, *Dictionary of Military Terms – Power Projection*, http://www.dtic.mil/doctrine/jel/doddict/data/p/04209.html (accessed 5 February 2008).
Voortmeyer, Bert and Nickisher, Carol, *Riding the Reef: A Pan American Adventure with Love* (McLean: Paladwr Press, 2005).
Washington Naval Treaty 1922, http://www.dtic.mil/doctrine/dod_dictionary/index.html (accessed 24 June 1999).
Weirather, Larry, *The China Clipper, Pan American Airways and Popular Culture*, (Jefferson: McFarland and Company, 2007).
Wiens, Harold, *Pacific Island Bastions of the United States* (Princeton: Princeton University Press, 1962).
Williams, Alison J., 'Hakumat al Tayarrat: The role of air power in the enforcement of Iraq's boundaries', *Geopolitics* 12/3 (2007), pp.505–28.
Wohl, Robert, *The Spectacle of Flight: Aviation and the Western Imagination, 1920–1950* (London: Yale University Press, 2005).

Part Two

Performance

Chapter 5

Affectivity and Geopolitical Images
Sean Carter and Derek P. McCormack

Introduction

This chapter considers the following question: In what ways does attending to processes of affectivity complicate or enhance our understanding of the relations between geopolitics and visual culture? We pose and pursue this question in the context of what appears to be something of an 'affective turn' across the social sciences and humanities concerned with how phenomenon including emotion, mood, feeling, affect and passion participate in social, cultural, economic and political life. This renewal of interest in affectivity has many strands and implications, not least for understanding the logics through which geopolitical cultures are produced and reproduced. And yet questions of affectivity, at least at first glance, would appear to move us away from attending to how images participate in such geopolitical cultures: particularly if a renewal of critical interest in affectivity is understood as part of the emergence of what have been called non-representational approaches to culture and politics: approaches that challenge the primacy of representation as the basis for thinking, knowing and politics (Thrift 2008). Images, after all, tend to be understood first and foremost in representational terms – through processes that reflect and/or construct the matter and meaning of the world. In contrast, affectivity is often understood as a process operating in the non-representational registers of social, cultural and political life. However, and as we argue in this chapter, conceiving of affectivity as non-representational does not necessarily encourage us to attend less to the politics and geopolitics of images; indeed, it encourages us to think further and think differently about what images are and, perhaps more importantly, about what images can *do* within and through contemporary geopolitical cultures.

Thinking through the relation between affectivity and geopolitical images in this way depends in turn upon at least three critical moves, each of which we seek to make and elaborate upon in this chapter. The first move involves differentiating the category of affectivity, particularly through attending to the difference between affect, feeling and emotion. The second move involves refusing the tendency to equate the concept of image with the process of representation. And the third move involves developing a vocabulary robust yet flexible enough to conceive of how images *move* (spatio-temporally and affectively) through processes and logics whose power is only ever partially accounted for by critical accounts of signs, scripts and codes, however performative.

By working through each of these moves, we pay particular attention to the relation between the visual culture of geopolitics and cinematic images. There is, of course, an extensive and growing body of scholarship on the relation between cinema and popular geopolitical cultures (Sharp 1998; Bleiker 2001; Power and Crampton 2005; Weber 2005; Behnke and de Carvalho 2006; Holden 2006). In much of this work, the relation between film and geopolitics/international relations has tended to be traced in terms of two related sets of logics. First, a range of critical commentators have sought to reveal the mutually implicated shifts in the *scripting* of geopolitical and cinematic interventions, in which the codes and signs of geopolitical intervention are articulated through the representational logics of film (Ó Tuathail 1996; Dodds 2003). Second, the relation between geopolitical and cinematic interventions has been understood as a matter of the production and reproduction of particular logics of perception and 'ways of seeing' (Virilio 1989, 2002; see also Ó Tuathail 1996; Mattelart 1996; Luke and Ó Tuathail 1998; Der Derian 2001).

Here, however, we wish to foreground the affective participation of film within complex fields of popular geopolitical cultures. And we do so through a brief discussion of three films – *The Thin Red Line* (1998), *United 93* (2006) and *Three Kings* (1999). Our choice of these films has been made in part because we both use them in our teaching to think through various issues. In discussing these films our point is not that they are only about affectivity or that their significance can be understood solely as a question of their affective qualities. Rather, we want to argue that a fuller understanding of the geopolitical significance of these films requires attending to how they mobilise different affective logics.

Geopolitics becoming (more) affective

To begin we want to outline how questions of affectivity have become more important to scholars interested in thinking through and interrogating geopolitical cultures. The events of 11 September 2001 provide a point of departure here. Clearly, '9/11' is not the first geopolitical event to have an intense geopolitical resonance. Nor indeed can it be claimed that it is more resonant than for any other geopolitical event. Yet, while critical and scholarly response to the events of 11 September 2001 has been manifold, one of the distinguishing features of the analysis of this event by those in the social sciences and humanities is the way in which notions of affectivity have been employed. This, in part, is something of a coincidence: after a period of latency, social sciences and humanities were beginning to take affectivity more seriously at just about the same time as the events of 11 September and the ongoing 'war on terror' which followed in its wake. At the same time, it is possible to claim that the intensity of these events have amplified such interest, insofar as they have required scholars to confront the importance of affectivity in thinking through political and geopolitical processes.

Such attention registers in a number of ways. First, through a general reflection on the political significance of concepts such as terror and fear, and a critical excavation of how such affects and emotions have been both understood historically and actively manipulated in various political regimes (see Badiou 2003). Then, and second, this attention registers through efforts to conceptualise how the affective nature of 9/11 was crucial to subsequent efforts to provide justification and legitimacy for military intervention. As Gearóid Ó Tuathail has argued, in the USA the affective logics of 9/11 became linked with the moral and geopolitical imperatives of military intervention in such a way that the intensity of the first came to work, at least for a time, as an inviolable support for the apparent necessity of the latter. For Ó Tuathail, drawing upon the political theorist William Connolly (2002), 'the affective tsunami unleashed by the terrorist attacks of 2001' came to work as a 'powerful somatic marker for most Americans', at the centre of 'an affect-imbued memory bank for the media and political class in the United States and, consequently, for the media-incited nation' (2003: 859). While Ó Tuathail's discussion arguably reinforces a suspicion of affectivity as something detrimental to argument and analysis, it nevertheless foregrounds the need to recognise that geopolitical cultures operate through and are sustained via processes that are always more than discursive.

Third, interest in affectivity registers in efforts to reflect upon the nature of political violence. On one level the affective fact of violence seems obvious. After all, violence is nothing if not affective: it is felt, even if it is not emotional. Yet as Nigel Thrift has argued recently, the affective space of violence is neither so concentrated nor so immediate: 'violence is not just the physical trauma of bullet penetrating body or fist impacting jaw or knife rending flesh, or indeed, bomb cutting a swathe through an unsuspecting street' (2007: 274). Rather, violence needs to be conceived as a set of distributed practices that involve bodies and objects in different kinds of alignment and association, often over great distances. Furthermore, argues Thrift, violence is becoming more performative and increasingly mediated. The point here is not just that we see more and more images of violence acted out on screens of various kinds. Rather, the point is that the very nature of violence, and the manner in which it is conducted, is organised at least in part to work through the affective logics of mediated spaces, whether this is through tactics of 'shock and awe' or suicide bombing.

Fourth, interest in affectivity registers in discussions of how geopolitical intervention post-9/11 has been organised around particular imperatives, the most important of which is pre-emption. Brian Massumi (2007) has argued that the object of intervention in the war on terror has become *virtual*, in the terms outlined in the now infamous words of the former US Defense Secretary, Donald Rumsfeld: 'unknown unknowns'. In a world of virtual threats, the fears and anxieties of which potential futures are generative become crucial to understanding how the logics of intervention are reorganised in the present around efforts to engage with threats that have not yet materialised (see also Anderson 2007).

Fifth, and finally, interest in affectivity is also registering through efforts to rethink the process of thinking and, by extension, the processes of thinking geopolitically. Importantly, while contemporary theories of affectivity rework the relation between the biological and the cultural, they also refuse to juxtapose affectivity to the serious business of thinking. Affectivity is not necessarily something that undermines thinking, nor is it something through which thinking must penetrate in order to reveal some deeper, more transparent truth. Rather, for better or for worse, affectivity is part of the moving grounds from which thinking – including thinking critically about geopolitics – emerges and is cultivated (Bennett and Shapiro 2001; Gibson-Graham 2006).

Differentiating affectivity through cinematic images

This interest in affectivity is also beginning to register in work on the relation between geopolitics and visual culture (Aitken 2006; Carter and McCormack 2006; Hughes 2007), and it is the question of this relation that we want to address here. Again, while the events of 9/11 were by no means the first to be witnessed via images, the scale and extent of 9/11 as an event of collective image-witnessing was particularly significant. Indeed, this image-event, and the invasion of Iraq that followed in April 2003, have been understood as spectacular interventions into a highly mediated image-economy. Furthermore, as various commentators have remarked, the comparison between events unfolding live on TV screens and the scripted scenarios of the Hollywood disaster movie was uncanny (Zizek 2002). Certainly, various comparisons can be made in this regard. It was precisely the pre-scripted and pre-digested aspect of these images that provoked certain ways of feeling: we had seen it all before and therefore, in some sense, already knew how it should feel. However, despite appeals to cinematic frames of reference, affective response to those images was often far more immediate, happening before any judgements or comparisons with previously viewed cinematic scenarios could be made, too quickly to be the consequence of the recognition of a script or scenario. If any pre-scripting took place, it was retrospective: a way of making sense of the significance of images long after the affective materiality of those images had registered as a sense of corporeal disquiet, a knot in the stomach, a visceral unease. Such images were affective before they were re-scripted via familiar frames of reference.

How might we make sense of the affective quality of such image-event? In order to do this, we need to consider first what it is we mean when we talk about affectivity and, more specifically, how the category of affectivity might be differentiated in ways that provide some purchase on the various ways in which images might be said to be affective. Crucial here is the distinction, increasingly recognised and debated across a range of disciplines, between categories of affect, feeling and emotion (Massumi 2002; McCormack 2003; Thrift 2004; Hemmings 2005; Shouse 2005; Anderson 2006). Emerging from a tradition of thinking that can be traced through figures such as Baruch Spinoza (1989), Gilles Deleuze (1989; 1992) and, more recently, Brian Massumi (2002), *affect* can be understood as a kind of turbulent background field of relational intensity, irreducible to and not containable by any single body or subject. Affect is never just personal, even if it can be registered, or sensed, in bodies. Then, and second, feeling can be understood as the registering of intensity in a sensing body before that intensity is recognised as a distinct emotion (see Shouse 2005; Anderson 2006). Feeling is the sense of disquietude experienced by a body before this sense becomes recognisable, or nameable, as fear. Emotion, in turn, is the qualification of the felt intensity of affect through its registering in socio-cultural webs of meaning. Emotion is affect felt and expressed, through language – but also through a look, a glance, a gesture – as fear, hope, joy, etc. This three-fold differentiation is, of course, rather artificial. What we take to be affectivity is an ongoing passage between affect, feeling and emotion, in which at various points for instance affect is felt but not expressed, or where the expression of emotion flows back into the distributed field of affects. Furthermore, this is not even to begin thinking about how such a three-fold typology might relate to or include categories such as passion. Nevertheless, this typology does provide a way to gain more conceptual purchase on the affectivity of images. In what follows we therefore want to discuss each of these categories in relation to an individual film, in order to exemplify the geopolitical significance of those films. In doing so our point is not that any film is only about any one element of affectivity; rather, in their different ways, each of the films allows us to draw out and exemplify the importance of a differentiated conception of affectivity to the critical analysis of geopolitical images.

Fields of affect

We want to turn first to the relation between cinema and *affect*. The writings of Gilles Deleuze on cinema (1985; 1986) provide some orientation here, and in particular his concept of affection-image.[1] For Deleuze the affection-image is distinguished by how it gathers together and registers the intensity and singularity of *affects*. Such affects are pre-personal in the sense that they are 'not individuated like people and things'. These affects exist instead as 'singularities'; and they 'enter into virtual conjunction and each time constitute a complex entity', in a process Deleuze compares to melting, boiling, condensation or coagulation (1986: 106). An affect in these terms is like an atmosphere, in which lots is going on, even if it is not yet visible, tangible or sensible. Yet affect is an atmosphere from which, and within given constraints, certain things might happen, in a process through which affect becomes 'actualised in an individuated state of things and in the corresponding real connections (with a particular space-time ... particular characters, particular roles, particular objects)' (Deleuze 1986: 106).

How do cinematic images register such affects and their actualisation? For Deleuze, it is primarily through the close-up and, more specifically, the close up of the face. In order to exemplify this claim, we can think about the cinematic depiction of battlefield intensity. Such depictions are hardly unusual, but even where films try hard to depict the intensity of battle (such as Spielberg's *Saving Private Ryan*, 1998), they rarely manage to register the multiple registers of affectivity to which Deleuze's writing directs our attention. In part this is because our attention is often directed towards the feelings or emotions of an individual as part of the unfolding of a tragic-heroic narrative or because the film works too hard to try to *reproduce* the experience of battle. A notable exception in this regard is Terence Malick's *The Thin Red Line* (1998). Against the backdrop of the Allied assault on Guadalcanal, *The Thin Red Line* foregrounds the affective intensity of battle-field experience in ways that have obvious similarities with films such as *Saving Private Ryan*. But there are important differences. As Bersani and Dutoit observe, 'extraordinarily for a so-called war film (especially one about World War II), there is not a single expression of patriotic sentiment in the film and there is no attempt whatsoever to provide a moral or historical justification or even explanation for the violence of war' (2004: 129). Where *Saving Private Ryan* opens with misty-eyed sentimentality triggered by a visit to war graves in Normandy, the opening of Malick's film features a crocodile sliding ominously into still, weed-covered water. Over subsequent shots of cathedral-like primordial forests, a voice poses a question: 'Why does nature vie with itself?' Immediately then, the heroic narrative of the individual is displaced in favour of a philosophical meditation on the moral ambivalence of a more-than-human world. While the voice is human, the field through which it moves is de-individualised: a distributed field of as yet unnamed affects, a sense of something not yet registered.

Faced with the ambivalence of such a world, one option for the film could be to recover a narrative of tragic heroism, in the manner of *Saving Private Ryan*. However, rather than reclaim the agency of the individual in this way, the film develops as a sustained attempt to depict the registering of affect – as something impersonal – through the faces of soldiers who never quite become the strong individual characters upon which heroic narratives depend for a degree of perspectival fixity and emotional reference. This sense of the film as a series of cinematic images moving through a distributed field of affect is developed further through the central role that non-human agencies such as grass and wind come to play in one of the pivotal assault sequences. Malick's shots take us through and within the grass, cutting at various points to shots of hillsides over which wind is gently blowing. Why? Because a gust of wind or a field of grass is like an affect: distributed, non-individualised, and yet sensed. And the participation of such affects in the world is not registered through obviously emotional narratives; instead, it is registered through close-ups in which the faces of the soldiers in the film come to possess a unique kind of expressiveness. While they do communicate some easily identifiable feelings, they are not primarily psychologically expressive. They are strongly individuated, but not on the basis of personality; rather, they individuate the different worlds we see them registering (Bersani and Dutoit 2004: 145).

By foregrounding affect in this way, Malick's film is not engaged in a strategy of de-humanising individuals. Nor does it serve merely to rehearse a story of the helplessness of the individual in the face of global geopolitical military machines. It does, however, work to privilege the experience of geopolitical conflict and makes obvious gestures to the aesthetic of the sublime. Yet such an aesthetic does not become reincorporated into an emotional experience. Rather, as Dana Polan observes, *The Thin Red Line* achieves something else: an image emerging from the 'glimpsing of experientiality itself, a pure immersion in temporality, in a duration that only vaguely adds up to either meaningfulness or anything resembling meaningfulness' (Polan 2005: 62).

Events as intensities of feeling

If *The Thin Red Line* works to illustrate how a distributed field of affect is registered without becoming individualised, the second film we want to talk about, *United 93*, provides a particularly important example of how affect is sensed as an intensity of feeling in individual bodies. Directed by Paul Greengrass, *United 93* is one of a number of films about the 'fourth plane' that was hijacked on 11 September 2001 and which crashed in Pennsylvania.[2] Cell-phone transcripts and the flight data recorder indicated that the passengers on this flight were aware of the situation in which they found themselves, generating speculation about whether or not they had overwhelmed the hijackers before the plane crashed.

Whether or not they did is not our concern here. *United 93* is interesting, we would argue, both because of how it depicts the events of that day and because of the nature of popular and critical response to its release, much of which centred on its intensely affective impact. Thus, and first, *United 93* foregrounds with particular skill the distributed and background technological infrastructures through which an affective image-event is registered, transmitted and managed. The hijacked planes may have become *publicly* visible through so many television screens, but they first showed up on the radar screens of the air traffic control system as a series of bodies being tracked and traced along fairly predictable lines of movement. At the same time, *United 93* cleverly reveals the sheer sense of disbelief felt by air traffic controllers when they are told that they might be dealing with a hijack. Hijacking no longer figured on the horizon of anticipation for air traffic controllers, unlike the 1970s and 1980s when the hijacking of airliners was central to the performative and mediated logics of terrorism – an atmosphere of expectancy simply did not exist.[3] At the same time, and entirely coincidentally, the consequences of this lack of anticipation were exacerbated by the occurrence on the same day of a military exercise off the Eastern Seaboard of the USA. Perversely, and as the film illustrates, it was precisely the space of anticipation of which that scenario was generative that prevented any attempt to take seriously the reality of what was happening. What the film does, therefore, is exemplify how both the lack of expectancy and the attempt to engineer anticipation became central to how subsequent events became visible as emerging problems across distributed assemblages of image and movement.

The film is also interesting because it works to choreograph the distributed events with which it is concerned in terms of the emergence and circulation of certain intensities of feeling; that is, as the event of the felt registering of affect in, through and between bodies. In part this is achieved through the casting of various individuals to play themselves; the director of air traffic control is most significant in this respect. It is also achieved through the almost real-time pacing of the narrative. And it is achieved through a deliberate attempt to avoid any explicit commentary on the geopolitical significance of the event. Indeed, despite its use of transcripts of actual phone conversations between passengers and their relatives and co-workers, the real significance of *United 93* is not so much its attempt to depict with any authenticity what actually happened. The real significance of the film is its attempt to suggest what it might have been like to have *felt* these events. Feeling is the primary affective logic of the film: feeling that circulates within and between the bodies of those on the aircraft; feeling which, due to the skill with which the film is constructed, cannot but be felt by the viewer – however critical. Indeed, its emphasis on the felt intensity of geopolitical events allows the film to act – at least potentially – as a cinematic reminder of how 9/11 functions as a somatic marker, 'an affect-imbued memory bank' (Ó Tuathail 2003) that worked to 'down-scale' the world into simple oppositional categories.

Re-scripting emotion and intervention

The third film we want to briefly consider here offers a deliberate attempt to generate certain intensities of feeling, while also seeking to re-script the emotional narratives through which these feelings are expressed and made meaningful. Directed by David O. Russell, and starring George Clooney, Mark Wahlberg, Ice-Cube and Spike Jonze, *Three Kings* is ostensibly a standard Hollywood action movie based around a predictable, heist-driven plot and set against the backdrop of the end of the 1991 war in the Gulf.[4] Under the leadership of Major Archie Gates (played by George Clooney), and with the help of a map, four US soldiers set out to steal gold bullion. What is initially a straightforward operation is complicated when the soldiers become involved in some of the after-events of the conflict and find themselves involved in the efforts of a group of Iraqis to escape from Saddam Hussein's Republican Guard. One of the few movies (with *Courage Under Fire* and the more recent *Jarhead*) to take as its central focus the first Gulf War, the significance of the film here is the extent to which it sets out to destabilise how that campaign was scripted and perceived in US popular culture.[5]

There are, we want to suggest, three aspects of the film that are of particular importance here. The first involves the extent to which it attempts to problematise the logics of vision and perception through which the 1991 Gulf War was framed. Influenced by the visual style of photo-journalists and by camera techniques used by CNN reporters, Russell's film is a deliberate attempt to problematise the role vision plays in mediating the relation between war and landscape: in the process, the desert becomes a cinematic landscape within which to play around not only with the possibilities of light and depth of field, but also with claims of moral clarity and visibility. Thus, the opening scene unfolds in a featureless environment that combines the potential for effortless mobility with a lack of visible points of orientation; for Russell, the 'billiard-table' flatness of the desert represented the 'moral-blankness that attended the end of the war'.

If the film seeks to problematise the perceptual logics of US intervention, it also foregrounds and challenges the affective logics through which this intervention was made meaningful and scripted. After the opening scene, the film cuts to a depiction of post-war euphoria, fuelled by alcohol and amplified by an accompanying soundtrack, over which a reporter asks if victory over Iraq has exorcised the ghost of Vietnam. It is this scripting of the affectivity of military intervention that Russell's film works to complicate. A key way in which the film attempts to do this is by foregrounding how bodies register the affects of military intervention. Thus, early on in the film, as the central characters drive into the desert in search of gold, three of them begin firing off live rounds because, we are told (by Jonze's character), they did not get to do much shooting during the war. Gates asks if any of them know what happens when someone gets shot, then describes the effects of a bullet wound, during which the view cuts to an image of the internal cavity of a human body showing the major internal organs. As it is being described, a bullet enters the body cavity and a pocket of green bile begins to form, before the same process is shown in reverse.[6] Subsequently, this scene becomes a minor refrain at various points throughout the film. Admittedly it is brief and contrived; but it is precisely its contrived nature that stands out. It is only, perhaps, by de-familiarising this process that it can come to stand out in geopolitical cultures in which the affective natures of acts of violence have become so mediated that they constantly run the risk of becoming routine, overly familiar (see Thrift 2007).

Where *United 93* amplifies intensity of feeling without any explicit commentary upon the geopolitical scripting of this feeling, *Three Kings* employs scenes such as those described above as cinematic-somatic markers through which to complicate the 'down-scaling' of the conflict in popular geopolitical discourse. Indeed, the film opens with a statement of intent in this regard, making explicit its effort to heighten the emotional impact of the film in order to challenge the popular scripting of the conflict. For example, Russell foregrounds the hypocrisy of George Bush Senior's call for the Southern Iraqis to rise up against Saddam Hussein's regime without providing any military support, articulating this through one of the key Iraqi characters, who sardonically summarises the fundamental contradiction lying at the heart of US intervention: 'The big army of democracy beats the ugly dictator and saves the rich Kuwaitis. But you go to jail if you help us escape from the same dictator.' In another scene, an Iraqi interrogator pours crude oil down the throat of Troy (played by Mark Wahlberg) in response to the latter's claim that the primary rationale for military intervention is 'regional stability'.

Admittedly, while the film goes some way to disrupt the geopolitical scripts of US militarism and foreign politics, it can and has been criticised on various fronts: its portrayal of female characters; its unsympathetic portrayal of one of the central US characters who rehearses all the prejudices of a caricatured Southern Redneck; its rather undifferentiated depiction of Iraqi characters, even those portrayed in a sympathetic light as articulate, insightful critics of the imperatives of US military intervention; and its rather ambivalent relation to consumer culture, which it sometimes seems to offer as a form of universal language. Perhaps the most significant critique of the film focuses on its relationship to hegemonic narratives about US military intervention. As Rowe (2004: 586) has argued: 'Through the biblical figures and redemptive humanitarianism of the "Three Kings" in the film, a familiar imperial narrative of US paternalism, of the white man's burden, plays itself out once again in terms almost identical to those criticized so thoroughly in nineteenth-century imperial narratives.' For Rowe, this narrative actually renders the film complicit with the kind of ideology of intervention underpinning the 2003 invasion of Iraq. Put another way, *Three Kings* complicates the manner in which US intervention in the 1991 war was conducted rather than challenging the legitimacy or necessity of intervention in the first place (Weber 2005).

Yet while they have some purchase, the force of such critical comments about the relation between the film and wider narratives of geopolitical intervention needs some qualification. To claim (as some critics did) that the film presents the USA as the destination to which the Iraqi characters in the film aspire is rather misleading: their actual final destination is Iran (Davies 2005). And to suggest that the geopolitical significance of a film such as *Three Kings* should ultimately rest on the extent to which it reproduces an overarching script through which the logics of geopolitical intervention are made meaningful is both overly simplistic and dangerously reductionist. By placing primacy on the narrative content of film, such a critique ignores how *Three Kings* is intended as an intervention into geopolitical cultures that are always more than discursive, layered in complex ways by different logics of affectivity.

Making more of moving images

It is important to reiterate that none of the films discussed above is only about one affective register – each mobilises affectivity in different ways and with different degrees of intensive emphasis. At the same time, by doing so, they force us to think further about the nature of their affective participation in geopolitical cultures and the conceptual vocabulary through which we understand this participation. In so far as we focus on the scripts, codes and signs through which films make geopolitical sense, we are accustomed to articulate the relation between film and geopolitics through terms such as reproduction, resistance and subversion. But, as we have suggested above, affectivity participates in ways that cannot necessarily be reduced to these terms. In addition to differentiating affectivity then, understanding the participation of cinematic images in geopolitical cultures requires two further moves.

The first involves considering exactly what we mean when we talk about affective images *qua* images in relation to visual culture. Key here has been the problematising of images as representations; as symbols or pictures that stand in the place of something in the world. In this critical vein, images have been thought about as internal (a mental 'picture') or external (a photo, painting or film, for example). This understanding of images provides a great deal of critical purchase because it opens up questions about the degree to which images reflect reality in an accurate way, the extent to which they participate in or are complicit with contested webs of signification and meaning, and the ways in which 'internal' images reflect 'external' images.

Such questions are important; indeed, much of the analysis of images in social sciences and humanities has tended to proceed by posing variations on one or more of these questions. And much recent critical analysis of images (including geopolitical images) concentrates on the twin tactics of destabilising the meaning of images as representations and critically picking through whatever ruins remain. There is, to be sure, much to be gained from thinking and engaging critically with images in these ways. Yet one of the crucial elements of this work, even at its most critically acidic, is that the basic status of images as representations (however contested, slippery or duplicitous) tends to remain in place. Because of this, something is lost in the process. That something is best understood as the non-representational quality of images (see Doel and Clarke 2007). One way in which this quality registers is precisely in terms of the materiality of sensation and affectivity: a registering that takes place before an image is processed representationally; a sensing that happens before something is made meaningful through any discursively scripted frame of reference (Shaviro 1993).

How then might we think of images without reducing them to the terms of representational thinking? The work of Henri Bergson is a useful point of departure here, precisely because it provides the basis for an account of images as both more and less than representational. For Bergson, images are not quite representations – they are not little symbolic reflections of the real world, cuts in its ongoing flow. Nor, however, do they have the quality of a thing. Instead, images can better be conceived in terms of duration. Bergson's claim in this regard is made originally in relation to what we often conceive of as 'internal' representations. But a similar claim can be made in relation to what we often conceive of as an 'external' image; again, rather than a fixed frame, an image becomes a process of duration. The key point here is that even still images are durational before they are representational. What moving or cinematic images do is make tangible or visible the durational quality of images, their existence as 'blocs of space-time' (Deleuze 1986: 63).

Importantly, thinking about images along these lines encourages us to recognise the ways in which images move in excess of the conceptual terms often employed in the critical geopolitical analysis of film. What moves is less a script or code than a bloc of affective space-time that is experienced with different degrees of intensity. In this way, the affective participation of images in geopolitical cultures can be understood through logics other than those framed so heavily by discourse. We might begin by thinking of images as participants in the contagion of affectivity (see also Thrift 2007). *Contagion* refers to the capacity of affectivity to circulate at speed through multiple sites and circuits of relay. As William Connolly has observed, contagion is a process by which the intensity of affectivity becomes extensive 'across individuals or constituencies by the timbre of our voices, looks, hits, caresses, gestures, the bunching of muscles in the neck, and flushes of the skin. Such contagion flows through face-to-face meetings, academic classes, family dinners, public assemblies, TV speeches, sitcoms, soap operas, and films' (Connolly 2002: 75).

The contagion of affectivity depends in turn upon the process of *amplification*. Amplification can be understood as a process through which the affectivity of events or experiences are intensified. This can occur live, as an event unfolds, through a range of practices and techniques. Mass media are crucial here insofar as they are 'amplifiers of affect, heightening and intensifying affects (by amplifying the tone, timbre and pitch of voices and, in the case of television, by means of close ups which provide a concentrated focus on facial expressions)' (Gibbs 2002). But amplification can also occur after the occurrence of a particular event. This is of particular significance with regard to film and to the relation between geopolitical and cinematic events. Films can be understood in terms of how they work to amplify the after-affects of geopolitical events – United 93 is the most obvious case in point. Indeed, if we understand 9/11 as (among other things) an ongoing geopolitical image-event, then United 93 provides an important cinematic site through which the affectivity of this image-event is (re)amplified. And for some, this was precisely the point – the film served as an all too visceral reminder of the felt of intensity of that event and a necessary corrective for those who would doubt the importance of the ongoing 'war on terror'.

All the better that in doing so it contributed to the idea that, however terrible, the events of that day allowed the USA, embodied in the athletic figures of those who take on the hijackers, to rediscover its muscle, bite and ability to stand up for itself. For others, however, it was precisely the film's emphasis on such felt intensity at the expense of commentary that made it so problematic. Why, precisely, was the cinematic recreation of such intensity necessary? Beyond a cinematic version of a particularly visceral fairground ride, what exactly was the point of the film? Why would one want to feel like this again?

Thus, the force of amplification is related to and depends in part upon the degree to which cinematic images resonate. 'Resonance' can be understood as the mutually reinforcing relay between different points of amplification at various scales and intensity (Kintz 1997; Connolly 2005). As Linda Kintz suggests (1997: 6): 'Resonance refers to the intensification of political passion in which people with very different interests are linked together by feelings aroused and organized to saturate the most public, even global issues.' The logics of amplification and resonance work together. The affectivity of what happens on TV will be picked up on talk radio or in op-ed columns, or *vice-versa*. Yet even if a film amplifies certain affective currents, it might not resonate or it might resonate differentially – the mixed reception to *United 93* is an example of how the amplification of affectivity was questioned by a range of critics.

In certain contexts, however, the affectivity amplified in films can work against the force of some of what William Connolly calls 'resonance machines' that operate at different scales and duration. Connolly (2005) discusses resonance machines in the context of an analysis of a political alignment between evangelical forms of Christianity and corporate capitalism. As he puts it:

> The major constituencies in this machine do not always share the same religious and economic doctrines. Affinities of sensibility also connect them across links and differences in formal doctrine. The complex becomes a powerful machine as evangelical and corporate sensibilities resonate together, drawing each into a larger movement that dampens the importance of doctrinal differences between them. At first, the parties sense preliminary affinities of sensibility; eventually they provoke each other to transduct those affinities into a massive political machine. And the machine then foments new intensities of solidarity between these constituencies. (Connolly 2005: 271)

Such resonance machines have their points of instability. Furthermore, they can be challenged through nascent coalitions that seek to produce and amplify alternative sensibilities through diverse constituencies. It is in this way that we can perhaps understand the significance of a film such as *Three Kings*: as a cinematic event that works to amplify counter affectivities in relation to a geopolitical resonance machine – one in which the logics of intervention are also sustained by intensities and affinities between scripts and affective currents. The film works in this way by amplifying certain minor but countervailing intensities of feeling associated with the war, but as yet unarticulated in mainstream media. As Russell suggested in an interview (2000); 'When people see the movie it hasn't created an uproar. I think it affirms what they felt in their guts, but just haven't wanted to deal with before.'

Crucially, the participation of images in processes of contagion, amplification and resonance does not necessarily involve the transmission of anything like a 'message'. As Eric Shouse argues: 'In many cases the message consciously received may be of less import to the receiver of the message than his or her non-conscious affective resonance with the source of the message' (Shouse 2005). That is not to claim that codes, scripts or signs are unimportant. But images participate in geopolitical cultures in ways that are excessive of the representational and discursive logics of such terms. In this analysis, rather than being ideological signs, cinematic images are refigured as blocs of affective intensity with differential speeds, durations and capacities to affect other kinds of bodies.

Conclusion: Affective images and geopolitical thinking-space

To argue, as we have in this chapter, for attending to the relation between affectivity and the geopolitical import of cinema is not to claim that certain processes might not be ideological, nor is it to deny that discursive formations can produce powerful geopolitical effects. But attending to affectivity moves us to think about the viscerally intense processes that provide the conditions of emergence for ideological and/or discursive formations, rather than seeing these processes as sugar-coating such formations after the fact of their emergence (see also Massumi 2002). The key point here is that understanding the geopolitical significance of cinema does not necessarily turn solely on their relation – along a continuum between complicity and subversion – to a certain set of performative geopolitical scripts. Some films have a geopolitical resonance precisely because they do not adhere to the critical rules of contextualizing. Rather, as in the case of the *Thin Red Line*, *United 93* and *Three Kings*, such films are significant precisely because they produce distinctive kinds of affective geopolitical images, in combination with experimentation with the logics of perception and, in some cases, with explicit attempts to re-script popular narratives of intervention.

Arguably, the power of affectivity has too easily been ignored in critical analyses of geopolitical cultures. As we have tried to suggest here, cinema provides one way of exploring the relation between affectivity, thinking and geopolitical cultures. But doing this requires thinking about cinema as an intervention into multilayered fields of affectivity. This is cinema as an assemblage of techniques and technologies of affective event amplification, through which the cultural and corporeal logics of intervention come to resonate. Thus, while a film like *Three Kings* deploys a barrage of conventional special effects, it is the particular way it combines narrative strategy and affective technique that makes it a (potentially) powerful cinematic intervention.

Thinking about cinematic images in this way has much to 'teach us about the cultural stimuli to thought and thoughtlessness, the layering of perception, and the role of affect in perception and thought' (Connolly 2002: 13–14). By foregrounding the participation of affectivity in our own thinking, both as scholars and as instructors, it encourages us to recognise the possibility that the production and circulation of geopolitical cultures is always layered into the affectivity of body-brain matrices (Connolly 2002). This, we want to suggest, should be read as an encouragement to pay more attention to and through the affective logics of cinematic interventions, even where such films do not, at least at first look, challenge explicitly geopolitical scripts, signs and codes. As film theorist Amy Herzog has written (2001: 5):

> Looking even at the most hackneyed, clichéd films, the attentive, inventive thinker might see within their stutterings and pauses waves of affect that move against the prevailing current. This affectivity might take an infinite number of forms: a strain of music that overwhelms the narrative flow, a glance between characters that gestures toward a whole world of unactualized becomings.

Herzog gestures towards the nub of the argument of this chapter: that films are important not only insofar as they provide geopolitical texts to be decoded and deconstructed. They can and should also be understood as critical-geopolitical thinking-spaces in which we might explore how images participate in geopolitical cultures. Admittedly, by foregrounding affectivity, such thinking-spaces might trouble some of the critical manoeuvres through which we often engage with popular geopolitical cultures. Yet, in their own minor way, they might also provide sites of amplification and points of resonance through which counter-affective currents might emerge, both in our own thinking and in the thinking of our students.

Bibliography

Aitken, Stuart, 'Leading men to violence and creating spaces for their emotions', *Gender, Place and Culture* 13/5 (2006), pp.491–506.
Anderson, Ben, 'Becoming and being hopeful: toward a theory of affect', *Environment and Planning D: Society and Space* 24/3 (2006), pp.733–752.
Anderson, Ben, 'Hope for nanotechnology: Anticipatory knowledge and the governance of affect', *Area* 39/2 (2007), pp.156–65.
Badiou, Alain, *Infinite Thought*, translated by J. Clemens and O. Feltham (London: Continuum, 2003).
Behnke, Andreas and de Carvalho, Benjamin, 'Shooting war: International relations and the cinematic representation of warfare', *Millennium: Journal of International Studies* 34/3 (2006), pp.935–6.
Bennett, Jane and Shapiro, Michael (eds), *The Politics of Moralizing* (London: Routledge, 2001).
Bergson, Henri, *Matter and Memory*, translated by N.M. Paul and W.S. Palmer (London: Zone Books, 1991).
Bersani, Leo and Dutoit, Ulysse, *Forms of Being: Cinema, Aesthetics and Subjectivity* (London: British Film Institute, 2004).
Bleiker, Roland, 'The aesthetic turn in international political theory', *Millennium: Journal of International Studies* 30/3 (2001), pp.509–33.
Carter, Sean and McCormack, Derek P., 'Film, geopolitics and the affective logics of intervention', *Political Geography* 25 (2006), pp.228–45.
Connolly, William, *Neuropolitics: Thinking, Culture, Speed* (London: University of Minnesota Press, 2002).
Connolly, William, 'The evangelical-capitalist resonance machine', *Political Theory* 33/6 (2005), pp.869–86.
Crosthwaite, Paul, 'Speed, war, and traumatic affect: Reading Ian McEwan's atonement', *Cultural Politics* 3/1 (2007), pp.51–70.
Davies, Jude, 'Diversity. America. Leadership. Good over evil. Hollywood multiculturalism and American Imperialism in *Independence Day* and *Three Kings*', *Pattern of Prejudice* 39/4 (2005), pp.397–415.
Deleuze, Gilles, *Cinema 2: The Time-Image*, translated by H. Tomlinson and B. Habberjam (Minneapolis: University of Minnesota Press, 1985).
Deleuze, Gilles, *Cinema 1: The Movement-Image*, translated by H. Tomlinson and B. Habberjam (Minneapolis: University of Minnesota Press, 1986).

Deleuze, Gilles, *Spinoza: Practical Philosophy* (San Francisco: City Lights Press, 1989).
Deleuze, Gilles, *Expressionism in Philosophy: Spinoza*, translated by M. Joughin (London: Zone Books, 1992).
Deleuze, Gilles and Guattari, Felix, *A Thousand Plateaus: Capitalism and Schizophrenia*, translated by B. Massumi (London: Athlone Press, 1988).
Der Derian, James, *Virtuous War: Mapping the Military-Industrial-Media-Entertainment Network* (Boulder, CO: Westview, 2001).
Dodds, Klaus, 'Licensed to stereotype: Popular geopolitics, James Bond and the spectre of Balkanism', *Geopolitics* 8/2 (2003), pp.125–56.
Doel, Marcus and Clarke, Daviod, 'Afterimages', *Environment and Planning D: Society and Space* 25.5, pp. 890–910.
Gibbs, Anna, 'Contagious feelings: Pauline Hanson and the epidemiology of affect', *Australian Humanities Review* 24 (December 2001–February 2002), available at http://www.australianhumanitiesreview.org/archive/Issue-December-2001/gibbs.html (accessed 31 October 2008).
Gibson-Graham, J.K., *Post-capitalist Politics* (Minneapolis: University of Minnesota Press, 2006).
Hemmings, Clare, 'Invoking affect: Cultural theory and the ontological turn', *Cultural Studies* 19/5 (2005), pp.548–67.
Herzog, Amy, 'Affectivity, becoming, and the cinematic event: Gilles Deleuze and the Futures of Feminist Film theory' (2001) available at http://media.utu.fi/affective/herzog.pdf (Accessed 7 October 2008).
Holden, Gerard, 'Cinematic IR, the sublime, and the indistinctness of art', *Millennium: Journal of International Studies* 34/3 (2006), pp.793–818.
Hughes, Rachel, 'Through the looking blast: Geopolitics and visual culture', *Geography Compass* 1/5 (2007), pp.976–94.
Jarhead, Directed by Sam Mendes (USA: Universal Pictures, 2005).
Kintz, Linda, *Between Jesus and the Free Market: The Emotions that Matter in Right-Wing America* (Duke University Press: London, 1997).
Luke, Timothy and Ó Tuathail, Gearóid, 'Thinking geopolitical space: The spatiality of war, speed and vision in the work of Paul Virilio', in Mike Crang and Nigel Thrift (eds) *Thinking Space* (London: Routledge, 1999), pp.360–79.
Manning, Erin, *Politics of Touch: Sense, Movement, Sovereignty* (Minneapolis: University of Minnesota Press, 2006).
Massumi, Brian, *Parables for the Virtual: Movement, Affect, Sensation* (Durham, NC: Duke University Press, 2002).
Massumi, Brian, 'Potential politics and the primacy of pre-emption', *Theory and Event* 10/2 (2007).
Mattelart, Armand, *Mapping World Communication: War, Progress, Culture*, translated by S. Emanuel and J.A. Cohen (Minneapolis: University of Minnesota Press, 1994).
Ó Tuathail, Gearóid, *Critical Geopolitics* (London: Routledge, 1996).
Ó Tuathail, Gearóid, ' "Just out looking for a fight": American affect and the invasion of Iraq', *Antipode* 35/5 (2003), pp.856–70.
Polan, Dana, 'Amateurism and war-teurism: Terrence Malick's war movie', in R. Eberwein (ed.), *The War Film* (London: Rutgers University Press, 2005), pp.53–61.

Power, Marcus and Crampton, Andrew (eds), 'Reel geopolitics – Cinematographing political space', *Geopolitics* 10/2 (2005), pp.193–203.

Rowe, John C., 'Culture, US Imperialism and globalization', *American Literary History* 16/4 (2004), pp.575–95.

Saving Private Ryan, Directed by Steven Spielberg (USA: Dreamworks, 1998).

Sharp, Joanne, 'Reel geographies of the new world order: Patriotism, masculinity and geopolitics in post-Cold War American movies', in Gearóid Ó Tuathail and Simon Dalby (eds), *Rethinking Geopolitics* (New York: Routledge, 1998), pp.152–69.

Shaviro, Steven, *The Cinematic Body* (Minnesota: University of Minneapolis Press, 1993).

Shouse, Eric, 'Feeling, emotion, affect', *M/C Journal* 8/6 (December 2005), available at http://journal.media-culture.org.au/0512/03-shouse.php (accessed 21 September 2007).

Spinoza, Baruch, *The Ethics* (London: Everyman, 1989).

The Thin Red Line, Directed by Terrence Mallick (USA: 20th Century Fox, 1998).

Three Kings, Directed by David O. Russell (USA: Warner Brothers, 1999).

Thrift, Nigel, 'Intensities of feeling: towards a spatial politics of affect', Geografiska Annaler, 86/1 (2004), pp.57–58.

Thrift, Nigel, 'Immaculate warfare? The spatial politics of extreme violence', in Derek Gregory and Alan Pred (eds), *Violent Geographies: Fear, Terror, and Political Violence* (London: Routledge, 2007), pp.273–94.

Thrift, Nigel, *Non-representational Theory* (London: Routledge, 2008).

Virilio, Paul, *War and Cinema: The Logistics of Perception*, translated by P. Camiller (London: Verso, 1989).

Virilio, Paul, *Desert Screen: War at the Speed of Light* (London: Continuum, 2002).

Weber, Cynthia, *Imagining America at War: Morality, Politics, and Film* (London: Routledge, 2005).

Zizek, Slavoj, *Welcome to the Desert of the Real* (London: Verso, 2002).

Chapter 6

Gameworld Geopolitics and the Genre of the Quest

Rachel Hughes

This chapter is concerned with the relationship between contemporary geopolitics and the popular domain of digital games. Recent research has argued for greater attention to the shared materialities, economies and imaginaries of commercial games and military campaigns, especially in the context of the 'War on Terror'. These existing analyses are, however, concerned with war-themed games to the exclusion of other game genres. These existing analyses also focus on what might be termed the 'representational logics'[1] of games, particularly the contextualising or 'background' images contained within games. I argue that other genres of game, particularly action-adventure games structured around a heroic quest, might also be considered both constitutive of and constituted by contemporary geopolitics. In examining this reciprocity between games and geopolitics, I pay attention to the ways in which both are 'more-than-representational', involving various doings, viewings and feelings (Lorimer 2005). Crucially, gaming and geopolitical practices draw from and add to well-established, yet dynamic, cultural genres. In what follows, I employ literary theorist John Frow's understanding of genre as a 'typified action' with a complex relation to a recurring social situation; 'the patterns of genre', he argues, 'are at once shaped by a type of situation and in turn shape the rhetorical actions that are performed in response to it' (Frow 2006: 14). Consciously or otherwise, genre is as integral to the meaning-making of political strategists and military generals as it is to game designers and players of digital games.

Cinematic and literary genres are often evoked by geopoliticians: Ronald Reagan's aping of the speech and gestures of the 'Western' movie hero is a well-noted example; Arnold Schwarzenegger's playing himself playing California's hero governor is even more involved. Similarly, game genres 'play at' geopolitics, they resonate with and profit from new technologies and ways of seeing made possible by the conduct of contemporary conflicts. The personal visual recordings of combat produced by soldiers can be seen to (re)produce the kind of doing and looking modelled by specific genres of digital games (see Power 2007). In this chapter, I introduce the concept of 'gameworld geopolitics' to refer to this generic resonance between geopolitics and gaming, as well as to an important basis for this resonance: the historical intimacy between commercial and state interests in the computation and simulation of conflict.

In the second part of the chapter, I examine more closely the genre of the heroic quest in the popular game series *Tomb Raider* and in various geopolitical situations arising in the late 1990s to 2003. Reference is made to the non-state (non-soldiering) agency of three character figures: tomb raiders, mercenaries and weapons inspectors. Finally, I interrogate the affects and effects of quested-for objects across both the *Tomb Raider* series and contemporary geopolitics: the powerful game-quest talisman, the weapons of mass destruction (WMD) and the antiquities 'looted' from the Iraqi National Museum in 2003.

Worldly games

To begin this story with an account of either games or geopolitics as discrete entities would fail to recognise their symbiotic development. Patrick Crogan argues that state interests in war-gaming were the original driver of the computational technology development, noting the accelerated interchange of personnel and software between military organisations, defence contracting firms, defence-funded academic research programmes and the commercial gaming and simulation industries in the mid-twentieth century (Crogan, in press; see also Der Derian 2003). Other commentators have noted more recent examples of the links between commercial games and military agencies. For example, the US Marines, US Department of Defense, US Army and the UK Ministry of Defence have been involved in developing or modifying a number of games, including *Doom*, *Spearhead*, *Operation Internal Look*, *America's Army* and *Half-Life* (see Stahl 2006; Power 2007). Of these, *America's Army* has drawn particular critical interest given its explicit marketing as a 'recruitment and outreach tool' of the US Army and its enormous popularity with players (see Stahl 2006; Power 2007).

Hardware, as well as software, is routinely shared between games and military manufacturers. For instance, Roger Stahl notes that the Sony PlayStation 2 console was classified by the Japanese government as a 'general purpose product related to conventional weapons' because the technology was found to be viable for use in missile guidance systems (2006: 112).[2] At the same time the US military was developing a controller for a small, unmanned, reconnaissance truck that was modelled on the PlayStation 2 console, in line with the assumption that incoming soldiers would already be partially trained to use it (Stahl 2006: 112; see also Power 2007). The advantages of console familiarity go further than the shape, size, configuration and operation of the object concerned: habits of touch are intimately attuned to those of the eye, ear and human computational core, the brain.

With regard to games images, geographers have argued that war-themed games assist in representing particular places and types of spaces (cities, desert landscapes) as little more than receiving points for US military ordnance (Gregory in Graham 2005: 6). Games images are undoubtedly simplistic depictions of the world, and renderings of some worlds are more aggressively simplistic than others (see Graham 2004, 2005; Gregory 2008). In attempting to move beyond such analyses, to account for what Carter and McCormack refer to as 'the non-representational quality of images', I have elsewhere reviewed work on the development of digital games as part of a discussion of a new kind of geopolitical visuality (Hughes 2007). My interest there was in what kind of 'looking' is modelled or afforded by digital games, and what this might tell us about the wider visuality of contemporary conflicts. I drew on Stahl's argument that a new visuality was evident in the 2003 invasion of Iraq. Stahl (2006) contrasts the 'televised media spectacle' of the 1991 Operation Desert Storm with a newer, 'interactive' mode of the coverage of Operation Iraqi Freedom in 2003, symbolised by the 'countdown clock' that appeared on news broadcasters screens in anticipation of the invasion. Stahl refers to this shift as the supplanting of 'the sedative of the spectacle' with 'the stimulant of gametime'[3] (Stahl 2006: 120). Several aspects of this shift towards an interactive or, as I prefer, an anticipatory visuality have attracted critical comment. As a part of this new visuality, many contemporary war-themed games require the player themselves to remain invisible, conducting 'secret missions out of sight and out of mind' (Stahl 2006: 119). In these and other games, the secrecy of the (usually militarised) mission is guaranteed only by invisibility. Other aspects of anticipatory visuality are a constant state of alertness, expectation of attack and pre-emptive action (manifesting as a 'shoot-first' or 'mashing'[4] approach). The looking of the 'first-person-shooter' or the 'virtual citizen-soldier' (Stahl 2006) is intimately attuned to movement through the gameworld. Often more rapid than an equivalent embodied movement (through the non-gameworld), this looking-moving-feeling is also productive of a particular kind of space. Looking-moving-feeling in this way produces space after space of increasingly difficult engagements and violent actions. For war-themed and contemporary action-adventure games, this practice of 'anticipatory looking' (and rapid response) arguably matters more than the player's game strategy, experience-level and dexterity in manoeuvring their avatar through the gameworld.

Thinking about the kind of looking that occurs within digital games, as additional to games images, shifts an analysis away from the familiar argument that games are simply poor, partial or distorting representations of the world. Games are 'methectic',[5] rather than mimetic or figurative (Harrison in Huizinga 1998: 15): they do not mirror but instead participate or partake in the world, functioning as a 'helping out of [an] action' (Marett in Huizinga 1944: 15). The playing out of an idea, plan or an operation is not the same as rendering, observing or engaging with an image, though images may of course be employed. As Ben Anderson notes of strategic gaming in the 1950s and 1960s, it is not that such war games 'represented' the future, but that their organisation of (simulated) space created a certain quality of experience in which unknown events could be *felt* (Anderson, in press). Examining contemporary digital war games, Marcus Power speaks to this more-than-visual operation of games when he claims that some games provide 'a space of cyber-deterrence', where it is possible to 'play through the anxieties that attend uncertain times and new configurations of power' (Power 2007: 271). Sean Carter and Derek McCormack's exploration of film as an affective assemblage is also useful for further thinking on games (see Carter and McCormack 2006; this volume). Pertinent to analyses of games – especially those war-themed or action-adventure games routinely decried as simply mirroring or replicating extant ideological positions – is Carter and McCormack's argument that 'the participation of images in processes of contagion, amplification and resonance does not necessarily involve the transmission of anything like a "message"' (Carter and McCormack, this volume). Games are no more conductive of 'messages' than any other visual medium. Although film remains largely impervious to the doing and feeling of the viewer, and games unfold immediately, variously and interactively depending on players' embodied responses, neither the film or game experience is predetermined or determining.

Somewhat paradoxically, interactivity has been given all sorts of determining powers in games analysis. Although a high degree of interaction between bodies and machines is facilitated by contemporary games, these embodied responses only ever register as translations into recognisable, computable input (just as responses to other visual media must undergo some form of translation and input, not necessarily computational, into the world). Tempering the more hyperbolic claims made about interactivity, it can be noted that interactivity

> consist of selections (rather than choices) that have been anticipated by the game designers. ... This pre-programming is implanted at a number of levels: technologically, in the capacities and valences of the machines players access; [and] culturally, in the nature of the scenarios and storylines chosen for development. (Kline et al 2003: 19)

Crogan also cautions against the hype of interactivity, arguing that games allow for a 'playing with the illusion of control, control, that is, of the model's illusion of a more complex system' (Crogan, in press). Along with James Newman, Crogan argues that one plays a computer game to learn how to 'think like a computer'. Mastery of the experiential whole of a game demands a synthesis perspective – taking in action, location, scenario – such that the gameworld can be managed to resolve game challenges (Newman in Crogan, in press). Games offer a form of affective immersion in which 'one can play out mastery of the indeterminate through a game of mastery over the model' (Crogan, in press). In this sense the popular hysteria about violent games producing violent players misses the mark: it is not violent feelings but the violence *of* feeling – the affective intensities of playing gameworlds – that arguably intoxicates players. The 'selections' of game designers, and the 'thinking' (like a computer) and 'managing' (the gameworld) performed by players, are all part of an anticipatory visuality that delivers something felt and celebrated as mastery.

The slippage between gameworlds and other worlds is facilitated by the scaling-up to a more complex situation of this anticipatory viewing and the sense of mastery engendered by playing a pre-programmed model. In gameworld geopolitics the affective states associated with anticipatory viewing and mastery of the model are transposed to the scale and sphere of the global indeterminate. In introducing the chapter, it was suggested that 'gameworld geopolitics' refers in part to the historical intimacy between commercial and state interests in computer simulations, an intimacy that has been explored further in this section. 'Gameworld geopolitics' can also be seen as a particular subset of geopolitical representations, practices and affects that participate in (and yet deny the illusory nature of) the practised simulation and the simulated world. Moreover, these representations, practices and affects are configured through particular genres; I want in particular to examine the genre of the quest.

The genre of the quest

In his comprehensive examination of genre, John Frow establishes:

> far from being mere 'stylistic' devices, genres create effects of reality and truth which are central to the different ways the world is understood in the writing of history, philosophy or science, or in painting, or in everyday talk. (Frow 2006: 19)

Frow also argues that genre is itself anticipatory or future-orientated, inasmuch as genre defines a set of expectations that guide engagement with a text, broadly defined (Frow 2006: 104). Digital games mobilise specific genres – often those borrowed from the realms of writing, television and film – to various future-orientated ends. Genres thus guarantee and extend the commercial popularity of particular games, they initiate players' expectations about particular forms of gameplay and character sets, and they structure and heighten gaming affects (see Carr 2003; King and Krzywinska 2006: 54–9). Generic games are thus doubly anticipatory: while genre itself allows for anticipation, the game as simulation, as previously noted, is not a reflective experience but an anticipatory one, demanding extensive temporal immersion and experimentation. Contemporary geopolitics, in its intensified engagement with simulation, also participates in this doubly anticipatory field. As in games, generic 'effects of reality and truth' in the writing and practice of global space come with expectations about forms of conduct, character sets and affective experiences. Such expectations are crucial to the legitimacy and futures of particular global actions and administrations.

Of course, multiple genres are at work in contemporary geopolitics: the oral genres of sermon, military command and reminiscence; the literary genres of allegory, drama, melodrama, political satire and science fiction; and, arguably, the legal genres of case and cross-examination, to name only a few. As genres are transacted across different contexts, they potentially comment on, reflect or parody both context and genre, while nonetheless bringing with them 'some of the force of [their] initial function' (Frow 2006: 17). The focus for my remaining discussion is a popular genre of contemporary geopolitics and digital games; indeed, the exemplary genre of gameworld geopolitics: the genre of the heroic quest.

The oral tradition of heroic quests first appeared in the twelfth century, and

> sought to rehabilitate the passing feudal order by integrating its values into the new centralized monarchy ... These stories ... define the ideal knight as the aristocratic warrior subject ... From this feudal origin, Arthurian romance develops into a religious genre ... later Grail romances devalue the court in favour of religious authority. [They redefine] knighthood in terms not of physical prowess but spiritual prowess, a development that, not surprisingly corresponds to the crusades and the Church's attempts to control an increasingly unruly secular authority. (Aronstein 1995: 4–5)

Susan Aronstein provides a perceptive reading of the *Indiana Jones* film trilogy (Paramount Pictures 1981, 1984, 1989) in terms of their detailed fidelity to what she identifies as the 'recuperative politics' of the Arthurian quest. She further argues that the quest genre is, both historically and thematically, an ideal vehicle for reintroducing or redefining a positive vision of authority in times of crisis. Aronstein is not alone in drawing connections between the figure of Indiana Jones and the crises that threatened (and crises threatened by) the Reagan administration (see Kellner and Ryan 1987). While Indiana was obviously a darling of 1980s 'Reaganite entertainment', critics were divided as to whether he was a paternal saviour, a dashing colonial adventurer, a superhero or a democrat (see Aronstein 1995: 26). Analyses of more recent developments in the geopolitical cultures of the US-led 'coalition of the willing' have also drawn attention to the emergence of an ideal figure, that of the 'professional Western warrior' (Dalby 2008), the active agent of what Bush unguardedly termed 'a crusade' in 2001.

Quests or crusades form the basis of many action-adventure and role-playing games. The traditional quest – an oral account of the many tasks and ordeals of a hero's journey – has a loose episodic structure that is particularly suited to games (King and Krzywinska 2006: 49). In quest games – such as the hugely popular *EverQuest*, *Primal* and *Tomb Raider* games – the quest destination is often less emphasised than the quest journey such that 'the majority of attention is devoted to the performance of the particular gameplay tasks required for progression' (King and

Krzywinska 2006: 49). Quests generally present a subject at a moment of realisation, the realisation that a central, patriarchal authority provides her or him with 'an encyclopaedia of desire, a locus of representations to which [she/he] wishes to be called' (Kolker in Aronstein 1996: 6). The journey of the hero begins with this moment of 'being hailed', marking the advent of righteous action. Such feudal conviction is apparent in the statements of recent geopolitical figures: witness George Bush complimenting Tony Blair in the wake of the invasion of Iraq by reference to his 'great ability, deep conviction and steady courage'.[6] Media and diplomatic commentators also attested to the 'moral certainty' and 'strong religious conviction' of Bush and Blair, suggesting that 'both of them, although [in] different ways, are driven by very strong principles and notions of faith' (D'Ancoma 2003; Meyer 2003). Some accounting for the popularity of quest games and the geopolitical quest comes with this simple yet powerful mechanism: the 'hailing' of a subject. This practice of 'hailing' has the potential to overspill the interiority of the gameworld and affectively engage the player, politician or citizen. It is also the starting point for the *Tomb Raider* game series to which I now turn, as a specific example of the quest genre and geopolitics.

Tomb Raider and the search for WMD

Tomb Raider is one of the most successful action-adventure genre games ever released. It is considered a 'third-person shooter' game in the sense that the player plays as the main character and heroine Lara Croft, but Lara also remains within the player's view. Originally developed by the Core Design group and first published in 1996 by the UK company Eidos, it is estimated that $500 million have now been spent on 21 million take-home Lara Crofts across seven versions of the game (Matrix 2006: 128).[7] EIDOS, together with the game's current developers, Crystal Dynamics, continue to enjoy success with the 2007 release: *Tomb Raider: Anniversary*. The intended Anniversary release date of 2006 was meant to mark the tenth birthday of the game. Despite this one-year delay, Anniversary has been well received, testifying to Lara's continued popularity and perhaps the interest of a new generation of *Tomb Raider* fans. A new edition, *Tomb Raider: Underworld*, was released in 2009.

When the original *Tomb Raider* was released in 1996, Lara appeared in far wider marketing and cultural domains than was common for game avatars of her time. Lara's cross-over into media, advertising and eventually film domains was apparently fuelled by her superior appearance. The game's graphics and animations were more sophisticated than those of any other game then available. But Lara was superior in other ways too. What Lara did and how Lara looked made her hugely popular with players. For her female fans especially, she embodied the post-feminist 'grrrl power' attitude of her time. She was strong, self-reliant, intelligent and willing to actively and aggressively pursue her desires. Some critics disagreed, and decried Lara is a sexualised cyberbimbo. Lara appeared to revel in both forms of attention. As *Face* magazine put it, Lara was 'bigger than Pammy, wiser than Yoda' (see Figure 6.1).[8] Lara is and has always been multiple, not only multiply mediated but, in the hands of her fans, she is playable in quite different ways.

Like other games, *Tomb Raider* offers a form of anticipatory viewing and affective immersion: training in movement command sequences and the curious experience of third-person narcissism (being and admiring Lara simultaneously) are especially key. To be immersed in the playing of a game, to inhabit 'the country of the half-second delay [of human reaction time]' (Thrift 2004: 67), is also to pursue a certain sort of erotic relation. Such techno-eroticism is variously defined as

> the pleasure of the cyborg myth, the seduction of symbiosis and potent fusions ... is the holding power of the machine and the screen, the seductive interface between humans and their computers ... [b]ased on virtual interdependence, trust, and even love ... we become passionately attached to our machines. (Matrix 2006: 121)

In the case of Lara, this passionate attachment is generally misrecognised as desire for the figure of Lara. The question of desire for 'pixel vixens' like Lara is one that has long exercised feminist critics. The standard debate is captured in titles such as: 'Lara Croft: Feminist Icon or Cyberbimbo?' (Kennedy 2002) and 'Does Lara Croft wear fake polygons?' (Schleiner 2001). As Sidney Matrix argues, this either/or debate largely misses the point. Lara's 'hook' lies not in her disproportionate curves, but in human-machine coupling: 'the seductive and intimate connection that is pre-requisite for keeping digital capitalism online' (Matrix 2006). Gameworld geopolitics is not immune from the pleasures and pitfalls of techno-eroticism; rather, the seductive and intimate connection of body and machine is part of the sense of mastery engendered by gaming, and in this way a pre-requisite for keeping digital conflict online.

Figure 6.1 Lara Croft crosses over: *The Face* magazine cover, June 1997.
Source: *The Face*, reproduced with permission

Thus, while at first glance quest genre games such as *Tomb Raider* may appear to be less directly aligned with the exigencies of the 'military-industrial-media-entertainment-network' (Der Derian 2001), the wet, quiet, subterranean and often unpopulated spaces of *Tomb Raider* (see Figure 6.2) are a far representational cry from the dry, urban or desert spaces of current war-themed games. The game is structured around a quest for objects, not the defeat of enemy forces. Given these specificities, it would be easy to assume that *Tomb Raider* is unconcerned with the production of what Stahl (2006) terms the 'virtual citizen-soldier'. But what remains on offer is a coupling with the computations of conflict. *Tomb Raider* invites a different game experience and a different kind of 'helping out' of the actions of gameworld geopolitics: participation in solitary, non-state agency and the effects and affects associated with talismanic objects.

Figure 6.2 *Tomb Raider Anniversary* wallpaper, 2008.
Source: EIDOS, reproduced with permission

Private violence

Much has been made of the imperial politics of *Tomb Raider* (see Breger 2008), but Lara is perhaps more feudal than she is imperial. She is unmistakably aristocratic in her accent, interests and familial background. Her father is an English peer, and her home an estate. Aristocrats are feudal residues, not imperial agents; their money and power stems from inherited lands and titles, not trade, bureaucracy or capital investment. As such they are leisured figures, free to pursue idiosyncratic interests, profiting where they may. From the outset, Lara's character and interests were conceived in decidedly exploitative and individualistic terms. An early development document for the game states that she is

> a modern-day adventurer and procurer of rare artefacts which she relieves from Johnny foreigner with the gay abandon of a five year old stealing mars bars [sic] from the corner shop. She then sells the heritage of these countries for profit, and perverse xenophobic pleasure. (Toby Gard/Tomb Raider Development Team 1995)

Tomb raiders – procurers of rare artefacts – have a rich and peculiar legacy. Unlike waging war, tomb raiding is typically the pursuit of mercenaries, renegades, connoisseurs, archaeologists, scholars and other non-state agents.[9] On the official game site, Lara is even referred to as an 'archaeologist-mercenary'.[10] In literary and cinematic representations, archaeologists of tombs are highly unstable figures. They must maintain careful moral distance from the 'grave robbers' with whom they are often in competition: grave-robbers are parasitic, anarchic and ignorant. Indiana Jones – on whom Lara was modelled[11] – and Lara are, rather, experts with superhuman drive. Both Lara and Indy are reluctant renegades, transient tomb raiders.[12] They may act on behalf of a state or state institution (like a museum), but private interests more often enlist their services and it is their independent resourcefulness that allows them to work as they do. Generally speaking, some form of crisis demands that they travel to an exotic locale, solve the riddles of ancient or iconic sites, beat a path through the bodies of any resistant human and non-human residents, and encounter the powerful object before it is encountered by evil-doing competition.[13]

Figures such as Lara and Indiana must steal objects because stealing occurs. Such a rationale participates in a realist geopolitical culture, where actors are self-interested and all means of maximising a states' security and power, even if those means are held in common with the enemy or antithetical group, are legitimate practice. Theirs is the pre-emptive steal, the steal that anticipates stealing, a recurrent theme of the genre. This take-it-and-run action is measured out in the gameworld when the player must 'pick up' objects – ammunition, keys to puzzles and various 'rewards' – to safely and profitably progress from one space or level to another. The action is more straightforwardly figured at various culminations of gameplay where central, talismanic objects become available for the taking. At times tomb raiders are assisted by native informant-type characters, in other cases by glamorous offsiders (in *Tomb Raider Legend*, for example, Lara maintains radio contact with a team of assistants). On the whole, however, tomb raiders are lone figures, operating in the interstices of the law and social order. For the most part, this suspension of law and social order is explained in terms of a 'lost civilisation' that leaves only its material traces: objects now dangerous because they have been forgotten by those who created them. As it is in contemporary geopolitics for Western nations seeking dangerous weapons in Other places, the forgetting of these Othered objects is proportionate not to the demise of an ancient order or defunct regime, but to an unwillingness to acknowledge the Self in their production.

The heroic, non-state agency of Lara resonates in two additional figures: the mercenary for hire and the weapons inspector. The mercenary may at times work for or identify with a nation-state, but he or she is not a member of the national armed services in a straightforward sense, and arguably draws agency precisely from a being outside the codes of conduct and rules (both legal and cultural) that states are subject to (see Chesterman and Lehnardt 2007). The weapons inspector is a figure whose expertise with specific objects (and their traces and trappings) is what brings them into play. The weapons inspector works for an international regime and according to multilateral dictates, albeit it with significant national interests at stake. Though perhaps not in the muscular fashion of Indy and Lara, the weapons inspector is charged with finding, recognising and neutralising a dangerous object in an exotic locale, while avoiding a great many obstacles along the way. It is to the talismanic objects prized by such figures I now turn.

Talismanic objects

While much has changed across the six *Tomb Raider* editions, the kind of talismanic object that lies at the heart of the game has altered little. In the first *Tomb Raider* (and in the *Anniversary* version), Lara must find the Scion of the lost city of Atlantis; in *Tomb Raider II*, Lara is on the trail of the Dagger of Xian, the Infada Stone in *III* and so on. In the next edition, the as yet unreleased *Tomb Raider: Underworld*, Lara finds that the root of all world mythology leads back to the European Norse, and that she will need 'Thor's Hammer' if she is to 'to kill a god'.[14] Lara's quested-for objects are most often weapons, many with citations to various geopolitical realities: 'Xian' is not only identifiably 'Chinese' as the name of the last Emperor of the Han Dynasty, but also the name given to a nuclear bomber, the Xian H-6, developed and used by the Chinese Liberation People's Army and Air Force in the 1950s and 1960s. 'Atlantis' is a clichéd site of geopolitical parable: an island-state whose naval power and extensive geopolitical reach could not prevent it from disappearing without trace. The 'Infada Stone' of *Tomb Raider III* – the game was released in 1998/99 – undoubtedly references the First Intifada or 'war of stones', the Palestinian uprising and ensuing conflict of 1987–93. 'Thor' was the name given to the first US intermediate range ballistic missile, later deployed by the UK. Again, these correspondences are not concerned to transmit a 'message'. Rather these correspondences are generic, generative and often less than conscious. My argument is that Lara's worldly quest is to seek out the weapons and talismans of contemporary geopolitics. Playing Lara is a 'helping out' of the actions associated with geopolitical quests. Her talismans measure out the dangerous objects of international discord: the 'smoking gun'[15] of terrorist complicity, the Weapon of Mass Destruction (WMD), the biological agent and the fissile substance. Like the Scion of Atlantis and Thor's Hammer, these objects have the power to affect an event so terrible that only the most heroic, those of purest motive, can be trusted with the task of their neutralisation.

From BAFTA Awards to Lucozade sales, Lara was claimed as a homegrown late 1990s British phenomenon. One of the most important geopolitical contexts for the emergence of Lara was Britain's involvement in the United Nation's search for WMD. Experts, along with agents of various states and supra-state bodies, were engaged in a very high-profile quest for the talismanic object of the time, the WMD. In this way, gameworld geopolitics was arguably inaugurated by a quest, not by an invasion. Following the end of the 1991 Gulf War, the United Nations Special Commission (UNSCOM) was established by the United Nations with the aim of ensuring Iraq's compliance in the production and use of weapons of mass destruction. UNSCOM supervised the destruction of weapons and weapons facilities throughout the 1990s. Controversy arose in 1998 when the Iraqi government levelled accusations that UNSCOM was US intelligence operatives' Trojan horse of choice. What was envisaged as an independent, international commission for arms control became an organisation that, simultaneous to its tracking of weapons, netted additional intelligence for interested nation-states, particularly the USA, Britain and Israel. With the inspectors removed from Iraq, the USA and Britain undertook bombing raids that 'did not respect any boundaries between the weapons sites claimed as the provocation for the attacks and sites associated with the regime itself' (Wright 1999).

In Britain, the saga of weapons inspections took an additional and tragic turn in light of the 2003 invasion of Iraq. David Kelly, an experienced weapons inspector and long-time member of UNSCOM, participated anonymously in a May 2003 interview with a BBC journalist about the Blair government's intelligence 'dossier' on Iraqi WMD. He voiced concerns about the dossier and intimated that 'the 45-minute claim' (a claim that Iraq was capable of firing biological and chemical weapons within 45 minutes of an order to do so) had been included in the dossier at the behest of Blair's own director of communications. When aired, the BBC report caused significant controversy and Kelly was eventually called to appear before a televised sitting of the Foreign Affairs Select Committee. Two days after this appearance, Kelly took his own life.

The exposure and debasement of Kelly, his death and the public responses that followed, including numerous films, investigative reports and conspiracy theories, say something of the heroism with which he was identified. Kelly was a dedicated and experienced national public servant who had served international disarmament causes in the former USSR and Iraq. He was also a present-day knight of sorts: a companion of the Order of St Michael and St George, the sixth-most senior of Britain chivalric orders and one reserved for members of the British Diplomatic Service and those who render service to UK interests overseas. The Order bears the motto '*Auspicium melioris ævi*', 'token of a better age'. Seen as an embodiment of a better and more principled political age, Kelly in death 'transform[ed] a range of disgruntlements into a profound sense that the [British] government had shown itself to be morally and politically bankrupt' (Gearty 2004).[16] This 'profound sense' can be seen as a form of affective resistance to British domestic and foreign policy practices, a resistance that suggests that a knight's heroism may transcend and thus diminish the central authority that he or she ostensibly serves.

The search for WMD was explicitly discussed by geopolitical figures in terms of a difficult quest: in the lead up to invasion the British Foreign

Secretary, Jack Straw, wrote that 'the chance that 300, or even 3,000, inspectors could criss-cross a country the size of France and successfully track down substances capable of being produced in an ordinary living room is absurd', thus emphasising the quest territory as large and the questing heroes as few (Straw 2003). After the commencement of invasion he reiterated this difficulty: '[w]hether or not we are able to find one third of one petrol tanker in a country twice the size of France remains to be seen' (Straw, 29 April 2003). In this reference to a possible store of Iraqi anthrax, Straw exaggerated Iraq's land area by incorrectly stating that it was twice that of France. As others have argued, in the lead up to the invasion it had become imperative to *not* find WMD such that the search for such objects remained ongoing and the case for war could be strengthened (see Luke this volume). In this situation, 'the closer the inspectors got to finding any Iraqi weapons of mass destruction and having them destroyed (or proved non-existent) the more panic – not relief – this caused in Washington' (Kiernan 2003: 847). As has been noted, in his persuasion for invasion address to the UN Security Council on 5 February 2003, Colin Powell employed the authoritative visuality of Microsoft PowerPoint. But Powell also waved his own talismanic object at members: a vial containing 'less than a teaspoon full' of model anthrax. While the vial was charged with the danger 'out there', Powell also brought home the affects associated with this danger by the conflation of the vial with the humble teaspoon, and by reminding his audience of the domestic anthrax attacks of 2001. He stated that this small amount of anthrax had 'forced several hundred people to undergo emergency medical treatment and killed two postal workers' in 2001, and concluded that the equivalent of 'tens upon tens upon tens of thousands of teaspoons' of dry anthrax were estimated by UNSCOM to be in Saddam Hussein's store (Powell 2003). In gameworld geopolitics, threat as continual and imminent is constantly visualised and materialised, albeit in changing modes and forms. The RETORT collective identifies this situation as 'permanent war' and refers to the American empire as a 'machine' that is 'normalized' and '[kept] running' by the repeated use of military force (RETORT 2005: 81–2). Where once international accord was threatened by a passing crisis or conflict, conflict is now briefly threatened by the end of stimulation: a geopolitical 'game over'.

As the game ran on and the quest for Iraqi WMD became overshadowed by the invasion of Iraq, media reports emerged of the looting of the Iraqi National Museum. Stories of hundreds of thousands of stolen ancient artefacts jostled for media time amidst accounts of key areas of Baghdad being taken and live footage of air strikes on the capital. These initial reports of stolen artefacts were later exposed as gross exaggerations. Some explanation for the exaggeration and prominence of these reports is found in the long-standing generic distinction between the hero and the grave robber. The anarchic, opportunistic thief in the tomb – as all around Baghdad was becoming a grave – provided a perfect foil to the heroism of US and allied forces. The objects themselves were spoken of in terms of the antiquity of human occupation of the region, the ancient 'Cradle of Civilisation', to which Saddam's Iraq could be unfavourably compared.

The case of the 'looting' of the Iraqi National Museum demonstrates something of the 'helping out' of the action (of military invasion) that *Tomb Raider* provides. The museum objects themselves resonated with the emotions associated with the search for Iraqi WMD: anxiety that these objects had been removed and that they remained unseen, frustration that their locations were unknown (and suspicion that they might have already been moved across national borders with the help of sympathetic intermediaries) and narcissistic aggression in the charge that 'humanity' was the loser. Speaking more broadly about Iraqi archaeological sites, Atwood gives voice to this anxiety and dismay, this not knowing:

> When ancient sites are excavated carefully and methodically by trained archaeologists, all of humanity can gain an understanding into how these societies lived ... When those sites are ransacked by looters, all that knowledge is lost. (Atwood 2004: 9)

Saying more than he knows, Atwood continues by intoning that 'looting robs a country of its heritage, but, even worse, it destroys everyone's ability to know about the past' (Atwood 2004: 9). The generic drama of 'looting' so fixed upon in media reports also amplified the sense that law and social order had entirely broken down in Baghdad (but also inferred that this was not entirely the Coalition's doing), undoubtedly assisting other actions to be taken by both residents and incoming forces and for these actions to go unseen. Much of the visual footage that accompanied the reports provided an 'eyewitness' looking-moving view of the cavernous interior space of the museum, with hand-held cameras wobbling over broken display cases and scattered glass, naked plinths and vestiges of artefacts. This gameplay view seemed to scan the scene for clues or reward objects hidden amongst the debris of violent encounter, in hope of an indication for the incoming raiders of where to next.

Rather than understanding games as ideologically driven attempts to mirror the world, gaming ought to be understood as a type of practice that participates in the world. In this chapter, I have suggested that games should be seen neither as predictably or dangerously prescriptive, nor as unprecedented and radically 'interactive' cultural forms. Genre, as a typified action, allows geopolitical power to be played out in games, and games carry with them some of the force of their original operation into the conduct of geopolitics. Both contemporary geopolitics and digital games facilitate anticipatory viewing and transact the illusion of mastery over the model to wider domains. I have specifically argued that the *Tomb Raider* game series offers players (and non-players) participation in mercenary rather than militarised agency. In this sense *Tomb Raider* and similar action-adventure games diverge from much of the current suite of war-themed games, but not from a constitutive role in global conflict. In mobilising the quest genre, a genre that works affectively to reinstall support for a central authority in times of crisis, *Tomb Raider* measures out a generic form of geopolitics made up of solitary, techno-eroticised, object-focused and objectifying play.

Bibliography

Anderson, Ben (in press), *'No Bad Surprises: Anticipating the Event of Terror'*.
Aronstein, Susan, ' "Not exactly a Knight": Arthurian narrative and recuperative politics in the Indiana Jones trilogy', *Cinema Journal* 34/4 (1995), pp.3–30.
Atwood, Roger, *Stealing History: Tomb Raiders, Smugglers, and the Looting of the Ancient World* (New York: St Martin's Press, 2004).
Breger, Claudia, 'Digital digs, or Lara Croft replaying Indiana Jones', *Aether* 2 (2008), pp.41–60, available at: http://geogdata.csun.edu/~aether/volume_02.html (accessed 5 November 2008).
Carr, Diane, 'Genre and affect in *Silent Hill* and *Planescape Torment*', *Game Studies* 3/1 (2003).
Carter, Sean and McCormack, Derek P., 'Film, geopolitics and the affective logics of intervention', *Political Geography* 25 (2006), pp.228–45.
Chesterman, Simon and Lehnardt, Chia, *From Mercenaries to Market: The Rise and Regulation of Private Military Companies* (Oxford: Oxford University Press, 2007).
Crogan, Patrick, 'Gametime: History, narrative, and temporality in Combat Flight Simulator II', in M.J.P. Wolf and B. Perron (eds), *The Video Game Theory Reader* (London and New York: Routledge, 2003), pp.275–302.
Crogan, Patrick, 'Gameplay mode: Between war, simulation and technoculture' (Minneapolis: University of Minnesota Press, in press).
D'Ancona, Matthew, PBS interview (11 March 2003), available at: http://www.pbs.org/wgbh/pages/frontline/shows/blair/interviews/dancona.html (accessed 4 November 2008).

Dalby, Simon, 'Warrior geopolitics: *Gladiator, Black Hawk Down* and *The Kingdom of Heaven*', *Political Geography* 27/4 (2008), pp.437–56.
Der Derian, James, *Virtuous War: Mapping the Military-Industrial-Media-Entertainment Network* (Boulder, Colorado: Westview Press, 2001).
Frow, John, *Genre* (London and New York: Routledge, 2006).
Gard, Toby (and *Tomb Raider* Development Team), *Tomb Raider Game Outline 1.3/Tomb Raider game design*, 20 March 1995, unpublished.
Gearty, Conor, 'A misreading of the law', *London Review of Books* (19 February 2004), available at: http://www.lrb.co.uk/v26/n04/gear01_.html (accessed 21 June 2008).
Graham, Stephen, *Cities, War And Terrorism: Towards an Urban Geopolitics* (Malden, MA and Oxford: Blackwell, 2004).
Graham, Stephen, 'Remembering Fallujah, demonising place, constructing atrocity', *Environment and Planning D: Society and Space* 23/1 (2005), pp.1–10.
Gregory, Derek, '"The rush to the intimate": Counter-insurgency and the cultural turn', *Radical Philosophy* 150 (2008), available at: http://www.radicalphilosophy.com/default.asp?channel_id=2369&editorial_id=26755 (accessed 1 November 2008).
Hughes, Rachel, 'Through the looking blast: Geopolitics and visual culture', *Geography Compass* 1/5 (2007), pp.976–94.
Huizinga, Johan, *Homo Ludens: a Study of the Play-Element in Culture* (London and New York: Routledge, 1998, originally published 1944).
[Indiana Jones and the] Raiders of the Lost Ark, Paramount Pictures (1981).
Indiana Jones and the Temple of Doom, Paramount Pictures (1984).
Indiana Jones and the Last Crusade, Paramount Pictures (1989).
Kellner, Douglas and Ryan, Michael, *Camera Politica: The Politics And Ideology Of Contemporary Hollywood Film*, (Bloomington: Indiana University Press, 1987).
Kennedy, Helen, 'Lara Croft: Feminist icon or cyberbimbo? On the limits of textual analysis', *Games Studies* 2/2 (2002), available at: http://www.gamestudies.org/0202/kennedy/ (accessed 3 January 2007).
Kiernan, Ben, 'Collateral damage', *Antipode* 35/5 (2003), pp.846–55.
King, Geoff and Krzywinska, Tanya, *Tomb Raiders and Space Invaders: Videogame Forms And Contexts* (London and New York: I.B.Tauris, 2006).
Kline, Stephen, Dyer-Witheford, Nick and de Peuter, Greig, *Digital Play: the interaction of technology, culture and marketing* (Montreal and Kingston: McGill-Queen's University Press, 2003).
Lorimer, Hayden, 'Cultural geography: The busyness of being "more-than-representational"', *Progress in Human Geography* 29/1 (2005), pp.83–94.
Matrix, Sidney E., *Cyberpop: Digital Lifestyles and Commodity Cultures* (London and New York, Routledge, 2006).
Meyer, Christopher, PBS interview, 18 March 2003, available at: http://www.pbs.org/wgbh/pages/frontline/shows/blair/interviews/meyer.html (accessed 4 November 2008).
Powell, Colin, 'Iraq: Failing to disarm', address to the UN Security Council (5 February 2003), available at: http://www.whitehouse.gov/news/releases/2003/02/20030205-1.html# (accessed 19 November 2008).
Power, Marcus, 'Digitized virtuosity: Video war games and post-9/11 cyber-deterrence', *Security Dialogue* 38/2 (2007), pp.271–88.

Retort, *Afflicted Powers: Capital and Spectacle in a New Age of War* (London and New York: Verso, 2005).

Schleiner, Anne-Marie, 'Does Lara Croft wear fake polygons? Gender and gender-role subversion in computer adventure games', *Leonardo* 34/3 (2001), pp.221–6.

Stahl, Roger, 'Have you played the War on Terror?', *Critical Studies in Media and Communication* 23/2 (2006), pp.112–30.

Straw, Jack, 'I joined the peace protesters in the Sixties. Believe me, this is different', *The Independent* (23 February 2003), http://www.independent.co.uk/opinion/commentators/jack-straw-i-joined-the-peace-protesters-in-the-sixties-believe-me-this-is-different-598525.html (accessed 11 November 2008).

Straw, Jack, Quoted in the Select Committee on Foreign Affairs' *Minutes of Evidence*, 29 April 2003, available at: http://www.parliament.the-stationery-office.com/pa/cm200203/cmselect/cmfaff/405/3042907.htm (accessed 19 November 2008).

Thrift, Nigel, 'Intensities of feeling: Towards a spatial politics of affect', *Geografiska Annaler Series B* 86 (2004), pp.57–78.

Wright, Susan, 'The hijacking of UNSCOM: United Nations Special Commission used incorrectly', *Bulletin of the Atomic Scientists* 55/3 (1999), pp.23–4.

Chapter 7

'I Used to Keep a Camera in My Top Left-Hand Pocket': The Photographic Practices of British Soldiers

Rachel Woodward, Trish Winter and K. Neil Jenkings

Introduction

A former British Royal Marine told us: 'I used to keep a camera in my top left-hand pocket. When we were out and about we used to whip it out and say "Would you like to take a phot?".' Taking a 'phot' – this soldier's specific shorthand for 'photograph' – was commonplace to him, he said, throughout his military life. It is these photographic practices of British soldiers that are the focus of this chapter, drawing on research we conducted on the construction, representation and negotiation of military identities.[1] As a method for eliciting narratives about identity, we framed interviews with former soldiers around a selection of the photographs they had kept from their military lives. All the quotations used in this chapter are taken from the soldiers' own accounts. What follows, then, are a set of stories that, while not explicitly addressing either the practices of popular geopolitics or the visual cultures of militarism, nonetheless speak to both these themes. Amongst other things, narratives emerged about the role and purpose of the soldier in the spaces and territories in which military activities take place, about the utility of photographs for communicating this participation in practical geopolitics to other people and about how soldiers' practice of photographing themselves doing military things constitutes a performance of soldierly identity. Our intention in this chapter is quite modest: to look at these narratives of identity and the photographic practices through which they are often mediated and ask how these soldiers' awareness of their own geopolitical agency permeates their sense of self as soldiers. Military personnel, charged with the execution of legitimated violence by the state, are agents of geopolitical power. A range of ideas, assumptions and anxieties are projected onto these agents of the state, including concerns about what it means for faceless warriors to have geopolitical agency. Our interviewees were alert to these anxieties, and this chapter tries to show how this geopolitical agency is negotiated in the lives of soldiers through practices that include the taking of photographs.

Our exploration of soldier photography brings two ideas to the broader topic of relating the visual and the geopolitical. Firstly, that soldier photography articulates connections between formal and popular geopolitical practices and that the visual is significant to that articulation. This idea arises from the positioning of these people and their photographs relative both to popular geopolitics – explorations of the operation of geopolitical power in and through popular cultural forms and practices – and to the formalised and explicit geopolitical practices of the state. We discuss here the images and commentaries of individuals who have used a popular cultural practice – mass photography – to record features of their lives. But these individuals are also soldiers, individuals selected and trained on the basis of personal attributes and granted the exclusive and legitimate right by the state to exercise lethal force in pursuit of its political territorial objectives. Whilst we emphasise in this chapter the personal and popular geopolitics performed within our corpus of visuals, we should acknowledge that there are other geopolitical scripts dictated by other themes and concerns within the genre of soldier photography specifically, and the visual culture of the armed forces more widely.[2]

The second idea that we develop concerns the value brought to the pursuit of a critical geopolitics from the small details furnished by ordinary people (MacDonald 2006: 61). Militarism and military activities are geographically constituted and expressed through the mundane, the normalised, the unobserved, the unremarkable and the routine, as well as through the spectacular, the newsworthy, the visible and the publicised; and there is empirical value in the interrogation of the ordinary (Woodward 2004, 2005). Nigel Thrift suggests that within the small details of people's lives lurk 'some of the most potent geopolitical forces' (Thrift 2000: 384); he argues for consideration of these 'little things' which 'are crucial to how the geopolitical is translated into being' (Thrift 2000: 380). Soldiers, as executors of the state's geopolitical strategies, translate geopolitical intention into action through their daily activities, but also – crucially – as individuals performing personal acts. Their own ideas and explanations thus add texture and detail to larger geopolitical narratives.

The practice of soldier photography

Militarism and photography have long been mutually constitutive (Trachtenberg 1985; Virilio 1989, 1994; Diller and Scofidio 1996). Military engagement has been, since the development of photography, an enduring photographic subject: the photographer shows what the civilian cannot see, through a medium singularly able to capture the spectacle and the human response it provokes, and offering a set of practices simultaneously fascinating and revolting (Price 2004). For the public, civilian gaze, the work of photo-journalists and photographers – embedded or independent, co-opted or dissident to the state – produces images of conflict and combatants. Specific photographic images of the soldier endure, their power transcending their origins and the banality of their repetition in visual media (Hariman and Lucaites 2007). For less public gazes, military photographers attached to platoons, companies and regiments record on a daily basis the actions of units and the lives of those who comprise them. Soldiers too snap away with cameras when they can. The walls of military buildings – the barracks, messes, offices, depots, stores and armouries – become galleries for the display of these images. The private spaces of soldiers – from the surfaces of the family living room to the headboards of barracks bunks, from the chronologically regimented albums to the carrier bag in the locker – contain the output of professional and amateur photographers capturing on film or pixel the image of the soldier. To be a soldier is to engage with photographs and with photographic practice; military life is a life of images.

Soldier photography has become a public and political phenomenon. Soldiers' photographs can be readily reproduced and widely circulated, particularly with the advent of digital reproductive technologies. Recently, certain soldiers' images, particularly those showing violence meted out to detainees by military personnel, have prompted extensive commentary on both the legitimation of unlawful military violence and the consequences of taking and viewing such imagery (see, for example, Judith Butler's chapter in this volume). The point we wish to advance here, against a backdrop of the public circulation of soldier photographs, is that such photographic practices are ubiquitous. Photographs showing the abuse of Iraqi civilians by British troops in a food distribution depot (Camp Breadbasket), which circulated in the British news media following courts martial of the perpetrators in 2005, generated public commentary as much for their very existence as for what they depicted. This was also the case in commentary surrounding (faked) photographs of the abuse of Iraqi civilians, published in 2003 in the British *Daily Mirror*. The surprise expressed at the existence of such photographs is itself interesting, indicating assumptions about the absence or restriction of photographic practices in military lives. And yet, as we have indicated, for many soldiers the camera is just another piece of kit, and photographic practices are a regular feature of soldiers' lives:

> 'cause I always took a camera around with me ... it was just like a little instant in my pocket, kept in my little plastic bag, to keep it water-proof. Every now and then [I] would whip the camera out and take a few photographs.

The motivations for taking and keeping photographs of military lives are shared with other photographic genres. They are a means of recording an event, place or time of life; a means of remembering another person or group; a device for fixing, spatially and temporally, a self in a situation:

> Me dad got me a camera when I first joined up, 'cause I wanted to take photographs of everywhere I went and different things ... Most tours, adventure training and things like that, I'd always take my camera with me.

The ubiquity of military photographic practice is also attested through that more established representational practice, the military memoir. These confirm through repetition the consistency and significance of photographic practice. A startling example is Phil Ashby's *Unscathed* (2002), an account of four Royal Marines' escape through rebel-held bush following the collapse of a peace-keeping enterprise in Sierra Leone in 2000. The marines include a camera amongst the minimal equipment they carry through the bush. Lying up after a day on the run, 'Paul even took a photo. I began to feel more confident that we might actually make it' (Ashby 2002: 252).[3] Having and using a camera is a routine part of military life. And while not all events and places are recorded (or are even recordable) and not all memories are assisted by the existence of a photograph – military photographic practices are, like any other, uneven – the point remains that it is a practice so commonplace as to constitute an identifiable genre, the 'soldier photograph'.

With a genre comes a cluster of themes or concerns that work in combination to describe or define that genre's characteristics. As Liz Wells notes, although the histories, practices, ideas and expectations that construct a genre may shift through time, there is a coherence to the themes through which the genre is constituted (Wells 2004). One of the themes through which the genre of soldier photography gains its coherence is that of the performance by soldiers of military activities across territory – the performance of practical geopolitics and the expression of a geopolitical agency. This observation was confirmed for us in the interviews on which this chapter is based. We conducted 16 interviews with serving and former British soldiers and Royal Marines. Our interviewees were self-selecting respondents to a local newspaper article and were primarily resident in the north-east of England, a former industrial region with a strong tradition of military recruitment. Our interviewees included both men and women across the ranks from Private to Captain, with varying lengths of service in a range of military occupations. There was a slight skew in the sample towards former Royal Marine commandos. Each interview was structured around a small sample of photographs (about ten), chosen by the interviewee, from their own collection, prior to the interview as meaningful in some way to that person's military life. In every interview, each photograph was discussed in turn to explore its content, its history and social life, and its significance to the interviewee. Our focus on photographs was methodological, with auto-driven photo-elicitation providing a means for exploring the soldiers' construction and negotiation of soldierly identities. We took copies of each photograph after the interview, and recorded and transcribed each interview in full.

Photographs derive their meaning from their context (Berger 1982; Sontag 1990, 2003). As David Campbell puts it:

> The dominant social understandings existing at the moment of production and reception are more important than the specific form or content of the image for the creation of meaning. When combined with issues of context that relate to the presentation of the image – the economy of display – the power of images cannot be said to result from qualities internal to the picture. (Campbell 2004: 71)

This certainly holds true for the photographs in our study. We coded the photographs using the contextual information contained in the transcripts. One code that emerged was that of 'place', our shorthand for instances when an individual drew on observations about the physical location and spatiality in the course of discussions of soldier identity. Although not all the place photographs spoke to the geopolitical exercise of military power, a significant proportion did, and it is these that we focus on here. Soldiering, and the photographic practices that frame it, are situated activities. Our interviewees talked about photographs taken in Iraq, Belize, the

Mediterranean Sea, Norway, Albania, Libya, Cyprus, the Falkland Islands, France, West Germany and partitioned Berlin, Bosnia, Singapore and of course the UK, including Northern Ireland.

Another code that emerged and that is significant to our argument here was 'performance'. This term, as it is used in post-structuralist theory, relies upon definitions of 'the performative' developed in linguistics and grammar (see Butler 1999). Such a conception has also found a secure purchase in much of the geographical literature (Nash 1996; Gregson and Rose 2000). But alongside this, we are interested in ideas of performance as it is commonly defined, in phrases like 'to perform a task' or 'to perform a role'. We consider that this multivalent term is useful for exploring the negotiation of identity and geopolitical agency through photographic practices.

Soldier photography is performative: photographic practices are part of how soldiers 'do' their soldiering, part of how they become British soldiers. Photographic practices are of course only an element in a wider repertoire of performative acts, through which the military body, individual and collective is constructed and consolidated. From the codified gestures of drill, to the routines of operational procedures, military acts produce and sustain the military body. There is a visuality inherent in these performative acts: they are watched for their efficiency and efficacy; they may be conducted purely in order to be observed, or carried out with the intention of concealment from the watching eye; they entail surveillance as a learnt way of looking at land, at others, at the activities of the enemy. The taking, collecting and displaying of photographs is part of that engagement with the visual and is in turn performative. Furthermore, this performativity is fundamental to the production and maintenance of military identities. As Judith Butler famously notes with respect to gender, it is through the repetition of acts that the ideal is secured, and this constant process of reiteration points to the transience and instability of the ideal; it has to be worked at, over and over again, to be maintained (Butler 1999). Elsewhere, we talk more generally about the centrality of performativity to military identity, particularly to gendered military identities (Woodward 1998, 2003, 2006; Woodward and Winter 2007). We want to emphasise here that for many of the soldiers we interviewed, there was an awareness and a self-consciousness about this process of performance, which includes recognition of the geopolitical context in which they had served. This is illustrated quite neatly with the comment of a soldier – an engineer – who served in Iraq alongside US forces in Iraq, about his photo of an Airborne Warning and Control System (AWACS) aircraft:

One of the Americans came up and says – he could see we had our cameras out – and said, 'Look, don't take any photos of the plane.' So when they all went for their lunch, us being squaddies,[4] just went up and took a couple of sneaky shots of it.

This soldier affirms not only a sense of self through the taking of the photograph ('us being squaddies'), but also a resistance, in his own small way, to the dictates of US military power. Our point here is that, although many of the people interviewed about their soldier photographs were low-ranking and anonymous foot soldiers in major international geopolitical entanglements, they were astute about both their performance of soldiering and its representational politics.

This alertness is evident in comments about the essentially fabricated nature of photographic performance. Our interviewees talked frequently about the posed quality of photographs of themselves and others. Sometimes this was deliberate and conveyed wider political intent. One photograph, taken for a PR piece in a British regional newspaper, shows a man (our interviewee) dressed in a warm-weather uniform, squatting on his haunches in front of a hand-drawn map resting on an easel: 'They went and got that [notebook] off a desk in the office and said "Hold that with a pen in your hand".' Or photographic fabrication can be ostensibly for fun: a picture of a man dressed in civilian clothes sitting at the wheel of an unmarked Landrover, and holding an Uzi sub-machine gun as if he were about to fire, is explained as 'just a pose-y photograph in the garage after we'd finished [a day's training]'. However, these two photographs are posed according to certain conventions: the men pictured are shown in classic soldier poses – reading the map, holding a ready gun. The posed performance is cognisant of iconic and universalised figures of the soldier. Two other photographs, shown by two different people, show small groups of soldiers in posed but informal group shots. They are dressed in a variety of camouflage uniform, with head-gear and camouflage cream, and stand against a backdrop of lush green tropical vegetation. 'It must have been like we were US troops in Vietnam', said one interviewee. 'It's a rugsy[5] phot. We are all looking Rambo-ish, all sweat bands', said the other. Soldier photographs reference wider cultural myths and historical geopolitical engagements.

Although they were alert to the fabricated performance of a photograph, this co-existed for many soldiers with an assertion of the photograph's validity: it captured a reality, verified a performance as accurate. One of the interviewees quoted above, while recognising the iconography of a fictionalised Vietnam war, was still emphatic about the non-fictional reality the photograph captured. This was an exercise with live ammunition in Belize by the Guatemalan border, where 'you really had to look after yourself in there because of trench foot, because you were wet all the time'. Another talked of a photograph of himself as a younger man, shown descending round a stairwell looking up at the photographer, expressionless: 'absolutely threaders.[6] I think it was a kind of a hero photo, of "we've done it". It was one of those just to prove to ourselves that it wasn't a dream.' He verifies the representation of extreme physical and mental fatigue, a result of his soldierly activities, but simultaneously identifies with a wider identity position, that of the soldier-hero. The hero position is claimed as a lived and embodied experience, and the photograph is proof.

The idea and vocabulary of performance, then, is useful for describing how so many soldier photographs come into being. What we illustrate here is the negotiation of two different understandings of representation: the photographic representation as a deliberate construction, a fabrication, a performance for the camera; and the photographic representation as documentation or evidence of lived experience. We are working, therefore, with an idea of the photographic performance as complex, negotiated and referencing a much wider collection of soldiering practices and experiences.

In the three sections that follow, we discuss three themes that have emerged from discussion of these photographs which assist in the consideration of soldier photos as geopolitical practice. These themes are: a soldier's physical presence in a location and the display of this for the camera; professional military expertise and its exposition through the photograph; and alternative narratives around the geopolitical events which these photographs record.

'The places that I've been'

Emergent from the interviews, and anticipated before we started, were those photographs that say to their owner 'I was there'. The owner may or may not appear in the photograph itself for this message to persist. As one former Royal Marine put it, 'the main reasons that I take the photographs, I like to be reminded of the places that I have been, the things, the situations we got up to and that'. The photograph may not speak self-evidently about location or place because some photographs stand as proxy for images that could not be taken: 'I think a lot of time it is because of the seriousness of it, you couldn't really take your camera out to take photographs. Because you were watching your back all the time.' Some photographs, though, plainly disclose their location to the outside observer. A photograph of two soldiers, taken from a distance of about 20 metres, shows them on patrol, back to back around five metres apart. They hold their rifles and wear webbing, and are similarly dressed in camouflage print smocks and khaki green trousers, boots and berets. They walk a pavement that runs alongside a wooden fence and the gable end of a brick-built terraced house. Where else but 'Northern Ireland, and there is a picture of me on the streets of Ardoyne in Belfast'. The picture replicates the iconic images of British troops patrolling the suburban streets of Northern Ireland during the 1970s and 1980s, but for this interviewee its significance lies entirely with what that engagement meant to him in the course of his own life:

> I went to my first unit, and probably the biggest experience of my life, at the tender age of 18, 19 years old. ... I mean, you sign up, don't you, knowing that you possibly or potentially go over to places. But as a young 18, 19-year-old lad, you don't expect to get dropped straight into it. I joined as a vehicle mechanic, and I thought 'Yeah, it'll be no problem, I'll be in the workshop spannering away'. I got to [name of regiment] and they goes 'Ah, we are going to Northern Ireland'. And said, 'you'll be going out on the streets, we are short of bodies'. They always say you are a soldier first, a mechanic second, in the Army. So there I am, trained as a vehicle mechanic ... patrolling the streets with a brick [a four-man patrol], attending riots, stopping cars and checking their identities, searching cars, house searches, cordons, even personnel searchings [sic] – you could stop anybody in the street and search them – and arresting people as well.

Entwined with a broader narrative about the performance of British state power in Northern Ireland through the military foot patrol is the disjuncture between what a teenage recruit anticipated on joining his regiment and his sudden acquisition of power through participation in Ulster's constabulary practices. The photograph places him there.

Another photograph from another interviewee shows five men wearing the green berets of the Royal Marines: 'It's basically a bit of a posey photograph, I'm sat on the top of a Panhard Armoured car in Stanley.' Four of the men stand in front of the Panhard, its gun barrel pointing towards the camera. Two look directly at the camera, smiling and relaxed, the hands of one resting on the flash guard of his upturned rifle. The fifth man, whose photograph it is, whose camera took it, smiles and sits with his left arm across his left knee on top of the vehicle. Two more armoured cars are visible in the background, with other Royal Marines around them. This photograph has been deliberately posed – one of the men shown is remembered as routinely adopting a specific stance when photographed – and is significant 'because it's over, Stanley, and a photograph with the lads and that, just the moment, that sort of thing'. This photograph places the man in the recapture of the Falkland Islands in 1982 and at the liberation of Port Stanley. It is performative of military victory, echoing iconic photographs of other military victories in other places and of the universalised figure of the victorious soldier astride captured enemy equipment. For this man, this photograph places him in that place, in that moment and in that tradition.

A third photograph, reproduced in Figure 7.1, is not immediately obvious as one of a soldier, but 'it's the only one of me in Berlin in 1975'. Caught by surprise, the man turns to the photographer, distracted from his ironing. The room is non-descript and institutional, high-ceilinged and sparsely furnished, and is staged for a scene of domesticity; the man is pressing his uniform and is surrounded by his laundry drying on the radiators. He is

Figure 7.1 'It's the only one of me in Berlin in 1975'.
Source: Soldier's own photograph, reproduced with permission

clad only in his underpants. Yet the interviewee, the man in the photograph, sees this photograph as proof of his role in policing the Cold War's boundaries. His conversation emphasises how 'weird' it was to be there at that time, to make the slow journey to West Berlin by sealed train through the German Democratic Republic, the drama of the border gates through which the train had to pass, the contrasts between this vibrant city and its rural hinterland. Above all, his conversation is about his own part in the NATO presence in Cold War Berlin, a partitioned city:

> We were stationed – actually where that is, it's Smuts Barracks, which was right next door to Spandau prison where Hess was being held; Hess was in when I was there.

The connection he makes to Rudolf Hess, imprisoned former deputy leader of the Nazi party, locates him spatially and temporally within the key geopolitical event of post-1945 Europe: the partition of Berlin, with all its tensions and defections:

> You could practically guarantee when the Russians were doing the guard one of them would jump over the wall, into Smuts Barracks and give himself up to the guardroom, practically guarantee it ... there was one done it when ... we were there.

This photograph, the only one the soldier has of that time, is proxy for vivid memories of dramatic military acts, such as crashing out of barracks: a routine of quick evacuation and standing to that was practised regularly and recorded photographically by both the unit photographer and by Soviet personnel atop the Brandenburg Gate, observing the Allied military strength.

This in turn was the cue for a further photograph (Figure 7.2): 'It's, alright, a bit emotive; what it is, I swore I would walk through the Brandenburg gate, and I did.' This shows the same man, now middle-aged and dressed in casual civilian clothes, framed by Berlin's Brandenburg Gate, a monument symbolic first of partition of Berlin and then of its reunification. The photograph was chosen as significant because 'the wall is down, you know, and I walked through the Brandenburg gate, that was ... one of those little promises you make to yourself'. Having participated in the partition of Berlin, this is a memento not only of a key episode in European geopolitics, but also of his own role in this wider picture: 'the fact that I was part of that, even in the '70s'. He recalled that the line of the

Figure 7.2 'I swore I would walk through the Brandenburg Gate'.
Source: Soldier's own photograph, reproduced with permission

now-dismantled wall was marked on the ground at the Brandenburg Gate: 'I didn't get emotive when I was walking through it [the gate] but I stopped on this line and I started to walk up that, and that's when I sort of got the shivers ... to me it was pretty awesome, that.' He recalled how television news coverage of the fall of the Berlin Wall in 1989 had affected him. He had been watching television

> and one of me kids sort of nudged the other one, 'What's wrong with me dad?' – I had tears coming down my face, it's just the wall coming down, it meant more than just – it wasn't just bricks and mortar coming down, it was a whole society, really, you know, the Russian society was crumbling, or the communist was crumbling.

Such pictures do personal memory work around larger public events, inserting a personal narrative into international stories. These photos are 'certificates of presence' (Barthes 1981: 87) authenticating being in space and time. As Barthes goes on to say, the photograph possesses an 'evidential force' with its testimony that bears not on the object but on time: 'the power of authentication exceeds the power of representation'. In this respect, soldiers' photos are no different from, say, tourist snapshots. But memories of presence in places that the photographs invoke signify not just a presence somewhere else, but a presence and a participation in globally significant events. 'I've been in these places', these pictures say, 'not as a passive observer but as an active participant'.

'We do the job'

The realism of the photograph, a concern of much critical writing about photography (Tagg 1988; Sontag 1990; McQuire 1998), was also of interest to our interviewees. For example, one interviewee spoke of a situation in Iraq as 'surreal', but then used her photographs to prove its veracity. A number of interviewees used photographs as communicative artefacts to testify to a particular lived experience, and for these people the realism of the photograph is fundamental and valuable. The power of authentication is invoked here as part of a communicative strategy in which the photograph's purported indexicality to the world uniquely comes into its own. The mimetic function of photography was, for some, its purpose; photographs were taken precisely because of their capacity to communicate something of the lived experience of soldiering. One such example shows a figure wrapped snugly in cold-weather clothing in the snow, next to two trucks parked under drooping fir trees. It was taken explicitly so that the man pictured could give his friends a sense of what it was like to go on exercise in Norway: 'How can they visualize what an 8-tonne wagon is, and how can they visualize what Norway is like? ... when you are talking to your mates, they haven't got a clue what you are talking about.' Significant here is the belief that the visual is the most appropriate and powerful communicative means for sharing experiences of a place's environmental quality or an action's embodied affect.

What, exactly, is being communicated, visually? As well as authenticating presence, as we outline above, these photographs participate in the construction of identity. They communicate the performance of soldiering to a wider audience, and they also consolidate ideas about the self, about what it is actually like to be a soldier. Another photograph shows a row of tanks lined up in a desert, camouflaged sand-coloured against a blue sky. The tanks fly flags of St Andrew and St George to denote national affiliation with Scotland and England, and men sit casually on each tank. The tanks recede into the distance, this perspective implying a mass of vehicles. The iconography echoes that of the men on the Panhard in Stanley; the soldiers are relaxed, smiling. Not all wear uniform. The photograph's owner explains that 'it's not just a picture of me, and it's not just a picture of my squadron or my vehicles ... it just shows us out, doing a job, and job finished'. It was taken, he says, in Kuwait's northern desert, three days before the start of Operation Telic 1. What is being represented here is not the environmental challenge or even the pressing physical danger. This photograph, the owner explains, is demonstrative of professional soldierly skill in getting a job done: he was a vehicle engineer, leading a group tasked with refitting tanks to cope with desert conditions prior to the invasion of Iraq. It constructs an identity around pride in professional competence.

The same man showed us another image (Figure 7.3): 'Bosnia again. ... I took this one to show that we work in any weathers.' It shows two white-painted Warrior armoured personnel carriers, with their stencilled UN markers visible on the side. It is snowing, blizzard conditions. Four green DPM (disruptive pattern military)-clad men mill around one of the Warriors, clearly busy. A large blue metal object sits in the foreground. The interviewee identified the object as an engine and explained its distinctive

Figure 7.3 'Bosnia again'.
Source: Soldier's own photograph, reproduced with permission

colour, emphasising and sharing his technical knowledge and expertise: 'it is duck-egg blue. All our engines are painted. On a lighter engine you can see the leaks easier, if you've got a dark engine, trying to see dark oil is nigh on impossible.' The engine is the focus of attention for one of the men:

> There the lads are, with the engine out of a Warrior, doing work on a Warrior. And you can see, snow on the ground, blizzards, and the lads just work through it, no choice, to get the vehicles back on the road. ... So we do the job, and we do it anywhere in any condition, and Bosnia was no different from anywhere else, from being a training exercise on Soltau to being actually out on operations here.

The work that this photograph does, for this interviewee, is to demonstrate soldierly perseverance and stoicism under poor working conditions, and his Bosnian experience is about just that:

> We do it in any conditions, anywhere, whatever the job asks you to do, and the lads do it. The majority of the times they do it with a smile on their face and they get very little praise for it, except from people like myself or people of their own peer groups or their own environment. It is the sort of thing the press would never show, the cameras never show and your normal civilian wouldn't understand quite truthfully. Some of the conditions the lads work in, I mean this is only 10 years ago, can you imagine that under Health and Safety? You wouldn't be able to go near it [because of the noise and heat] ... but if they don't do it, the big wheel grinds to a halt, the cog doesn't turn anymore, unfortunately.

The photograph, then, shows not just professional competence, but constructs this as an unrecognised attribute of army life. The photograph presents a lived experience of which this man is proud. The setting in Bosnia is relevant, but as an environmentally and politically inclement backdrop to this performance.

These photographs, then, in their construction and their circulation, are about the performance of identity: they are communicative devices for sharing what it means personally to be a soldier, often with those outside the military. The function of these photographs extends to the self: pictures are taken to remind a future self of what military experience was like at the time and are used in subsequent lives as reminders of times past. What is interesting here is the use of the photograph to verify experience as accurate and the emphasis through this of the lived experience of soldiering.

Part of that verification comes through the invocation of physical memory, of embodiment. As Nigel Thrift puts it: 'embodiments must be extraordinarily important to critical geopolitics, not just as vectors of force, but as sites of performance in their own right' (Thrift 2000: 383). These sites of performance are recorded photographically in order to use the medium's realist representational capabilities to record the military life as a lived, embodied experience. Furthermore, it is often through the recollection of the embodied experience that an alternative story about military activities is told, a story that counters the dramatic and newsworthy tales dominating public civilian perceptions of what being a soldier is actually like, and offers instead a nuanced account of the demands on the body of the soldier.

'One of the good reasons why we were out there'

The idea that soldier photographs can offer an alternative account of soldiering or of a specific military engagement came through very strongly in the explanatory narratives around these photographs. We now turn to the work that these photographs do, for their owners, in asserting narratives about specific military engagements that extend or counter dominant explanations of the purpose and outcome of such engagements. The critical geopolitics tradition is, of course, alert to how dominant narratives and discourses, constructed primarily by the state around the play of power over territory, function to consolidate state power and public support. Visual representational practices, including photography, contribute to establishing dominant explanations of armed conflicts. In our corpus of photographs and their accompanying narratives, we note the ways in which these dominant narratives are variously supported or contested by soldiers themselves through their recourse to personal stories. It is to these we now turn.

These alternative stories do not necessarily deny the wider narratives around specific conflicts. Figure 7.4 is 'a photograph of me on patrol in Northern Ireland, next to a mural to Bobby Sands'. It shows a DPM-clad Royal Marine, cradling his rifle, standing against the gable end of a brick house on which has been painted a mural commemorating the death through hunger strike of a prominent IRA member.[7] The soldier looks straight to camera and the picture has been deliberately posed, although the way in which his weapon is held suggests a snapshot of a routine patrol. The mural shows a flag-draped picture of a coffin, three IRA

'I Used to Keep a Camera in My Top Left-Hand Pocket' 159

Figure 7.4 'Me on patrol in Northern Ireland'.

paramilitaries in a guard of honour, a reproduction of an iconic photograph of Sands from his time in prison and a quotation by Sands that is not legible. Our interviewee commented on the ubiquity of republican and loyalist murals on the estates of Belfast (which was reflected in his own photograph collection) and on the significance of this particular photograph as a certificate of presence in dangerous territory, explaining it as an example of real soldiering despite its appearance as a tourist photograph: 'again it was really something to show people back home, "look what a dangerous area I'm in"'. This photograph, then, accords with the themes that we have discussed so far, of identifying the individual in place, performing a geopolitical act and of emphasising a lived and embodied experience, a reality of the job. But, in addition, this photograph is an assertion of military power – one man's story of performing the armed British military presence in republican Belfast – that extends a wider state narrative, circulated primarily through print media, about the control of republican resistance. Interviewer and interviewee discuss the wider symbolism of this:

> [Interviewee:] It is a trophy isn't it, because there is people there, the people live in that house, you don't know, but you assume that they have okayed

> this sort of painting, so they are very pro IRA, and you are right, I am saying 'Look at me, I am not scared of you'. Just standing next to the wall, and me mates taking a happy-snappy of me, I am not scared of you.
>
> [KNJ:] And you are almost taking the picture off them by saying, 'look this is a really [Catholic] thing, I am standing in front of it, having my photograph taken', to take it home, and it is my photograph of somewhere. 'Cause you've almost taken something; they didn't put it there for you to take a photograph in front of.
>
> [Interviewee:] It was their sort of trophy, their trophy and I've gone in and taken it away from them I suppose. I hadn't thought about that, that is very much the case.

This photograph, then, personalises a bigger geopolitical act and by so doing extends and consolidates it.

Other photographs engage with bigger narratives around armed conflict, but do very different work, asserting alternative stories around such engagements for their owners. One such example shows two men wearing jeans and casual shirts, sitting on a big blue sofa. There are racks of CDs in the background, a large black, white and blue flag on the wall behind them, packets of crisps on the table in front of them and one holds a bottle of beer. The photograph's owner explains that these two men are German civilians he became friends with when he was based in Germany in the 1980s as part of the British military presence there. They had bonded over their shared love of football and music, and the three have remained friends to the present:

> When I first met them, they were a bit apprehensive of me, because I was British, 'cause the only contact they had with them, was British soldiers fighting with them. These two guys used to carry CS canisters, because they always had trouble with British soldiers. But I am very good friends with them. ... It shows that you can overcome the stereotypes that exist around soldiers, and you can move on, which I did. I made friends with the local community.

This photograph and its explanatory narrative asserts an alternative view of the garrisoned British soldier to that of the socially and culturally isolated occupant of foreign territory. It has personal significance for its owner in the context of his own life-story, but also because it opens the possibility of alternative narratives of that Cold War British engagement in Germany.

Another alternative narrative for some interviewees entailed the extraction of something positive, personally, from an otherwise destructive and violent military engagement. We were shown a photograph of a young woman dressed in desert DPM uniform, her blonde hair tied back, standing in an office. She is smiling directly at the camera and is flanked by two older men, Arab in appearance, dressed in smart civilian shirts and trousers, who are sharing the joke. She is holding an ornament – a ceramic camel. She explained her relationship with the two men, Iraqi civilians in charge of two technical training institutes in Basra, as friendly and positive, and based on their mutual engagement with reconstruction work at the institutes. On leaving Iraq at the end of her tour, they had presented her with a gift, the figurine camel. The photograph was symbolic of her wider story about her time in Iraq, where she was involved in reconstruction work in 2005:

> I think it is like a happy ending. We were all laughing and joking, it reminds me of memories of what my job was and one of the good reasons why we were out there, not *the* reason, but a good reason. Another happy snapshot of good times.

Her narrative, of the positive and beneficial consequence of the British presence in Iraq, counters quite explicitly that more dominant story of violent resistance to the invading Coalition forces in the British sector of southern Iraq. Whilst she does not deny this other more dominant story, her own personal narrative of her military experience, confirmed for her through this photograph, emphasises a positive, beneficial contribution.

The photographs and their explanatory narratives were also used to contest culturally dominant constructions of soldier identity, particularly those identifying the British soldier as the brutish embodiment of state-sanctioned violence. The photograph reproduced as Figure 7.5 provides for its owner this theme of a positive outcome from a destructive military engagement, but also resurrects a detail from the Falklands War that he argued had been obscured in the dominant narrative about this conflict, with its emphasis on the reclamation of sovereign British territory. The photograph shows two young men, teenagers really, dressed in drab brown overalls, looking up at the camera. One holds a bowl of food. They look uncertain, a little frightened. The photograph's owner recalls being the member of a company of Royal Marines tasked with the transfer of

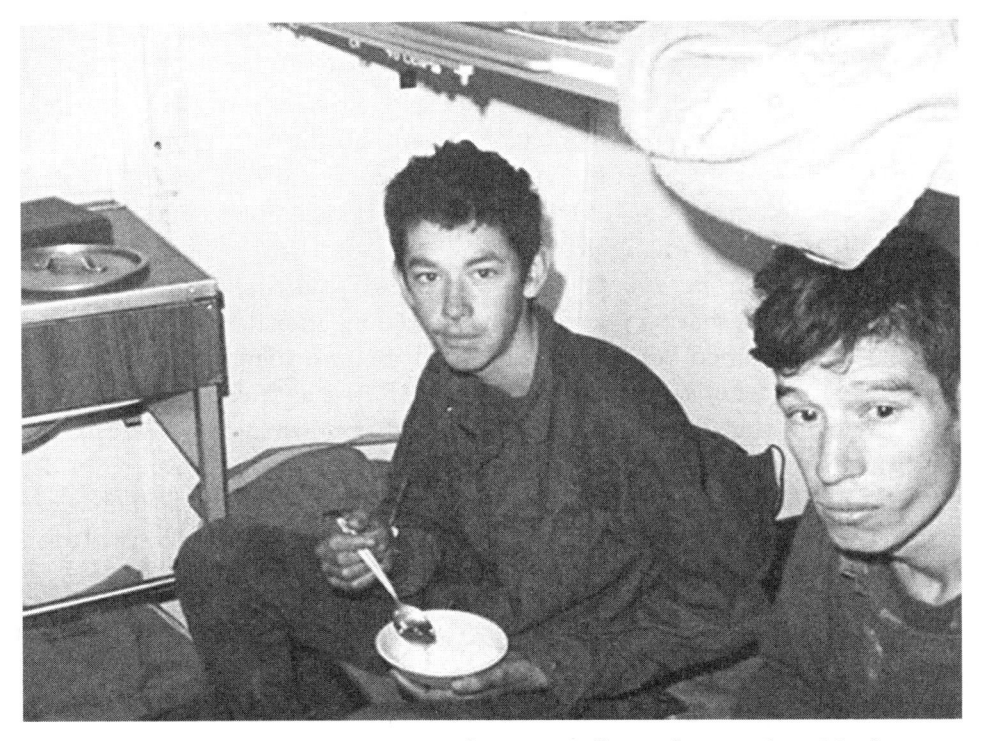

Figure 7.5 'Two Argentineans who were suffering from malnutrition'.
Source: Soldier's own photograph, reproduced with permission

Argentinean prisoners of war from the theatre of active operations on the Falkland Islands to Montevideo in Uruguay:

> This photograph shows two Argentineans who were suffering from malnutrition and these were the lads suffering from malnutrition not because of the British troops, but because of their own people. ... these lads were young conscripts who couldn't really look after themselves in the field. One has got a dish in their hand. We were feeding them a special diet to try and get them malnutrition [sic] up, so again it is the nice side of looking after these prisoners.

The interviewee expanded on the poor physical condition of these conscripted soldiers, a consequence of their lack of training in survival skills; many of them had persistent diarrhoea, for example. The photograph mattered to its owner because it signified the existence of a story from the war that he felt was missing from dominant narratives. Whether this is an accurate representation is, in one sense, beside the point; for this interviewee, the assertion of an alternative representation of the soldier as humanitarian appeared to be an essential part of his identity as a military man. He went on to draw parallels and contrasts between his role as military humanitarian during the Falklands campaign and contemporary stories of the abuse of prisoners of war (and indeed of civilians) emerging from the war in Iraq.

Conclusions

Soldiers' photographs constitute one of the many practices through which the relationship between geopolitics and visuality is constituted. Military activities are performed at the behest of the state for the achievement and consolidation of geopolitical objectives. These performances, recorded on camera, often with a degree of self-consciousness, rehearse and repeat through a repertoire of visual images a set of ideas about the subject position of the soldier and of his or her geopolitical agency. Moreover, the very act of taking photographs is in and of itself contributory to the exercise of geopolitical power (an idea we are unable to explore here, that is nonetheless pertinent to the discussion in this chapter).

We want to conclude with some observations about the work that these photographic performances do, and we want to do this through a consideration of their generic qualities. Soldier photographs share many of the preoccupations of other photographic genres, such as family album photos, tourist snapshots, documentary photo forms and personal portraiture. The examples we have used to illustrate this chapter are cases in point. Some of these images are remote from conventional representations of the figure of the soldier, others echo the discursive figures that abound in popular cultural representations. The point we take forward here is that soldier photographs domesticate military life. Through the images and the practices of their capture and display, the practical geopolitics of the state are literally subjectivised through affective registers that are more closely associated with civilian modes of sociality.

One of the photographic genres with which soldier photographs resonate is that of personal or family photographs. Family photographs reconstruct a version of the past, setting personal narratives against public accounts (Spence and Holland 1991; Rose 2003; Holland 2004). This is indeed what soldier photographs do, establishing personal narratives to set against wider geopolitical narratives about the maintenance of the nation-state. Furthermore:

personal photography remains a minor discourse, a knowledge without authority, designed to be *used* by a limited number of individuals. It is precisely because of this special quality, this everyday unimportance, that we would do well to attend to what it has to tell us. (Holland 2004: 158)

This observation resonates with Thrift's comment, that it's the 'little things ... which are crucial to how the geopolitical is translated into being' (Thrift 2000: 380). Geopolitical acts are carried out, performed, by individuals, engaged in their own small, personal acts of soldiering. Photographic practices are significant because of their constitutive, memorializing and communicative functions around these geopolitical acts. The personal is geopolitical, in this sense.

But soldier photographs cannot lightly be conflated with family photographs. Although they speak to the personal and the private, and to unauthoritative knowledge, and although they do this through limited circulation, they never break away from their origins in events around which much bigger narratives circulate. They press up against these broader narratives, variously questioning, supporting, confirming and resisting them. Soldiers' photographs and their explanatory narratives may constitute a less visible social practice – the mass circulation of graphic abuse photographs notwithstanding – but they remain as one of the multiple practices through which geopolitical power continues to be constituted and expressed.

Bibliography

Ashby, Philip, *Unscathed: Escape from Sierra Leone* (London, Pan, 2002).
Barthes, Roland, *Camera Lucida: Reflections on Photography* (New York: Hill and Wang, 1981).
Berger, John, *Another Way of Telling* (London: Readers and Writers, 1982).
Butler, Judith, *Gender Trouble: Feminism and the Subversion of Identity*, second edition (London: Routledge, 1999).
Campbell, David, 'Horrific blindness: Images of death in contemporary media', *Journal for Cultural Research* 8/1 (2004), pp.55–74.
Campbell, David, 'Geopolitics and visuality: Sighting the Darfur conflict', *Political Geography* 26/4 (2007), pp.357–82.
Diller, Ricardo and Scofidio, Elizabeth, *Back to the Front: Tourisms of War* (Princeton: Princeton Architectural Press, 1996).
Gregson, Nicky and Rose, Gillian, 'Taking Butler elsewhere: Performativities, spatialities and subjectivities', *Environment and Planning D: Society and Space* 18 (2000), pp.433–52.

Hariman, Robert and Lucaites, John Louis, *No Caption Needed: Iconic Photographs, Public Culture and Liberal Democracy* (Chicago: Chicago University Press, 2007).
Holland, Patricia, ' "Sweet it is to scan..." ': Personal photographs and popular photography', in Liz Wells (ed.), *Photography: A Critical Introduction*, third edition (London: Routledge, 2004), pp.113–58.
MacDonald, Fraser, 'Geopolitics and "the vision thing": Regarding Britain and America's first nuclear missile', *Transactions of the Institute of British Geographers* 31 (2006), pp.53–71.
McQuire, Scott, *Visions of Modernity: Representation, Memory, Time and Space in the Age of the Camera* (London: Sage, 1998).
Nash, Catherine, 'Performativity in practice: Some recent work in cultural geography', *Progress in Human Geography* 24/4 (1996), pp.653–64.
Price, Derrick, 'Surveyors and surveyed: Photography out and about', in Liz Wells (ed.), *Photography: A Critical Introduction*, third edition (London: Routledge, 2004), pp.65–111.
Rose, Gillian, 'Family photographs and domestic spacings', *Transactions of the Institute of British Geographers* 28/5 (2003), pp.5–18.
Sontag, Susan, *On Photography* (New York: Anchor Books, 1990).
Sontag, Susan, *Regarding the Pain of Others* (Harmondsworth: Penguin, 2003).
Spence, Jo and Holland, Patricia (eds), *Family Snaps: The Meanings of Domestic Photography* (London: Virago, 1991).
Tagg, John, *The Burden of Representation: Essays on Photographies and Histories* (University of Minnesota Press, 1988).
Thrift, Nigel, 'It's the little things', in Klaus Dodds and David Atkinson (eds), *Geopolitical Traditions: A Century of Geopolitical Thought* (London: Routledge, 2000), pp.380–7.
Trachtenberg, Alan, 'Albums of war: On reading civil war photographs', *Representations* 9 (1985), pp.1–32.
Virilio, Paul, *War and Cinema: The Logistics of Perception*, translated by Patrick Camiller (London: Verso, 1989).
Virilio, Paul, *The Vision Machine* (British Film Institute/Indiana University Press: London and Bloomington, 1994).
Wells, Liz, 'On and beyond the white walls: Photography as art', in Liz Wells (ed.), *Photography: A Critical Introduction*, third edition (London: Routledge, 2004), pp.245–94.
Woodward, Rachel, ' "It's a man's life!": Soldiers, masculinity and the countryside', *Gender, Place and Culture* 5/3 (1998), pp.277–300.
Woodward, Rachel, 'Locating military masculinities: The role of space and place in the formation of gender identities in the Armed Forces', in Paul Higate (ed.), *Military Masculinities: Identity and the State* (Westport CT and London: Praeger, 2003), pp.43–56.
Woodward, Rachel, *Military Geographies* (Oxford: Blackwell, 2004).
Woodward, Rachel, 'From Military Geography to militarism's geographies: Disciplinary engagements with the geographies of militarism and military activities', *Progress in Human Geography* 29/6 (2005), pp.718–40.

Woodward, Rachel, 'Warrior heroes and little green men: Soldiers, military training and the construction of rural masculinities', in Michael Mayerfeld Bell, Hugh Campbell and Margaret Finney (eds), *Country Boys: Masculinity and Rural Life* (Penn State University Press, 2006), pp.235–50.

Woodward, Rachel and Winter, Trish, *Sexing the Soldier: The Politics of Gender and the British Army* (London: Routledge, 2007).

Chapter 8

The Scopic Regime of 'Africa'
David Campbell and Marcus Power

> Travelling in Africa is adventurous enough as it is, without any fiction.
> (H.M. Stanley, *How I Found Livingstone*, 1872)

> The history of the European view of non-European peoples has always reflected Europeans' history of imaging themselves. (Landau 2002: 2)

From natural history museums to imperial exhibitions, from postcards to comic strips, from travel writings to accounts of exploration and missionary activity, from colonial photographs to contemporary cinema, 'Africa' has been consistently (re)produced and enacted across a wide range of cultural sites. Just as Frantz Fanon once described the racialisation of subjectivity in late colonial Algeria as being 'fixed by a dye', the performance of 'Africa' through various technologies of observation, reproduction and display has been remarkably consistent and enduring. The continent has been infantilised, feminised and homogenised, whilst being repetitively reduced to what is 'seen' to be deficient (Andreasson 2005).

In this sense it is important to consider how this 'Africa' has been enacted, circulated and consumed historically through performance (Ebron 2000), and how these historical encounters create the place of Africa in the world. The 'Africa' that the world imagines (often through dystopian images) is always a thing of illusion, magic and contradiction, but the performance of this construct and the meanings attached to it have particular temporalities. The ideological space that 'Africa' occupied in the popular Western imagination from the last decades of the nineteenth century to the beginning of

World War II was coherent if not always fixed. The continent envisioned was at once savage, threatening, exotic and productive, in ways which varied depending on the political exigencies of the particular historical conjuncture (Coombes 1994). To understand these performances of 'Africa' we need to consider the historicity of its visual enunciation, as well as the political consequences of its persistent re-enactment. In principle, this involves taking into consideration the entire 'domain of images' (Elkins 1999), as well as the intertextual spaces of the visual. Although we cannot accommodate all that could be understood in terms of images or visuality, in this chapter we consider a wide range of visual practices that have contributed to the enactment of 'Africa'. We begin with a review of the literary tradition because we understand writing to be a visual technology central to the construction of the continent. The argument then moves on to the practices of collecting, curatorship and display in the context of museums and imperial exhibitions, before turning to the technologies associated with cinema, photography and digital computer games.

We take the idea of 'scopic regimes' to be an important heuristic category through which the enduring performance of Africa can be understood. Martin Jay (1988) famously developed the idea of scopic regimes from the work of film theorist Christian Metz (1982), who argued that a given sensory regime was hegemonic in a particular historical period. Jay argued that Cartesian perspectivalism – which combined Renaissance notions of perspective with Cartesian ideas of subjective rationality – produced a dominant if not hegemonic scopic regime in which the singular eye of the observer coldly arrested all before it in ways consonant with a scientific world view. Derek Gregory (2003: 224) drew from this the idea of a systematic structuring of the visual field which produced a 'constructed visibility that allows particular objects to be seen in determinate ways', while Allen Feldman argued a scopic regime was the sum of the

> agendas and techniques of political visualization: the regimens that prescribe modes of seeing and object visibility and that proscribe or render untenable other modes and objects of perception. A scopic regime is an ensemble of practices and discourses that establish the truth claims, typicality and credibility of visual acts and objects and politically correct modes of seeing. (Feldman 2005: 224n)

The idea of the scopic regime is far from being uncontested, at least in so far as it can be read as promoting an ocularcentrism that fails to accord senses such as the auditory and haptic a constitutive place in observant practice (MacDonald 2008). While we argue that the visual can be read discursively, we do not regard it as a discourse distinct from all other senses. In this context, our argument intersects with Judith Butler's (2007) account of the frames that produce a field of perceptible reality and establish the recognisability of certain figures of the human. While Butler argues the visual is vital in transmitting the norms that establish the conditions of possibility for an ethical response to the Other, other practices are also at play in this. The scopic regime, therefore, is one element, albeit an historically significant element, in the performance of perceptible places. As such, we identify with Butler's (2007: 966) call to 'thematize the forcible frame, the one that conducts the dehumanizing norm'.

It is our contention that, although contested, there has been produced in the last century or so a dominant scopic regime that plays a major role in enacting a place in the world called 'Africa', largely through the repetition and reiteration of colonial tropes. As James Ferguson (2006: 2) argues: 'For all that has changed, "Africa" continues to be described through a series of lacks and absences, failings and problems, plagues and catastrophes.' This 'suspiciously dark' account of a continent surely hides much that goes uncovered, but we concur with Ferguson (2006: 8, 10) that we should neither shy away from the abundant evidence that supports elements of these characterisations, nor retreat into a particularist defence that refuses to engage with the category of 'Africa' itself. In our account, the scopic regime is a repertoire of perspectival practices, embedded in a global visual economy, which establishes the relationship between the observer and observed, producing both subject positions in the process. At its most powerful this scopic regime contributes greatly to a forcible frame. It is not singular, nor is it unchallenged, but it is powerful in the performances it elicits over time. And above all else, it is significant in establishing the conditions of possibility for an ethical response to the events and issues it makes available to us.

Literary envisionings of 'Africa'

Between 1870 and 1960, during which time there was a huge increase in Western 'non-fiction' writings about Africa from explorers, scientists, travel writers, journalists, colonial administrators and missionaries, the continent was increasingly plunged into 'darkness' (Brantlinger 1988). Writing is itself a visual technology: 'a gaze actually graphs and an eye can write' (Ó Tuathail 2000: 390). In this sense, we want to begin with literary visions of 'Africa' since the visual should be understood discursively, as a range of social practices (not just technologies) that contributed to the production and performance of this social construct. In particular, the writing of Africa through the metaphor of darkness and light has been a central and recurring theme (Brantlinger 1988, 2003). As Jacques Derrida (1978: 27) has argued, this metaphor of darkness and light (of self-revelation and self-concealment) '[is] the founding metaphor of Western philosophy as metaphysics ... The entire history of our philosophy is a photology, the name given to a history, or treatise on, light'. This homogenising metaphor of Africa as the 'dark continent' 'flattens places and people' (Jarosz 1992: 105), and serves as a negatively valued foil for Western notions of superiority and enlightenment (Ryan 1997). Joseph Conrad's *Heart of Darkness* and Henry Morton Stanley's *Through the Dark Continent* were seminal here, depicting the continent and its peoples as 'savage', 'exotic', 'cannibal' and 'primitive'.

European travel writings also played an important role in enframing and visualizing Africa, creating the domestic subject of European imperialism and engaging metropolitan reading publics with the expansionist enterprises of Empire (Pratt 1992). Imperial travel existed alongside settler literatures in European languages, including short stories, poems, romance novels, essays and memoirs (McClure 1994; Boehmer 1998). Written by imperial adventurers, colonial administrators, missionaries, propagandists and poets, they reflected the diverse responses to colonial experience. Although this writing of Africa was far from monolithic (Pratt 1992; Blunt 1994), a number of rhetorical modalities have persisted (Spurr 2002), and, whilst these are not necessarily unique to Africa (and not all of them occur in every colonial text), they do represent an important part of the repertoire of colonial discourse and constitute a very significant range of tropes and conceptual categories. According to Spurr (2002), these include surveillance, appropriation, aestheticisation, classification, debasement, negation, affirmation, idealisation, insubstantialisation, naturalisation, eroticisation and resistance.

The observation and description of indigenous peoples, landscapes and territories would often involve various forms of surveillance. The 'commanding view' or 'writer's eye' that many textual enactments of Africa articulated sought to take possession of African landscapes by ordering and arranging what was seen, making possible the mapping and exploration of colonial territory. This 'Monarch-of-all-I-survey scene' (Pratt 1992: 201) is enacted, for example, in Henry Morton Stanley's account of the rescue of Emin Pasha in *Darkest Africa*. Allied to this is the 'relation of mastery predicated between seer and seen' (Pratt 1992: 204), as the writer produces the landscape for their audience by conveying the impression that what is seen is all there is and that the landscape was intended to be viewed from this particular (static) vantage point. Further, many Western writers made the experience of 'Africa' into an inner journey, rendering that world as insubstantial in the process or as the backdrop against which was played 'the drama of the writer's self' (Spurr 1993: 142).

Explorers, scientists, travel writers, journalists, colonial administrators and missionaries generally scripted Africa in a way which implicitly claimed the territory surveyed as the colonisers' own, often disguising this appropriative strategy in the form of an appeal to nature, humanity and the colonised themselves. Here the exploitation of African colonial territories becomes a moral as well as a political and economic imperative. Often writers would emphasise the exotic, the bizarre, the grotesque or the elemental in outlining (for example) the abundance of nature, the ease of subsistence, the lack of private possessions, the 'romantic' simplicity, the pleasures of day-to-day life, or the unfamiliarity of scents, sounds and images (which have for centuries been common topoi in the representation of 'exotic' African societies). The rhetorical device of debasement saw indigenous people reduced to beings of an inferior status (usually as 'animals'), with European identities contrasted against this Other in order to create a clear-cut Manichean division between coloniser and colonised, almost as an act of preservation. The ultimate horror here was to 'go native' (like Kurtz in Conrad's novella), to lose one's sense of difference and superiority, and to regress or revert to a 'savage' past. Here the natives are reviled for their non-Western Otherness, but also ridiculed for their attempts to imitate the forms of the West. According to Chinua Achebe (1988), debasement is a fundamental characteristic of Western attitudes towards Africa, where the continent serves merely as a setting or backdrop. Envisioning 'primitive peoples' as living a 'natural life' in 'natural surroundings' led to a view that saw indigenous communities as extensions of the landscape, 'as wilderness in human form' (Spurr 1993: 165). Portrayals of the 'noble savage' similarly emphasised the exotic Other's closeness to nature, gentleness or innocence. European domination and control over nature becomes another way of justifying Empire since such relations with the natural world were central to the presumption of 'civilisation'. The persistent assignment to Africa and Africans of a close proximity to nature serves to make the contemporary apocalyptic imagery of war, violence, disaster and social unrest appear as something 'natural', since the continent is seen to be governed by the forces of nature and not those of reason or civilisation.

Many explorers and travel writers also envisioned Africa as a largely uninscribed and primeval continent. The 'blank space on the map' that Marlow invokes in Conrad's novella is a continent awaiting exploration and, ultimately, colonisation. As a fantasy space, 'Africa' quickly became the ideal setting for a masculinist daydream. The absences and blanks created a desire to go there and fill the void left by 'Africa's essential nothingness' (Spurr 1993: 92). Since Africa is presented as having no history or pre-existing social order of its own, it is the presence of the male European explorer and discoverer that is then considered to create such order. Colonial rule and authority are thereby constructed as creative rather than violent acts. This legitimacy is also produced through the rhetorical device of self-affirmation, where the presence and power of colonialism is justified and legitimated by idealising the project and its protagonists. Thus, many colonial literatures affirmed the collective values of the colonial enterprise and the selflessness and obligations of trusteeship or the 'white man's burden', of bringing 'light' to the dark continent.

In other important ways the dark continent was feminised, with colonial literatures and travel writings often ascribing feminine or even erotic qualities to Africa, the continent figured as the explorer's mistress, both mysterious and tempting. The 'African woman' (a singular and homogenising construct frozen in time and space) became the classic figure of sexual adventure and a synecdoche for the whole continent constructed as an immense, prolific, fertile body (Schiebinger 1995). 'Africa' thus offered 'the aphrodisiac of the unknown' (Hodeir 2002: 233). The 'reality' of Africa was often depicted as concealed, veiled and mysterious, constructing colonial exploration as an act of unveiling through penetration deeper into the continent's interior as 'virgin territory'. While the European colonist presented himself as disciplined and rational, it is an unrestricted sexuality that characterises the exotic Other. In emphasising the exotic nature of Africa, a distance is produced that is instrumental in purveying further images of the atavism of the inhabitants of African societies. As a consequence, barbarism, madness and disaster are naturalised, and Africa and its peoples are held at arms length, becoming 'object[s] of beauty, horror, pleasure and pity' (Spurr 1993: 59).

The museum and the Imperial Exhibition

In the context of Enlightenment thinking and the enactment and performance of Africa, the museum was an important cultural site for the dissemination of 'scientific' knowledge regarding Africa to a diverse public. Hooper-Greenhill (1992) argues that the public/private division of knowledge hardened in the nineteenth century, with a new role emerging for the state. It was in this context that the public museum emerged, an enterprise and a technology producing a vast and expanding network of new classifications that systematised knowledge about the world (Crang 2003). With the rapid development of regional and national collections under British imperial expansion, the nascent discipline of museum ethnography struggled to demonstrate its relevance to both the state and the public. In this context, ethnographic displays became increasingly important. Museological dramas were also crucial to the performance and projection of a 'publicly imagined past' (Blatti 1987: 7), and can be considered an important part of what Cantwell (1993) calls 'ethnomimesis' or the performance of a particular group identity to an audience.

The physical arrangement of an ethnographic collection within the space of a major metropolitan museum often involved typological classifications of material culture. These were arranged from primitive to advanced, demonstrating the evolutionary theories of anthropology and justifying the need for technological advancement in the guise of colonisation. These micro-geographies of museums and their ordering and arrangement of space were typical of a disciplinary knowledge whose object it was to fix: 'it is an anti-nomadic force ... [which] uses procedures of partitioning and cellularity' (Foucault 1977: 218-19). It was no coincidence that just at the moment when Bentham produced his planned panopticon of enclosed surveillance, a few miles away the Crystal Palace Imperial Exhibition site was being built. The Crystal Palace was followed a few years later by the 'Albertopolis' of museums and exhibitionary institutions in Kensington in London (including the Natural History Museum, the Museum of Mankind, the Victoria and Albert Museum, the Albert Hall and the Royal Geographical Society). We need to think then about the historical emergence of a wider 'exhibitionary complex' in the nineteenth century (Bennett 1988) that came about with the moving of objects from private into public displays (in museums and exhibitions), which served to broadcast other messages of power.

World fairs and imperial expositions were an important part of the process of exhibiting European imperialism to domestic audiences and offer a useful point of entry into critical considerations of the performance of 'Africa'. Such exhibitions have been understood as sites where a commodity world was on show, but it could also be argued that the performances of Africa enacted in these spaces also circulated as commodities.

Exhibitions were thus imperial spectacles and pictures of a capitalist 'world of resources' (Olds and Ley 1998). Between 1854 and 1911, over 30 colonial exhibitions opened to the public across the British Empire from Calcutta to Melbourne, from Delhi to Queensland, all demonstrating the unprecedented energy of cultural professionals, scientists, administrators, entrepreneurs, colonial officials and bureaucrats across British territories interested in recreating the Empire in their own image. From London's Great Exhibition in 1851 to the Universal Exposition of Paris in 1889, these spaces exhibited landscapes of bourgeois and imperial ideology, privileging Western science and 'civilisation' and their putative contribution to progress and modernity.[1] Collectively, imperial exhibitions rested upon a highly particular way of thinking about, being in and visualising the world (Gregory 1994), in part based on a particular process of enframing that seemed to exist apart from and prior to the objects displayed and to be peculiar to European modernity (Mitchell 1989).

The ephemeral architecture of some exhibitions was in many cases analogous to a film set, producing a kind of cinematographic effect (Hodeir 2002). The individual buildings representing the French colonies at the 1931 International Colonial Exhibition, for example, were built higher than the treetops to increase panoramic visibility. According to Hoffenberg (2001), post-1851 exhibitions which incorporated the use of large-scale cultural events and institutions were more dynamic and effective in luring the public to imperial visions than their predecessors had been, and were designed specifically to integrate the masses and forge a sense of imperial unity by having them explore the Commonwealth or other forms of imperial 'federation'.

Featuring more popular forms of spectacle and fantasy, post-1851 exhibitions were essential parts of the 'new' imperialism, offering spectacles that dazzled consumers with the dual aura of imperial fantasy and technological advancement. Exhibitions also anticipated the creation of public spaces that imaged a peaceful social order and the grandeur of imperial rule (Hoffenburg 2001). The *experience* of the exhibition was also important, involving a walking, observing, touching, sensing, consuming and learning public. Exhibitions often evoked in the public a sense of wonder and awe by presenting things 'in motion', while also stimulating their desires to buy and collect things fantastic and foreign. Buttons and cranks were essential interactive tools that encouraged hands-on engagement with the displays of machinery, while artisanal products heightened fascination with collectibles and memorabilia.

At the 1889 Paris Universal Exposition, model 'native African villages' were simulated on site and African subjects repeatedly performed particular dances, customs, rituals, craftsmanship and hunting-and-gathering techniques in and around these 'villages'. The model villages were sanitised in order to offer an imagined landscape for European visitors who might be made uncomfortable by the idea of a 'real' trip to Africa. Parisian women quickly developed an ethos of maternal charity towards the African subjects, often bringing sweets or candies in the belief that these curious people were simply overgrown children (Hodeir 2002). Such infantilising performances were staged alongside symbols of European technology and modernity. At the 1931 International Colonial Exhibition in Paris, visited by 33 million people, a weekly procession appeared along the *Grande Avenue des Colonies* that would publicise theatrical performances in the exhibition such as *An African Fairy Tale, Dancing and Singing from the Colonial World, Colonial Nights* and *Farewell to the Colonies* (Hodeir 2002).

Many expositions positioned European imperial powers such as Britain, France or Portugal as 'pioneers' within this evolutionary process of human history, and celebrated this 'superior' contribution alongside a concomitant parodying of the 'inferior' non-West. Thus one of the significant tropes of such exhibitions was a celebration of progress that involved juxtaposing the old and the new: the traditional, even 'savage' past and the 'civilised' present. Indigenous peoples were often depicted as locked in battle; their 'primitive' technologies of war would be exhibited alongside more 'modern' European versions. The complexity and contradictions in these tropes is explored by Morton (2000) in relation to the International Colonial Exhibition in Paris in 1931, where the tensions between the colonial project of civilisation and the need to represent colonised cultures as 'backward' and timeless (in order to justify this civilising mission) were acutely evident. In the Franco-British exhibition of 1908, 'Africa' was figured differently because it had become important to visualise Africa as a continent that was 'civilisable'. Each exhibition offered a staging of the modern (Mitchell 2000) and each claimed a certain universality for modernity, whilst trying to render a particular take on the global and hybrid history of modernity. Yet exhibitions also centred on forms of difference that introduced the possibility of a discrepancy between the proclaimed universality of modernity and unity of Europe and the specificity of different forms of Empire. Exhibitions thus often produced what Pred (1995) calls 'repress-entations', where some elements were actively silenced in ways that were similar to the symptomatic repressions, amnesic gaps and *forgetting* of Africa that characterise the narrative corpus of Conrad's novella.

Coombes (1994) writes of how exhibitionary 'spectacles' between 1890 and 1913 represented 'Africa' differently, reinventing it from the land of 'savages' that only military intervention could redeem, to a dark and mysterious continent, full of unusual rituals and strange behaviour. The latter was an Africa that could be helped with the aid of colonial 'care' and a metropolitan sense of responsibility. This change in view was not so much due to new philosophies or enlightenment as much as pecuniary desires to capitalise upon the huge public interest in all things African that was being manipulated by exhibition promoters at the end of the nineteenth and start of the twentieth centuries. Anthropological theories regarding racial difference were conveyed to the public through exhibitions of African material culture and displays of Africans themselves. Further, in the heart of a range of imperial cities, zoological gardens also played an important and associated role in visualising 'savage Africa' (Anderson 1995).

In many exhibitions, black performers billed simply as 'Africans' would be drawn from a particular society that held a topical fascination for British, French or Portuguese audiences because of their notoriety through recent conflicts (Coombes 1994). Thus, exhibitions constructed racial difference through spectacle. Although exhibition organisers often denied that their product was fiction and emphasised the exhibition visit as distinct from a theatrical experience, literary and exhibition constructions of racial 'types' and identities overlapped and corresponded with one another quite closely. For example, the official guidebook for the 1899 'Briton, Boer and Black' exhibition compared the inhabitants of a 'Zulu Kraal' to a Rider Haggard novel (Coombes 1994).

Cinema and photography

Visual practices of enacting 'Africa' were taken to a new dimension with the invention of cinema in 1895, billed as a universally comprehensible form of visualisation. Cinema began to discover its true narrative potential only when it explored the real possibilities of *movement*, which was an important point of distinction from parallel media such as photography. Within years of the colonial emergence of cinematographic practices in Africa in the 1920s, the medium was being inserted into the problematic of the historical record, re-making the boundaries of fact and fiction, truth and falsehood. In so doing, cinema followed on from the ways in which colonial photography had functioned as a form of geographical discourse that visualised the non-European world as Other. While colonial photography, especially in its anthropological mode as a classificatory practice cataloguing indigenous colonial subjects, was part of the apparatus of surveillance required by imperialism, it was also a fractured practice which served the critics of Empire at home and abroad (Ryan 1997).

Like their still counterparts, and alongside the press, education, international exhibitions and popular art, film images served an important role as information, scientific record and novelty in colonial propaganda (Ryan 1994). After World War I, cinema became part of all expeditions into the African continent, underlining the link between cinematographic practice and colonial conquest. Colonial film units began to emerge in Africa at the beginning of World War II in an attempt to supplement the propaganda power of the radio broadcast. In Britain the 1926 creation of the government-sponsored Empire Marketing Board (EMB; which had also been part of the organisation of imperial exhibitions) led to a number of experiments with documentary films about the Empire. With the outbreak of war the EMB's successor was split into the Crown Film Unit and the Colonial Film Unit. In the years up to 1952 the two units had produced between 3000 and 5000 35-mm films (Film Images 2007).

World War II also drew the attention of the French authorities in Algeria to the propaganda potential of film. In Algeria a *Service de diffusion cinématographique* (SDC) was established in 1943 to bring *ciné-bus* units to rural communities, showing films to some 1 million Algerians by 1948 (Malkmus and Armes 1991). The majority of French colonial films were made in the course of travels, expeditions, missions, voyages and other colonial 'adventures', with films as 'travelogues'. French and many other Western cinematic representations of Africa produced under colonialism helped to reinforce the dominant vision of Africa as a continent with no history and no culture (Murphy 2000). A variety of films were made by the French government with the goal of showing and celebrating French colonial 'achievements'. According to Slavin (2001), French colonial cinema played an important role in making and re-making an assumed difference between the supposedly superior French civilisation and the exotic, colonised African Other. It was in the 1920s and 1930s, partly in the arena of colonial film, that Frenchness became a distinctly white identity, with many films warning about the perils of miscegenation. Slavin (2001) explores the masculine fantasies that dominate French films about North Africa and the 'blind spots' (the avoidance or denial of colonial realities) that these produced among workers in Europe. Many films tried to capture the mobility inherent in the French colonial enterprise and can be read as testimonies to the French translation of colonial space. Maps of Africa appeared at the start of a large number of colonial films and were representations of the colonial fantasy of possessing Africa. Many of these maps showed an Africa that was 'empty' and ready to be 'possessed', envisioning Africa as approachable by anyone watching the movie. A variety of colonial films thus showed an Africa that was only enlivened through the agency and sorcery of the coloniser, with the presumed primitiveness of the continent an important backdrop for this performance.

Early colonial films failed to acknowledge any of the Africans involved in their production and played down the difficulties that colonial conquest had encountered in terms of disease or climate. Despite the variety of African locations that colonial films represent, an undifferentiated figure of 'the African' was often employed. These films can thus tell us a lot about the nexus of imperial interests in African affairs and about the racist ideologies at work in the cinematographic imagination of European imperial powers such as France. Many films sought to underline the technological advancement of the coloniser (often showing images of new forms of transport in action) or sought to highlight the corresponding 'backwardness' of the technologies of the colonised. Cinema was thus an instrument of conquest, a medium used in the representation of history largely through the eyes of the conqueror (at least until the advent of anti-colonial cinema in the late 1950s). In many colonies indigenous people were excluded from cinema theatres and were instead offered 'wandering cinemas' (mobile cinema units), which projected imperial propaganda in rural areas. There were thus separate circuits of exhibition for the indigenous and settler communities.

Some of the first colonial films were short newsreels and documentaries (many of which were made by groups of amateur cinema enthusiasts) that tried to convey 'progress' in arenas such as infrastructure or agriculture. By 1927, Kodak cine-cameras were becoming increasingly popular and there were many amateur films that document the adventures of the 'photographer–explorer' in Africa. New camera technologies were marketed in magazines such as *National Geographic*, which also sought 'to deliver advice on how to deal with camera-shy natives' (Gordon 2002: 216). Soon almost every American, British, French, Italian or Portuguese expedition into Africa included a cinematographer. Documentary or 'actuality' filmmaking first emerged in Europe and North America in the late 1890s. In France, all non-fiction films (including documentaries) were initially termed *actualités*, a term that originally meant conversational topics of the hour (including, of course, imperial rule). From 1956 the production of this kind of newsreel/documentary style of film-making accelerated within Portugal's African colonies, when colonial state administrations began to sponsor the production of *Journais Das Actualidades* (newsreels) covering the national events of political significance. The object of these films was to focus attention on the apparatus of the colonial state, conveying information about its latest political decisions or documenting the visits of officials across colonial territory. These newsreels were also linked to 'psycho-social' campaigns to convince indigenous people not to join the liberation struggles and to recognise the benefits of Portuguese colonialism.

In Mozambique, none of the documentary films sponsored by the colonial state mentioned resistance to colonialism, each seeking to justify the place of the Portuguese colonist in this African country (Power 2004). In these films, remarkably little filming took place outside the offices, administrative posts, and industrial and commercial organisations of colonial rule. The 'filmic spaces' of colonial cinema were constructed almost in inverse proportion to the realities of colonial power in that they were dominated by the colonial bourgeoisie, as if the Mozambican public did not exist or was somehow temporarily absent. In the dying days of colonialism in Mozambique, the ratio of Portuguese settlers to indigenous people was 1:10, whereas in films such as the *Actualidades* we see at least ten Portuguese settlers for every African. The images of Mozambique shown in such films might easily have been mistaken for images of Lisbon or of any other European capital. Just as these *Actualidades* and other films sponsored by the colonial state were being made, however, anti-colonial movements across lusophone Africa were beginning to experiment with the medium themselves. These films set out to decolonise visual culture in order to project back alternative understandings and visions of the continent and its struggles. In Mozambique, films such as *Venceremos!* (*We Will Win!*) (1966), *A Luta Continua* (*The Struggle Continues*) (1971) and *Viva Frelimo!* (1967) depict the ideological motives of the liberation war of Frelimo and were made with support from foreign film-makers, often from the Socialist bloc. In Angola, Sarah Maldoror's *Sambazinga* (1972), a fictional narrative film about the Angolan liberation struggle, shot in the Congo using anti-colonial guerrillas from the Popular Movement for the Liberation of Angola (MPLA) as actors, sought to legitimate nationalist discourses and to highlight colonial exploitation.

In his discussion of film spectatorship and voyeurism, Metz (1982) explores the essential property of the voyeuristic gaze as keeping the desired, seen object at a safe distance from the viewing subject. He argues that cinema shows us the world at the same time as it takes it away from us: 'What defines the properly cinematographic scopic regime is not the maintained distance, not the care exerted in maintaining it, but the sheer absence of the seen object. ... Cinema is ... founded on an unbridgeable distance, on a total inaccessibility.' This is particularly true in the case of colonial cinematographic practice, where the Other is kept at a distance partly by the predominance of white faces, the sheer absence of non-white subjects and by the way in which colonial cities were depicted as entirely European spaces. The myth of a naive, credulous and gullible viewer of such films – one unable to differentiate between representation and reality – dominated many of the assumptions made about the reception of colonial propaganda by colonial film-makers (Burns 2000; Oksiloff 2001). Movies encouraged not gazing but 'glancing: shallow accumulative looks' (Gordon 2002: 215). In the 1930s, as film industries in Western countries grew, misconceptions of Africa and Africans began to proliferate and perpetuated colonial modes of thinking (Murphy 2000). Edgar Rice Burroughs' *Tarzan* novels, which were first published in 1912, fixed the image of Africa in the American imagination as a 'jungle playground for masculine innocence' (Landau 2002: 4). Western films made in the 1930s about Africa – including *Trader Horn* (1931), *Tarzan the Ape Man* (1932), *Tarzan and his Mate* (1934), *Sanders of the River* (1935), *Tarzan Escapes* (1936), *King Solomon's Mines* (1937), *Tarzan Finds a Son!* (1937), *Four Feathers* (1939) and *Stanley and Livingstone* (1939) – reiterated this image. One of the most popular interwar movies, *King Kong* (1933), revolves around the 'travel into darkness' motif centred on a scientific cinematographic expedition that ends up catching the giant ape.

Of all the images of Africa employed during the 1930s, one of the most pervasive is Africa as a dream/nightmare. On the one hand, Africa was presented as a beautiful land that was ripe for settlement; on the other, Africa was a terrible, untamed wilderness that required taming by white men. The experience of 'Africa' thus becomes another 'inner journey', rendering Africa as the insubstantial backdrop against which is played the drama of the European self. As the dream/nightmare begins, all certainties are dissolved and European encounters with the continent reproduce the crisis of the Western subject. In such accounts, the colonised were portrayed as lazy and inept, while nightmare Africa is populated by 'savage' natives, further highlighting the need for colonisation. Subsequent images of Africa as an untamed 'void', open zoo and keeper of lost treasures further encouraged white settlement.

A good example is the film *Africa Speaks!* (1930, Columbia Pictures), which features the Colorado-based explorer–naturalist Paul Hoefler leading a safari into the Belgian Congo (Figure 8.1). The narrative focuses on

Figure 8.1 Paul Hoefler leads a cinematographic safari in the Belgian Congo for the film *Africa Speaks!* (1930) as the expedition team seeks to 'shoot' and 'capture' Africa's wildlife and wilderness.
Source: Columbia Pictures, 1930

the 'unusual' customs and rituals of the 'tribes' encountered during the expedition into the 'dark continent', and images of these 'tribes' are interspersed with shots of zebras, elephants and hippos. Hoeffler's book of the same title, published shortly after the release of the film, differs insofar as it records that the expedition travelled from East to West, rather than the reverse, as in the film, where events were adapted to produce more dramatic/cinematic action scenes. The film opens with a largely blank map of Africa and offers the viewer a journey into 'Africa the sinister, the mysterious, the unknown ... Africa the land of savagery and dangerous adventure ... where nature is without mercy and deadly beasts of the jungle are supreme'. In this film 'Africa' is seen to 'speak' for the first time by being captured on film and the continent (although not allowed to represent itself) is seen as a single entity, with a single voice. The movie also contains several scenes of the film crew – shot subsequently in California and spliced into the film – that accompanied the 250-person expedition, underlining the centrality of this medium to the exploration, penetration and colonisation of 'Africa'.

Many colonial films included an ethnographic focus and encouraged viewers to glance at the bodies of native/indigenous people from a safe distance. Oksiloff (2001) has explored the visualisation of 'primitive' bodies in early German films, either in the 'research films' made by anthropologists or in colonial and adventure films produced by the state, and argues that 'screened images of primitive bodies were in many ways more real than actual bodies, even the ones displayed in the popular live spectacles of fairs, exhibitions, and human "zoos".' Other colonial films were dominated by scenes of 'tribal dances' (one example is found in *The*

Figure 8.2 Man dressed as an 'African' standing besides a poster advertising the movie *Africa Speaks!* in front of the Capitol Theatre, State Street, Wisconsin.
Source: The Wisconsin Historical Society

Bushmen, a documentary produced during the Denver African Expedition of 1925) or other performances of primitiveness in musical or theatrical form. In other films from this period, missionaries, explorers, hunters and colonial authorities are often pictured (heroically) taming the jungle. Africa was thus constructed as a physical/psychological challenge, as inhospitable to whites, reinforcing a sense of the dangers of Africa for white audiences (Figure 8.2). The *au naturel* savage and colonised servants were the 'before' and 'after' examples of the effects of colonisation. Africans were portrayed as untrustworthy and shiftless: 'If there was a "good" African in the film, he was defined by the characteristics admired in servants: honesty, courage, submission and unflagging loyalty' (Murphy 2000: 170). In many ways cinema proved to be a more cost-effective way of circulating 'primitive bodies' than, for example, colonial expositions, and remained an important 'meeting place for science and fantasy' (Gordon 2002: 214).

Hollywood, as one of the most influential producers of images, 'has always loved colonialism' (Mayer 2002: 3) and has had a special fondness for the British Empire in particular. The typical Hollywood colonial scene depicts stock figures such as the ape-man, the white hunter and the colonial lady. More generally the adventure tale (a paradigmatic mode for exoticising the Other) and the autobiography (a paradigmatic mode for exploring the Self) continue to shape popular understandings of colonial Africa: 'Quartermain the adventurer, Tarzan the ape-man, Hemingway's white hunters and Baroness von Blixen' (Mayer 2002: 19). While it cannot be assumed that audiences passively absorbed these representations, they were consistently bombarded with such representations and met with few significant alternatives. As such these dominant cinematic representations came to shape popular Western thinking and attitudes towards Africa as the 'dark continent'.

Contemporary performances

Africa remains almost as much of a 'dark continent' for movie-goers today as in the past. According to Rosaldo (1993: 68), a spirit of 'imperialist nostalgia' emerged in 1980s Hollywood cinema in which 'the white colonial societies portrayed in these films appear decorous and orderly, as if constructed in accordance with the norms of classic ethnography'. Sidney Pollack's 1985 film version of Isak Dinesen's *Out of Africa* (originally written in 1938), for example, explicitly disclaims colonialism, but endows the colonialist framework (both in Europe and in Africa) with the glamour of an exotic order of the past. The movie depicts Karen Blixen's sojourn in Kenya largely in terms of her donning the right clothes to fit in *and* stand out. Being the same (as a white) *and* different (as a woman) is fetishised in the film and overlays a subtext on the risks of going native (Mayer 2002). Colonialism becomes a spectacle, a huge masquerade of outfits, styles and gestures against a backdrop of an exotic environment. The 1985 remake of *King Solomon's Mines* similarly presents an Africa cut off from the historical and political realities of imperialism in the form of 'Kukuanaland' of Rider Haggard's original novel (written in 1885). Here Africa is staged as a timeless and familiarly 'exotic comic-book space with African warriors in leopard skins who carry spears, cook their enemies in huge pots, play drums and – naturally – don masks' (Mayer 2002: 35). While the film's main protagonist, Quartermain, drives a car through the desert, his African companion, Umbopa, ridiculously afraid of Western technology, is seen running alongside. This image rehearses many of the tropes of earlier visual forms, in an Africa that appears as a giant US adventure theme park.

The white man's quest in the wilderness is also the theme of Clint Eastwood's *White Hunter, Black Heart* (1990), a film which differentiates fact and fiction along the lines of film-making and hunting (its two main themes). Like so many other white-hunter narratives, the movie enacts a journey into the heart of darkness as a trip of self-discovery and self-fashioning. During the 1980s and 1990s, Hollywood produced a number of films about jungle life which were reminiscent of earlier colonial visions: *Gorillas in the Mist* (1988), about a scientist who comes to Africa to study an endangered species; *Congo* (1995), about an expedition into the African jungle; and *Greystoke* (1996), which pits a decorously vicious England against a primeval and timeless Africa. A film version of Conrad's *Heart of Darkness* was also made in 1994, directed by Nick Roeg.

In recent years there have been a number of movies in which Africa becomes a setting for the performance of what might loosely be termed postcolonial 'guilt': *Hotel Rwanda* (2005), *The Interpreter* (2005) and *In My Country* (2005). Others, such as *Black Hawk Down* (2001), use Africa as a stage for imperial projections of US geopolitical imaginations (Lisle and Pepper 2005; Carter and McCormack 2006). The last of these films says little about the historical or political context of the war or of Somalia more generally, and the Somalis in the film are depicted as undifferentiated hordes that die in anonymous waves. Recently too, cinematic renderings of desolation in Africa have become ever more popular. *Blood Diamond* (2006) and *The Last King of Scotland* (2006) have gathered Oscar nominations and plaudits for their assault on Western consciences. Like *The Constant Gardener* (2005), Africa functions in these films as a backdrop for a white man's odyssey and articulations of humanitarianism and responsibility, an Africa defined by underdevelopment, suffering, death and disease. In many of these films, such as *Tears of the Sun* (2003), African voices are often submerged. What the viewer is allowed to witness in this film is the classic portrayal of 'Africans' that has been in existence since the movie industry began. One such timeless theme appearing in *Tears of the Sun* is that of the saviour (in this case played by a white woman) of the 'indigenous' population, a population who reciprocates with love and zeal for their saviour. African men and women are here styled helpless, afraid and devoid of any personality, except in crucial moments.

Such cinematic themes are replicated in much contemporary photojournalism and documentary photography. Since the 1980s, 'Africa' has become synonymous with famine images and *vice versa* (Campbell 2003; Campbell et al 2005) (Figure 8.3). Famine images remain powerful and salient in modernity because they recall a precarious pre-modern existence that industrialised society has allegedly overcome. Understood as a natural disaster in which there is a crisis of food supply, famine is seen as a symptom of the lack of progress that results in the death of the innocent

Figure 8.3   'Korem, Ethiopia, 1984' by Mohammed Amin.
Source: Mohammed Amin

(Edkins 2000). It is for this reason that famine images are, more often than not, of individuals, frequently including children, barely clothed, staring passively into the lens, flies flitting across their faces.

Content analyses of news images through time reveals that, regardless of the context in which famine has been observed, the same images recur (Moeller 1999). They recur because they are the icons of a disaster narrative in which complex political circumstances are interpreted through an established journalistic frame of reference. As in colonial films, outsiders come from afar to dispense charity to victims of a natural disaster who are too weak to help themselves (Benthall 1993). Instead of this discursive formation having to be explained in full each time, the recurrence of the iconic image of the starving child triggers this general and established understanding of famine, thereby disciplining any ambiguity about what is occurring in famine zones.

These visual performances have effects on 'observers' at the same time as they give meaning to the 'observed'. Indeed, they establish a series of identity relations that reproduce and confirm notions of Self/Other, developed/underdeveloped, North/South, masculine/feminine, sovereignty/anarchy and the like. Given that most contemporary famine imagery comes from one continent, it reproduces the imagined geography of 'Africa', so that a continent of 900 million people in 57 countries is homogenised into a single entity represented by a starving child. This homogenisation is reiterated and reinforced by the media's use of similar imagery to depict situations such as that in Darfur, even though the political violence and possible genocide in Sudan is fundamentally different to a natural disaster or humanitarian crisis (Campbell 2007).

Africa is also envisioned through the emerging domain of digital technologies. While not figuring extensively in arcade, computer, console and mobile games, where Africa does appear the attendant images and themes are depressingly familiar. One particular theme is 'wilderness Africa', as in the case of PC games such as *Safari Adventures* (Global Star 2005), *Wildlife Tycoon: Venture Africa* (Dreamcatcher Interactive 2006), *Zoo Tycoon 2: African Adventure* (Microsoft 2006) and *Wild Earth Africa* (Xplosiv 2007). In these games, which often have console equivalents, Africa is the empty container for the simulation of ecology, wildlife or wildlife management, and many offer 'safari experiences'. Online *virtual* safari tours of Africa are also now widely available. In addition to the performance of Safari and wilderness 'Africa', console games (those available for hardware such as the Playstation or Xbox) also often use the continent as a cinematic backdrop or exotic setting. This is true for the spy adventure *Metal Gear* (first released in 1987)

The Scopic Regime of 'Africa'   187

and the rally game *GTC Africa* (Majesco Games 2002). The opening battles between 'Master Chief' and the 'covenant aliens' in the popular Xbox release *Halo 2* (2005) are, for example, set on the picturesque island of Zanzibar.

The African landscape has also been the setting for a range of military adventure games such as *Call of Duty 2* (a World War II themed game set in North Africa) and the game *Black Hawk Down*. There is also now a multiplayer online game called *Africa* (Rapid Reality Studios 2006), where gamers pay a monthly subscription to delve into a land of thirteenth-century African civilisation and mythology, crossing the virtual Sahara on a camel, journeying to Timbuktu and fighting as a Zulu warrior against a 'were-lion'. The game's designers argue that games like this can improve players' understandings of Africa, appealing to the recent emergence of self-proclaimed 'games for change'. These games apparently seek to use the virtual spaces of the gaming world to change ways of thinking and seeing various places and peoples. A similar claim might be made for the game *Darfur is Dying* (2007). The idea for this game came out of a partnership between the Reebok Human Rights Foundation and the International Crisis Group that together launched the Darfur Digital Activist contest. Designed largely by students at the University of Southern California in conjunction with humanitarian aid workers with experience in Darfur, the game is a narrative-based simulation where the user adopts the perspective of a displaced Darfurian and negotiates the forces that threaten their chosen refugee camp. According to the game's website, it 'offers a faint glimpse of what it's like for the more then 2.5 million who have been internally displaced by the crisis in Sudan'. A faint glimpse indeed. Characters must forage for water (while being chased by the Janjaweed militias) or must procure food or build shelters within the refugee camp.

In a satirical account of 'how to write about Africa' ('some tips: sunsets and starvation are good'), the Kenyan writer Binyavanga Wainaina (2006) advised:

> never have a picture of a well-adjusted African on the cover of your book, or in it, unless that African has won the Nobel Prize. An AK-47, prominent ribs, naked breasts: use these. If you must include an African, make sure you get one in Masai or Zulu or Dogon dress.

It is no surprise, given the truth of Wainaina's excoriating observations, that the majority of outsiders (more than 80 per cent of UK respondents in one survey) view 'Africa' in wholly negative terms as a place of disease, distress and instability.² The scopic regime of 'Africa' has reduced and condensed the continent into a kind of exotic comic-book space, a backdrop of baseless fabric against which a series of identity relations (Self/Other, North/South) are staged and enacted. As such, the scopic regime of 'Africa', itself a 'visual performance of the social field' that establishes perceptible reality, provides the conditions of possibility for geopolitics through the relationship between sites and sights that it installs (Campbell 2007).

The scopic regime of 'Africa' has thus created a place in the world marked by either war and disaster or exotic natives and animal tourism. It achieves and sustains this through the structure of iteration that is at the heart of performativity, whereby discourse produces the effect that it names through reiterative and citational practices (Campbell 1998: 25–8, 200). The persistence of negative or exoticised imagery over time, recalling past representations in each contemporary production, stands as testament to the power of iteration (Figure 8.4). Yet the problem is not so much the *presence of* such imagery because it would be foolish to deny the actuality of much that takes place before the lens, but, rather, the *absence* of other views amongst the imagery the global visual economy transmits to audiences. As Wainaina (2006) notes: 'Taboo subjects [include] ordinary domestic scenes, love between Africans (unless a death is involved), references to African writers or intellectuals, mention of school-going children who are not suffering from yaws or Ebola fever or female genital mutilation.'

The easy response to this situation is to call for more 'balanced' or 'positive' views, as the World Bank did in 2003 with its photographic exhibition 'Africa in Pictures', designed to 'showcase another side of Africa' (World Bank 2003). The Bank undertook this project because of an understanding that negative perceptions of Africa lead to under-investment and poor economic growth (see Ferguson 2006: 7). Such efforts at fostering alternative images are not without merit, and the difficulty of achieving even some distance from colonial tropes should not be underestimated.³ In this context, *National Geographic*'s September 2005 special issue on Africa is a stark reminder of the power of the scopic regime, even when alternatives are sought.⁴ While the cover declares 'Africa – whatever you thought you should think again', it also advises readers that inside is a free map of the 'wild continent'. The contents page is illustrated by four images, three of which involve fighting zebras, desert dunes and dancing 'pygmies'. The Society's month-long focus on Africa was headlined by streamed video images from Pete's Pond in Botswana's Mashatu Game Reserve; the first colour spread in the magazine pictured a baby elephant walking through the reception of a Zambian lodge; the largest of three

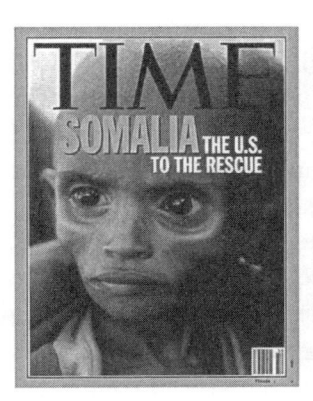

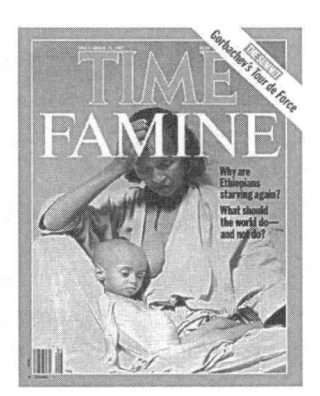

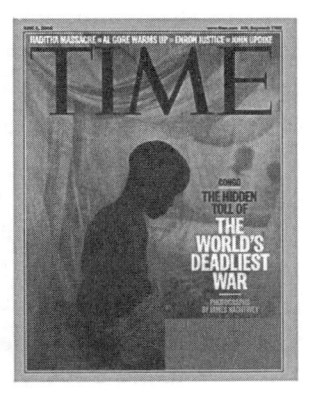

Figure 8.4 *From TIME to TIME* by Alfredo Jaar.
Source: Alfredo Jaar

photographs illustrating the 'Africa in Fact' section was of a Congolese militiaman swaddled in ammunition; the Africa Quiz begins with a question about Burroughs' *Tarzan* novels and focuses on Hollywood films; and Jared Diamond's overview article privileges the continent's geography and history as determinants of its contemporary condition.[5] To be sure, there is some attempt at a more contemporary, nuanced account of a heterogeneous place – as in the article on Nairobi, written by Binyavanga Wainaina – but in light of the final photograph in the magazine, an archive shot of Teddy Roosevelt posing with a rhino he shot during a 1911 safari, Wainaina's satire seems more than justified, and the structure of iteration is clear.

There are alternatives that seek to counter the power of the scopic regime of 'Africa'. With regard to still photography, the artistic work of Carrie Mae Weems (1995), the 'Depth of Field' collective in Lagos (World Press Photo 2006), the exhibitions of Okwui Enwezor (2006) and the agency 'majorityworld.com' are significant. At the same time, the pursuit of alternatives should not mean the abandonment of compelling artistic and documentary work by the likes of Alfredo Jaar (Figure 9.5), Simon Norfolk and Gilles Peress that deals with the negatives (Norfolk 1998; Mirzoeff 2005). With regard to cinema, there are films that attempt to 'shoot back' (Thackway 2003) alternative imaginings of 'Africa' or that have situated themselves within the traditions of 'third cinema'. These films are increasingly gaining international recognition, particularly through the contributions of African film-makers such as Ousmane Sembene, Idrissa Ouedraogo, Haile Gerima, Djibril Diop Mambéty, Souleymane Cissé and Safi Faye (amongst many others). Many such films seek to revisit and reinterpret colonial history (often satirically), or otherwise unsettle and disturb the nostalgic recollection in Western films of an (illusory) exotic order of white colonial societies. They do so by envisioning resistances to colonialism or the circumstances of its demise or rebirth as neocolonialism.

The scopic regime of Africa establishes the conditions of possibility for an ethical response to the events and issues it makes available. It makes 'Africa' a place in the world that is most often understood as an object of humanitarianism or a destination for exotic tourism, with little in between. There remains a need to displace and unsettle the historical frames that occlude so much of the continent's richness and diversity. At the same time it must be ensured that alternative framings expand to fill that space in-between and in turn denaturalise the scopic regime in order to make possible other responses.

Bibliography

Achebe, Chinua, 'An image of Africa', in *Hopes and Impediments: Selected Essays 1965–1987* (London: Heinemann, 1988).
Allimadi, Milton, *The Hearts of Darkness: How White Writers Created the Racist Image of Africa* (Black Star Books: New York, 2002).
Anderson, Kay, 'Culture and nature at the Adelaide Zoo: At the frontiers of "human" geography', *Transactions of the Institute British Geographers* 20 (1995), pp.275–94.
Andreasson, Stefan, 'Orientalism and African development studies: The "reductive repetition" motif in theories of African underdevelopment', *Third World Quarterly* 26/6 (2005), pp.971–86.
Bennett, Tony, 'The exhibitionary complex', *New Formations* 4 (1988), pp.73–102.
Benthall, Jonathan, *Disasters, Relief and the Media* (London: I.B.Tauris, 1993).
Blatti, Jo (ed.), *Past Meets Present: Interpretation and Public Audiences* (Washington, DC: Smithsonian Institute Press, 1987).
Blunt, Alison, *Travel, Gender and Imperialism: Mary Kingsley and West Africa* (New York: Guilford, 1994).
Boehmer, Elleke (ed.), *Empire Writing: An Anthology of Colonial Literature 1870–1918* (Oxford: Oxford University Press, 1998).
Brantlinger, Patrick, *Rule of Darkness: British Literature and Imperialism 1830–1914* (Ithaca: Cornell University Press, 1988).
Brantlinger, Patrick, *Dark Vanishings: Discourse on the Extinction of Primitive Races 1800–1930* (Ithaca: Cornell University Press, 2003).
Burns, James, 'Watching Africans watch films: Theories of spectatorship in British colonial Africa', *Historical Journal of Film, Radio and Television* 20/2 (2000), pp.197–211.
Burns, James, 'John Wayne on the Zambezi: Cinema, empire, and the American Western in British Central Africa', *International Journal of African Historical Studies* 35/1 (2002), pp.103–17.
Butler, Judith, 'Torture and the Ethics of Photography', *Environment and Planning D: Society and Space*, 25 (2007), pp.951–66.
Calhoun, Dave, 'African cinema – White guides, black pain (White conscience films set in Africa)', *Sight and Sound* 17/2 (2007), pp.32–5.
Campbell, David, *National Deconstruction: Violence, Identity and Justice in Bosnia* (Minneapolis: University of Minnesota Press, 1998).
Campbell, David, 'Salgado and the Sahel: Documentary photography and the imaging of famine,' in Francois Debrix and Cindy Weber (eds), *Rituals of Mediation: International Politics and Social Meaning* (Minneapolis: University of Minnesota Press, 2003), pp.69–96.
Campbell, David, 'Geopolitics and visual culture: Sighting the Darfur conflict 2003–05', *Political Geography* 26/4 (2007), pp.357–82.
Campbell, David, Clark, Dave and Manzo, Kate, *Imaging Famine* (2005), at http://www.imaging-famine.org (accessed 4 November 2008).
Cantwell, Robert, *Ethnomimesis: Folklife and the Representation of Culture* (Chapel Hill: University of North Carolina Press, 1993).

Carter, Sean and McCormack, Derek, 'Film, geopolitics, and the affective logics of intervention', *Political Geography* 25/2 (2006), pp.228–45.
Coombes, Annie, *Reinventing Africa: Museums, Material Culture and Popular Imagination in Late Victorian England* (New Haven, London: Yale University Press, 1994).
Crang, Mike, 'On display: The poetics, politics and interpretation of exhibitions', in M. Ogborn, A. Blunt, P. Gruffudd, J. May and D. Pinder (eds), *Cultural Geography in Practice* (London: Hodder Arnold, 2003).
Darfur is Dying (2007), at http://www.darfurisdying.com/ (accessed 4 November 2008).
Derrida, Jacques, *Writing and Difference* (London and New York: Routledge, 1978).
Domosh, Mona A., ' "Civilized" commerce: Gender, "race" and empire at the 1893 Chicago Exposition', *Cultural Geographies* 9 (2002), pp.181–201.
Dunn, Kevin, 'Lights ... camera ... Africa: Images of Africa and Africans in Western popular films of the 1930s', *African Studies Review* 39/1 (1996), pp.149–75.
Ebron, Paulla, *Performing Africa* (Princeton: Princeton University Press, 2002).
Edkins, Jenny, *Whose Hunger? Concepts of Famine, Practices of Aid* (Minneapolis: University of Minnesota Press, 2000).
Elkins, James, *The Domain of Images* (Ithaca: Cornell University Press, 1999).
Engelen, Leen, 'The black face of cinema in Africa', *Historical Journal of Film, Radio and Television* 26/1 (2006), pp.103–9.
Enwezor, Okwui, *Snap Judgments: New Positions in Contemporary African Photography* (2006), at http://www.icp.org/site/c.dnJGKJNsFqG/b.1432339/k.9484/Snap_Judgments.htm (accessed 4 July 2007).
Feldman, Allen, 'On the actuarial gaze: From 9/11 to Abu Ghraib', *Cultural Studies* 19/2 (2005), pp.203–26.
Ferguson, James, *Global Shadows: Africa in the Neoliberal World Order* (Durham, NC: Duke University Press, 2006).
Film Images, 'COI footage file background' (2007), at http://www.film-images.com/index.jsp?ID=0&CollectionID=87/ (accessed 4 November 2008).
Geada, Eduardo, *Imperialismo e o Fascismo na Cinema* (Lisbon: Morães Editores, 1977).
Gordon, Robert, ' "Captured on film": Bushmen and the claptrap of performative primitives', in P.S. Landau and D. Kaspin (eds), *Images and Empires: Visuality in Colonial and Postcolonial Africa* (Berkeley: University of California Press, 2002).
Gouda, Frances, *Dutch Culture Overseas: Colonial Practice in the Netherlands Indies 1900–1942* (Amsterdam: Amsterdam University Press, 1995).
Gregory, Derek, *Geographical Imaginations* (Oxford: Basil Blackwell, 1994).
Gregory, Derek, 'Emperors of the gaze: Photographic practices and productions of space in Egypt, 1839–1914', in J.M. Schwartz and J.R. Ryan (eds), *Picturing Place: Photography and the Geographical Imagination* (London: I.B.Tauris, 2003).
Harrow, Kenneth (ed.), *African Cinema: Postcolonial and Feminist Readings* (London: Africa World Press, 1998).
Harvey, Penelope, *Hybrids of Modernity* (New York and London: Routledge, 1996).
Hodeir, Catherine, 'Decentering the gaze at French colonial exhibitions', in P.S. Landau and D. Kaspin (eds), *Images and Empires: Visuality in Colonial and Postcolonial Africa* (Berkeley: University of California Press, 2002).

Hoffenberg, Peter, *An Empire on Display: English, Indian, and Australian Exhibitions from the Crystal Palace to the Great War* (Berkeley: University of California Press, 2001).
Hooper-Greenhill, Eilean, *Museums and the Shaping of Knowledge* (London: Routledge, 1992).
Hughes, Deborah, 'Kenya, India and the British Empire Exhibition of 1924', *Race and Class* 47/4 (2006), pp.66–85.
Jarosz, Lucy, 'Constructing the dark continent: Metaphor as geographic representation of Africa', *Geografiska Annaler (B)* 74/2 (1992), pp.105–15.
Jay, Martin, 'Scopic regimes of modernity', in H. Foster (ed.), *Vision and Visuality* (Seattle: Bay Press, 1988).
Kirriemuir, John, 'A history of digital games', in J. Rutter and J. Bryce (eds), *Understanding Digital Games* (London: Sage, 2006).
Landau, Paul, 'Introduction: An amazing distance: Pictures and people in Africa', in P.S. Landau and D. Kaspin (eds), *Images and Empires: Visuality in Colonial and Postcolonial Africa* (Berkeley: University of California Press, 2002).
Lisle, Debbie and Pepper, Andrew, 'The new face of global Hollywood: *Black Hawk Down* and the politics of meta-sovereignty', *Cultural Politics* 1 (2005), pp.165–92.
MacDonald, Fraser,. 'Visuality', in N. Thrift and R. Kitchin (eds), *International Encyclopaedia of Human Geography* (Elsevier, 2009).
Majesco Games, *GTC Africa* (PS2 console game) (Edison: New Jersey, 2002).
Mayer, Ruth, *Artificial Africas: Colonial Images in the Times of Globalization* (Hanover/London: University Press of New England, 2002).
Maxwell, Anne, *Colonial Photography and Exhibitions: Representations of the Native and the Making of European Identities* (London: Continuum, 1999).
McClure, John, *Late Imperial Romance* (London: Verso, 1994).
Metz, Christian, *The Imaginary Signifier: Psychoanalysis and the Cinema* (Bloomington: Indiana University Press, 1982).
Mirzoeff, Nicholas, 'Invisible again: Rwanda and representation after genocide', *African Arts* 38 (2005), pp.36–9, 86–91, 96.
Mitchell, Timothy, *Colonizing Egypt* (Cambridge: Cambridge University Press, 1989).
Mitchell, Timothy, 'Introduction', in T. Mitchell (ed.), *Questions of Modernity* (Minneapolis: University of Minnesota Press, 2000).
Mitchell, W.J.T., 'Showing seeing: a critique of visual culture', *Journal of Visual Culture* 1 (2002), pp.165–81.
Moeller, Susan, *Compassion Fatigue: How the Media Sell Disease, Famine, War and Death* (New York: Routledge, 1999).
Morton, Patricia, *Hybrid Modernities: Architecture and Representation at the 1931 Paris Exposition* (Cambridge: MIT Press, 2000).
Murphy, David, 'Africans Filming Africa: Questioning Theories of an Authentic African Cinema', *Journal of African Cultural Studies* 13/2 (2000), pp.239–49.
National Geographic, 'Africa: Whatever you thought, think again', special issue, 208/3 September 2005, at http://www7.nationalgeographic.com/ngm/0509/index.html (accessed 4 July).
Norfolk, Simon, *For most of it I have no words* (Stockport: Dewi Lewis Publishing, 1998).

Oksiloff, Assenka, *Picturing the Primitive: Visual Culture, Ethnography and Early German Cinema* (New York: Palgrave, 2001).
Olds, Kris and Ley, David, 'Landscape as spectacle: World's fairs and the culture of heroic consumption', *Environment and Planning D: Society and Space* 6 (1988), pp.191–212.
Ó Tuathail, Gearoid, 'Dis/placing the geo-politics which one cannot not want', *Political Geography* 19 (2000), pp.385–96.
Paris, Michael, 'Africa in post-1945 British cinema', *South African Historical Journal* 48 (2003), pp.61–70.
Poole, Steven, *Trigger Happy: Video games and the Entertainment Revolution* (London: Arcade Publishing, 2000).
Power, M., 'Post-colonial cinema and the reconfiguration of Moçambicanidade', *Lusotopie* (2004), pp.261–80.
Power, Marcus and Sidaway, James D., 'Deconstructing Twinned Towers: Lisbon's EXPO '98 and the occluded geographies of discovery', *Social and Cultural Geography* 6 (2005), pp.865–83.
Pratt, Mary Louise, *Imperial Eyes: Studies in Travel Writing and Transculturation* (London: Routledge, 1992).
Pred, Allan, *Recognizing European Modernities: A Montage of the Present* (London and New York: Routledge, 1995).
Rapid Reality Studios, *Africa* (PC Game) (Marietta, Georgia, 2006).
Roberts, Andrew, 'Africa on film to 1940', *History in Africa* 14 (1987), pp.189–227.
Robinson, Jennifer, '(Post-)colonial geographies at Johannesburg's Empire Exhibition, 1936', in A. Blunt and C. McEwan (eds), *Post-colonial Geographies* (Melbourne: Cassell, 2002).
Rosaldo, Renato, *Culture and Truth: The remaking of Social Analysis* (Boston: Beacon Press, 1993).
Rose, Gillian, *Visual Methodologies* (London: Sage, 2001).
Ryan, James R., 'Visualising imperial geography: Halford Mackinder and the Colonial Office Visual Instruction Committee, 1902–1911', *Ecumene: A Journal of Environment, Culture, Meaning* 1/2 (1994), pp.157–76.
Ryan, James R., *Picturing Empire: Photography and the Visualization of the British Empire* (Chicago: University of Chicago Press, 1997).
Schiebinger, Londa, *Nature's Body: Gender in the making of Modern Science* (London: Beacon Press, 1995).
Slavin, David, *Colonial Cinema and Imperial France, 1919–1939: White Blind spots, Male fantasies, Settler Myths* (Baltimore: John Hopkins University Press, 2001).
Smyth, Rosaleen, 'The British colonial film unit and sub-Saharan Africa, 1939–1945', *Journal of Film, Radio and Television* 8/3 (1988), pp.285–98.
Smyth, Rosaleen, 'The postwar career of the colonial film unit in Africa 1946–1955: Instructional films for Africans', *Journal of Film, Radio and Television* 12/2 (1992), pp.163–77.
Söderström, Ola, 'Expo.02: Exhibiting Swiss identity', *Ecumene* 8 (2001), pp.497–501.
Spurr, David, *The Rhetoric of Empire: Colonial Discourse in Journalism, Travel Writing, and Imperial Administration* (Durham, NC: Duke University Press, 1993).

Stollery, Martin, 'The question of Third Cinema: African and Middle Eastern cinema', *Journal of Film and Video* 52/4 (2001), pp.44–56.
Strohmayer, Ulf, 'Pictoral symbolism in the age of innocence: material geographies at the Paris World's Exposition of 1937', *Ecumene* 3 (1996), pp.282–304.
Sweeney, Carole, '"Le Tour du Monde en Quatre Jours": Empire, exhibition, and the surrealist disorder of things', *Textual Practice* 19/1 (2005), pp.131–148
Thackway, Melissa, *Africa Shoots back: Alternative Perspectives in Sub-Saharan Francophone African Film* (Bloomington: Indiana University Press, 2003).
Ukadike, Frank, 'Western film images of Africa: Genealogy of an ideological formulation', *Black Scholar* 21/2 (1990), pp.30–48.
Van der Gaag, Nikki and Nash, Cathy, *Images of Africa: The UK Report* (1987), at http://www.imaging-famine.org/images_africa.htm (accessed 4 November 2008).
Vera, Hernán and Gordon, Andrew, *Screen Saviours: Hollywood Fictions of Whiteness* (London: Rowman and Littlefield, 2003).
Wainaina, Benjamin, 'How to write about Africa', *Granta* 92 (2006), at http://www.granta.com/Magazine/92/How-to-write-about-Africa/Page-1 (accessed 3 July 2007).
Weems, Carrie Mae, *From Here I Saw What Happened and I Cried* (New York: Museum of Modern Art, 1995), at http://www.moma.org/collection/browse_results.php?object_id=45579 (accessed 4 July 2007).
World Bank, '"Africa In Pictures" Exhibit Opens Worldwide' (10 January 2003), at http://go.worldbank.org/CPDZWBMWG0 (accessed 4 November 2008).
World Press Photo, 'Picture Power', *Enter* (May 2006), at http://www.enterworldpressphoto.com/editie4/ppower.php?hilow (accessed 4 July 2007).

Part Three

Observant Practice

Chapter 9

Combat Zones that See: Urban Warfare and US Military Technology
Stephen Graham

Introduction: Surveillance, war, urbanisation

> For Western military forces, asymmetric warfare in urban areas will be the greatest challenge of this century ... The city will be the strategic high ground – whoever controls it will dictate the course of future events in the world. (Karen Dickson[1])

> Some people say to me that the Iraqis are not the Vietnamese! They have no jungles of swamps to hide in. I reply, 'Let our cities be our swamps and our buildings our jungles'. (Tariq Aziz, former Iraqi foreign minister[2])

Western military theorists and researchers are increasingly interested in how the geographies of Global South cities, and processes of Global South urbanisation, may influence the geopolitics and the techno-science of post-Cold War political violence.[3] Almost unnoticed within 'civil' urban geography and social science, a large shadow system of military urban research is quickly being established. This overlooked domain of military research is concerned with how intensifying global processes of urbanisation are reconfiguring the traditional battlespace environment (Graham 2004). This research is important, I would argue, in that it gives imaginative shape to the so-called 'urban terrain' of the Global South as a theatre of future Western military operations. There has been a growing realisation that the scale and significance of contemporary processes of urbanisation across the world may significantly recast military doctrine within the new realities of post-Cold War Western strategy. The central consensus amongst the wide variety of Western military theorists pushing for such shifts is that 'modern urban combat operations will become one of the primary challenges of the 21st century' (DIRC 1997: 11). In 2004, Major Kelly Houlgate, a US Marine Corps commentator, notes that 'of 26 conflicts fought over by US forces' between 1984 and 2004, '21 have involved urban areas, and 10 have been exclusively urban' (Houlgate 2004: 1).

The widening adoption of 'urban warfare' doctrine follows centuries when Western military planners preached Sun Tzu's mantra from 1500 BC that the 'worst policy is to attack cities'. It follows a Cold War period marked by an obsession with mass, superpower-led 'Air–Land' engagements centred on the North European plain, within and above the spaces between *bypassed* European city-regions. Whilst numerous wars were fought by Western forces in developing-world cities during the Cold War as part of wider struggles against independence movements and 'hot' proxy wars, such conflicts were seen by Western military theorists as unusual side-shows to the imagined superpower 'Air–Land', and tactical and global nuclear engagements (Davis 2004a).

In the place of such neglect of Western military doctrine, which specifically addresses the challenges of counter-insurgency warfare within cities, a highly contested, diverse and complex set of institutional and techno-scientific battles are now emerging to try and reshape Western military forces, so that counter-insurgency operations within large urban areas become one of their *de facto* functions (Hills 2004). Prevailing conceptions of Western military engagement are thus being widely challenged to address the perceived perils of engaging in 'military operations on urban terrain' (MOUT). In the process, Global South cities are being imagined in military circles as domains which interrupt the technological gaze of overhead surveillance platforms. This reimagining sits at a complex intersection between the perceived physical morphology of rapidly urbanising terrain and a Western military techno-science which relies ever more on the 'visual' capabilities of machines, linked over computer networks, as prosthetic, cyborganised, sensor systems. Perceptions that urbanised areas interrupt Western military surveillance and targeting systems are crucial because, as Jordan Crandall has argued, the current age of panoptic data processing means that Western nations increasingly wage war through what he calls 'processual infrastructures' (Crandall 2005: 3). Integrating the capabilities of digital sensors to sustain 'strategic seeing' and 'persistent surveillance', military command and control systems increasingly delegate decisions to track, undertake surveillance and target the software algorithms that connect such sensor systems to computer databases. The result is a techno-militarised, control society where computerised tracking of various flows and movements (bodies, vehicles, data, finance) produces what Jordan Crandall terms 'an anticipatory form of seeing', conducted by a kind of continuous, anticipatory, 'armed vision'. In this, the continuous agency of computerised algorithms pre-emptively traces and identifies individuals, signals and movements, deemed in some way to be 'targets' to be tracked or attacked (Crandall 2005: 5). This can happen through identifying apparently 'abnormal' behaviours in comparison with the statistical patterns of a general urban background of 'normality'. Or it can occur when people, behaviours, vehicles or flows are identified because of their similarity to the electronic signatures of alleged targets within databases embedded within computer memory (Crandall 2002).

Importantly, such anticipatory tracking systems are being installed within both the securitised cities of Western 'Homelands' and those frontier cities in the Global South 'war zones', which have become sites of expeditionary Western warfare. However, the functions of such systems are startlingly different and exemplify the stark biopolitical geographies that mark the 'war on terror' (Graham 2006). In Western cities, then, risk-profiling systems are used to identify 'targets' for the further scrutiny of various 'homeland security' policies. In the occupied cities of Iraq, meanwhile, the algorithms are not only being used to track and identify 'targets', but, increasingly, to instigate automated military attacks to attempt to destroy them.

As the world's pre-eminent military power, the military forces of the USA provide a key example of how discursive constructions of the interruptive effects of 'urban terrain' on technologies of electronic tracking and seeing are being used to justify attempts at the 'transformation' of the technologies, tactics and strategies of national military intervention more broadly (Ek 2000). US military forces will be our central concern here because their research on 'urban operations' dwarfs that of all other nations combined. The USA is also more reliant on the agency of algorithms and electronic surveillance, tracking and targeting systems than other Western militaries.

The bloody experience of the Iraq urban insurgency already looms large in these debates. A major review of urban warfare 'doctrine' for US forces prepared by Major Lee Grubbs in 2003, for example, baldly stated that 'as the Iraq plan evolves, it is clear that the enemies of the US military have learned a method to mitigate the Joint [US] Force's dominance in long range surveillance and engagement. The enemy will seek the city and the advantages of mixing with non-combatants' (Grubbs 2003: 1). There is a strong emphasis here on how the three-dimensional complexity and scale of Iraq's cities has worked to undermine the USA's obvious advantages in surveillance, targeting and killing through 'precise' air and space-based weapons systems.[4]

All of this speaks to recent discussions about geopolitics and visuality (MacDonald 2006; Campbell 2007; Hughes 2007) in that these developments encourage us to move beyond a sole focus on discourse and representation when considering the circulation of geopolitical power within popular culture (Sharp 1996; Dodds 2003). The problematisation of urban space in military doctrine and the concomitant attempt to render such space 'visible' through military techno-science is a reminder that the power of the visual always exceeds the simple matter of representation. New techniques of visualisation have long been central to the ability of the state and its militaries to enact geopolitical power. In this respect my discussion of visuality is in some sense deeply literal: my concern with the mechanics of visual data runs counter to the abstract discursive treatment of the visual that has characterised much critical geopolitics. This chapter thus considers the nature of *technologised* visuality and visualisation: the use of machinic systems of surveillance, increasingly independent on the human eye, for tracking and constituting subjects, rendering 'targets' and orchestrating the new geopolitics of visuality (Crandall 2002).

In what follows, my discussion is three-fold. In the first instance, I analyse the discursive problematisation of Global South cities as interrupters of networked surveillance and targeting systems by US military urban researchers. I emphasise how developing world cities are depicted as labyrinthine, chaotic and deceptive physical environments that frustrate the wider US strategy known as the 'Revolution in Military Affairs' (RMA). The second part of the chapter goes on to analyse the proposal of technophiliac 'solutions' to the purported erosion of US geostrategic power through Global South urbanisation. I identify an 'urban turn' to the RMA which has seen a shift from discussions of planet-straddling weapons systems to innovations which could control the micro-spaces of developing world 'megacities'. Centred on the concept of 'persistent area dominance', such strategies entail the saturation of 'adversary' cities with large numbers of miniature surveillance and targeting systems. The final part of the chapter makes some concluding remarks on how these developments might inform recent discussions of the relationship between geopolitics and visual culture.

Dreams frustrated? Urbanisation and the revolution in military affairs

The orbital weapons currently in play possess the traditional attributes of the divine: omnivoyance and omnipresence. (Paul Virilio[5])

Urban operations represent a black hole in the current Revolution in Military Affairs pantheon of technological advantage ... the technologies traditionally ascribed to the current Revolution in Military Affairs phenomenon will have negligible impact on Military Operations in Urban Terrain. (Andrew Harris[6])

The military strategies to sustain and entrench US geopolitical power in the post-Cold War period (Kirsch 2003; Barnett 2004; Roberts et al 2004) rest on the 'transformation' of US military power through the much heralded revolution in military affairs (RMA) (Ek 2002; Pieterse 2004). The RMA has widely been hailed amongst US military planners as the means to sustain US dominance in the post-Cold War world by enlisting technologies of 'stealth', 'precision' targeting and satellite geo-positioning (Stone 2004) (see Figure 9.1).

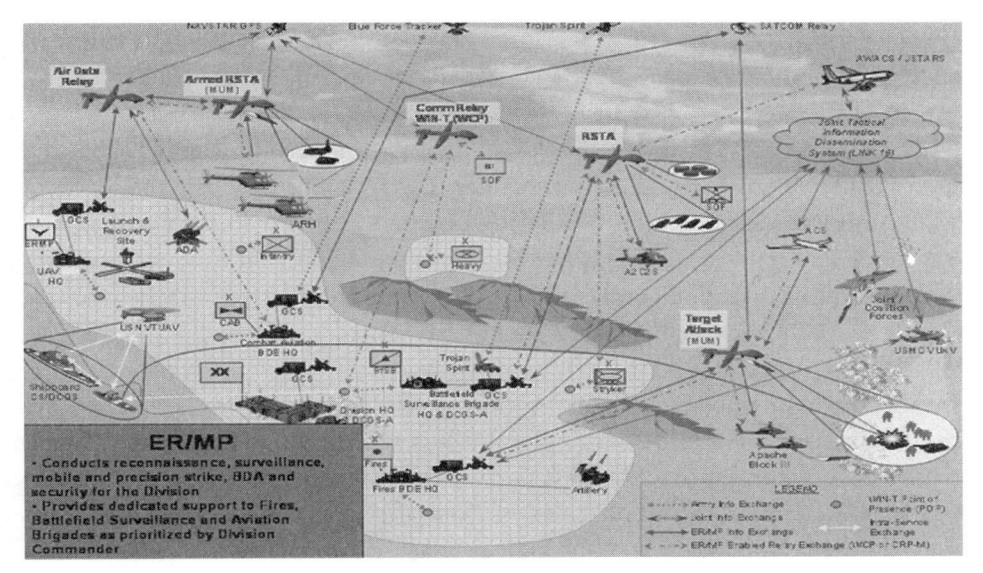

Figure 9.1 The US military's 'revolution in military affairs', signifying ageographical mastery through uninterrupted surveillance and networking.

Of particular importance is the notion that 'military operations are now aimed at defined effects rather than attrition of enemy forces or occupation of ground' (Cohen 2004: 395). Through the interlinkage of the US military 'system of systems', RMA theorists argue that a truly 'network centric warfare' is now possible through which US forces can continually dominate societies deemed to be their adversaries through an omnipotent surveillance and 'situational awareness', devastating and precisely targeted aerial firepower, and the suppression and degradation of the communications and fighting ability of any opposing forces (Arquilla and Ronfeldt 2001; Graham 2005). Thus, RMA theorists imagine US military operations to be a giant, integrated 'network enterprise': a 'just-in-time' system of posthuman, cyborganised warriors which utilises many of the principles of logistics chain management and new-technology based tracking that are so dominant within contemporary management models (Gray 2003).

Crucial here is the argument that this reduced risk affords the confidence to launch pre-emptive attacks, which is now the central basis for US strategy (Barocas 2002). Such perceptions were central to the Bush Administration's 'pre-emptive' and unbounded 'war on terror' after the 9/11 attacks. They were also central to the influential pronouncements of the neoconservative *Project for a New American Century*, in 2000, that US forces needed to be redesigned in the post-Cold War so that they could 'fight and decisively win multiple, simultaneous major theatre wars' (Project for a New American Century 2000; Roberts et al 2004). Typical of such arguments, the 'air power theorist' Raymond O' Mara (2003) argues:

> It is now possible to use America's military might with a greatly reduced chance of suffering friendly casualties or equipment loss. The reduction of American casualties afforded by the marriage between stealthy aircraft and precision guided munitions has had a profound effect on America's willingness to intervene militarily ... the military must also adapt to its new role as a tool of choice, rather than a tool of last resort.[7]

Importantly, however, such technophiliac discourses which depict a new reduced-risk, 'clean' and seemingly painless strategy of US military dominance have assumed that the vast networks of sensors and weapons would work *uninterruptedly*. Global scales of flow and connection have thus dominated RMA discourses; technological mastery, omnipotent surveillance, real-time 'situational awareness' and speed-of-light digital interactions have been widely portrayed as processes which would usher in 'Full Spectrum

Dominance' for the USA on a planetary scale, irrespective of the geographical terrain that was to be dominated.

RMA discourses have, in this sense, been notably ageographical. Crucially, for our purposes here, little account has been taken of the spaces or terrains inhabited by the purported adversaries of the USA in the post-Cold War period, or how these are changing through processes of urbanisation and globalisation. A key axiom of RMA rhetoric has been the idea that the USA is now able to prosecute its global strategies for geopolitical dominance through a 'radical non-territoriality' (Duffield 2002: 158). In response to this neglect of global urbanisation within the RMA and spurred on by the catastrophic and ongoing urban insurgency since the US–UK invasion of Iraq in 2003, an increasingly powerful range of counter-discourses have emerged within the US military. Through these, a second group of US military theorists have asserted that the technophiliac dreams of RMA will either fail, or be substantially undermined, by global processes of urbanisation, especially in the Global South cities where they imagine US forces being most often engaged. The pronouncements of those advocating an 'urban turn' in the RMA have had two main features.

Signal failures: Urban environments as physical interrupters to 'network-centric warfare'

> In simple terms walls tend to get in the way of today's battlefield communications and sensor technologies. (Hewish and Pengelley 2001: 14[8])

In the first instance, proponents of an 'urban turn' in RMA strongly suggest that the urban terrain in poor, Global South countries is a great leveller between high-tech US forces and their low-tech and usually informally organised and poorly equipped adversaries.[9] The complex and congested terrain below, within and above cities is seen here as a set of physical spaces which limit the effectiveness of high-tech, space-targeted bombs, surveillance systems and automated, 'network-centric' and 'precision' weapons. The US defence research agency, the Defense Intelligence Research Center (DIRC), for example, argues that 'the urban environment negates the abilities of present US military communications equipment resulting in dead spots, noise, the absorption of digital signal, propagation problems which severely undermine the principles and technologies of "network-centric warfare" ' (DIRC 1997).

The architects Misselwitz and Weizman are amongst the very small number of critical urban researchers who have addressed the ways in which urbanisation undermines the technologies produced by the RMA. They conclude that, within contemporary cities:

> high-tech military equipment is easily incapacitated. Buildings mask targets and create urban canyons, which diminish the capabilities of the air force. It is hard to see into the urban battlespace; it is very difficult to communicate in it, because radio waves are often disturbed. It is hard to use precision weapons because it is difficult to obtain accurate GPS satellite locations. And it becomes more and more difficult (but not impossible) for the military to shoot indiscriminately into the city. For all these reasons, cities continue to reduce the advantages of a technologically superior force.[10]

The 'urbanisation of battlespace' is seen by US urban warfare commentators to reduce the ability of US forces to fight and kill at a distance (always the preferred way because of their 'casualty dread' and technological supremacy). Cities are considered riskier for US forces fighting preemptive, expeditionary wars: 'from refugee flows to dense urban geography, cities create environments that increase uncertainty exponentially' (DIRC 1997). Military operations in cities are thought to run the risk of a Trojan horse-style event that might allow weak and poorly equipped insurgents to gain victory of the world's remaining military superpower (Glenn et al 2001).

The 'urbanisation of insurgency': Global South cities and verticalised military power

> Opposition forces will camouflage themselves in the background noise of the urban environment. Within the urban environment, it is not the weapon itself rather the city which maximizes or mutes an arm's effectiveness. In claustrophobic alleys and urban canyons, civilians are impossible to control or characterize as friendly or not. Weapons hidden beneath a cloak, in a child's carriage or rolled in a carpet can get past security personnel undetected. (DIRC 1997)

A second main feature of US urban warfare discourse moves the focus away from the alleged political challenges of 'failed states' to focus on the urban, rather than national, scale. The supposed military and political challenges of well-armed insurgent groups hiding within, and controlling, fast-growing urban areas are a primary focus here. Highly influential here is the

US military commentator Richard Norton's concept of 'feral cities' – highly disordered urban areas which are controlled by violent, non-state militia of various sorts (DIRC 1997).

Some protagonists in this debate argue that the failure of high-technology sensors and weapons to correctly interpret the physical morphology of cities is leading to an increasing tendency amongst the USA's political adversaries to take refuge within cities (Norton 2003). 'The long-term trend in open-area combat', writes the leading US urban warfare commentator Ralph Peters, 'is toward overhead dominance by US forces' (Peters 1996: 4). As a result, he predicts: 'Battlefield awareness [for US forces] may prove so complete, and "precision" weapons so widely available and effective, that enemy ground-based combat systems will not be able to survive in the deserts, plains, and fields that have seen so many of history's main battles' (Peters 1996: 4).

As a result, Peters argues that the USA's 'enemies will be forced into cities and other complex terrain, such as industrial developments and inter-city sprawl'.[11] Grau and Kipp concur, suggesting that:

> urban combat is increasingly likely, since high-precision weapons threaten operational and tactical manoeuvre in open terrain. Commanders who lack sufficient high-precision weapons will find cities appealing terrain ... provided they know the city better than their opponent does and can mobilize the city's resources and population to their purposes. (Grau and Kipp 2001: 14)

Central to this perception of the incentives underlying what RAND theorists Taw and Hoffman have termed the 'urbanization of insurgency'[12] is the notion that insurgents exploiting the material geographies of Global South cities can force US military personnel to come into close physical proximity, thereby exposing US politicians to much higher casualty rates than stipulated within RMA doctrine. The DIRC argue that

> the weapons [such insurgents] use may be 30 to 40 years old or built from hardware supplies, but at close range many of their inefficiencies are negated. The most effective weapon only needs to exploit the vulnerabilities that the urban environment creates. Each new city will create a different pool of resources and thereby create different urban threats. (DIRC 1997)

Dreams reclaimed? From pre-emptive war to 'persistent area dominance'?

> The time has come to change the perception that the high-tech US war machine fights at a disadvantage in urban areas. (Kelly Houlgate 2004[13])

> Urban areas should become our preferred medium for fighting. We should optimize our force structure for it, rather than relegating it to Appendix Q in our fighting doctrine, treating it as the exception rather than the norm ... It is time to tell Sun Tzu to sit down ... Instead of fearing it, we must own the city [sic]. (Lt. Col. Leonhard, US Army 2003[14])

With the widespread perception that the intensifying urbanisation of the parts of the Global South that the US military envisage as their dominant areas of operation is radically undermining their broader efforts at techno-scientific transformation, a wide range of deeply technophiliac projects and initiatives are emerging aimed at tailoring the 'RMA' to the specific geographies of these southern urban areas. With the urban insurgency in Iraq as an ongoing fulcrum war, a 'transformation' based on the technophiliac celebrations of the death of geography through new technologies is, ironically, being transformed into a major techno-scientific effort to develop and experiment with surveillance, communications and targeting systems that are specifically tailored to the fine-grain physical and human geographies of Global South cities.

It is now widely argued within US military strategic organisations and think-tanks that the RMA needs to be reconfigured to address the challenges of tightly built Global South cities; that new bodies of 'urban' research need to be built up to understand how to use military violence to deliver precise 'effects' in such cities; and that the doctrine, weaponry, training and equipment of US forces need to be comprehensively redesigned so that urban military operations are their de facto function. A large output of conceptual, techno-scientific and research-and-development material has been created by the 'urban turn' of the RMA, especially since the Iraq invasion (Grubbs 2003). The overwhelming rhetoric in such efforts emphasise that new military techno-science, specifically developed to address cities, will turn Global South urban environments into areas that US forces can completely dominate, using their technological advantages, with minimum casualties to themselves. The language and discourse here is deeply woven with long-standing fantasies of omnipotence and control, especially within US military culture (Franklin 1988). It shows deep crossovers with long-standing tropes of cyberpunk science fiction (Gannon 2003). And it renders the future as technologically pre-determined and inevitable, rather than shaped through a myriad of small-scale, technosocial events in practice (Thrift 2000).

The 'urban' turn in the RMA is also backed up by a wide range of projects which develop physical and electronic simulations of Global South urban environments. War games and simulated urban conflicts can be rehearsed and new doctrines, weapons and technologies tested. There is, for the military, a remarkable and productive synergy between these simulations and the popularity of urban warfare video games (Power 2007). In the most important electronically simulated urban war game entitled 'Urban Resolve', a huge swathe of eight square miles of Jakarta (the capital of Indonesia) has been carefully digitised and 'geo-specifically' simulated in three dimensions. This has been done down to the interior of the (1.6 million) buildings and also involves 109,000 mobile 'vehicles' and 'civilians', as well as the subterranean infrastructures. The initiative is being used as the basis for a series of massive military simulations, between 2003 and 2008 (see Figure 9.2). These project the city as the site of a massive urban war involving US forces in 2015, complete with a range

Figure 9.2 The digital rendition of Jakarta as part of the 'Urban Resolve' war games which simulate a major insurgency in 2015.

of imagined new US sensors and weapons geared towards warfare in a megacity. In this imaginative geography, the primary recognition of urban citizens is as dumb software avatars within a landscape of targets. Thus, the time-space rhythms of the virtualised 'Jakarta' have even been simulated, but only to add realism to the urban battlespace: 'roads are quiet at night, but during weekday rush hours they become clogged with traffic. People go to work, take lunch breaks and visit restaurants, banks and churches' (Walker 2004).

Technophiliac unveilings of Global South cities: Dreams of 'real-time situational awareness'

The first key effort to redirect the RMA to the domination and control of Global South cities involve programmes designed to saturate the urban environment with myriads of networked surveillance systems. The dream of US military theorists is of the automatic identification of targets and exposing them to the high-technology tracking and killing powers of 'network-centric' weapons. Such visions imagine pervasive and interlined arrays of 'loitering' and 'embedded' sensors, overcoming the limits and interruptions of megacity environments. Ackerman, for example, suggests that these sensor suites will be designed to automatically trace dynamic change rather than merely soaking up data from unchanging environments: observing 'change' rather than observing 'scenery', as he puts it. In other words, algorithms will be designed to function only when definable changes occur. They will thus identify purported notions of 'normality' against the 'abnormal' behaviours and patterns that can then be assessed as targets (Ackerman 2002).

A notable example of this development is the tellingly titled 'Combat Zones that See' (CTS) project led by the US Defense Advanced Research Projects Agency (DARPA) (Figure 9.3). Launched at the start of the Iraq insurgency in 2003, CTS 'explores concepts, develops algorithms and delivers systems for utilizing large numbers (1000s) of algorithmic video cameras to provide the close-in sensing demanded for military operations in urban terrain' (DARPA 2003). Through installing computerised CCTV across whole occupied cities, the project organisers envisage that, when deployed, CTS will sustain 'motion-pattern analysis across whole city scales', linked to the tracking of individual cars and people through intelligent computer algorithms designed to recognise number plates and human faces. The launch report, *Combat Zones that See*, suggests that it:

Combat Zones That See
Multi-Camera Surveillance for Urban Operations

Briefing to Industry

BAA 03-15

Thomas M. Strat
Information Exploitation Office
tstrat@darpa.mil

Figure 9.3 The 'Combat Zones that See' project under development by the Pentagon's Defense Advanced Research and Projects Agency (DARPA).

will produce video understanding algorithms embedded in surveillance systems for automatically monitoring video feeds to generate, for the first time, the reconnaissance, surveillance, and targeting information needed to provide close-in, continuous, always-on support for military operations in urban terrain. (DARPA 2003)

A direct response to the perceived interruptive effects of city environments on older notions of air- and space-based network-centric warfare, it is envisaged that, once it has been developed, CTS 'will generate, for the first time, the reconnaissance, surveillance and targeting information needed to provide close-in, continuous, always-on support for military operations in urban terrain' (DARPA 2003). It will be designed to specifically address the 'inherently three-dimensional nature of urban centres, with large buildings, extensive underground passageways, and concealment from above' (DARPA 2003).

The central challenge of CTS, according to DARPA, will be to build up fully representative data profiles on the 'normal' time–space movement patterns of entire subject cities so that algorithms could then use statistical modelling, and comprehensive 'target' databases, to 'determine what is normal and what is not'.[15] This will be a purported aid to identifying insurgents' activities and real or potential attacks, as well as warning of the presence or movement of target or suspect vehicles or individuals. The report states that the CTS project will:

> include ... analysis of changes in normalcy modes; detection of variances in activity; anomaly detection based on statistical analyses; discovery of links between places, subjects and times of activities; and direct comparison and correlation of track data to other information available to operators. Predictive modelling, plan recognition, and behavior modeling should alert operators to potential force protection risks and hostile situations. Forensic information (where did a vehicle come from, how did it get here?) should be combined and contrasted to more powerful 'forward-tracking' capabilities (where could the vehicle go?, where is the vehicle going?) to allow operators to provide real-time capabilities to assess potential force threats. (DARPA 2003)

After a stream of protests from US civil liberties groups, DARPA stressed that, whilst the initial test of mass, urban tracking will take place at a US Army base within the USA (Fort Belvoir, Virginia), the deployment of CTS will only take place in 'Foreign urban battlefields' (Sniffen 2003). Other DARPA programmes rest similarly on dreams of saturating complex urban landscapes with millions of networked sensors, which render all physical barriers transparent to the electronic gaze of algorithmic 'processual infrastructures'. The 'Visibuilding' programme, for example (Figure 9.4), aims to develop sensors through which ground forces and unmanned aerial vehicles can remotely sense the people and objects within buildings.

'Persistent area dominance': Towards robotic killing systems in urban warfare?

The second main area of defence research and development to help assert the dominance of US forces over Global South cities focuses on a shift towards robotic air and ground weapons which, when linked to these surveillance and target identification systems, will continually and automatically destroy purported targets in potentially endless streams of automated killing. It seems that the urban turn of RMA is now influenced by dual military fantasies of divine omnipotence and omniscience. In the first instance, there is the fixation with a 'sentient' surveillance – an almost God-like 'situational awareness' – which can oversee the intrinsically 'unruly' megacities of the Global South (see Figure 9.5). But even more

Figure 9.4 DARPA's Visibuilding programme: an attempt to build and deploy sensors that render urban-built fabric transparent.

Figure 9.5 Raytheon's vision of future urban combat, in which a range of sensors and weapons allow US forces to dominate an occupied city.

intimidating is that this surveillance infrastructure is dovetailed with automated machines for killing.[16] A telling example comes from the discussion of a model, near-future US 'urban operation', described by *Defense Watch* magazine during its discussions of DARPA's CTS Programme just discussed.[17] In their scenario, swarms of micro-scale and nano-scale networked sensors pervade the target city, providing continuous streams of information to arrays of automated weaponry. Together, these systems would produce continuous killing and 'target' destruction: a kind of robotised counter-insurgency operation, with US commanders and soldiers doing little but overseeing the cyborganised and automated killing systems from a safe distance. *Defense Watch* thus speculate about 'a battlefield in the near future' that is wired up with the systems which result from the CTS programme and its followers. Here, unbound technophiliac dreams of urban control blur into long-standing fantasies of cyborganised and robotised warfare. 'Several large fans are stationed outside the city limits of an urban target that our [sic] guys need to take', they begin:

> Upon appropriate signal, what appears like a dust cloud emanates from each fan. The cloud is blown into town where it quickly dissipates. After a few minutes of processing by laptop-size processors, a squadron of small, disposable aircraft ascends over the city. The little drones dive into selected areas determined by the initial analysis of data transmitted by the fan-propelled swarm. Where they disperse their nano-payloads. (*Defense Watch* 2004)

'After this, the processors get even more busy', continues the scenario:

> Within minutes the mobile tactical center have a detailed visual and audio picture of every street and building in the entire city. Every hostile [person] has been identified and located. From this point on, nobody in the city moves without the full and complete knowledge of the mobile tactical center. As blind spots are discovered, they can quickly be covered by additional dispersal of more nano-devices. Unmanned air and ground vehicles can now be vectored directly to selected targets to take them out, one by one. Those enemy combatants clever enough to evade actually being taken out by the unmanned units can then be captured or killed by human elements who are guided directly to their locations, with full and complete knowledge of their individual fortifications and defenses ... When the dust settles on competitive bidding for BAA 03-15 [the code number for the 'Combat Zones That See' programme], and after the first prototypes are delivered several years from

now, our guys are in for a mind-boggling treat at the expense of the bad guys. (*Defense Watch* 2004)

Such omnipotence fantasies extend even further to the automated surveillance, through emerging brain-scanning techniques, of people's inner mental attitudes to any US invasion. This allows 'targets' deemed to be resistant to be automatically identified and destroyed:

> Robotic systems push deeper into the urban area ... Behind the fighters, military police and intelligence personnel process the inhabitants, electronically reading their attitudes toward the intervention and cataloguing them into a database immediately recoverable by every fire team in the city (even individual weapons might be able to read personal signatures, firing immediately upon cueing ... Smart munitions track enemy systems and profiled individuals ... Satellites monitor the city for any air defense fires, curing immediate responses from near-space orbiting 'guns'. Drones track inhabitants who have been 'read' as potentially hostile and 'tagged'. (*Defense Watch* 2004)

Such dreams of continuous, automated and robotised urban targeting and killing are far from being limited to the realms of futuristic speculation, however. Rather, as with the CTS programme, they are fuelling contemporary weapons research aimed at developing ground and aerial vehicles which not only navigate and move robotically, but which, on the basis of algorithmically driven 'decisions', select and destroy targets without 'humans in the loop'.

Maryann Lawlor, for example, discusses the development of 'autonomous mechanized combatant' air and ground vehicles or 'tactical autonomous combatants' for the US Air Force (Lawlor 2004). These are being designed, he notes, to use 'pattern recognition' software for what he calls 'time-critical targeting': linking sensors to automated weapons so that fleeting 'targets' both within and outside cities can be continually destroyed. Such doctrine is widely termed 'compressing the kill chain' or 'sensor to shooter warfare' in US military parlance (Herbert 2003). The 'swarming of unmanned systems' project team at the US Forces Joint Command experimentation directorate, based in Norfolk, Virginia, he states, are so advanced in such experimentation that 'autonomous, networked and integrated robots may be the norm rather than the exception by 2025'.

By that date, Lawlor predicts that 'technologies could be developed ... that would allow machines to sense a report of gunfire in an urban environment to within one metre, triangulating the position of the shooter and return fire within a fraction of a second', providing a completely automated weapon system devoid of human involvement. She quotes Gordon Johnson, the 'Unmanned Effects' team leader for the US Army's 'Project Alpha', as saying of such a system:

> if it can get within one meter, it's killed the person who's firing. So, essentially, what we're saying is that anyone who would shoot at our forces would die. Before he can drop that weapon and run, he's probably already dead. Well now, these cowards in Baghdad would have to play with blood and guts every time they shoot at one of our folks. The costs of poker went up significantly ... [are] the enemy ... going to give up blood and guts to kill machines? I'm guessing not. (Lawlor 2004)

Lawlor predicts that such robo-war systems will 'help save lives by taking humans out of harm's way'. In this model, however, only US forces fall within the category 'human'.

In a further development, unmanned aerial vehicles armed with 'intelligent munitions' are already being designed, which will, eventually, be programmed to fire on, and kill, 'targets' detected by US force's real-time surveillance grids, in a completely autonomous way. Crucially, such munitions will be equipped with algorithms designed to separate 'targets' from 'non-targets' automatically. The ultimate goals, according to Pinney, an engineer at weapons company Raytheon, is what he calls a 'kill chain solution' based on '1st look, 1st feed, 1st kill', where each armed, unmanned vehicle continuously 'seeks out targets on its own' (Pinney 2003) (see Figure 9.6). Tirpak, a US Air Force specialist, envisages that humans will be required to make the decisions to launch weapons at targets only 'until unmanned combat air vehicles (UCAVs) establish a track record of reliability in finding the right targets and employing weapons properly'. Then the 'machines will be trusted to do even that' (Tirpack 2001).

Conclusions

This chapter suggests that it is important to incorporate the sentient and 'visual' capabilities of machines and cyborganised systems into discussions about geopolitics and visual culture. In particular, it is clear that a major strand of Western military research and development aims to render the complex three-dimensional geographies of Global South cities transparent

AUTONOMOUS TARGET RECOGNITION

See-Through-the-Wall Radar

- Adaptive Learning
- Advanced Processor
- Biometrics
- Cognitive Computing
- Data/Image Exploitation
- Distributed ATR
- Distributed Tracking
- Human Aided ATR
- Information Fusion
- Situational Awareness

Future Force Visualization

From UAV   From Smart Grenade

Smart Grenade

Distributed Robotics

Autonomous UAV

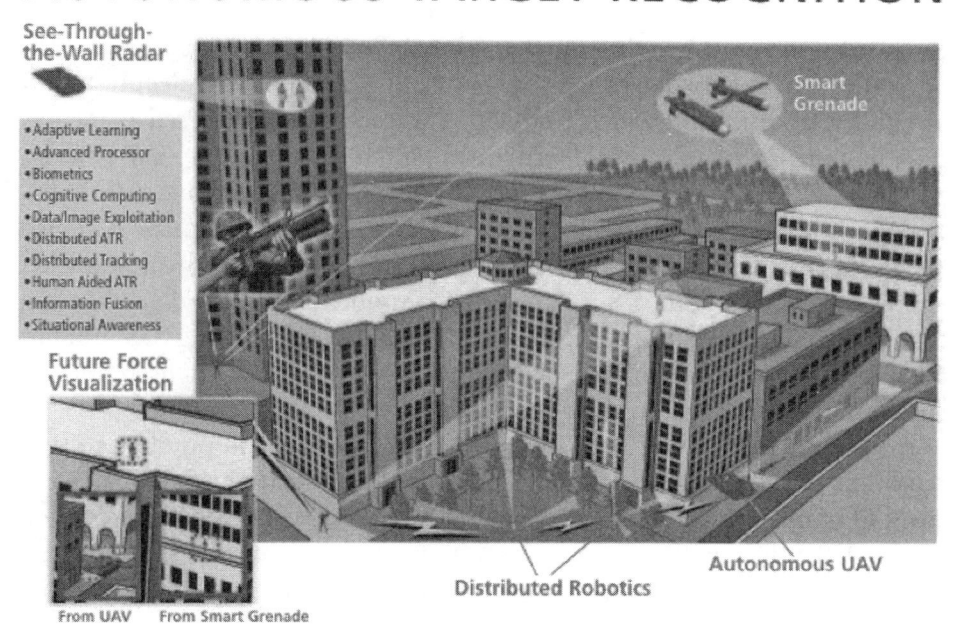

Figure 9.6 An image from a Raytheon military sales brochure envisaging a range of near-future surveillance and weapons systems which can recognise 'targets' automatically.

to the machinic and algorithmic gaze of military technologies. The recent disasterous engagement in Iraq has lent a particular momentum to this 'urban turn' in the RMA. Its constituent programmes are a result of a major 'supply push' by an increasingly integrated complex of surveillance, corrections and military corporations, who are trying to exploit the disastrous experience of US forces in Iraq's cities since 2003. In this context, it is relatively easy to sell dreams of omniscience and, crucially, the promise of removing the bodies of US personnel far from the dangers of the urban streets they are attempting to occupy. Scenarios in which sentient robot warriors autonomously dispatch any adversary emerging from the urban labyrinth add to the political attractiveness of the ultimate in 'asymmetric' war. It is a model in which the archetypal insurgent, necessarily relying on their corporeal presence and locality, sacrifices themselves in futile exchanges with autonomous robot drones tied to distantiated webs of command and control. Such dreams of autonomous surveillance, targeting and killing machines, tailored to overcome the interruptive effects of urban geographies, raise three further points for discussion.

Firstly, the promise of delegating the military gaze to autonomous machines, animated by computer algorithms, is more than just a military tactic to control the cities of the Global South. It also connects very powerfully with broader trances of Western visual culture, deeply tied to orientalist traditions in which Arab cities are invariably rendered as intrinsically devious and labyrinthine structures which are opaque to the penetrative gaze of Western geopolitical power. They are places where, in Derek Gregory's words, 'deceit and danger threaten ... at every turn' (Gregory 2004: 202). Take, for example, the popular range of urban warfare video games produced by the US military for commercial and popular use using the electronic simulations originally developed for training US military personnel for urban combat. Such games rely entirely on stylised and orientalised depictions of Arab urban areas.

A universal feature of both urban RMA discourses and popular cultural renditions of Arab cities in video games is the reduction of Global South cities to uninhabited spaces whose geographies resist the verticalised power of the US military. These discourses sustain the dehumanisation of the urban citizens through the hyper-militarised and technophiliac rhetoric that dominates the US military. This process, in turn, renders the lives, deaths and citizenship of these inhabitants of no account. For, in trying to render physical cityscapes transparent to the both algorithmic gaze of Western military techno-science and the immersed, voyeuristic gaze of the video game player, paradoxically, the inhabitants and social worlds of such cities simultaneously become invisible. 'Cities' are reduced to pure 'battlespace'. Urban populations become 'targets' to be tracked, surveyed and, if necessary, 'neutralised'. One of the casualties of this system is the notion of the civilian: discussions about 'asymmetric', 'network-centric' or 'unrestricted' warfare effectively means that all bodies, everywhere, must be treated, *a priori*, as adversaries (Gregory 2006).

Secondly, I would argue that the 'urban' turn in the RMA involves an important rescaling process in the geographical and geopolitical imaginaries of the Western military. Instead of rendering the globe as a single, integrated 'battlespace' to be controlled through the real-time systems of network-centric warfare – as was typical in the first generation of RMA discussions – military planners now address the microgeographical landscapes of streets, buildings, tunnels and cities. The world of the city once again becomes the pre-eminent space of geopolitical contest. Heralding the possibility of a new relationship between warfare, techno-science and the organisation of space, these encounters bring with them a highlycharged politics of seeing – a geopolitics of differential exposure and (in)visibility.

But such a politics moves beyond familiar postcolonial concerns with the gaze and the imaginative geographies of orientalism. Rather, it forces the consideration of what media theorist Jordan Crandall (2005) calls the 'tracking-gaze' and how the social matrix of anticipatory seeing, with computer algorithms as key agents, brings with it a new geopolitics of visuality. For Crandall, this complex of tracking technologies 'moves away from a focus on perspective and position to one of movement-flow'. It 'is a convenience- and security-driven network ontology that requires its own threatening other'. Moreover, it brings with it a post-optical politics of (attempted) control and subordination, which is now being closely inscribed into the geographies of Western military incursions in the rapidly urbanising Global South.

Thirdly, however, it is important to stress that the 'urban turn' of the RMA is both contested and contingent. Even within the US military, many are deeply sceptical that new tracking and targeting systems will ever offer anything like the levels of persistent military control over extended urban areas portrayed by those selling the hardware. Many in the US Army and Marines, especially, are unconvinced that these autonomous and robotic weapons will ever challenge the need for a large infantry presence to cover the extending geographies of cities occupied by US forces.

Clearly, as the war in Iraq has demonstrated, the 'fog of war' persists despite such systems. Urban surveillance systems always amount to an 'oligopticon' rather than an all-seeing panopticon. As Caroline Croser (2007) has shown, when one looks beyond these apocalyptic posthuman fantasies to address the ways in which new military technologies are actually used, a much less certain picture emerges. Systems fail or work in unexpected ways. Trajectories and encounters are complex, counter-intuitive and unpredictable. Human agency emerges through technosocial assemblages which are shaped by the 'little things' of practice rather than the grand imaginings of technophiliac fantasy (Thrift 2000). It is also important to look beyond the assumptions of absolute technological omniscience to stress that many urban spaces inevitably remain unknown and unknowable, even with the intensifying power of tracking technologies.

The contestation of the 'urban' turn in the RMA also involves a range of social movements, who are problematising the imperial urban geographies of the 'war on terror'. Here, attention is focusing on the broader installation of tracking and surveillance systems covering Western cities and urban infrastructures. As with the mobilisation against the 'Combat Zones That See' initiative discussed above, the possibilities that algorithmic tracking systems might be applied in Western cities is the primary concern of such critiques. All of this is just the latest in a long line of innovations in urban planning, security, surveillance and military technology, which rapidly diffuse from the sites of first application in colonised cities to the urban heartlands at the core of Empire.

For all the criticism of the 'urban turn' in the RMA, to which this essay is itself a contribution, the opponents of this development face some formidable obstacles. The scale of resources currently being devoted to automated urban war mean that military systems are being developed that might offer US commanders a continuous, robotised and largely invisible counter-insurgency warfare in Global South cities within the medium-term future. Some of the weapons discussed here are already on the verge of deployment; many more capable ones seem likely to follow. The clear risk here is that discourses emphasising the biopolitical rights of US soldiers to be withdrawn from the streets of urban war zones might add justification to the deployment of automated killing systems which bring urban civilians into the cross-hairs of an aggressive military hegemon.

All of this is affirmed in the Pentagon's military doctrine of 'The Long War', which gives further weight to new surveillance, tracking and targeting systems in the form of drones which are robotic, unmanned, armed and increasingly autonomous. With a political retreat from large-scale expeditionary war looking very likely following the disaster in Iraq, low-intensity and persistent incursions based on the continuous presence of robotic drones will become even more politically attractive. It is clear then that the military effectiveness and omniscient reach of algorithmic tracking and targeting systems can never exceed the fantasies that support their development. It is also clear that urban incursions will always be more risky and problematic than these fantasies suggest. At the same time, however, the new military surveillance complexes and the geopolitics of Global South urbanisation are now irretrievably entwined, not least because the massed invasion of Iraq's cities by large numbers of traditional infantry has been such a conspicuous failure. Further interventions will probably follow this same strategic imperative, one that attempts to see without being seen.

Bibliography

Ackerman, Robert, 'Persistent surveillance comes into view', *Signal Magazine*, available at www.afcea.org/signal/ (accessed February 2005).

Arquilla, John and Ronfeldt, David (eds), *Networks and Netwars* (RAND: Santa Monica, 2001).

Barnett, Thomas, *The Pentagon's New Map: War and Peace in the 21st Century* (Putnam: New York, 2004).

Barocas, Solon, '9-11: A strategic ontology: Pre-emptive strike and the production of (in)security', *InfoTechWarPeace* (6 August 2004), www.watsoninstitute.org/infopeace/ (accessed 4 January 2010).

Bellamy, Craig, 'If the cities do not fall to the Allies, there may be no alternative to siege warfare', *Independent* (28 March 2003), p.3.

Campbell, David, 'Geopolitics and visuality: Sighting the Darfur conflict', *Political Geography* 26 (2007), pp.357–82.

Crandall, John, *Drive: Technology, Mobility, and Desire* (Ostfildern-Ruit: Hatje-Kranz, 2002).

Crandall, John, 'Envisioning the homefront: Militarization, tracking and security culture', *Journal of Visual Culture* 4 (2005), pp.1–22.

Croser, Caroline, 'Networking security in the space of the city: Event-ful battlespaces and the contingency of the encounter', *Theory & Event* 10 (2007), available at: http://muse.jhu.edu/journals/theory_and_event/v010/10.2croser.html (accessed January 2008).

DARPA (2003) *Combat Zones That See Program: Program Information*, www.darpa.mil (accessed February 2004).

Davis, Mike, 'The urbanization of Empire: Megacities and the laws of chaos', *Social Text* 22 (2004a), pp.9–15.

Davis, Mike, 'The Pentagon as global slum lord', *TomDispatch*, http://www.tomdispatch.com/ (accessed 19 April 2004b).

Defense Intelligence Reference Center (DIRC), *The Urban Century: Developing World Urban Trends and Possible Factors Affecting Military Operations* (Quantico, VA: Marine Corps Intelligence Agency, 1997).

Defense Watch (2004), 'Combat zones that "see" everything', http://www.argee.net/DefenseWatch/Combat%20Zones%20that%20See%20Everything.htm

Dickson, Karen, 'The war on terror: Cities as the strategic high ground' (Mimeo, 2002).

Dodds, Klaus, 'Licensed to stereotype: Popular geopolitics, James Bond and the spectre of Balkanism', *Geopolitics* 8 (2003), pp.125–56.

Duffield, Mark, 'War as a network enterprise: The new security terrain and its implications', *Cultural Values* 6 (2002), pp.153–65.

Ek, Richard, 'A revolution in military geopolitics?', *Political Geography* 19 (2000), pp.841–74.

Franklin, Bruce, *War Stars: The Superweapon in the American imagination* (Oxford: Oxford University Press, 1988).

Gannon, Charles, *Rumors of War and Infernal Machines: Technomilitary agenda-setting in American and British speculative fiction* (Liverpool: Liverpool University Press, 2003).

Glenn, Russell, Steeb, Randall and Matsumura, John (eds), *Corralling the Trojan Horse: A Proposal for Improving US Urban Operations Preparedness in the Period, 2000–2025* (Santa Monica, California: RAND, 2001).

Graham, Stephen, 'Vertical geopolitics: Baghdad and after', *Antipode* 36 (2004), pp.12–19.

Graham, Stephen, 'Switching cities off: Urban infrastructure and US air power', *City* 9 (2005), pp.190–2.

Graham, Stephen, 'Cities and the "war on terror"', *International Journal of Urban and Regional Research* 30 (2006), pp.155–76.

Grau, Lestor and Kipp, Jacob, 'Urban combat: Confronting the spectre', *Military Review* (1999), pp.9–17.

Gregory, Derek, *The Colonial Present* (Oxford: Blackwell, 2004).

Gregory, Derek, 'The death of the civilian', *Environment and Planning D: Society and Space* 24 (2006) pp.633–8.

Grubbs, Lee, *In Search of a Joint Urban Operational Concept* (Fort Leavenworth, Kansas: School of Advanced Military Studies, 2003).

Harris, Andrew, 'Can new technologies transform military operations in urban terrain?', *Small Wars Journal* (2003), available at: www.smallwarsjournal.com/documents/harris.pdf (accessed [?]).

Hewish, Mark and Pengelley, Rupert, 'Facing urban inevitabilities: Military operations in urban terrain', *Jane's International Defence Review* (August 2001), pp.13–18.

Hills, Alice, *Future Wars in Cities* (London: Frank Cass, 2004).

Houlgate, Kelly, 'Urban warfare transforms the Corps', *Naval Institute Proceedings* (November 2004), available at: http://www.military.com/NewContent/0,13190,NI_1104_Urban-P1,00.html (accessed February 2005).

Huber, Peter and Mills, Matt, 'How technology will defeat terrorism', *City Journal* 12 (2002), pp.22–4.

Hughes, Rachel, 'Through the looking blast: Geopolitics and visual culture', *Geography Compass* 1 (2007), pp.976–94.

Kirsch, Scott, 'Empire and the Bush doctrine', *Environment and Planning D: Society and Space* 21 (2003), pp.1–6.

Lawlor, Maryann, 'Robotic concepts take shape', *Signal Magazine*, available at: www.afcea.org/signal/ (February 2005).

Leonhard, Robert, 'Sun Tzu's bad advice: Urban warfare in the information age', *Army Magazine* (April 2003), available at: http://www.ausa.org/www/armymag.nsf/0/AA1C74DA9302525585256CEF005EED3D?OpenDocument (accessed February 2005).

MacDonald, Fraser, 'Geopolitics and "the vision thing": Regarding Britain and America's first nuclear missile', *Transactions of the Institute of British Geographers* 31 (2006), pp.53–71.

Misselwitz, P. and Weizman, E., 'Military operations as urban planning', in Franke Anselm, Chase Jefferson and Klaus Bisenbach (eds), *Territories* (Berlin: KW Institute for Contemporary Art, 2003), pp.272–5.

Norton, Richard, 'Feral cities', *Naval War College Review* 56 (2003), pp.97–106.

O'Mara, Raymond, 'Stealth, precision, and the making of American foreign policy', *Air and Space Power Chronicles* (June 2003), available at: www.airpower.maxwell.af.mil/airchronicles/cc/omara.html (accessed February 2005).

Peters, Ralph, 'Our soldiers, their cities', *Parameters* 26 (1996), pp.43–50.

Pieterse, Jan, 'Neoliberal empire', *Theory, Culture and Society* 21 (2004), pp.118–40.

Pinney, Chuckan, *UAV Weaponization* (Washington, DC: Raytheon, 2003).

Power, Marcus, 'Digitized virtuosity: Video war games and post 9/11 cyber-deterrence', *Security Dialogue* 38 (2007), pp.271–88.
Project for the New American Century, *Rebuilding Americas Defenses* (Washington: Project for the New American Century, 2000).
Roberts, Susan, Secor, Anna and Sparke, Matt, 'Neoliberal geopolitics', *Antipode* 35 (2004), pp.886–97.
Sharp, Joanne, 'Hegemony, popular culture and geopolitics: *The Reader's Digest* and the construction of danger', *Political Geography* 15 (1996), pp.557–70.
Stone, John, 'Politics, technology and the revolution in military affairs', *Journal of Strategic Studies* 27 (2004), pp.408–27.
Taw, Jennifer and Hoffman, Bruce, *The Urbanization of Insurgency* (Santa Monica, California: RAND, 2000).
Thrift, Nigel, 'It's the little things', in Klaus Dodds and David Atkinson (eds), *Geopolitical Traditions: A Century of Geopolitical Thought* (London: Routledge, 2000), pp.380–7.
Tirpak, J., 'Heavyweight contender', *Air Force Magazine* 85 (2001), available at: http://www.afa.org/magazine/July2002/ (accessed 15 August 2005).
Virilio, Paul, *Desert Screen: War at the Speed of Light* (London: Continuum, 2002).
Walker, Richard, 'Urban resolve', *Small Wars Journal* (2004), available at: http://www.smallwarsjournal.com/blog.htm/UrbanResolve (accessed 15 August 2005).

Chapter 10

Eye to Eye: Biometrics, the Observer, the Observed and the Body Politic
Emily Gilbert

> Everyone is unique. Let us keep it that way.
> (UK Home Office, Identity and Passport Service[1])

A man in a dark business suit approaches a counter at the international airport. Leaning in towards an automated teller, a fine line of infrared light pans across his eye (Figure 10.1). The complex texture of his iris patterns is read, coded and checked against multiple databases. Seconds later, when the machine registers approval, the man marches past the security line-ups and into the members' lounge, where he loosens his tie and flips open his laptop computer. His identity has been secured. This is the easy passage that awaits thousands of air travellers who have joined border pre-clearance programmes that rely on biometrics to expedite security clearance. The securitisation of identity based on unique, bodily characteristics is increasingly widespread, helped by technological advances that make them less intrusive in their application. Special instruments capture and record the patterns of body parts – fingerprint swirls, retinal blood vessels, face scans, etc. – rendering three-dimensional bodies into two-dimensional representations. The biometric is then linked up to a wide array of information that can span across legal, financial, medical and educational domains. It is against this information that identities are verified – a confirmation is made, as in the example above, that the subject is who he says he is. Alternatively, information in the database could flag this individual as a potential risk who warrants additional security measures.

Figure 10.1 Clear traveller at kiosk at Oakland International Airport, USA.
Source: Clear, reproduced with permission

Touted as a key prong in the 'war on terror', biometrics have become integral to national security programmes, specifically with regard to the regulation of borders (see Gill 2004). States are also turning the biometric gaze inwards to secure their domestic populations; proposals for national identity cards proliferate, and some countries, such as Canada, have already implemented biometric identity cards for non-nationals. After the 2011 census in India, a new biometric Multi-Purpose National Identity Card (MNIC) will be introduced as part of the compulsory regulation of all citizens and non-citizens in the country. But biometrics are not only deployed by the state. They are increasingly used at sporting events, including the Olympics in Atlanta and Athens; for hotel workers and patrons, at the boutique Nine Zero Hotel in Boston; and at clubs in the Netherlands and the UK, where they are used to control the entry of blacklisted patrons or simply to monitor those taking outdoor smoking breaks. Commercial applications have also expanded, from biometric security features on laptop computers, to SmartScan locks that are fingerprint activated. Iris-recognition products in bank ATMs are underway in the USA, UK and Japan, and in 2007, Hitachi announced the development of a finger vein reader to be used in a cash-less credit payment system. Several Piggly Wiggly stores in South Carolina have used a fingerprint reader in lieu of a debit card since 2005.

In each of these cases, the sorting of the population through biometrics reinforces notions of belonging, entitlement and authenticity (Lyon 2002). This chapter examines the geopolitical dimensions of this biometric sorting, attending to the ways that technologies of visualisation are mobilised to reconfigure social relations in time and place. To investigate this dynamic, I draw upon critical research in geography that considers the spatial politics of the visual. Much of this work demonstrates a particular interest in the discipline's own heavy investment in representations such as surveys, maps and GIS. Gillian Rose, for instance, criticises geography's ocularcentrism for a disembodied visualization that all too often reinforces gender dichotomies (Rose 1993). Research on visuality and critical geopolitics poses further questions about territory and political power (see MacDonald 2006; Amoore 2007; Campbell 2007). Fraser MacDonald, for example, traces the ways that geographical power 'operates through sites and spectacles' with respect to the performativity of military visual fields (MacDonald 2006: 53). As he eloquently asserts, 'to have a target in sight is already to have changed the relation between subject and object' (MacDonald 2006: 57). An analysis of military targeting thus requires moving beyond identifying what sites are made visible, to a more embodied examination of the practices through which they are made visible, to whom and in what contexts (see also Kearnes 2000).

In this chapter, I engage with these geographical critiques alongside the cultural work on vision, particularly that of Jonathan Crary. In his groundbreaking *Techniques of the Observer*, Crary raises two key questions (1991: 2). First: 'how is the body, including the observing body, becoming a component of new machines, economics, apparatuses, whether social, libidinal or technological?' And second: 'in what ways is subjectivity becoming a precarious condition of interface between rationalised systems of exchange and networks of information?' These questions frame my analysis here, much as they frame Crary's own project to destabilise the evolutionary accounts of visual transparency and accuracy. He charts the shift in scopic regimes across the nineteenth century, from camera obscura through to the stereoscope, which entailed a reorganisation of visual registers and a reconstitution of the observer. This paper extends Crary's historical analysis into the present to consider the proliferation of biometrics and what this means for understanding the bodies of the observer and the observed, the social body and geopolitical relations. In what follows, I begin by briefly outlining Crary's analysis which I use to identify three lines of enquiry for the study of biometrics. How is the relationship between the body and the body politic being recalibrated? How are space and time reconfigured through new technologies of visualisation? And finally, in what ways do biometric technologies reconstitute the observer and the observed? Do they see eye to eye?

Scopic regimes

In *Critical Geopolitics*, Gearóid Ó Tuathail asserts that traditional geopolitics has been 'ocularcentric ... with a natural attitude, a philosophical approach to reality grounded in Cartesian perspectivalism' (MacDonald 2006: 54). In this way, geopolitics is aligned with the dominant scopic regime of modernity that Martin Jay describes as 'rational, ordering and controlling' (Heffernan 2000: 348). There is a tendency towards both mimetic and 'authentic' visual representations and an imposition of this sense of natural order on the ground. Urban planning, with the 'geometric, isotropic, rectilinear, abstract and uniform space' manifest in grid cities, is one such example (Jay 1993: 125). Multiple attempts have been made to disrupt claims to a singular, visual Cartesian truth. Jay does so by underscoring the suspicion to the visual that emerges in early twentieth-century French thought. Surrealist art, for example, revealed an acute loss of innocence and confidence in the power of the eye. The visual contortions of war – from the blinding gunfire of the trenches, to the gas-induced haze of the battlefield, to the trickery of camouflage – all contributed to the destabilisation of the ocular, and the emergence of an alternative visual register of disillusion (Jay 1994: 174).

Crary's examination of the technical and discursive dimensions of visual technologies is equally disruptive. In *Techniques of the Observer* (1991), he undermines the evolutionary accounts that cast nineteenth-century representational innovations – such as photography and film – as heir to the camera obscura and its rendering of perspective. From the late 1500s the camera obscura, with its projection of an accurate, objective and authentic image, had become the model for understanding the relationship between

Figure 10.2 Camera obscura, 'Fig. 3' from A. Rees' *Cyclopaedia, or Universal Dictionary of Arts and Sciences*, 1786.
Reproduced with kind permission of the National Maritime Museum, Greenwich, London

observer and the world. The device, generally box-shaped but of almost any size, is pierced with a pinhole through which a stream of light penetrates (Figure 10.2). An image is projected, upside-down, onto the back wall of the box, so that the three-dimensional image is rendered onto a two-dimensional field, in correct perspective. This became the foundational model of 'authentic' or 'truthful' representation, conveyed by 'an infallible vantage point' (Crary 1988a: 31–2). It features widely in seventeenth-century thought, from Descartes' *Dioptrics*, to Locke's *Essay on Human Understanding* (and Leibniz's critique of Locke), and is central to the technical and cultural practices of Kepler and Newton. These accounts celebrated a decorporealised vision and insisted upon a stark differentiation between inside and outside space which the camera obscura so clearly required. The observer is posited as 'a free sovereign individual ... who is also a privatised isolated subject enclosed in a quasi-domestic space separated from a public exterior world' (Crary 1991: 39). The model of the camera obscura thus entrenched a categorical distinction between subject and object, inside and outside, and public and private spheres in mimetic representation.

Crary, however, turns to the writings of figures such as Kant, Goethe, Blake and Schopenhauer to uncover a latent, 'subject-centered epistemology', whereby the visible is lodged 'within the unstable physiology and temporality of the human body' (Crary 1988b: 5). Goethe, for example, draws upon the camera obscura in very different ways. He shifts his attention to the retinal after-images created when the observer stares first into the light and then into darkness. The lingering orb of light, rounded by a floating spectrum of colours, suggests to Goethe that colour and vision are not properties that exist outside the observer, but rather are produced by the individual's own 'corporeal subjectivity' (Crary 1991: 69). Moreover, Goethe's ruminations imply that 'optical truth' is realised not in the clarity of full light, but in the 'turbid, cloudy or gloomy' moment when light has been extinguished, when the after-image lingers (Crary 1991: 71). Crary situates this alternative epistemological model of vision alongside the explosion of physiological studies in the early nineteenth century, when vision itself became subject to the clinical gaze and the eye became a 'field of statistical information' (Crary 1988a: 36). In the realm of visual technologies, the camera obscura is displaced by the thaumatrope, phenakistiscope, kaleidoscope and stereoscope, which all rely upon visual 'tricks' or optical illusions to render complex representations. The jumble of planes and surfaces of the stereoscope, for example, relied on the 'work' undertaken by the observer's eyes to render a three-dimensional visual order (Crary 1991: 132).

Crary's alternative narrative of visual technologies, like much of the critical work in geography, thus insists that the subject is not detached from that which is observed, but is intrinsic to the very production of the scopic regime. But Crary pushes his analysis still further to examine how these alternative visual technologies recalibrated space and time. The differentiation between 'interior representation and exterior reality' that is intrinsic to the camera obscura is dissolved in favour of a 'single surface of affect ... cut from any spatial referent' (Crary 1991: 71). The scenic field is no longer privileged; rather, vision depends upon a visual propinquity between viewer and visual device that is not dependent on location. Moreover, vision and temporality become wedded, in that mimesis is projected through tricks of speed, light and movement, as evidenced with the stereoscope's appearance of depth. The fading impress of the after-image as it passes through the spectrum of colours reinforces this temporal emphasis. But although these alternative technologies permitted the observing subject to be liberated from a specific referent in space and time, they existed alongside new forms of biopolitical governance that were exercised in and through the body. Vision and the visual were increasingly ordered, even as the eye appeared to be loosened from context. Thus, as Crary illustrates, the observer came to be understood in the full sense of the term, as a subject who *observes* rules, codes, regulations and practices (Crary 1991: 5).

Crary's analysis of alternative visual technologies offers three important registers for understanding biometrics. First, the relentless narratives of visual mimesis, whereby the 'truthfulness' or 'accuracy' of representation rely on an abstract observer, are destabilised. By illustrating how technologies make the visible visible through processes of mechanisation, calculation, measurability and exchangeability, Crary reconstitutes the observer from a passive spectator to the producer of events. Second, this analysis provokes an engagement with the time-space dimensions of visual technologies. Historical and geographical contextualisation are implicit to this, and attention to representation, interpretation, circulation, consumption and commodification are required. Mimetic technologies such as the camera obscura, he suggests, are resolutely spatial in that they fix relations in terms of inside and outside, private and public, internal and external worlds. By contrast, the optical devices that rely on visual tricks emphasise the temporal in that they rely on the speed of light and the after-image. Although such neat categorisations of technologies as either time- or space-bound may be too simplistic, Crary's differentiation suggests the importance of identifying moments when new technologies help to open up alternative temporal or spatial epistemologies. Third, the interruption of evolutionary Cartesian perspectivalism challenges the persistent 'fiction of the "free" subject' (Crary 1991: 133). Crary attends to the visual play (illusion, hallucination, deception) that are part and parcel of mass and elite cultures, which implicitly complicate the integrity of a rational, autonomous, transparent self. Yet in so doing, he also draws attention to new forms of ordering as biopolitical governance is exercised in and through the body. The observer is not only a subject who bears witness, but a compliant subject. Visual technologies thus demand an analysis that extends beyond embodied subjectivity to consider the social and political dimensions of how observer and observed, bodies and body politic are constituted and reconstituted. These are issues that are explored in the following section, where I consider the geopolitical implications of biometrics in light of these three registers.

Techniques of the observer

On the surface, biometrics appear to cohere with the traditional model of the camera obscura, particularly with respect to the pervasive narratives of accuracy and truthfulness. Each model relies on the presumption of transparent and transcendent vision. But as Crary's work suggests, the disembodied scientific gaze is a fiction. What is necessary, then, is to examine how and why these narratives of accuracy and truthfulness endure by interrogating the mechanisms through which biometrics operate, and bringing into view the hidden ways that biometrics order information. Biometrics generally work by transforming a feature of the body (iris, retina, fingerprint, etc.) into a visual or numeric code (see Figure 10.3). As an identifier specific to the individual, the two-dimensional code becomes a unique mechanism for identity verification. In practice, however, the usefulness of the biometric relies upon how it is attached to databases of information which are used to sort the population. Even with this secondary step, biometric scans are touted to have great accuracy. Professor John G. Daugman, who developed the sophisticated algorithms which are used in all commercially developed iris-recognition technologies, refers to the border-crossing programmes in the United Arab Emirates as an example of biometric success. Daily about 6000 non-nationals have both irises scanned at the country's 27 land-, air- and sea-ports, with over 7.2 billion iris comparisons made daily and over 5 trillion comparisons since the programme's inception in 2001. The biometric is compared against a 'negative' watch-list of over 300,000 individuals who have been deemed untrustworthy or have been denied entry to the country. In this time, more than 47,000 people have been caught with false documentation. Daugman celebrates the success of the process, noting 'that so far there have been no matches made that were not eventually confirmed by other data' (2006: 1928).

As with many surveillance technologies, the putative successes of the programme are used to legitimise their use. Only rarely are errors noted, and at 1 per cent the rate of false matches is certainly low. Yet false matches are endemic to biometric sorting and, as Daugman notes elsewhere in his report, likely to increase proportionally with the size of the database

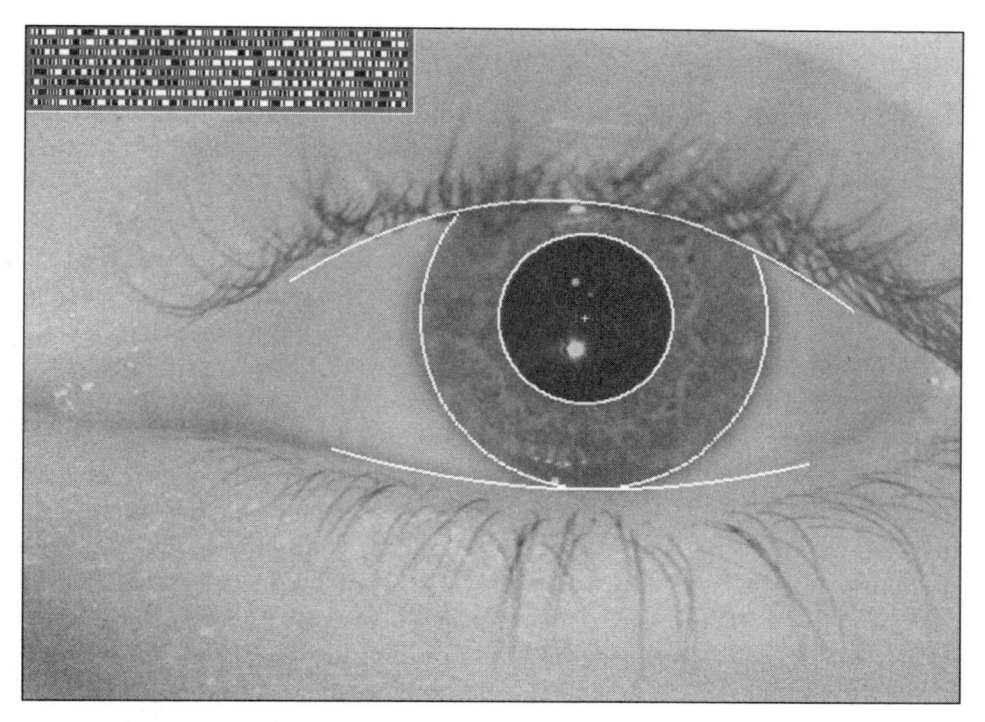

Figure 10.3 Example of an iris pattern, imaged monochromatically at a distance of about 35 cm. The outline overlay shows results of the iris and pupil localisation and eyelid detection steps. The bit stream in the top left is the result of demodulation, with complex-valued two-dimensional Gabor wavelets to encode the phase sequence of the iris pattern.
Source: Reproduced with kind permission of Professor John Daugman, Cambridge University

(Daugman 2006: 1934). Moreover, even the low rate of false matches can have a significant impact. Petermann, Sauter and Sherz remark that in a situation where up to 50 million travellers pass through an international airport in a year, 'even a false acceptance rate of only 1 per cent would trigger hundreds of false alarms per day' (Petermann et al 2006: 158). With other biometric technologies the numbers of false matches may be even higher. A variety of external conditions can effect face-recognition technology using CCTV: where the photograph is taken (inside or outside), whether the individual is solitary or in a busy public space, the time of day or if the subject has aged (Introna and Wood 2004).

These questions about the potential fallibility of visual technologies are important to keep in mind as they disrupt the simple narratives of biometric accuracy. So too does Daugman's observation that as databases expand, retaining a 1 per cent false match rate requires adjustments to the decision threshold policy. It is a reminder that biometrics are not sorted by an abstract, disembodied sovereign eye, but rather are susceptible to human decision-making. This partiality emerges in some of the critical work that has been undertaken on algorithms. As mathematical sets of instructions, algorithms seem to lie outside the realm of politics. Yet in their work on face-recognition surveillance, Introna and Wood (2004) illustrate that bias is embedded in the standard template and the patterns of recognition that are inbuilt. There is a great variability in rates of recognition on the basis of age, gender and race (see Introna and Wood 2004: 190). Faces that deviate from the standard (such as the faces of visible minorities) are more likely to trigger a mechanised and/or human response. Thus, a standard is inbuilt to which normalcy gets affixed, while those whose facial characteristics differ are implicitly construed as abnormal and targeted as potential 'risky subjects'. These processes are especially hard to detect when the underlying decision-making (the decision threshold policy) is obscured, and the comprehension of its mechanisms is in the hands of only a small number of experts. Moreover, the experts themselves perpetuate biases in the management of the data as a 'security continuum' is drawn across multiple and disparate realms – such as crime, unemployment and immigration – by security professionals (Bigo 2002). Inbuilt biases may by themselves be minimal, but they can become 'multiplied and magnified as they become tied to other practices' and spread across multiple networks (Introna and Wood 2004: 191).

With respect to the US-VISIT programme, for instance, migrants are checked against a wide and disparate group of databases, including foreign and exchange students, national crime watch and Interpol, foreign nationals claiming benefits, and an array of other databases on health, finance, banking and education (Amoore 2006: 339). This bundling of data is endemic. The national identity card to be introduced in India, while ostensibly introduced for the purpose of national security, will also be used to access financial, educational, medical, travel and social services. Very small transgressions or errors in one domain can easily trigger alerts in other unrelated areas. How the databases are derived is also a contentious issue. In Iraq, for example, police recruits are screened by US military personnel against the US Department of Defense's Biometric Identification System for Access (BISA) and the FBI's Integrated Automated Fingerprint Identification System (IAFIS) – which it promotes as the largest database in the world. But ironically, given its antipathy to the former government, part of this database is derived from Ba'ath Party records held by Saddam Hussein (Singel 2007). The situation is alarming given the suggestion that the growing biometric database might eventually be transformed into an Iraq-wide identification programme along the lines of the US social security registry. There are particular concerns that linking biometric information with other identifiers such as religion could have a devastating impact if used maliciously, a concern raised by the Electronic Privacy Information Center (Schachtman 2007).

What these examples suggest is that the sorting at the heart of biometrics is not neutral, transparent or benign. Rather, as Crary illustrates historically, there are hidden politics embedded in processes of mechanisation, calculation and measurability. Bringing this politics into view is especially important to dispel the rhetoric of neutrality and transparency that lingers with forms of representation that make claims to mimesis. But there is also a second order of politics that needs to be interrogated, and this concerns the translation of biometric data into a two-dimensional code. Nikolas Rose and Carlos Novas refer to this process of representation as the production of 'biovalue', whereby 'the depths of the body' are rendered 'visible, intelligible, calculable and capable of intervention at a molecular level' (Rose and Novas 2003: 30). This is a flattening of the body, but also its affirmation. The visual field is not the distant landscape of the camera obscura, but unique bodily signifiers. There is thus a new kind of scopic regime at work and a new kind of optical trickery, whereby the vital processes of the body are 'flattened' so that 'surfaces' 'become equivalent with one another at the most basic biological level [which enables] them to be enfolded within processes of capital or social accumulation' (Rose and Novas 2003: 30). Biometrics denote a moment of convergence between narratives of representational accuracy and the physiological, medical body of the early nineteenth century – the body that was made visible in the technologies of optical illusion. This new 'biologisation' of life has been likened by some to another 'reorganisation of the gaze of the life sciences', whereby identities 'appear at least potentially to be explicable in biological terms and increasingly in terms of their genetic make-up' (Rose 2000: 44, 6). As I will explore further below, the essentialisation of human life in terms of the body has significant political and geopolitical consequences.

Time and space

Visual technologies have both temporal and spatial dimensions, but they can also prioritise different ontologies of time and space. Crary suggests that the camera obscura fixed the observer in space – in the blackness of the machine – while also fixing the outside landscape, both in terms of its projection and later representation. It reinforced a differentiation between observer and observed, inside and outside, and private and public space. The technologies of optical illusion, by contrast, were more temporally oriented as they relied upon movement and speed to render order to their representations. The scenic landscape of the Cartesian perspective dissolved from view as the observer and the observed were positioned in a direct and embodied relationship. On the surface, biometrics appear to resonate with the mimetic model of the camera obscura and its absolute differentiation of space. As many of the examples cited in this chapter's introduction suggest, biometrics are repeatedly deployed to control access to place. National territory is secured by regulating the movement of peoples across borders, whether keeping out or enabling limited access, as with the 'trusted traveller' programmes that enable expedited travel for their members.

Yet non-national spaces are also increasingly securitised and secured. These include the ways that biometrics are being used to regulate access to sporting events, at hotels, at nightclubs, both for patrons and for workers. The four Walt Disney World theme parks in Orlando, Florida use biometric fingerprint scanners to match ticket holders with their tickets so as to prevent their resale. Since the mid-1990s this has been 'the largest, single commercial application of biometrics' in the USA, and Disney personnel have been consulted by the federal government post 9/11 in the development of their national security projects.[2] Disney, however, will shortly be overtaken by the US military initiatives in Iraq, where biometrics have been used to regulate mobility into US-secured strongholds such as Fallujah, and to secure identity for police recruits and voters in the national elections.[3]

Yet at the same time that spaces seem to be more starkly differentiated, biometric technologies also work to 'mystify' or to complicate space in the sense that distinctions between public and private are muted. Scholars suggest, for example, that the prevalence of urban CCTV reconstitutes public space as a private sphere (Coleman 2004). Security matters, even at the national scale, are increasingly reliant on public-private partnerships. Accenture was controversially awarded a 10-year contract for US $10 billion to work on the biometrics for US VISIT at land, sea and air borders (Amoore 2006: 337).[4] In February 2008 it was announced that Lockheed Martin, the nation's largest defence contractor, had won a ten-year contract worth US $1 billion to develop the world's biggest security database. Not only is this a testament to the privatisation of security, but with the possibility that the database will be expanded to the UK, Canada, Australia and New Zealand, national security issues are being rescaled in new ways. With respect to the individual, biometrics are also challenging the hitherto sacrosanct demarcations of the inner and outer limits of the body, as they involve more invasive and intrusive forms of examination and identification, as technologies such as iris scanning become commonplace (van der Ploeg 2003).

Ironically, as David Lyon has remarked, the securitisation of public spaces speaks to a desire for modern, 'private' existence; hence 'the quest for privacy *produces* surveillance, because privacy is also looked to as protection *against* surveillance' (Lyon 2002: 2; original emphasis). Private and public are thus not easily disentangled, but constituted as an interpenetrating Möbius ribbon that 'has replaced the traditional certainty of boundaries' (Bigo 2002: 76). But space is also being reconfigured in other ways. Coleman notes that CCTV surveillance captures public life – street protest, street trading or even homelessness – with little sense of the contingency of the event. All actions in public space are 'defined through the lens of crime and disorder' and hence rendered suspicious (Coleman 2004: 300). As with the devices of optical illusion, the landscape dissolves from view as the spatial context is severed.

At the same time, temporality is reworked. The precautionary paradigm that governs surveillance elides past, present and future. The contemporary ethos of risk demands that calculations are made 'about probable futures in the present, followed by interventions into the present in order to control the potential future' (Aradau and Van Munster 2007: 97; citing Rose 2001: 7). Individual profiles stored in databases 'precede' one's arrival, thus fixing identities in the present, while projecting them into the future, but relying on past information (Dodge and Kitchin 2005: 859). For François Ewald, who has written extensively in this area, 'to calculate a risk is to master time, to discipline the future' (Ewald 1991: 207). It presumes a certain control over one's fate that situates responsibility for the future in one's own hands rather than in the hands of the gods. The individual thus becomes the site of power/knowledge, but is also responsibilised to monitor external risks and to regulate their own behaviour so that they are not deemed to be risky subjects.

Time is reconfigured in a second way by virtue of the attachment of speed to surveillance and risk. Biometrics rely on constructions of accuracy, but their efficacy relies equally on their ability to generate results almost instantaneously. On the one hand this denotes efficiency, but it also speaks to the urgency that underlies the risk attached to the 'war on terror'. On the other hand, the emphasis on speed reconfigures democratic process and the role of bureaucratic gatekeepers and security professionals (Adanau and Van Munster 2007: 107). The desire for speed favours strong administrative practices over the 'slow procedures of law' (Aradau and Van Munster 2007: 107). The presumption of culpability shifts the burden of proof onto the individual and away from the state (Adanau and Van Munster 2007: 106). Exceptional means of detention and isolation which govern the population through spatial segregation are facilitated. The push for speed challenges the viability of deliberative democracy and mutes dissent as security decisions are reframed in terms of false or positive identification, rather than in terms of a common understanding of what constitutes risk (Huysmans 2004: 332; Aas 2006). Given that decisions are taken not on the basis of fact, but probability based on previous histories projected into the future, these transformations become especially problematic, especially when considered in parallel with the biases that are inbuilt into biometric identification. Biometrics thus portend to transform conventional state politics, and even inter-state politics, in manifold ways.

Bodies and the body politic

Biometrics are complicit with the molecularisation of human life and the essentialising of identity in terms of the body: differentiations are made between people because of and through the differences read through their bodies. As the slogan from the UK Home Office Identity and Passport webpage at the beginning of this paper proclaims: 'Everyone is unique. Let us keep it that way.' Biometrics thus affirm and reinforce a unique identity that is foundational to the 'free' liberal subject (Gilbert 2009). But it also speaks to the pernicious fear around identity-fraud or identity-theft that fuels many biometric applications. Paradoxically, with the ability for biometric technologies to better differentiate between bodies, the panic that one's identity can be assumed illicitly grows correspondingly. And there is a further paradox, for this radical individualisation is being made possible through collective forms, such as the national identity card that is being promoted by the UK Home Office. Bodies are rendered commensurable precisely through the very individuated differences that biometrics are said to be able to secure; social order is rendered through the very articulation of individuality. There is thus a tension between the individualising and totalising aspects of biometrics, a tension that is endemic to liberal governance (Gordon 1991: 3). The governing through life also speaks to a form of liberal governance in terms of contingency. Daugman asserts: 'The key to biometric identification is random variation among different persons, since this is the origin of uniqueness, and the basis for discrimination' (Daugman 2006: 1928). The aleatory is made visible and intelligible, and hence open to governance. Biopower is exerted on what makes life life – its random and contingent character – and it is through that arbitrary sliver of that life that bodies are governed (Dillon 2007b: 46).

Governing through the aleatory also has significant ramifications for how the body politic is conceived, an issue raised by Michel Foucault in the early lectures of *Security, Territory, Population* (2007). It denotes a shift away from a sense of community organised around a juridico-political and cultural concept of the population, to one that is rooted in a notion of shared biological species (see Dillon 2007b: 44). One manifestation of this discourse is the concept of universal human rights that emerged in the early twentieth century, with rights attached to membership in the human species – a biological argument – not to political membership. This discourse of shared humanity informed the liberal internationalism of Western geopolitics of the era. Yet this same period is also notable for the wholesale genocide of populations who have been deemed 'un-human'. Politics of exclusion and refusal persist within the global liberal humanism, but they are couched in different logics. The enemy or the 'un-human' is not simply decidable on the basis of their juridico-political and cultural identity: it is no longer simply a matter of state on state violence. Rather, the enemy is reconstituted as one who poses a threat to how the very notion of life is constituted. Julian Reid eloquently captures this tension: 'It is in encountering the existence of life in its indeterminacy that liberal regimes establish the conditions upon which they are able to draw the boundary between which forms of life they secure in the name of the interests of the population and which forms of life they disqualify as the source of their insecurity, and consequently, the object of their wars' (Reid 2006: 43). The ongoing 'war on terror' and the dehumanisation that has taken place in its name at various sites – at Guantanamo Bay, at Abu Ghraib or Iraqi cities more generally (see Graham 2006) – makes this new logic of inhumanity explicit.

Biometrics have thus become a crucial tool in the contemporary processes of differentiation. They render bodies legible and eligible, codifying people in terms of who is a threat; who is responsible or irresponsible; desirable or undesirable; capable or incapable; deserving or undeserving. Biometrics work to identify who qualifies and who doesn't. In some instances, as with trusted traveller programmes, biometrics are used to identify subjects who are regarded as less risky who are then bestowed with privilege. More and more, however, biometrics are used to target risky subjects. Yet this speaks to a troubling tendency of conflating potentially *risky subjects* and *subjects who are at risk*, to portray subjects whose lives are insecure and precarious as the source of insecurity. Irma van der Ploeg observes that 'the groups targeted for (obligatory) biometric identification disproportionately include criminals, recipients of welfare, Medicaid or other benefits, workers, asylants, and immigrants' (van der Ploeg 1999: 296). Indeed, biometrics are increasingly used to arbitrate the distribution of resources. This is the case in India where since 2005 the state of Andhra Pradesh has been using iris scanning to manage and control its state-issued ration cards. By the time of full implementation, it is expected that 80 million users will be registered. The UN High Commission for Refugees is also using iris pattern recognition technology at the Takhta Baig Voluntary Repatriation Centre, on the Pakistan–Afghan border. Biometric technologies are used for identification in the administration of cash grants to over 350,000 refugees returning to Afghanistan from surrounding countries, with an aim to eliminate fraud and be more accountable to donors (Aas 2006). In both these examples, it is precisely the most needy who are enrolled in the biometric databases, who become the most carefully scrutinised and subject to multiple layers of compliance.

Minoritised populations are affected in other ways. In urban areas, public and private CCTV is used to target the 'anti-social' population, such as the homeless (Coleman 2004: 303). All activity in public space becomes suspect. Visual trickery is also deployed. While biometrics propose to render the invisible visible and the unknown known, surveillance strategies operate by intervening on suspect populations and removing them from sight. Coleman argues that surveillance engenders social removal, 'a removal that attempts to render "invisible" unequal relations both on the streets and in public and political debate' – to 'disguise-through-exclusion' (Coleman 2004: 303). This form of social sorting through risk denotes a different kind of social organisation in the contemporary moment. From the early twentieth century, risk profiling and risk pooling were used to collectivise the population, as instruments such as social insurance spread risks across the population (Rose 2006). A kind of social responsibility was at work that echoed with the ethos of the Keynesian state. Risk is flexible in its application, however, and has been reconfigured in recent years, thanks in part to technologies such as biometrics (Valverde and Mopas 2004). A sense of the social still lingers in that security threats are presented as threats that affect the population as a whole (Aradau and Van Munster 2007: 104). Yet risk is individualised and targeted, so that the social is muted. Individuals are held accountable for their own profile and for the riskiness attached to it. The severing of space and the projection through time of individual profiles further encourages a disengagement from the social and political. This dovetails nicely with the twin pressures of individualism and privatisation under neoliberalism. The dismantling of the welfare state and the restricted redistribution of resources rely upon and require social sorting technologies such as biometrics to regulate precarious access to provisions and programmes.

Insecurity permeates the 'war on terror'. Michael Dillon observes that 'what most characterizes global terror we are persistently told is the very certainty of its radical uncertainty. We don't know when terrorists may strike, we do not know how they will strike, and we do not know with what terrifying effect they will strike. We only know for sure that they will strike' (Dillon 2007a: 3). The very strategies of security that are meant to secure and reassure generate insecurity and neurosis (Isin 2004). Biometrics are presented as a form of risk profiling that 'relies upon the representation of a world that would be safer if only ambiguity, ambivalence and uncertainty could be controlled', and as one prong in making the world more certain (Amoore 2006: 338). The aspiration to security is thus misguided and certainly unachievable. As Foucault (2007) has remarked, security is not a state to be realised; it is always elusive, an absolute end that cannot be attained. But it is also through this pervasive sense of insecurity that populations are governed, from the scale of the body to the realms of international politics. Biometric technologies seek to regulate the subject through their contingency and uncertainty. The aleatory nature of the human subject is affirmed, even as it is proposed that this uncertainty can be erased. Thus, the 'war on terror', Julian Reid suggests, is less about defining a common 'enemy that is inimical to life', but rather is a 'conflict over the political constitution of life itself ... specifically over the questions of *what human life is* and *what it may yet become*' (Reid 2006: 38, 13; emphasis in the original). Questions regarding whose lives are deemed secure and whose lives are insecure are thus some of the most pressing in the contemporary context. As biometrics and other forms of surveillance generate a 'generalised suspicion' so that 'the political body becomes a criminal body', these questions are at the heart of how the political is being reconstituted in the contemporary world (Agamben 2005).

Conclusions

Biometrics are a form of visual technology that reconstitute the relationship between body and body politic across space and through time. The pervasive emphasis on biometrics as a crucial prong in the increasing securitisation of society demands that they be critically interrogated. The intensification of the military-industrial-academic complex warrants particular attention. There has been an exponential growth in the biometric economy. The industry's global revenues in 2007 were US $3.01 billion, about double their worth in 2005. Projections are for an increase to US $7.41 billion by 2012,[5] with much of that growth arising from developments at big-name computer and technology companies such as Microsoft, Panasonic, IBM and Hitachi. Through research and teaching, universities are playing an increasing role in these developments. Pace University in Manhattan has been designated as a 'Centre of Academic Excellence' in the field of Information Assurance Education, which includes information security and biometrics, with graduates employed in fields such as airport and passport biometrics. The designation, endowed by the US National Security Agency and the Department of Homeland Security, enables Pace to secure additional resources and student funding, along with other, select partner universities such as the US Military Academy at West Point, Carnegie-Mellon and Johns Hopkins. The National Security Biometric Project, created with the assistance of US Congress after 9/11, has sought to guide university curriculums, such as the first undergraduate degree in biometrics at West Virginia University. A 'Biometric Education Working Group' has been initiated, to bring together university, government and industry representatives 'to propose a draft Biometric Curriculum to pave the way for certifying schools as Programs of Excellence in Biometrics'.[6]

For academics (and others) this intrusive complicity between universities, government and industry, right down to the level of curriculum planning, warrants careful vigilance. The fulcrum of attention on university campuses, however, might offer potential sites of resistance. In *Techniques of the Observer*, Crary makes it clear that he has not attended to forms of resistance: 'What is *not* addressed in this study are the marginal and local forms by which dominant practices of vision were resisted, defected or imperfectly constituted. The history of such oppositional moments needs to be written, but it only becomes legible against the more hegemonic set of discourses and practices in which vision took shape' (Crary 1991: 7; emphasis in the original). Like Crary, I too have focused attention on the hegemonic discourses rather than on moments of opposition, and I concur with his assessment that this work needs to take place. Some scholars have begun to do so (Mann et al 2003; see Amoore 2006). As sites of surveillance prove hard to resist – they so often operate just out of sight, in highly securitised areas where subjects are already exceptionally vulnerable – universities might offer ideal places where critical attention and defiance can take place. In these venues greater attention can be addressed as to the local and global dimensions of how biometrics work to reconstitute the relation between the body and the body politic, and to reconfigure our understanding of what constitutes life itself.

Bibliography

Aas, Katja Franko, ' "The body does not lie": Identity, risk and trust in technoculture', *Crime, Media, Culture* 2/2 (2006), pp.143–58.
Agamben, Giorgio, 'No to biometrics', *Le Monde*, 5 December 2005, available at: http://www.notbored.org/agamben-on-biometrics.html (accessed 4 January 2010).
Amoore, Louise, 'Biometric borders: Governing mobilities in the War on Terror', *Political Geography* 25 (2006), pp.336–51.
Amoore, Louise, 'Vigilant visualities: The watchful politics of the war on terror', *Security Dialogue* 38/2 (2007), pp.215–32.
Aradau, Claudia and Van Munster, Rens, 'Governing terrorism through risk: Taking precautions, (un)knowing the future', *European Journal of International Relations* 13/1 (2007), pp.89–115.
Bigo, Didier, 'Security and immigration: Towards a critique of the governmentality of unease', *Alternatives* 27 (2002), pp.63–92.
Campbell, David, 'Geopolitics and visuality: Sighting the Darfur conflict', *Political Geography* 26 (2007), pp.357–82.
Coleman, Roy, 'Reclaiming the streets: Closed circuit television, neoliberalism and the mystification of social divisions in Liverpool, UK', *Surveillance & Society* 2/2–3 (2004), pp.293–309.
Crary, Jonathan, 'Modernizing vision', in Hal Foster (ed.), *Vision and Visuality* (New York: The New Press, 1988a), pp.29–44.
Crary, Jonathan, 'Techniques of the observer', *October* 45 (1988b), pp.3–35.
Crary, Jonathan, *Techniques of the Observer: On Vision and Modernity in the Nineteenth Century* (Cambridge, MA: MIT Press, 1991).
Daugman, John, 'Probing the uniqueness and randomness of iris codes: Results from 200 billion iris pair comparisons', *Proceedings of the IEEE* 94/11 (2006), pp.1927–35, available at: http://www.cl.cam.ac.uk/~jgd1000/ProcIEEEnov2006Daugman.pdf (accessed 4 January 2010).
Dillon, Michael, 'Governing terror: The state of emergency of biopolitical emergence' (2007a), available at: http://www.hull.ac.uk/cass/downloads/governingterror.pdf (accessed 4 January 2010).
Dillon, Michael, 'Governing through contingency: The security of biopolitical governance', *Political Geography* 26/1 (2007b), pp.41–7.
Dodge, Martin and Kitchin, Rob, 'Codes of life: Identification codes and the machine-readable world', *Environment and Planning D: Society and Space* 23 (2005), pp.851–81.
Ewald, François, 'Insurance and risk', in Graham Burchell, Colin Gordon and Peter Miller (eds), *The Foucault Effect: Studies in Governmentality* (Chicago: The University of Chicago Press, 1991), pp.197–201.

Foucault, Michel, *Security, Territory, Population* (New York: Palgrave Macmillan, 2007).
Gilbert, Emily, 'Liberalism', in Nigel Thrift and Rob Kitchin (eds), *International Encyclopedia of Human Geography* (Oxford: Elsevier, 2009).
Gill, Felix, *The Implications to International Law of Biometrics and Trans-border Data Flows on Restricting Migration*, Master of Laws, submitted to the programme in International and Comparative Public Law, University of Exeter, 2004.
Gordon, Colin, 'Governmental rationality: An introduction', in Graham Burchell, Colin Gordon and Peter Miller (eds), *The Foucault Effect: Studies in Governmentality* (Chicago: The University of Chicago Press, 1991), pp.1–51.
Graham, Stephen, 'Cities and the "war on terror"', *International Journal of Urban and Regional Research* 30/2 (2006), pp.255–76.
Heffernan, Michael, 'Balancing visions: Comments on Gearóid Ó Tuathail's critical geopolitics', *Political Geography* 19/3 (2000), pp.347–52.
Huysmans, Jef, 'Minding exceptions: The politics of insecurity and liberal democracy', *Contemporary Political Theory* 3/3 (2004), pp.321–41.
Introna, Lucas D. and Wood, David, 'Picturing algorithmic surveillance: The politics of facial recognition systems', *Surveillance & Society* 2/2–3 (2004), pp.177–98.
Isin, Engin, 'The neurotic citizen', *Citizenship Studies* 8/3 (2004), pp.217–35.
Jay, Martin, 'Scopic regimes of modernity', reprinted in *Force Fields: Between Intellectual History and Cultural Critique* (New York: Routledge, 1993), pp.114–33.
Jay, Martin, 'The disenchantment of the eye: Surrealism and the crisis of ocular-centrism', in Lucien Taylor (ed.), *Visualizing Theory: Selected Essays from V.A.R. 1990–1994* (New York: Routledge, 1994), pp.173–201.
Kearnes, Matthew, 'Seeing is believing is knowing: Towards a critique of pure vision', *Australian Geographical Studies* 38/3 (2000), pp.332–40.
Lyon, David, 'Editorial. Surveillance studies: Understanding visibility, mobility, and the phonetic fix', *Surveillance & Society* 1/1 (2002), pp.1–7.
MacDonald, Fraser, 'Geopolitics and "the vision thing": Regarding Britain and America's first nuclear missile', *Transactions of the Institute of British Geographers* 31 (2006), pp.53–71.
Mann, Steve, Nolan, Jason and Wellman, Barry, 'Sousveillance: Inventing and using wearable computing devices for data collection in surveillance environments', *Surveillance & Society* 1/3 (2003), pp.331–55.
Petermann, Thomas, Sauter, Arnold and Sherz, Constanze, 'Biometrics at the borders – the challenges of a political technology', *International Review of Law, Computers and Technology* 20/1 (2006), pp.149–66.
Reid, Julian, *The Biopolitics of the War on Terror* (Manchester University Press, 2006).
Rose, Gillian, *Feminism and Geography: The Limits of Geographical Knowledge* (Cambridge: Polity Press, 1993).
Rose, Nikolas, 'The biology of culpability: Pathological identity and crime control in a biological culture', *Theoretical Criminology* 4/1 (2000), pp.5–34.
Rose, Nikolas, 'The politics of life itself', *Theory, Culture, Society* 18/6 (2001), pp.1–30.
Rose, Nikolas, *The Politics of Life Itself: Biomedicine, Power, and Subjectivity in the Twenty-First Century* (Princeton: Princeton University Press, 2006).
Rose, Nikolas and Novas, Carlos, 'Biological citizenship', paper prepared for Aihwa Ong and Stephen Collier (eds), *Global Assemblages: Technology, Politics and Ethics as*

Anthropological Problems (Oxford: Blackwell, 2003), paper available at: http://www.lse.ac.uk/collections/sociology/pdf/RoseandNovasBiologicalCitizenship2002.pdf (accessed 4 January 2010).

Schachtman, Noah, 'Iraq's biometric database could become "hit list": Army', *Wired* (15 August 2007), http://blog.wired.com/defense/2007/08/also-two-thirds.html (accessed 4 January 2010).

Singel, Ryan, 'Saddam's biometric spy files re-used by new Iraqi democracy', *Wired* Blog Network (27 April 2007), http://blog.wired.com/27bstroke6/2007/04/saddams_biometr.html (accessed 4 January 2010).

Valverde, Mariana and Mopas, Michael, 'Insecurity and the dream of targeted governance', in Wendy Larner and William Walters (eds), *Global Governmentality: Governing International Spaces* (London: Routledge, 2004), pp.233–50.

Van der Ploeg, Irma, 'The illegal body: "Eurodac" and the politics of biometric identification', *Ethics and Information Technology* 1 (1999), pp.295–302.

Van der Ploeg, Irma, 'Biometrics and the body as information: Normative issues of the socio-technical coding of the body', in David Lyon (ed.), *Surveillance as Social Sorting: Privacy, Risk, and Digital Discrimination* (London: Routledge, 2003), pp.57–74.

Chapter 11

Vigilant Visualities: The Watchful Politics of the War on Terror
Louise Amoore

It's the sense of touch ... I think we miss that touch so much that we crash into one another just so we can feel something. (Haggis and Moresco 2005)

If the hand is integral to, active in, seeing – then seeing itself must happen differently. (Cooley 2004: 133)

Introduction: 'I am Highway Watch'

In 1998 the American Trucking Association (ATA) founded Highway Watch, a programme designed to teach truck drivers 'what to look for when witnessing traffic accidents and how to assist emergency vehicles to find crash sites' (Boston Herald 2004). In the wake of 9/11, this guidance on what to look for, how to look, how to use the windscreen as a screening device for times of emergency, became something of a gift to the US Department of Homeland Security (DHS). By 2004 the DHS's Transportation Security Administration (TSA) had entered into an agreement with the ATA, providing US$40 million to extend the programme to 'school bus drivers, highway maintenance crews, bridge and tunnel toll collectors and others', so that they would be able to 'recognize and report suspicious activity' (DHS 2004a). Against a backdrop of the burning twin towers, the promotional video represents truck drivers as first responders, displaying 'I am Highway Watch' badges alongside the US flag on their uniforms. 'All of those eyes out there on our nation's highways', proclaims the voiceover, 'they see things that maybe don't fit into the picture somehow. We want them to watch out for unusual activity and call the Highway Watch call center.'

Highway Watch is but one example of a vigilant mode of visuality that is deployed routinely on the 'homefront' of the so-called war on terror. Of course, there is nothing substantively new about engaging the eyes of people in their everyday routines and journeys in order to identify suspicious behaviour or the apparently 'out of the ordinary'. In many ways, this is a rearticulation of the 'behind the blinds' surveillance of 1950s suburban neighbourhood watch. Yet, contemporary modes of watchful politics are particularly geared to the anticipation of events, deploying a kind of precautionary principle that governs through the suspicion of a possible future threat (Ewald 2002). As Highway Watch moves from the reporting of accidents, crashes and incidents during or after the event (where sight provides 'eyewitness' evidence) to the post-9/11 pre-emption of terrorist attack, before the event (where sight becomes foresight), the emerging watchful politics is vigilant: it 'looks out' with an anticipatory gaze.

Set in post-9/11 Los Angeles, Paul Haggis' film *Crash* reveals something quite different about the watchful politics of a fearful life lived predominantly on the highway. The watchful look is present in its many (dis)guises – through windows and windscreens, via glances at passers-by in hoodies or hijab, in a police officer's decision to stop and search. Yet, Haggis' film conveys also what is assumed but concealed in programmes such as Highway Watch: that this watchful look plays out as profiling, the usually racialised stereotyping of 'Arab', 'Muslim', 'immigrant' and so on. Life in cities that 'use freeways and wide boulevards to divide people by race and class', says Haggis (2006) in an interview, is a life 'encased behind glass: in our home, our cars, at work'. In our quest for safety and security, argues Haggis, 'we no longer truly feel the touch of strangers as we brush past them on the street'. Following a car accident in the opening scene of the film, a character muses on how the sense of touch is lost, so much missed that 'we *Crash* into one another just so we can feel something' (Haggis and Moresco 2005). *Crash* reminds us that the fearful and vigilant watching for the 'Other' through the windscreen is one specific and particular representation of visuality that asks that we look but do not touch. Indeed, so dependent is it on the drawing of lines between self and other, homeland and strangeland, safe and unsafe, ordinary and suspicious, that it must feign the prohibition of touch if it is to sustain the distancing that allows the dividing practices to continue. Haggis' film succeeds in capturing the ambivalence of contemporary watchful politics, conveying both the bleak and violent realities of racist suspicions and the sense that even this looking is ambivalent; it also craves the touch of others.

In this chapter, I engage with a form of visual culture that is, W.J.T. Mitchell (2002: 170) reminds us, 'not limited to the study of images and media', but extends also 'to everyday practices of seeing and showing'. In the spirit of this openness to multiple manifestations of the domain of the visual and visual practices, I will explore two questions. The first asks how a particular mode of vigilant or watchful visuality has come to be mobilised in the homefront of the so-called war on terror. Has vision come to be represented not only as the primary sense (more 'reliable' and verifiable than touch, taste, smell, etc.), but also as, precisely, the sovereign sense – the sense that secures the state's claim to sovereignty and legitimates violence on its behalf? Second, taking our illustrative cue from *Crash*, and from a body of work that conceives of touch as 'integral to' and 'active in' seeing (Cooley 2004: 133), how might we subvert watchful politics by seeing seeing differently?

Because we see: Sight and sovereignty

In his discussion of the myth that is a 'purely visual' media, W.J.T. Mitchell asks how the visual 'became so potent as a reified concept' (Mitchell 2005: 260). Given what he describes as the 'intricate braiding and nesting of the visual with the other senses', how, he asks, did the visual 'acquire its status as the sovereign sense?' (Mitchell 2005: 265). Such questions have become the principal concerns of critical writing on visual culture that seeks to expose the assumptions about visuality that render the visual sovereign. How, critical writers on visual culture ask, has visuality come to be represented as 'the superior, most reliable' of the senses? (Bal 2003: 13). And, why is it that images are afforded status as 'natural and visible signs' with an 'inherent credibility' that cannot be found in the tactile or aural senses? (Jay 2002: 269; see also Crary 1990). It is not that the visual is the sovereign sensory domain, then, or indeed that it can be meaningfully abstracted from other sensory perception, but rather that its representation as sovereign has important and material effects. The representation of a sovereign visuality has played an important role, for example, in the making of rational and responsible subjects. If sight is understood to be the sense most nearly and dispassionately under our control, or, as Heidi Rae Cooley (2004: 135) puts it, 'if people become distanced observers, whose vision is objectified, quantifiable, manageable', then the act of seeing is central to the defining of a coherent, autonomous subject. The image itself becomes an artefact that is, of all media, least vulnerable to 'subjective intrusion or ambiguity' (Daston and Galison 1992: 82).

Mitchell's claims about the sovereignty of the visual, though, can be usefully extended to thinking about contemporary articulations of state sovereignty. Not only is the visual reified as sovereign among the senses, but it is also uniquely implicated in the representational practices that make state sovereignty possible. As David Campbell (1998) has argued compellingly, a state must 'write' its security; it is dependent on representational practices that identify 'us' and delineate 'us' from the untrustworthy aliens. Understood in these terms, we cannot see ourselves clearly or know who 'we' are until we have recognisable representations of the Other. For Michael Shapiro (1997: xi), it is 'architectures of enmity', projected via images and stereotypes, that make threat and antagonism possible. 'People go to war', writes James Der Derian (2002: 5), 'because of how they see, perceive, picture, imagine and speak of others'.

Let me be clear here that I am not arguing that the visual realm is the realm through which the state secures its sovereignty via representations of the Other. Rather, a particular mode of visuality is called up and into being in contemporary articulations of sovereignty: a visuality that categorises and classifies people into images and imaginaries of many kinds. Sovereignty is performed, as Edkins and Pin-Fat (2004) suggest, through the drawing of lines, and the drawing of those lines is made credible, at least in part, by the reification of the visual:

> Visual culture finds its primal scene ... in the face of the Other: the face-to-face encounter. Stereotypes, caricatures, classificatory figures, search images ... As go-betweens ... these images are the filters through which we recognize and of course misrecognize other people. (Mitchell 2002: 175)

Where images become the filters through which we recognise/misrecognise ourselves and the Other, Mitchell's insights are critical for thinking about what I will call here an emergent watchful politics. The watchful politics of the war on terror has come to use the image – broadly defined as a picture of a person, a visuality of a scene, or the pattern of data on a screen – precisely as the primal scene in which it recognises and misrecognises 'Other' people.

Recognition has become pivotal to the watchful technologies of sovereignty deployed in this war. Facial- and gait-recognition surveillance, biometric identity cards, and expedited airport security clearance programmes, for example, are at the forefront of the drive to secure the state from the threat of the Other, and to do so via identity (see Sparke 2005; Amoore 2006). Predicated on the assumption that the image can fix, verify and authenticate identity, and in spite of evidence of clusters of false hits among black and Asian faces, the visual is used here as the basis for belonging and expelling. Similarly, the Highway Watch programme's appeal to 'report suspicious activity' is only intelligible if there is some basis for recognising who or what is alien, who or what is unusual, who or what is outside. In this sense, the identity of a 'we' – whether patriotic truck drivers, or 'we' the nation, or 'we the people' – is realised via the claim to be able to see and to recognise a threat.

Of course, any claim to recognise is always also a misrecognition. Since identity is never fully constituted, can never be fixed, is always in process of becoming identifiable, the visual filter is bound to misidentify, to misrecognise. In Haggis' *Crash*, a Persian shopkeeper, confronted with vandalism and racist graffiti in his shop, asks his daughter, 'Why do they think I am Arab? When did Persian become Arab?' (Haggis and Moresco 2005). He feels himself to be misrecognised, falsely identified as Arab. Yet, in the terms of a sovereignty that has designated him as Other, he is, nonetheless, rendered recognisable. In the context of our 'anxiety, rage, and radical desire for security', writes Judith Butler (2004: 39), we shore up the borders 'against what is perceived as alien', engaging in 'a heightened surveillance of anyone who looks vaguely Arab in the dominant racial imaginary'. As Butler suggests, misrecognition (of Sikhs, Hindus, Israelis, Arab-Americans, Persians and so on) scarcely seems to matter, as long as 'everyone is free to imagine and identify the source of terror'.

In the vigilant mode of visuality, though, it is not simply the recognition of an alien outside that is at stake, but also the demand that the Other inside be recognisable as Other in order to remain inside. In a further scene from Haggis' *Crash*, a white television executive asks the black director to re-take a scene:

> 'Is Jamal seeing a speech coach or something?'
> 'What do you mean?'
> 'Haven't you noticed – this is weird for a white guy to say – that he is talking a lot less black lately?'
> 'You think that because of that the audience won't recognize him as a black man?'

'It's not in character. Eddie is supposed to be the smart one, not Jamal. I mean, you're the expert here, but to me it rings false'.
(Haggis and Moresco 2005)

The white executive fears the misrecognition of the black character. In order for the audience to 'see' a black character, he must 'sound' recognisable. Jamal must, in order to be recognised by the audience, stand clearly behind a line that designates him as Other.

How might we make sense of the implications of these lines and of the role of the visual in their mapping and delineation? Didier Bigo (2001: 115), in his trope for contemporary security, suggests the Möbius strip – the twisted, conjoined figure in which inside and outside are interpenetrated, where one does not know 'on which face of the strip one is located'. Rather, as in Giorgio Agamben's (2005: 39) sense of sovereignty that is enabled by exception, the Möbius-style entanglement of interior/exterior allows for the inclusion of the Other by means of its very exclusion. As in the *Crash* scene, the black actor's character can be incorporated within what can be safely seen so long as he remains recognisably Other. Similarly, the authority of the black director can be tolerated if he does not breach what is recognisably black. What is at stake, then, at least as Bigo sees it, is not strictly the sovereignty performed via the physical borders of the state, but instead that performed via the lines of 'a new security device: the monitoring of minorities and diasporas' (Bigo 2001: 115). The watchful politics I analyse here is absolutely at the heart of this monitoring – a constantly vigilant mode of looking that produces what I have elsewhere described as a 'ubiquitous border' (Amoore 2006: 348). If, as Bigo (2001: 112) asserts, the policing of the lines between Self and Other is to become a matter of 'everyday securitisation' from 'the enemy within', then the visuality of the vigilant onlooker is the very means of the ubiquitous border. The visual becomes the sovereign sense that participates in the emergence of new forms of state sovereignty. It, quite literally, projects the lines through images and stereotypes, and it projects them forward in time. It is to this projection into an uncertain future that I now turn.

Because we see, we can decide: Sight and foresight

One week after the London bombings of July 2005, novelist Iain Sinclair (2005) observed the ghostly images and cinematic repertoires of the mobile phones used on the day of the bombings, and the desire of the authorities to somehow apprehend the images:

> Now we have a new cinema, requiring minimal light, no technical expertise (switch on and hold above your head like a torch). The people's cinema of the mobile phone: careless and magical ... At the moment of crisis, phones shift from being mere tools of convenience. They begin to create a poetry of unease. The authorities want you to send in all your digital improvisations, your snapshots, your small vanities.

Sinclair observes here a significant and politically troubling move in the watchful politics of the war on terror: the suturing together of people's fears, suspicions and everyday visuality with 'mobile screenic devices' (Cooley 2004) – mobile phones, palm computing devices, handheld electronic organisers – that can translate prosaic inexpert visualities into 'expert' data. One way to think about this move is to reflect on the role of 'eyewitness' accounts in practices of justice and procedures of law. As Martin Jay (2002: 269) writes, 'the legal distinction between eyewitness evidence and hearsay, or between a photograph of a crime and a verbal account of a crime' performs the very credibility of the visual. Understood this way, the call for people to submit their images and video clips – repeated on posters in the months following the bombings – is primarily about sight, about what has been seen but perhaps missed, about what can be shown from what is seen. Yet, the watchful politics at work here is not simply about sight and the gathering of evidence after the event. Instead, it is primarily about foresight and the anticipation of the event. Commuters were asked to send all images, even those depicting banal and ordinary 'normal' activities and events. In the careless or playful pictures taken on the daily commute are the images of the 'norm' against which, it is assumed, transgression of the norm – the 'out of the ordinary' – can be identified. Contemporary modes of watchful visuality are geared to the anticipation of events, deploying what François Ewald (1991; 2002) considers to be a 'precautionary' approach to risk.

Ewald takes his cue from Michel Foucault's (1975/2003: 19–20) work on techniques of normalisation and their incorporation into expert knowledge and judicial power that reveals 'how the individual already resembles his crime before he has committed it'. Here, calculative practices are deployed, in effect, before a crime takes place, in order to see or to envisage the individual as criminal. The act of seeing thus becomes an act of foreseeing, pre-empting or anticipating. Ewald (2002: 288) depicts the contemporary manifestation of such pre-emptive practices in the 'precautionary principle' that 'invites one to anticipate what one does not yet know, to take into account doubtful hypotheses and simple suspicions'. This does not mean that suspicions or prejudices or stereotypes are deployed randomly to anticipate an uncertain or unknown future. Rather, the profiling of a 'norm' of behaviour – whether via mobile-phone images or by CCTV footage, or by passenger manifests on transatlantic flights – becomes algorithmic; it becomes encoded so that deviations can be identified and decisions can be taken.

In a war on terror that actually redeploys 'dataveillance' systems in operation long before 9/11, it is this algorithmic logic that is distinctly novel. When suspicions and fears are called in to the Highway Watch or Life Savers hotline, the call centre uses an algorithm on a screen to turn simple suspicions into 'actionable intelligence', with the gloss of techno-science. As Ewald (2002: 294) notes, the precautionary logic implies that action is taken precisely on the basis of uncertainty: 'decisions are therefore made not in a context of certainty, nor even of available knowledge, but of doubt, premonition, foreboding, challenge, mis-trust, fear, and anxiety'. In the logic of the precautionary principle, we might say decision is taken on the basis of a particular mode of visuality, one that is captured by the 'screening' of the entire population to establish algorithmic norms and anomalies. From financial transactions to air-passenger data, 'smart' electronic profiles of daily life are deployed as though they could anticipate an uncertain future (Amoore and de Goede 2005). In these systems, the assumption is that it is possible to 'build a complete picture of a person', to quite literally see who they are before they board a plane or transfer money, by relating them to the norms of a wider population and identifying their degree of deviance (de Goede 2006). Indeed, for those who are able to exempt themselves from screening practices, there is now a booming market in pre-screening via programmes such as Privium Plus or PEGASE. In these instances, the electronic visualisation of a person becomes a specific kind of foresight, mediated via the screen as a 'touch screen', a biometric scanner or the computer-based results of data mining.

Is it the case, then, that the screens of post-9/11 dataveillance techniques extend the vigilant visuality across the more prosaic screens of the windscreen and the mobile phone? Sinclair's observation that 'we have a new cinema' in the flickering images of the mobile phone echoes Anne Friedberg's (2002: 184) sense that 'the automobile is a viewing machine ... the visuality of driving is the visuality of the windscreen, operating as a framing device'. Tracing the conjoined Californian histories of widening cinema screens and the wraparound windscreen, Friedberg's (2004: 190) work considers the screen as an interface between observer and observed and a site of projection. Citing Paul Virilio's claim that 'what goes on in the windscreen is cinema', Friedberg is concerned with the screen as a boundary in and of itself. 'Driving', she writes, 'transforms the mobilized pedestrian gaze with new kinetics of motored speed and with the privatization of the automobile capsule sealed off from the public and the street' (Friedberg 2002: 184). The screen as boundary produces a capsularized experience of being able to see, watch and look out, but not to be seen, watched or looked at.

In one sense, the screen here precisely enables the distancing of Self from Other, and provides a domain in which the precautionary principle can flourish and suspicions can become the basis of decisions. Certainly, the US homeland security project is coupling the windows of neighbourhood watch to the screens of automobile and mobile phone in new and troubling ways. Sponsored by Microsoft, Hewlett Packard and Nextel, for example, the Department of Homeland Security has toured US town halls calling for citizens to 'report questionable incidents and circumstances', via the communications companies and networks who 'have become trusted partners in a global neighborhood watch' (DHS 2004b: 12–14). The personal computer or mobile-phone screen thus becomes a means of shoring up the visual as the sovereign sense, giving the appearance of a detached, smart and data-driven basis for decision. Yet, as in Sinclair's observation of the careless and magical quality of the underground images, there is a kind of cinematic conceit associated with the screen – a theatrical suspension of disbelief. 'For the film spectator', writes Anne Friedberg (2002: 188), 'the darkness that surrounds the frame calls us to play upon its boundaries', and invites us to immerse ourselves in an 'imaginary, endless space'. The screen is ambivalent: it performs borders and boundaries, but it also invites us to play upon them.

Other ways of seeing

The vigilant visualities dominating the war on terror rely upon particular representations of sight and seeing. The visual is sustained as the 'sovereign sense', through which the Self is secured and the Other identified. In order to sustain the visual in this way, however, the vigilant and watchful mode must occlude the possibility of seeing differently. Specifically, it must say 'look, but don't touch'. To clarify my point here, it is not that vigilant visualities successfully decouple one sense (sight) from one other (touch). Instead, they feign the detachment of sight from all other senses that allow us to be 'touched' or moved. Not only is tactility inherent to visuality, but touch itself is to allow the taste, the sound, the scent of an experience literally to 'move' or 'displace' oneself (Bal 1997: 61).

To explore the tactility of visuality is to begin to locate some of the vulnerabilities of the vigilant mode of looking. 'On closer inspection', writes W.J.T. Mitchell (2005: 257), 'all the so-called visual media turn out to involve the other senses, especially touch and hearing'. Sustaining the impression of a purely visual experience, then, involves the prohibition of touch. That is why, suggests Mitchell (2005: 260), in the space of the gallery, 'we are so rigorously prohibited from actually touching the canvas ourselves'. Touching the image would in some way expose the elevated fiction of a purely visual experience. Like the representational practices necessary to elevate the myth of the state as untouchably sovereign, the visual is dependent for its sovereignty on representations that exclude the tactility of vision.

Understood in these terms, the images called for and collected by the authorities after the London bombings or those embodied in the Highway Watch programme, though they demand a distancing of observer from the observed, are actually both optical and tactile; they are as much about multisensory feeling as they are about seeing. Heidi Rae Cooley (2004: 143) analyses what she calls 'mobile screenic devices' in terms of the 'fit' between visuality and the involuntary tactility of the screen in the palm:

> The shift from window-ed seeing to screenic seeing reconfigures one's relationship to that which is seen. Whereas a window distances viewers from what they are looking at, the screen draws them toward the images that are displayed ... Window-ed seeing institutes a detached engagement, while screenic seeing encourages an experience of encounter ... that which is being viewed (and perhaps recorded) no longer exists separate from that which is framing it.

Cooley introduces ambivalence into our sense of the screen as the means of distancing the viewer from what is viewed, creating a privatised, capsularised space of invulnerability. For Cooley, 'screenic seeing' should be understood as co-present within 'window-ed seeing', precisely because the screen offers an interface, a possible means of breaching its own boundary. The screen, in Cooley's (2004: 145) terms, is a liminal space that is 'permeable and without definitive borders'. Experiencing this liminality, she argues, involves a temporality 'without linear historical time', an instinctive experience 'of flowing and spreading, not one of focused concentration' (Cooley 2004: 149). The mobile screenic device that has become so central to the watchful politics of the war on terror, then, potentially involves an ecstatic experience of being 'transported beyond oneself', or 'implicated in lives that are not our own' (Butler 2004: 24–5).

Read alongside Judith Butler, Cooley's sense of the 'absent minded' and 'distracted' screenic way of seeing evokes the experience of a decentred self. This has significant implications for the vigilant visuality that would seek to appropriate what is captured via the screens of consumer technologies and automobiles. The assumption that the screen allows for rational, distanced and data-led seeing is seriously challenged by the tactility of visuality that is suggested by Cooley and others. Tactile vision such as that involved in screenic seeing disrupts the precautionary logic of vigilance and subverts the sense of sight that is necessary to foresight. By contrast with a mode of visuality that claims to able to capture and profile everyday images in order to anticipate the future, screenic seeing reveals precisely the indeterminacy of the future. As Cooley (2004: 151) understands the 'distracted' viewer's capacity for surprise when 'the hand's engagement allows for a resonance in seeing':

> At such moments the vibrancy and surprise of now bursts forth to shatter the mundane, the routine ... It may be a matter of catching a moment that typically would go unrecognized, or activating a seeing that enables one to glimpse the ordinary anew ... It is in this way that vision becomes tactile.

In an exposure of the ambiguity of the vigilant visuality's deployment of everyday seeing to prevent shock, accident, violence and surprise, here the tactility of vision precisely allows one to see the ordinary anew, to see the banal or trivial as extraordinary, to see our relationship with the Other differently. In a scene from Haggis' *Crash*, there is something of a momentary tear in the distantiated windowed seeing of stereotypes and profiles, revealing the screenic seeing of how things might be otherwise. A police officer arrives at the scene of a road traffic accident where a woman is trapped inside a car that has flipped onto its roof. Petrol is leaking from the vehicle and firefighters are tackling blazing fires nearby. The officer crawls through the broken window of the car to try to rescue the woman. In the moment that they see one another they appear to know exactly who they see. In a previous scene, after stopping and searching a car driven by the woman's African-American husband, the officer has sexually assaulted the woman. In linear time she sees the villain, the perpetrator and her abuser, a white racist cop and a threat to be feared. He sees his victim, the light-skinned wife of a black, wealthy, SUV-driving film director:

> 'Get away from me. Not you, anyone else, not you. Don't touch me. Please don't touch me.'
> 'Look, I'm not going to hurt you.'
> 'Please don't touch me.'
> 'I'm not going to touch you.'
> 'Are you going to get me out?'
> 'Look at me. I'm going to get you out ... Look at me. Everything is going to be fine'.
> (Haggis and Moresco 2005)

The shock and trauma of the accident produces a different kind of looking in Haggis' scene. Inside the burning car they momentarily see one another differently. He uses 'look at me' to reassure and to breach the lines that were drawn between perpetrator and victim. Officer Ryan's colleagues pull him back through the window as the flames reach the car, but he goes back and pulls the woman from the car. Haggis reveals here some of the ambivalence of visuality that Cooley suggests in her study, as well as the potential for trauma to 'tear us from ourselves' that Butler identifies. The windowed seeing that dominates much of the film – distantiated, privatised, suspicious – is broken in the scene's shattered windscreen, revealing the co-presence of something more akin to Cooley's screenic seeing – tactile, surprising, immediate and affective.

In Jenny Edkins' work on the memorialisation of trauma in political community, she depicts a similar momentary rupture and emergence of the real in traumatic events. 'In the rational west', writes Edkins (2003: 13), 'we tend to seek certainty and security above all. We don't like not knowing. So we pretend that we do.' For Edkins (2003: 12), this feigning of control serves to conceal or forget the traumatic real so as to protect 'the imaginary completeness of the subject'. It is precisely this feigning of control that is attempted by the windowed seeing of the watchful politics of the war on terror. Indeed, the call for people's prosaic images of the trauma of the London bombings seeks exactly to incorporate what cannot be readily spoken or expressed into a narrative of bearing witness. Rather, as Cooley's windowed seeing captures the illusion of the complete watchful subject, Edkins shows how the state moves to quickly incorporate trauma or violence into a linear narrative that designates heroes, victims and perpetrators.

Similarly, Edkins' use of trauma time produces the sense of distraction and shock that Cooley suggests with screenic seeing. 'Trauma', writes Edkins (2003: 59), 'demands an acknowledgement of a different temporality, where the past is produced by – or even takes place in the present. We need to find a way of remaining faithful to its different temporality, a way to mark or encircle the trauma.' Edkins finds, in the architecture of some memorials to war, genocide or famine, exactly this capacity to encircle the trauma, to bear witness in a way that remains open and resists incorporation. Of course, trauma is not necessarily or inherently a condition for what Kaja Silverman (1996: 2) calls 'excorporative' processes of identification with 'bodies we would otherwise repudiate'. For Silverman, as for many critical analysts of visual culture, 'visual violence' can be undone in the architectures of the cinema screen and the windscreen that 'encircle the audience', inviting an escape from 'the binds of time' (Silverman 1996: 11; Friedberg 2002: 188). The flashbacks that Haggis' characters experience inside the burning car, flashbacks that Edkins (2003: 39) describes as images 'we do not have access to other than as images', find their expression also in the 'flashback fluid temporalities of cinema' (Friedberg 2002: 189). Far from producing a visuality that is distanced and dispassionate, or images that can be readily appropriated and interpreted, then, the screen is potentially also a means of flashback visuality, in which the image can be accessed only as image.

To put the argument simply, watchful modes of visuality, in their many guises, assure us that an image secures the presence of a rational observer. What I want to suggest here is that there are ways of seeing seeing that absolutely invert this: seeing can be about the absence of an observer in the sense that the 'usual' everyday order is disrupted. It is not the case that screenic ways of seeing offer political alternatives to vigilant visualities, but that they are always already present. Vigilant visualities of the war on terror rely upon the rational screening of normality in order to identify transgression. If the screen is positioned as the impenetrable boundary, as it is in the dataveillant and vigilant seeing of the war on terror, then we 'foreclose vulnerability, banish it' (Butler 2004: 30) in such a way that we crave the touch of passers-by. In the tactility of visuality, though, the viewer is transported out of herself (whether by trauma, by the tactile fit of hand to technology, by cinematic experience ...) and the anchor in a complete subject is threatened. The prohibition of touch in watchful and vigilant modes is revealed to be an impossibility.

The unseen, the unforeseen and the undecidable

As I have argued here, central to the vigilant mode of visuality is an anticipatory logic. Such a logic implies that the unforeseen can be made foreseeable, can be somehow folded into present decision. As for François Ewald (2002: 289), 'one must take all hypotheses into account, even the most dubious; one must be wide open to speculation, to the craziest imagined views'. The gap between knowing and deciding, considered by Ewald to be central to precautionary logics, in the visual domain appears as a gap between seeing (so that one can know) and deciding (on the basis of what is foreseen). Anticipatory modes of looking seek to act in advance of an event so that future events might be pre-empted.

One possible route into questioning the anticipatory logic of watchful visualities, as I have discussed, is to think about seeing differently. Another is to question the capacity to decide on the basis of what is seen or foreseen. How do images of commuters on a subway platform have to be seen, ordered and categorised in order for a decision to be taken? If suspicion is central to the vigilant visuality, who is to decide and how, on the basis of whose suspicions? In the case of Highway Watch, the suspicions, hypotheses and 'crazy imagined views' of the truck drivers appear on the screens of the 'highly trained analysts at the Highway Watch call centre' (Highway Watch 2005). Here, the gap between what is seen and what is later decided is filled with apparent 'expertise' and designated as a data-driven process. Indeed, even where the war on terror's dataveillance deploys complex algorithms to encode patterns of behaviour and identify suspicious activity, this only conceals the raw stereotyping of what can be seen. The technologies deployed to translate the unforeseen into the foreseeable, of course, fail everywhere and for much of the time. When they do, we see a glimpse of what they otherwise conceal: the absolute undecidability of all decision and the unforeseeability of most of what we think is seen.

Haggis' *Crash* beautifully exposes the twists and turns that take place in the attempts to manage uncertainty by identifying stereotypes and securing against them. The Persian shopkeeper, who is suffering racial violence, buys a gun to secure himself and his property. In the firearms store he faces further abuse by the store owner, who says: 'Hey, Osama, we're not planning the Jihad here' (Haggis and Moresco 2005). An argument ensues and the man is ejected from the store, leaving his daughter to buy the ammunition. Later in the film, the shopkeeper calls in a locksmith to repair a troublesome lock in his shop. When the Latino locksmith tries to tell him that it is the door that needs replacing, the shopkeeper is angry: 'I suppose you got a friend who can sell me a new door, you cheater.' Of course, the weak door is smashed again and, this time, because the lock company has reported that the advice was ignored, the insurance company considers the shopkeeper negligent and refuses to pay out for the vandalism. The shopkeeper sets out with his loaded gun and waits outside the locksmith's house.

The locksmith, meanwhile, has assured his five-year-old daughter that there will be no more bullets through her bedroom window – he comforts her with the gift of an invisible and impenetrable fairy cloak. When the child sees the man pointing his gun at her father, she moves from the bedroom window to stand behind the porch screen: 'It's OK, daddy. I'll protect you ... It's a really good cloak.' She runs into her father's arms as the shopkeeper fires his gun. As the Latino locksmith checks his daughter's body for what he thinks must be a fatal wound, he finds that she is unharmed. The gun that the shopkeeper bought to secure himself was loaded with the blanks that his daughter bought as a precautionary measure. In this scene, Haggis suggests to his audience the very impossibility of foreseeing the effects of actions taken to protect and to secure. We cannot be sure, he seems to say, which acts will protect or secure and which will further endanger. Neither can we be sure, throughout the film, of the identities of those whom we think threaten us – we misidentify at every turn. In a final scene, the Persian shopkeeper says of the young daughter of his apparent enemy, 'She is my angel. She came to protect me, to protect us' (Haggis and Moresco 2005). Each anticipatory move in the film, made on the back of suspicion and racial prejudice, fails somehow along the way: the SUVs crash or are carjacked; the gun fires blanks; the carefully manicured and gated home becomes an isolated place where accidents happen. Meanwhile, the apparently fictitious talismans – the girl's invisible cloak, a Saint Christopher on the dashboard, a lucky charm on a key ring – produce a kind of fragile justice of their own.

The moments of decision in *Crash* serve to disrupt the precautionary logic. To act on the basis of what one thinks one sees in order to anticipate future threat is revealed to be intensely problematic. As Jacques Derrida reminds us, 'the decision, if there is to be one, must advance towards a future which is not known, which cannot be anticipated'. In these terms, a decision that is anticipatory is not a decision at all, but merely 'the application of a body of knowledge' (Derrida 1994: 37; see also Derrida 1992). To be a decision, then, an act must invoke that which is somehow outside of the subject's control, it must be made in the face of a future that cannot be known. In the context of sight deployed as foresight, the apparently informed decisions taken on the basis of norms are not actually decisions at all, but simply rearticulated calculations. What is seen on the highway, in the subway or on the screens of tech-enabled border guards can never be the basis for decision, much less responsible or just decision.

Visual culture offers useful ways of thinking about how visuality might remain open to an unknown future and 'advance where it cannot see' (Derrida 1994: 39). By contrast with modes of visuality that use what is seen to anticipate the unforeseen, critical visual culture does not tightly tie knowledge to decision (we have the visual data, so we can know, so we can decide). Instead, it opens up to allow in the aporia, the undecidable. In photography, for example, the opening and closure of the shutter is simply one moment of decision, but the image that is produced is open to other future possible decisions. A photograph is a means of 'translating the unseen or unseeable into something that looks like a picture of something we could never see' (Mitchell 2005: 260). The intelligibility of the use of the visual in watchful politics is disrupted by this sense of the photograph. The visual in the war on terror is offered as a means of translating the unseen or unseeable into an actual picture of something, or someone, we think we see all of the time – an Arab, an immigrant, and so on. Mitchell's picture is of 'something we could never see', someone always beyond our reach. A critical ethics of vision, as Mieke Bal (2005: 160) has articulated it, would engage a 'commitment to look', an act of 'seeing through', not in the sense of deciphering some deeper truth behind the surface of an image, but in 'halting to see the overlooked'.

Installation artworks have become particularly significant in this pausing to see what is overlooked. Perhaps because they can be physically positioned to make us stop, walk around them, or see them in our peripheral vision as we pass by, installations seem to demand a commitment to look through and to see what is overlooked. What is interesting to me about the potential for installation artworks to open up the unseeable/undecidable is the way that they intervene in our mundane routines and trivial everyday journeys. Where the watchful politics of Highway Watch, for example, uses the visuality of daily routines in order to settle out the norm and identify suspicious deviation, artists are using the everyday visuality of the highway precisely to unsettle what comes to be normalised.

Tijuana artist Marcos Ramirez sought to make his 2003 installation 'Road to Perdition' a daily intervention on the highways of Reading, Pennsylvania. Commissioned in the 'Mexico Illuminated' series, Ramirez's work was to be mounted on a highway sign on the Bingaman Street bridge. 'Road to Perdition' lists eight cities bombed by the USA, alongside their distances from Reading and the dates of the bombings (see Figure 11.1). The sign was wholly ambiguous: it looked like something we see every day, and yet it also looked like something we could never see. The raw data of the distances to sites of violence is a calculation that is always already assumed but rarely seen. In the event, Ramirez was refused permission to site his work on the highway and exhibited a projected image of the Bingaman billboard at Albright College. Ramirez's work, rather like Haggis' *Crash*, represents a refusal to stand behind the lines that segregate the glass-walled privatized visualities of the highway from the violent actions that make them possible.

Conclusions: Visuality before justice

I do not wish to overemphasise the novelty of the watchful politics in the war on terror. Of course, in many ways the categories and judgements of the vigilant visuality only rearticulate prejudicial classifications long in operation. It does seem to me, though, that vigilant visualities are extending, via algorithmic screening, to incorporate ever more prosaic and playful uses of the screen in our daily lives – and this is deserving of urgent critical attention. At the time of writing, the DHS has announced the primary bidders for the Secure Border Initiative (SBI) – a 'virtual fence' connecting the USA's land border guards to technological infrastructures – including 'smart weapons' manufacturers Raytheon and Lockheed Martin, alongside Swedish telecommunications company Ericsson. The SBI illustrates precisely what I have been concerned with here: it conceals the raw stereotyping of what is assumed can be seen in a cloak of high-tech data-driven precaution. A close reading of the DHS's (2006) outline for contractors reveals the vision of a system that can 'classify the level of threat prior to the point of interdiction/encounter by law enforcement personnel'. At the

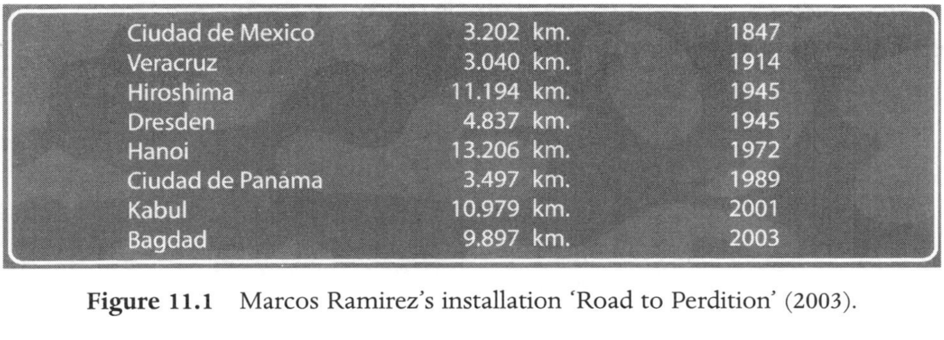

Ciudad de Mexico	3.202 km.	1847
Veracruz	3.040 km.	1914
Hiroshima	11.194 km.	1945
Dresden	4.837 km.	1945
Hanoi	13.206 km.	1972
Ciudad de Panamá	3.497 km.	1989
Kabul	10.979 km.	2001
Bagdad	9.897 km.	2003

Figure 11.1 Marcos Ramirez's installation 'Road to Perdition' (2003).

point that the border guard appears to decide, the calculation is already made within the algorithm. The data-led watchful politics of the SBI, then, seeks the visualisation of a threat in advance of law, prior to justice in the strict sense.

It is this visualisation before justice that is so integral to the watchful politics I have discussed here. The etymological sense of prejudice – *praejudicare*, or 'to judge before' – embodies the anticipatory logic of judgement before justice, or prior judgement. The screening of Highway Watch and the mobile phone images from the London bombings, then, are given the appearance of distantiated, data-led objective knowledges, a basis for anticipatory governance and prejudgement. Yet, the suspicions and stereotypes essential to vigilant visualities are, strictly, pre-judicial, pre-justice. The call for images to support justice or to provide evidence for decisions is in fact a call for prejustice, even prejudice.

If Ericsson's mobile screens become the visuality of the SBI, will they institute only the windowed and distantiated seeing of watchful politics? 'Sight, no matter how disincarnated it may appear', writes Martin Jay (2002: 276), 'never loses its links with the flesh in which it is embedded'. Windowed seeing is the sovereign fiction of securability; it is illusory. Far from two different incarnations of the screen, the vigilant visuality and the screenic touch are always co-present. Where the technologies of vigilant visuality apparently fail, we see momentarily the concealed logic of prejustice and feel momentarily the touch of the Other. As Judith Butler (2004: 24) writes: 'Despite one's best efforts, one is undone, in the face of the other, by the touch, by the scent, by the feel, by the prospect of the touch, by the memory of the feel.' The vigilant mode of visuality demands that we somehow remain intact, that we can be complete subjects capable of objective seeing. But, the lines of sight that we have are not ever only 'shields' or windscreens, but always also screens or windscreens, in which we see multiple reflections and shifting views, through which we miss the touch of others. To keep open this alternative visuality, even and especially in the face of the drive to recognise, identify and secure, is to expose the incompleteness and contingency of the vigilant homeland security programmes.

Bibliography

Agamben, Giorgio, *State of Exception* (Chicago, IL: University of Chicago Press, 2005).
Amoore, Louise, 'Biometric borders: Governing mobilities in the War on Terror', *Political Geography* 25 (2006), pp.336–51.

Amoore, Louise and de Goede, Marieke, 'Governance, risk and dataveillance in the War on Terror', *Crime, Law and Social Change* 43/2 (2005), pp.149–73.
Bal, Mieke, 'Looking at love', *Diacritics* 27/1 (1997), pp.59–72.
Bal, Mieke, 'Visual essentialism and the object of visual culture', *Journal of Visual Culture* 2/1 (2003), pp.5–32.
Bal, Mieke, 'The commitment to look', *Journal of Visual Culture* 4/2 (2005), pp.145–62.
Bigo, Didier, 'The Möbius ribbon of internal and external security(ies)', in M. Albert, D. Jacobson and Y. Lapid (eds), *Identities, Borders, Orders* (Minneapolis, MN: University of Minnesota Press, 2001), pp.91–116.
Boston Herald (9 July 2004), 'Trucker's eyes are on the road – and you!'.
Butler, Judith, *Precarious Life* (London: Verso, 2004).
Campbell, David, *Writing Security: United States' Foreign Policy and the Politics of Identity* (Minneapolis, MN: University of Minnesota Press, 1998).
Cooley, Heidi Rae, 'It's all about the fit: The hand, the mobile screenic device and tactile vision', *Journal of Visual Culture* 3/2 (2004), pp.133–55.
Crary, Jonathan, *Techniques of the Observer: On Vision and Modernity in the 19th Century* (Cambridge, MA: MIT Press, 1990).
Daston, Lorraine and Galison, Peter, 'The image of objectivity', *Representations* 40 (1992), pp.81–128.
de Goede, Marieke, 'The war on terrorist finance as biopolitical practice', paper presented at workshop on 'Governing by risk in the War on Terror', International Studies Association, San Diego CA (21 March 2006).
Department of Homeland Security (DHS), 'TSA teams up with American Trucking Associations', press release, Washington, DC (23 March 2004a).
Department of Homeland Security (DHS), 'Homeland security from the citizens' perspective' (Washington, DC: Council for Excellence in Government, 2004b).
Department of Homeland Security (DHS), 'Solicitation, offer and award', HSBP1006R0463 (Washington, DC: DHS, 2006).
Der Derian, James, 'The war of networks', *Theory & Event* 5/4 (2002), at http://muse.jhu.edu/journals/theory_and_event/v005/5.4derderian.html (accessed 19 November 2008).
Derrida, Jacques, 'Force of law: The mystical foundation of authority', in D. Cornell, M. Rosenfeld and D.G. Carlson (eds), *Deconstruction and the Possibility of Justice* (London and New York: Routledge, 1992).
Derrida, Jacques (in conversation with Richard Beardsworth), 'Nietzsche and the machine', *Journal of Nietzsche Studies* 7 (1994), pp.7–65.
Edkins, Jenny, *Trauma and the Memory of Politics* (Cambridge: Cambridge University Press, 2003).
Edkins, Jenny and Pin-Fat, Veronique, 'Life, power, resistance', in J. Edkins, V. Pin-Fat and M. Shapiro (eds), *Sovereign Lives: Power in Global Politics* (London and New York: Routledge, 2004).
Ewald, François, 'Insurance and risk', in G. Burchell, C. Gordon and P. Miller (eds), *The Foucault Effect: Studies in Governmentality* (London: Harvester Wheatsheaf, 1991), pp.197–210.
Ewald, François, 'The return of Descartes's malicious demon: An outline of a philosophy of precaution', in T. Baker and J. Simon (eds), *Embracing Risk* (Chicago, IL: Chicago University Press, 2002), pp.273–302.

Foucault, Michel, *Abnormal: Lectures at the College de France 1974–1975* (New York: Picador, 1975/2003).
Friedberg, Anne, 'Urban mobility and cinematic visuality', *Journal of Visual Culture* 1/2 (2002), pp.183–204.
Friedberg, Anne, 'Virilio's screen', *Journal of Visual Culture* 3/2 (2004), pp.183–93.
Haggis, Paul, 'On the origins of *Crash*' (2006), at http://www.movienet.com/crash.html (accessed 3 March 2006).
Haggis, Paul and Moresco, Bobby, *Crash* (Santa Monica, CA, New York and Vancouver: Lions Gate Productions, 2005).
Highway Watch, 'FAQ' (2005), at www.highwaywatch.com/about_us/faq.html (accessed 12 February 2006).
Jay, Martin, 'Cultural relativism and the visual turn', *Journal of Visual Culture* 1/3 (2002), pp.267–78.
Mitchell, W.J.T., 'Showing seeing: A critique of visual culture', *Journal of Visual Culture* 1/2 (2002), pp.165–81.
Mitchell, W.J.T., 'There are no visual media', *Journal of Visual Culture* 4/2 (2005), pp.257–66.
Shapiro, Michael, *Violent Cartographies: Mapping Cultures of War* (Minneapolis, MN: University of Minnesota Press, 1997).
Silverman, Kaja, *The Threshold of the Visible World* (London and New York: Routledge, 1996).
Sinclair, Iain, 'The theatre of the city', the *Guardian*, 14 July 2005.
Sparke, Matthew, *In the Space of Theory: Postfoundational Geographies of the Nation-State* (Minneapolis, MN: University of Minnesota Press, 2005).

Chapter 12

Perpendicular Sublime: Regarding Rocketry and the Cold War

Fraser MacDonald

Unto thee lift I mine eyes, O thou that dwellest in the heavens.
(Psalm 123:1)

This is an essay about looking upwards. It documents a particular moment in the twentieth century when the horizontal perspective of the European landscape tradition shifted to an altogether different axis – a sublime verticality. This development was not without precedent: in his famous *Philosophical Enquiry*, Edmund Burke celebrated the perpendicular as having 'more force in forming the sublime, than an inclined plane'. Many artists and travellers of the period favoured the view from a precipice; others found a certain sublimity at the base of a towering cliff. But in the eighteenth century, Burke could scarcely have imagined the new aesthetic possibilities that would be opened up by the development of rocketry: the neck-craning, eye-straining, ear-splitting awe at witnessing the propulsion of a vehicle into Earth's atmosphere at hypersonic speed. At the time of the *Apollo XI* launch in July 1969, a million people gathered to watch the event in the back roads near Florida's Kennedy Space Center. A similar enthusiasm greeted the launch of the US Space Shuttles in the 1980s. In the early days of rocketry, however, launches had yet to become national events of this kind. Testing was a more covert affair, with selected press correspondents giving supportive accounts on the latest triumph of engineering to an interested but generally uninformed public. On the one hand, military secrecy was necessary to protect what were flagship weapons projects from the intelligence-gathering of rival states. On the other hand, the whole point of a doomsday guided missile was that it would instill the confidence of the citizenry in the defence capabilities of the state, as well as offering a certain diplomatic leverage in international affairs. In short, it had to be known and seen in order to be effective.

This chapter considers this tension between public spectacle and military secrecy in relation to the British testing of the US-made Corporal missile, the vehicle for Britain and America's first guided nuclear warhead. The first launch took place on 23 June 1959 on the remote island of South Uist in the Scottish Hebrides. One local crofter, whose land was within a mile of the launch pad, described how he saw it ascend 'straight into the sky with a blaze of light behind it'.[1] 'It was', he added, 'a most beautiful thing to watch'. *The Glasgow Herald* reported that the noise of the launch was so loud that it could be heard all over the island. 'Army's success with the Corporal' was the triumphant headline that would have relieved the senior command at the British army. They had, after all, bought an American missile that was inaccurate, unreliable and expensive. Local and national protests had dogged the construction of the Hebridean testing range. Even this first launch – which had initially been scheduled for the Queen's official birthday – had been delayed for two weeks on account of 'technical difficulties'. Supportive media coverage of the Corporal's debut performance was thus particularly important, both for shoring up domestic support for Britain's home-grown nuclear weapons programme and also, more strategically, for asserting Britain's status as an independent player in the Cold War. The sight of the ascending Corporal, it was hoped, would testify to the continuing presence of the UK on the international stage.

As the first NATO weapon authorised to carry a guided nuclear device, the Corporal represents the ultimate progenitor of contemporary weapons of mass destruction (WMD). If the nuclear-armed guided missile has, for half a century, cast an apocalyptic shadow over civilian life, the Corporal is its very first embodiment. But unlike other launch vehicles that took humans to the moon and unlike other nuclear weapons that caused immeasurably greater suffering, the Corporal has been somewhat neglected by historical scholarship (MacDonald 2009). My primary interest here is in the missile as an object of visual enquiry and curiosity. Indeed, one of my central arguments is that force of the missile was monumental rather than technical, that being seen in 'peacetime' was more constitutive of its function than being fired in conflict (see Figure 12.1). The missile's power was represented less by its ability to propel a 680 kg, 20 kiloton XW-7 nuclear fission warhead 40 km high, than it was by being a object that carried both transcendent ideas about the discovery of new worlds, as well, of course, as the dread of nuclear destruction. Such ambiguity – a wavering between transcendence and annihilation, between peace time research vehicle and a Cold War WMD – is evident even in the terms 'rocket' and 'missile'. I use these words interchangeably as there is little, technically speaking, to differentiate them. If 'rocket' is more associated with space exploration and 'missile' with intent to destroy, the technology itself is more or less the same.

The historical significance of the Corporal can be attributed to this dual role. Its immediate predecessor, the Bumper WAC Corporal, was the first man-made object to leave Earth's atmosphere. Originally designed for upper-atmosphere research, the exigencies of the Cold War saw the Corporal rapidly weaponised for use along the borders of Eastern Europe. In one sense, my argument about the visuality of space technology applies

Figure 12.1 Monumental visibility: a replica of the newly-purchased US Corporal missile stands alongside the Scott Monument in the centre of Edinburgh, 1958.
Source: The *Scotsman* archive, © *The Scotsman* Publications Ltd, reproduced with permission

least of all to the Corporal: there are other rockets such as Atlas or Titan which more effectively embody the dual logics of exploration and nuclear destruction, space-cargo vehicle and Intercontinental Ballistic Missile (ICBM). But my argument applies to the Corporal precisely because this is the first time when these incongruous roles were required of the same instrument. Space exploration and weaponry have been shackled together ever since. To see the Corporal on display or in flight was thus to witness a particular historical moment in which the ascent into space represented a triumph not only on its own terms, but as a victory over the Soviet superpower rival. I consider the Corporal as a type of monument and as the object of a visual, even sublime, interest. Not only did the Corporal instill a new vertical imagination – the first images of Earth from space came from the Bumper WAC Corporal – but its capacity for destruction invoked the martial authority displayed to such barbarous effect at Hiroshima and Nagasaki. The historian David Nye has argued that rocketry represented a 'technological sublime' in that it fulfilled certain Burkian and Kantian criteria of awe, moral enlightenment and transcendence (Nye 1994). At the same time, the sublimity of this technology was always liminal and uncertain as the horror of nuclear weaponry was apt to negate any uplifting sentiment. But there is another echo of the sublime at work here. The spectacle of French revolutionary violence that Burke abhorred with such vehemence nevertheless veered dangerously close to the aesthetics of the sublime that he had outlined earlier in his career. And there is a correspondence, perhaps, between the revolutionary overhaul of the social order described by Burke and the reconfiguration of geopolitical power in the Cold War by the barbarous majesty of the atomic bomb. To examine the meaning of Cold War rocketry through the lens of the sublime is useful in that it restores an emphasis on the multi-sensory character of aesthetic experience. This in turn provides a useful corrective, I would argue, to the ways in which vision is too frequently isolated from other sensory modalities in much humanities scholarship.

The primary theme of this paper then is that of the embodied eye as the means of situating the ordinary citizen within the political world of the state. In one sense, something of this is encompassed by ideas of spectacle and spectatorship. Scott Kirsch has discussed how the early atomic explosions in the USA created a 'spectator democracy', where the public were reduced to 'a spectator's role in the management of political affairs' (Kirsch 1997: 229). I am wary, however, that this analysis tends to construct the observant subject as being somewhat passive. A reassertion of the active nature of the observant subject seems particularly apposite in relation to the visual culture of nuclearism. In their account of the Trinity test – the world's first atomic explosion – Rachel Fermi and Esther Samra describe how in the countdown to detonation, project staff gathered outside the control bunkers and were told to lie face down, flat, with feet pointing towards ground zero. Edward Teller, the so-called 'father of the bomb', recalled that 'no-one complied. We were determined to look the beast in the eye' (quoted in Fermi and Samra 1995: 149). The nuclear physicist Isidor Rabi described it as 'the brightest light I have ever seen or that I think that anyone has ever seen. It blasted; it pounced; it bored its way right through you. It was a vision that was seen with more than the eye' (quoted in Nye 1994: 228). Even if Teller and Rabi were hardly typical observers watching the explosive impact of a weapon rather than its launch and ascent, there is nevertheless a sublimity to the nuclear spectacle that belies a passive viewing. It is both visual and in excess of the visual.

In what follows, I explore a series of different visualities in which the Corporal was figured. I begin by briefly outlining the ways in which visuality has hitherto been considered as a constitutive part of the geopolitical tradition, making the case that this discussion has been almost entirely abstract. Vision is used primarily as a metaphor for the unreflexive role of the geopolitical theorist or tactician. An emphasis on the alleged 'ocularcentrism' of Western philosophy in general, and geopolitical thought in particular, oddly ignores the business of looking itself. An underlying theme of this essay is that, even aside from the significance of representation, the simple act of looking is a political act. And unlike much of the literature in both geopolitics and visual studies, I consider vision as indivisible from other sensory modalities. In this context, I use the term 'observant practice' to think about how the faculty of sight is practised, embodied, connective and situated. This theoretical re-casting of vision is supported by my subsequent enquiry into the visual culture of rocketry in which I show how Cold War geopolitics are in part sustained by these ordinary sensory engagements. Lastly, this essay turns to the experience of Duncan Lunan, a 13-year-old boy who was determined to see the Corporal for himself. His story is a suitable antidote not just to the state-dominated field of geopolitics, but also to the no less state-dominated histories of nuclearism (Hughes 2004). This sort of biographical approach is by no means new in geography (Lorimer 2003) and falls within a wider re-orientation of critical geopolitics, from the manoeuvres of elite men to the 'little details' of 'ordinary' people and the construction of an everyday or popular geopolitics (Sharp 1996, 2000; Thrift 2000). The conception of the 'popular' in operation here is less concerned with texts (narrowly defined) than with popular practices, in this case the schoolboy desire to witness in person that which had been previously imagined through science fiction.

Geopolitics and observant practice

In the last two decades, critical geopolitics has highlighted the agency of geographers and geography in the scripting of global space. In Gearóid Ó Tuathail's influential book of this title, he describes the geopolitical tradition as being 'ocularcentric' insofar as the competition between states was regarded 'with a natural attitude, a philosophical approach to reality grounded in Cartesian perspectivalism' (Ó Tuathail 1996: 23). In a break with this tradition, Ó Tuathail argues that the geographer is an active agent rather than a passive observer of geopolitical phenomena. Indeed, the notion of observation as an expression of, and metaphor for, geopolitical power lies at the heart of his critique. Occasionally, Ó Tuathail uses an example – such as Halford Mackinder atop Mt Kenya – of actual practices of observation, but for the most part his analysis is concerned with using the philosophical model of Western visuality, as outlined by Martin Jay, to explain the textuality of geopolitics (Jay 1993). Ó Tuathail's interest in the visual is primarily as a metaphor for the failure of geopolitical theorists to be aware of their own agency in the shaping and scripting of global space. While acknowledging the value of this wider conception, I think it necessary to reconceive the visuality of geopolitics in more specific and empirical terms that run against the grain of the Cartesian model.

Both Michael Heffernan and Neil Smith have been critical of Ó Tuathail's restricted interest in what Smith, borrowing a Bush-ism, refers to as 'the vision thing' (Heffernan 2000; Smith 2000). The substance of Heffernan's critique is that '[d]espite its message, *Critical Geopolitics* is a very textual account in which the techniques used by cultural critics to analyze, deconstruct, and challenge visual media have no place' (Heffernan 2000: 348). He laments the absence of 'any serious analysis of precisely how specific visual images have been deployed within Western geopolitics'. In his response, Ó Tuathail acknowledges that he could 'have more effectively pursued the question of visuality through an analysis of certain specific images as geopolitical texts in their own right', adding that he 'hope[s] that such work will emerge in the future' (Ó Tuathail 2000: 389). This is a comparatively small concession, however, alongside his insistent refusal to recognise a meaningful distinction between image and text in the first place. He argues instead that there is a need to demonstrate 'the dependence of the geopolitical gaze upon that which it tries to occlude: writing in general. The vision thing, in other words, is always more than just a vision thing' (Ó Tuathail 2000: 390).

This last line is significant. It is necessary to move beyond the detached model of the Cartesian subject towards an idea of perception as more expansive than merely the human body as a discrete and bounded seat of awareness. As the anthropologist Tim Ingold argues, 'the gaze is caught up in a dialogic, exploratory encounter between the perceiver and the world' (Ingold 2000: 263). An emphasis on the embodied practice of vision substantially complicates the alleged ocularcentrism of geopolitical discourse and takes us towards the 'more extensive theorization of particular techniques of observation and sight', which Ó Tuathail suggests 'would ... have enriched' his *Critical Geopolitics* (Ó Tuathail 2000: 390). In common with Ó Tuathail, much work in critical geopolitics has tended to focus on representation in one form or another. Even if I am sceptical of Nigel Thrift's punchy claim that critical geopolitics has been 'taken in' by representation, the recent widening of geopolitical enquiry to include matters of percept and affect is a welcome development (Thrift 2000: 385). As part of this turn, my approach here is less concerned with analysing particular images *per se*, than with using such images to open up questions about what I have called 'observant practice'. Having used this term before, let me (perhaps belatedly) be more explicit about what it might suggest.

In the first instance, it insists that vision is, above all, a perceptual practice: vision is an active human response to inhabiting the world. This would be a very elementary assumption for scholars in optometry, cognitive science or anthropology, but apparently less so for those in the humanities. There is a sense in which we have been too tied up with visuality as metaphor – 'the gaze', 'scopic regime' and so on – that we have forgotten that it is also a matter of empirical enquiry. Secondly, the term 'observant' suggests a bodily attentiveness that may not be confined to the visual. Part of the problem with the treatment of vision in both the geopolitics and visual studies literatures is that it is too glibly isolated from other sensory modalities. Tim Ingold, by contrast, conceives of looking-and-listening as aspects of one bodily activity rather than two individuated actions. Drawing on insights from phenomenology, he thinks of perception not as something which happens inside the head, but rather as something which 'takes place in circuits that cross-cut the boundaries between brain, body and world' (Ingold 2000: 244). In this way we can think of vision as a constantly rehearsed extra-ocular competency that is connective with, and integrated into, a wider bodily sensorium. Thirdly, the verb 'observe' also suggests a certain discipline: an adherence to social convention (Crary 1991: 5). This is a particularly appropriate association when one thinks of how looking is ineluctably social in its operation; it is the learned outcome of particular communities of practice (see Laurier and Brown, forthcoming). Fourthly, vision is political, a point that has long been maintained by theorists of art, psychoanalysis, feminism and postcolonial studies. Unlike some earlier critiques, I do not think of vision as somehow more political than other senses. This would require an odd individuation of the senses based on their apparent moral characteristics, a model that the historian of sound Jonathan Sterne has dismissed as 'audiovisual litany' (Sterne 2003: 18). What I mean by 'political' is best described by John Berger, when he wrote over 30 years ago that 'we only see what we look at' and thus 'to look is an act of choice. As a result of this act, what we see is brought within our reach.' The ability to include or exclude something from one's field of vision is thus an act of extraordinary power. To return to geopolitics for a moment, one could think of how a citizen looks at a flag or how one sovereign leader looks at their rival. This also raises the sheer heterogeneity of visual experience (gazing, glancing, peeking, gawking, looking away) which is too seldom acknowledged. Lastly, there is the question of how observant practice relates to language. The geographer Matthew Kearnes points out that while there is no simple correspondence between sight and articulation, we can still think of knowledge as being 'composed of rough bifurcating combinations of the seeable and the sayable' (Kearnes 2000: 332). Drawing on Foucault, Kearnes argues that 'one does not simply see, but rather objects and phenomena are "seeable" or "visible" in specific contexts ... when the [embodied] eye is placed in machinic combination with discourses, knowledges and spaces' (Kearnes 2000: 335). In the narrative that follows, the Corporal is differently visible to a variety of observant subjects, a multiplicity of visual experience that should challenge the conceptual homogeneity of 'the gaze'.

Monumental security, from New Look to VIOLET VISION

> And the Lord said unto Moses, Make thee a fiery serpent, and set it upon a pole: and it shall come to pass, that every one that is bitten, when he looketh upon it, shall live. (Numbers 21:8)

For all my criticism of an emphasis on visuality as metaphor, it is to this I want to now turn. Ocular metaphors seem particularly prominent in strategic and foreign policy. One thinks of the George H. Bush phrase 'the vision thing', implying strategic doctrine; others are specific to the discourse of Cold War militarism. Eisenhower's 'New Look' policy is one such instance, implying a suitably modern course of action that vigilantly surveys the changing security environment. New Look was a new strategic approach which promised 'massive nuclear retaliation', while simultaneously making peace with the Soviet Union and protecting America's economy. With military labour being scaled down from its expensive wartime heights, nuclear weapons were thought to offer a more cost-efficient form of geopolitical muscle. Both British and American policy in the 1950s was centred on the twin pillars of nuclear reliance and nuclear deterrence (Navias 1991: 2). Britain had always strived to be a nuclear power, but by the time it started to develop its own nuclear device at the end of the 1940s, the USA and the USSR had already tested theirs. One might argue that this failure to 'keep up' with the superpowers has haunted British nuclear policy ever since, underscoring the international retrenchment of its geopolitical power with the waning of Empire in the middle of the twentieth century. However, the fact that Britain succeeded in developing *any* independent nuclear capability was enough for it to gain limited admittance to the American stockpile; indeed, this has been the persistent goal of successive British governments since 1945 (Twigge and Scott 2000: 100). For both Britain and America, a compromise had to be found, however, between a policy of massive nuclear retaliation and the doctrine of a 'flexible response', which might include the large-scale deployment of conventional forces as well as small-scale 'tactical' nuclear weapons. The changing security environment in Eastern Europe meant that the American policy, and that of NATO more broadly, was geared to the possibility of fighting a 'limited' nuclear war using lower yield tactical weapons. This scenario, first outlined by a team of academics under the ocular auspices of 'Project Vista', set the strategic context for the Corporal, being the first operational guided missile capable of carrying a nuclear warhead (Elliot 1996).

As Britain's home-grown missile programme was insufficiently advanced to offer an independent deterrent, and the V-bomber nuclear strike force had other constraints, the UK looked across the Atlantic for a stop-gap measure until its own generation of rockets would come into service. The Corporal was considered the ideal solution. Such an exchange of information and technology would be important evidence of the bilateral ties that could be developed between nuclear allies (Twigge 1993). Sir Richard Powell, Permanent Secretary at the War Office, acknowledged that 'the

Corporal problem' would be 'a very important test of our proclaimed policy of increasing co-operation with the United States and taking American weapons when they are suitable'.[2] The 'problem', however, was that, while Britain was interested in the Corporal as the vehicle for carrying an atomic warhead, the USA had legislation under the 1946 McMahon Act that explicitly prohibited the sharing of its nuclear secrets (Ball 1995). Britain would have to be content with the missile minus its payload.

In 1954, America agreed to sell the Corporal programme, complete with 113 missiles, ground launchers, handling, guidance and control equipment (Army Ballistic Missile Agency 1961: 263). Initially the warhead problem was not considered insurmountable. Britain was already developing its own nuclear warhead for a freefall bomb under the code name RED BEARD (a refined version of its earliest nuclear device, BLUE DANUBE), which was thought could be modified to fit into the Corporal casing.[3] The project to develop this new tailored warhead was assigned the code name VIOLET VISION (Twigge and Scott 2000: 196). These colour code names, followed by a noun, routinely had been given to the major British weapons projects since 1945.[4] VIOLET VISION, however, is particularly suggestive: as the active component of Britain's first nuclear missile, it inevitably invokes the spectacular outcome of the explosion. In the famous photograph of the first atomic explosion, published in *Life* magazine, much was made of the 'mysterious violet haze' that appeared at the top of the mushroom cloud (Kirsch 1997: 227). This particular VIOLET VISION, however, was never to be realised. Eisenhower succeeded in amending the McMahon Act in 1958 with the result that Britain was able to receive American warheads by 1960, sparing the prohibitive cost of the home-grown programme as well as the difficulty in procuring sufficient fissile material (Navias 1991: 87).

The British purchase of the Corporal missile required a suitable area within the British Isles for missile testing and training, an extensive activity that was directed to the most marginal corner of the UK – the Outer Hebrides – where space could be more freely appropriated without undue political cost. This proposed 'rocket range', as it came to be known, required a rangehead base three miles long by one mile deep (on South Uist); a suitable area of flat land for a runway (Benbecula); a sea danger area, 250 miles by 100 miles, free from intensive shipping and with a conveniently located and uninhabited island (St Kilda), from which to monitor the trajectory of the guided missile. The Hebridean landscape and seascape not only became a theatre in the specular sense, but a theatre of military operations and the arena of clandestine military intelligence.

For all the remoteness of the rocket range, the arrival of the Corporal in Britain was scarcely an inconspicuous event. On the one hand, details of the most prized weapon in the country's arsenal were a state secret, and managing its security was itself a major operation. On the other hand, the whole principle of 'deterrent' was premised on the explosive potential of the missile being internationally *visible*. The ideology of defence needs to create an image of power and sovereignty that will affirm the confidence of citizens in the legitimacy and inviolability of the state, while also deterring rival colonists and hostile powers (Gold and Revill 2000). For that reason, the apparatus of defence, while its technical workings are kept secret, must still be seen in order to be effective. People must look at the Corporal missile in much the same way as the God of the Old Testament instructed the Israelites to survive the plague of snakes: behold the serpent on the pole and live! The citizen must look upon this very emblem of apocalyptic destruction with the political faith that it alone could deliver them from death.

The visibility of defence was also a question of geography: the missile had to be taken out of the silo and into the street. The Territorial Army toured the nation's towns and cities with a Corporal as a prop to encourage recruitment. A replica was erected alongside the Scott monument in Edinburgh's Princes Street, a primary space of national representation (Figure 12.1). Bryan Taylor, reinvigorating the ailing genre of 'nuclear criticism', has argued that the paradoxical conditions of Cold War deterrence 'effectively *fused* nuclear arms and monuments' (Taylor 2003). Because both superpowers built up sufficient arsenals to ensure mutual destruction, nuclear weapons 'could only be used as symbols of national capability and intention'. In Derrida's famous formulation, missiles thus became 'fabulously textual': that is to say that the referent of nuclear narratives could only be realised with the erasure of narration itself (Derrida 1984). This culture of display on Edinburgh's Princes Street, then, *is* the power of the missile; we are dealing with the effect (and not the referent) of representation (Taylor 2003: 6). The visibility of military hardware, however, is not always that which is deliberately sanctioned by the state. When the Corporal was exhibited in Edinburgh, it certainly made demands on the visual attention of passers by: it asked that the wandering eyes of the passive observer rest, if only for a moment, on the missile. But as we shall see, the Corporal would become the subject of a more determined and enraptured gaze.

Grandstand: 'Rocket Boy' and the NATO chiefs

Space was Duncan Lunan's passion.[5] As a 13-year-old schoolboy from Troon, near Glasgow, he avidly read science-fiction comics, kept abreast of emerging developments in rocket engineering and collected an array of space-related models (Figure 12.2). So when the British military developed a rocket range in the Scottish Hebrides, Duncan was naturally interested in what might take place there. He had even started writing a novel about the British space programme and had included South Uist as the site of his fictional launch complex (Lunan 2002: 36). Duncan's first step was to write to the Commanding Officer (CO) on the Hebridean range, Lt Col E.G. Cooper, asking if he could come and watch. 'I have been studying rockets since I was seven and know no Russians', wrote Duncan, amid other details of his space-related reading and with an assurance that he hoped to join the army cadets when he was old enough (MacNicol 1959). Cooper's reply was encouraging but ultimately non-committal, stressing that 'security regulations prevent me from giving you dates or from allowing you to be within a prescribed distance at the time of launching' (Lunan 2002: 37).

| VISITOR AT UIST—AND THE NAME'S LUNAN |

Rocket boy's 250-mile trek

By DUNCAN McNICOL

DUNCAN LUNAN, a 13-year-old Troon schoolboy, wants to be the first man on the moon.

This week, the boy with the name that fits took a tidy step along the way to the stars when he saw Britain's Corporal guided missile soar into a blue Hebridean sky and streak out over the

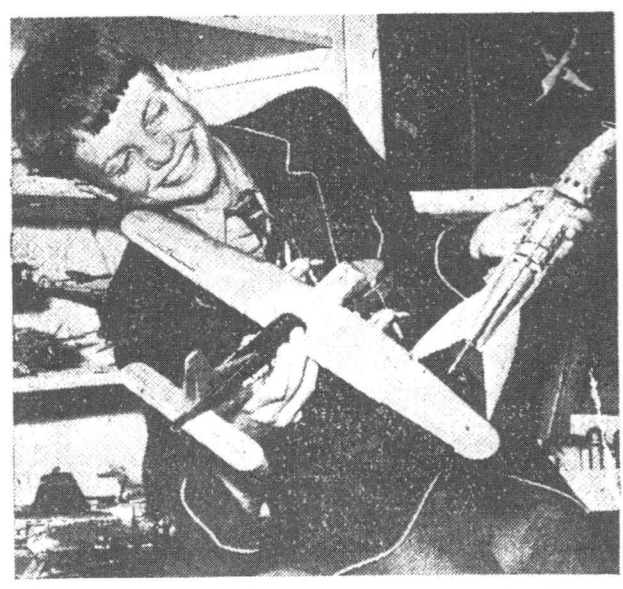

Duncan at home with his collection of model aircraft.

Figure 12.2 News article.
Source: *Glasgow Evening Citizen*, 26 July 1959

This uncertainty about dates was soon clarified by another article in *The Glasgow Herald* that particularly caught his eye. The paper reported that, on 11 July, a Corporal launched in front of Christopher Soames, the Secretary of State for War, had failed to develop sufficient power and struggled to get even beyond the land before its operatives aborted the flight. Amid the details of this conspicuous failure, it was reported that there were still another three launches before the end of the firing season.[6] For Duncan, this was the information he needed. Assisted by family and friends at connecting points of the journey, Duncan used his savings to travel to Uist. On arriving at the Carnan Inn, South Uist, he discovered that he was only just in time: two of the last three rockets in that season's firing had already gone and the third was due for the following morning. Having hitched a lift to the range the next day, the primary difficulty was gaining admittance. His only identification was a positive, if rather vague, letter from Lt Col Cooper. Mentioning the name of the CO at the gate persuaded the sentry to let him through, with instructions to report to the Regimental Sergeant Major (RSM). What Duncan did not know was that, being the last firing of the season, the Army had invited all the heads of the armed services in NATO to witness the event, constructing a special grandstand 400 metres from the launch pad, from which to view the spectacle (Figure 12.3). The RSM was confused as to how Duncan had been allowed in, but decided to pass the responsibility to another RSM – RSM Jennings – leaving a rather inexperienced Private in charge of directing the boy in the meantime. As RSM Jennings was reported to be up at the rocket, the Private drove through another security cordon to the very base of the Corporal missile, with Duncan hanging excitedly out of the window, camera in hand.

'The scene that followed', wrote Duncan over 40 years later, 'was pure farce'. Although the noise of the fuelling process was so loud that the conversation was impossible, they were left under little doubt that the ground crew were desperate for them to leave the immediate danger area and that RSM Jennings was not there (Figure 12.4). When RSM Jennings was eventually found, he was greatly concerned at what Duncan had just seen, but decided to allow him to stay for the launch given that he had already witnessed matters that were potentially much more sensitive. The 12.30 p.m. launch was running late and Col Cooper was busily engaged in giving a commentary to the assembled dignitaries at the grandstand. Being a formal military occasion, Cooper was in full dress uniform, wielding his 'swagger stick' – a ceremonial prop – to command the audience and point to features of interest (Figure 12.5). 'You may have heard', Col Cooper told

Figure 12.3 The grandstand vacated by the heads of NATO armed forces after the delay in launch.
Source: Duncan Lunan, reproduced with permission

the NATO chiefs, 'that there have been technical difficulties with the Corporal missile. Well, gentlemen, I am here to tell you on behalf of the British Army that, having the Corporal in service and complaining about technical problems, is like being married to Brigitte Bardot and complaining about the shape of the bedpost.' This, it should be emphasised, was a quite ordinary way of talking about the Corporal. Carol Cohn has shown how nuclear language often works through this discourse of competitive male sexuality, constructing a particular form of heterosexual identification in which men are controllers of machinery and women's bodies alike (Cohn 1987a,b).

It became clear, however, that there was a major problem. Having been tested and developed in the desert environment of White Sands Missile Range, New Mexico, the Corporal was experiencing some performance anxiety, induced, no doubt, by the cold Hebridean showers that were

Figure 12.4 Missile erection on the machair.
Source: Duncan Lunan, reproduced with permission

playing havoc with the missile's telemetry system (Army Ballisitic Missile Agency 1961: 138). As the delay for this particular launch lengthened and the NATO dignitaries eventually left, Duncan wandered around, taking notes and asking questions. He was even allowed to look through one of the optical trackers 'which brought the missile almost as close as I had already been to it for real' (Lunan 2002: 39). A mobile radar operator, who powered up his machine especially so that Duncan could witness it working, picked up an unexplainable echo, which the telescope aligned with the antenna revealed to be a golden eagle flying over the sea (Figure 12.6). Far from being the detached Cartesian observer, Duncan is encompassed by that which he came to see; these instruments of vision become prosthetic extensions of his own body, recruiting him into a web of military hardware that fostered unexpected visual intimacies with both raptor and rocket. By 8.30 p.m. permission to launch was eventually given, in part because it was

Figure 12.5 Lt Col. Cooper holds his 'swagger stick' upright.
Source: Duncan Lunan, reproduced with permission

simply too dangerous to dismantle the missile now primed with highly dangerous red fuming nitric acid and analine. Except for a 13-year-old boy and his three military minders, the grandstand for this historic firing was empty (Figure 12.3).

The numerical countdown to 'fire' was followed by a 'count-up' the phonetic alphabet – 'Alpha, Bravo, Charlie, ...'. At 'Charlie', Duncan recalled that 'the first red flash of the ignition occurred under the rocket, and I never got to hear "Delta" ':

> The sound was much too loud to hear, just a dry rattle in the ear drums ... the rocket was surrounded by smoke which was turned a deep red by the diffused light from the rocket flame, but turned black as it pulled away. The flame was so dazzling that the missile was through its four-second hover and climbing before my eyes adjusted to see it again ...
>
> At first all I could see was the black nosecone and fins, with the incandescent red flame below about three times as long as the rocket itself, and a thin straight tail of smoke ...

Figure 12.6 Mobile radar.
Source: Duncan Lunan, reproduced with permission

Watching it climb at that steep angle made the whole sky suddenly three-dimensional. ... As the Corporal entered the cloud the flame illuminated a big circle around it in pink, amazingly beautiful. (Lunan 2002: 40)

A more vivid account of the technological sublime would be hard to imagine. One could analyse this description with its integration of looking-and-listening in terms of 'percept' and 'affect', even if this complicates our understanding of what constitutes a field of vision (Wylie 2005: 236). These terms might begin to open up the odd configurations of light and dark, stillness and movement, silence and uproar, anticipation and awe, greyness and hue, from which boy and projectile emerge as points in a circulation of percept and affect, rather than the discrete and stable 'observer' and 'observed' (Wylie 2005: 236). It is clear, I think, that Duncan's attention

Figure 12.7 Corporal launch, 8.30 p.m., South Uist, July 1959.
Source: Duncan Lunan, reproduced with permission

to the detail of colour and motion is too finely wrought to have been seen through a camera viewfinder; with the NATO chiefs gone, the task of capturing the scene on Duncan's camera was delegated to Col Cooper's second-in-command. The resulting photograph picks out the ascending rocket, a strange emissary between the terrestrial and the celestial (Figure 12.7). Inasmuch as this was a visual spectacle, it also required Duncan's body to respond (sometimes too slowly) not just to colour and contrast, but to sound as well as mechanical perturbations. The sensory experience is also, of course, about a wider perception of space. The spectacle of launch is arguably the spectacle of the perpendicular; of diminishing glow and fading sound.

After the event, Col Cooper arranged for Duncan to be accompanied back to Glasgow with a party of soldiers going on leave, from whom the boy was to glean more information about future missile plans, all of which went into his diary. But Duncan's witnessing the Corporal at such close quarters was to become a problem for both the military and the civil service. The Scottish Office, keen to prevent a breach of security from being embarrassingly public, summoned Duncan to a meeting immediately after his return home. Photographs and his detailed diary were handed over, but only the former were returned. Arranging an 'interview' for Duncan with Glasgow's *Evening Citizen* was a decisive move intended to turn a bad situation to military advantage; such a pre-emptive media strike was also able to iron out an 'official' version of *what Duncan saw*, largely unencumbered by the experience of the observant subject himself. That the story appeared – 'Visitor at Uist – and the Name's "Lunan" ... "the boy with the name that fits"' – without any inappropriate detail, did not prevent the arrival of a string of new visitors to the Lunan household in Troon: in addition to Scottish Office personnel came CID, Army Intelligence, MI5 and even the CIA. All wanted to be able to trace the breaches in security to individual soldiers, but, fortunately for those concerned, Duncan had not recorded the names of his sources and no action could be taken. One of the investigators confided to his parents 'that all the technical information had long since been published in the USA and would doubtless be well known to the Soviets: it was only the British public (who were paying for it) from whom it had to be kept secret, just to prove that we could' (Lunan 2002: 41).[7] The rites of secrecy had to be observed for the sake of diplomacy, not because information had to be concealed from the enemy. One of the supreme contradictions of secrecy in this case is that the 'enemy' is assumed to be the privileged bearers of visual intelligence; it is the state's own citizens who must be kept in the dark. Secrecy, then, is generative of further secrecy, even if maintaining the appearance of covert behaviour outlived the original rational for bounded knowledge. As Brian Balmer has argued, military secrecy has its own geography, controlling where people can go and what they can do (Balmer 2004: 199). The trail of besuited men at the Lunan household were less worried about the schoolboy leaking the state's military secrets than the reputation of state security being visibly compromised. Any evidence that the boundaries of military intelligence had been breached, not least by a teenager from Troon, could crucially weaken the bi-lateral trust that had been built up between the UK and the USA as the nuclear axis of NATO.

★ ★ ★

What then can we conclude from this *Boy's Own* adventure? There are four points of analysis I want to draw out of this episode. Firstly, it speaks powerfully of the central paradox in the military strategy of the modern state; state and supra-state power straddle the dialectic that it must be transparent in order to be an effective deterrent, and yet it must also be sufficiently opaque to retain its competitive military capacity. As the argument about what Duncan saw makes clear, there is a sort of schizoid military tension between being known, seen and understood on the one hand and being secretive and protective of visual intelligence on the other. Into this awesome realm of competing tensions blunders a teenage boy, whose passion for outer space reveals the extent to which military hardware was sustained by a popular longing to get beyond a terrestrial perspective, whether it was landing on the moon or seeing Earth from space. There is no doubt that Duncan Lunan's 11th-hour privileged access to the missile was, lax security notwithstanding, predicated on the (perhaps misjudged) notion that his story could be valuable to the military at a time when local and national opposition to the tests was still significant. The significance of Duncan's story is that it reveals a hapless and unsanctioned crossing of the closely maintained boundary between public spectacle and military intelligence.

Secondly, Duncan's presence on the rocket range also re-orientates the question of agency in geopolitics. The sub-field of popular geopolitics has made considerable progress in demonstrating how geopolitical power operates through the domain of popular culture, as well as through the formal and practical application of statecraft. Even here, however, there is a need to expand the emphasis beyond representation (in the form of literature, film, media and so on) to ordinary and less-ordinary events, biographies, practices and encounters. Duncan's visit to South Uist was to see a rocket, a vehicle for aspirations greater than nuclear destruction. The NATO chiefs, meanwhile, had travelled to see for themselves the flight of a missile: the premier weapon in their Cold War arsenal. Their status as decision-makers – or as agents of geopolitical power – is already assured by military rank. That Duncan outstayed the NATO chiefs in waiting for the launch says something about the persistent significance of popular imaginings. Playing with the slippage between 'missile' and 'missive', Derrida has asked what – or rather who – is the vector of nuclear delivery?

> Nuclear war is not only fabulous because one can only talk about it, but because the extraordinary sophistication of its technologies – which are also the technologies of delivery, sending, dispatching of the missile in general, of mission, missive, emission and transmission, like all technè – the extraordinary sophistication of these technologies coexists, cooperates in an

essential way with sophistry, psycho-rhetoric, and the most cursory, the most archaic, the most crudely opinionated psychagogy, the most vulgar psychology. (Derrida 1984: 24)

We can easily conceive of the Corporal as the ballistic delivery system of a nuclear warhead. It is harder perhaps to also conceive of a 13-year-old boy as the delivery system; as an unlikely mechanism by which the passage of the missile is eased into the political culture of the era.

That this is an agency that operates through visual culture brings me to my third point. To come to terms with the power of the missile it is necessary to understand how it was configured as an object of visual curiosity. This is a power relation that cannot be easily reduced to a matter of 'spectacle' – with the linear power relations that this implies – but rather invites an analysis that takes seriously the active character of observant practice. 'We only see what we look at', wrote John Berger (1972: 8). 'To look is an act of choice. As a result of this act, what we see is brought within our reach.' There is of course an inevitable problem in attempting to translate this sort of visual experience into written form – that is to say, into the sense-making space of articulation (Kearnes 2000: 332). It should be clear that there is nothing 'obvious' about either sight itself or the processes which rendered this particular object into a subject for visual experience.

Lastly, if the conceptual starting point of this paper has been Gearóid Ó Tuathail's critique of the alleged 'ocularcentrism' of geopolitics (apparently supported by the naming of New Look and VIOLET VISION), then thinking through Duncan's story has made me much less certain about the traction of this argument. I am more circumspect about Ó Tuathail's claim that 'ocularcentrism is the condition of *all* geopolitical texts' (Ó Tuathail 2000: 390; my emphasis). The observant subject of Cartesian perspectivalism, with its detached, remote and disembodied eye/'I', is certainly analogous to the Olympian (but ultimately unreflexive) perspective of the geopolitical tactician. Geopolitical agency, however, is more diverse and diffuse than this singular figure of the theorist/tactician. Ó Tuathail's critique of ocularcentrism succeeds, then, in drawing attention to the co-constitutive character of geopolitics and visual culture. The problem is that while vision in his account remains almost entirely at the level of philosophical abstraction, the active character of observant practice (which is situated, embodied and connective with other sensory registers) is itself lost. Duncan's story may be about a visual spectacle, but the model of 'ocularcentrism' does not readily fit his integrated perceptual experience of the ascending missile. Nor, in a metaphorical sense, does Duncan easily occupy the Olympian place of the tactician. All of this affirms that there is much to be done on the relationship between geopolitics and visual culture, which can go beyond an analysis of texts or images, to address more searching questions about what it means to see.

Bibliography

Anon, 'Missile firing starts in Hebrides: Army's success with Corporal', *The Glasgow Herald*, 24 June 1959.
Army Ballistic Missile Agency, *Development of the Corporal: The Embryo of The Army Missile Program*, Vol. I, ABMA unclassified report (Alabama, 1961).
Ball, S.J., 'Military nuclear relations between the United States and Great Britain under the terms of the McMahon Act 1946–1958', *The Historical Journal* 38 (1995), pp.439–54.
Balmer, Brian, 'How does an accident become an experiment? Secret Science and exposure of the public to Biological Warfare Agents', *Science as Culture* 13 (2004), pp.197–232.
Berger, John, *Ways of Seeing* (London, 1972).
Cohn, Carol, 'Sex and death in the rational world of defense intellectuals', *Signs: Journal of Women in Culture and Society* 12 (1987a), pp.687–718.
Cohn, Carol, 'Slick'ems, glick'ems, Christmas trees, and cookie cutters: Nuclear language and how we learned to pat the bomb', *Bulletin of Atomic Scientists* 43 (1987b), pp.17–24.
Crary, Jonathan, *Techniques of the Observer: On Vision and Modernity in the Nineteenth Century* (Cambridge, 1991).
Derrida, Jacques, 'No apocalypse, not now (full speed ahead, seven missiles, seven missives)', *Diacritics* 14 (1984), pp.20–31.
Elliot, David C., 'Project Vista and nuclear weapons in Europe', *International Security* 11 (1996), pp.163–83.
Gold, John R. and Revill, George, 'Landscapes of defence', *Landscape Research* 24 (2000), pp.229–39.
Heffernan, Michael, 'Balancing visions: Comments on Gearóid Ó Tuathail's critical geopolitics', *Political Geography* 19 (2000), pp.347–52.
Hughes, John, 'Deconstructing the bomb: Recent perspectives on nuclear history', *British Journal for the History of Science* 27 (2004), pp.455–64.
Ingold, Tim, *The Perception of the Environment: Essays on Livelihood, Dwelling and Skill* (London, 2000).
Jay, Martin, *Downcast Eyes: The Denigration of Vision in Twentieth-Century French Thought* (Berkeley, 1993).
Kearnes, Matthew, 'Seeing is believing is knowing: Towards a critique of pure vision', *Australian Geographical Studies* 38 (2000), pp.332–40.
Kirsch, Scott, 'Watching the bombs go off: Photography, nuclear landscapes, and spectator democracy', *Antipode* 29 (1997), pp.227–55.

Laurier, Eric and Brown, Barry (in press), 'Cultures of seeing: Pedagogies of the riverbank', unpublished manuscript accessed online at www.geos.ed.ac.uk/homes/elaurier/texts/seeing_fish.pdf (accessed 9 September 2008).

Lorimer, Hayden, 'Telling small stories: Spaces of knowledge and the practice of geography', *Transactions of the Institute of British Geographers* 28 (2003), pp.197–217.

Lunan, Duncan, 'Visitor at Uist (or what I did in the summer holidays – 1959)', *Journal of the Royal Artillery* 139 (2002), pp.36–41

MacDonald, Fraser, 'High empire: Rocketry and the popular geopolitics of space exploration 1944–1962', in Simon Naylor and James Ryan (eds), *New Spaces of Discovery: Geographies of Exploration in the Twentieth Century* (London, 2009).

Navias, Martin, *Nuclear Weapons and British Strategic Planning 1955–1958* (Oxford, 1991).

Nye, David, *The American Technological Sublime* (Cambridge, MA, 1994).

Ó Tuathail, Gearóid, 'Dis/placing the geo-politics which one cannot not want', *Political Geography* 19 (2000), pp.385–96, p.389.

Sharp, Joanne P., 'Hegemony, popular culture and geopolitics: The Reader's Digest and the construction of danger', *Political Geography* 15 (1996), pp.557–70.

Sharp, Joanne P., *Condensing the Cold War: The Reader's Digest and American identity 1922–1994* (Minneapolis, 2000).

Smith, Neil, 'Is a critical geopolitics possible? Foucault, class and the vision thing', *Political Geography* 19 (2000), pp.365–71.

Sterne, Jonathan, *The Audible Past: Cultural Origins of Sounds Reproduction* (Durham, NC, 2003).

Taylor, B.C., ' "Our bruised arms hung up as monuments": Nuclear iconography in post-Cold War culture', *Critical Studies in Media Communications* 20 (2003), pp.1–24.

Thrift, Nigel, 'It's the little things', in Klaus Dodds and David Atkinson (eds), *Geopolitical Traditions: A century of geopolitical thought* (London, 2000), pp.380–7.

Twigge, Stephen, *The Early Development of Guided Weapons in the UK 1940–1960* (Amsterdam, 1993).

Twigge, Stephen and Macmillan, I., 'Britain, the United States, and the Development of NATO Strategy, 1950–1964', *Journal of Strategic Studies*, 19 (1996), pp.260–82.

Twigge, Stephen and Scott, Len, *Planning Armageddon: Britain, the United States and the command of Western nuclear forces 1945–1964* (London, 2000), p.100.

Wylie, John, 'A single day's walking: Narrating self and landscape on the South West Coast Path', *Transactions of the Institute of British Geographers* 30 (2005), pp.234–47.

Notes

Introduction

1. Rory McCarthy, 'Rights group hails video as new weapon against Israeli army', the *Guardian*, 22 July 2008, http://www.btselem.org/english/Video/Shooting_Back_Background.asp.
2. See Luke and Ó Tuathail (1997); Campbell (2004, 2007); Griffin (2004); MacDonald (2004); Parks (2006); Stahl (2006); Dodds (2007, 2008); Hafez (2007); Christiansen (2008).
3. For the necessary context to this remark and a discussion of its significance, see Lentricchia and McAuliffe (2003).
4. This bid was in addition to the original UN resolution 1441 which, in combination with earlier resolutions 678 and 687, were claimed by UK Attorney General Lord Goldsmith to provide sufficient legal authorisation for the war. This was a minority legal opinion.
5. See the discussion of this episode by Retort (p.16).
6. See Rooney (2003).
7. Colin Powell, 'A policy of evasion and deception', *Washington Post*, 5 February 2003, http://www.washingtonpost.com/wp-srv/nation/transcripts/powelltext_020503.html (accessed 6 August 2008).
8. Report of the Select Committee on Intelligence on the US Intelligence Community's Prewar Intelligence Assessments on Iraq, together with Additional Views, p.423, http://intelligence.senate.gov/108301.pdf (accessed 5 September 2008).
9. Stark and Paravel (2008), p.22.
10. Many international newspapers wrongly claimed that the flag had originally come from the rubble of the Pentagon on 11 September.
11. Al-Jazeera offices were bombed in Kabul in 2001 and in Baghdad in 2003, despite the station having disclosed their presence to the US military.
12. See Ryan (1994) for a more empirical discussion of Halford Mackinder's visuality.

13 We would go further, agreeing with Ingold that it is simply wrong (Ingold 2000: 251).

Chapter 1

1 Based on techniques first developed in the 1870s by the founder of eugenics, Francis Galton, in which photographs of criminals were superimposed into a 'natural kind', Burson's digitalised images of the 1980s subverted the notion of ideal and racial types, including 'Beauty' (a composite of Hollywood starlets Jane Fonda, Brooke Shields, Meryl Streep, Diane Keaton and Jacqueline Bisset) and 'Mankind' (a proportional composite of Asian, African, Caucasian and other races).
2 I would like to thank Tom Levin for the gift of the phrase 'Age of Adobe Photoshop'.

Chapter 2

1 See Sontag (2004), http://www.nytimes.com/2004/05/23/magazine/ 23PRIS-ONS.html, and my 'Photography, war, outrage' (2005b), which includes an earlier discussion of some of the issues covered in this essay.
2 Geoffrey Miller, Major General in the US Army, is generally regarded as responsible for devising torture protocols at Guantanamo, including instituting dogs for the purposes of torture, and for transposing those protocols to Abu Ghraib (see *Salon* 2006).
3 See http://www.zonaeuropa.com/20050413 2.htm.
4 See http://www.salon.com/news/abu ghraib/2006/03/14/introduction/.

Chapter 4

1 The archival research upon which this chapter is based was undertaken as part of my PhD research at the University of Hull, which was funded by an ESRC Competition Award. David Atkinson and Andy Jonas, who supervised my thesis, are thanked for their support and encouragement in this endeavour. Thanks also to the staff of the Archives and Special Collections section of the Otto Richter Library, University of Miami, where the Pan American Airways archives are held. Finally, thanks to the editors of this collection for their insightful comments on an earlier draft.

Chapter 5

1 An obvious omission from our discussion is psychoanalysis. In relation to the geopolitical, psychoanalytic theories have a great deal to say about the importance

of traumatic affects and their relation to the production, experience and instability of various symbolic economies (see Crosthwaite 2007). At the same time, they tend to reduce the terms of engagement with cinema to processes of symbolic interpretation.
2. Others include the 2006 TV movie *Flight 93* and the TV docudrama *The Flight that Fought Back* (2005).
3. For a brilliant cinematic depiction of this atmosphere, see *Dial H-I-S-T-O-R-Y* (1998), directed by Johan Grimonprez.
4. There is, of course, a great deal of critically informed written material on this war and its relation to popular geopolitical cultures (e.g. Ó Tuathail 1993; 1996).
5. In the commentary that accompanies the DVD version of the film, the director, Russell, is explicit about this intention:

> The juice of this film lies in the information, lies in the fact that I'm taking people's perceptions of this war and turning them on their head, and hopefully blowing their minds in some respect, saying all the assumptions you had about this war need to be looked at and turned over, including the sense of satisfaction you had as a moral victor, as an American, so you begin with these confident, self-satisfied Americans ... So we're basically playing with people's perception of information and challenging that – that's what's driving the film.

6. This scene reprises Clooney's role in the popular hospital drama *ER*, while also gesturing to his role in contemporary celebrity geopolitical cultures.

Chapter 6

1. See Carter and McCormack, this volume.
2. Accordingly, the Japanese government applied export controls on PlayStation 2, requiring that a special licence be obtained by distributors (Stahl 2006: 112).
3. The term 'gametime' was coined by Crogan (2003) to refer to the way in which the 'anticipatory impulse' of gaming closes the temporal gap between experience and history. Stahl (2006: 119) further argues that 'gametime collapses the temporal space between real world events and the ability to "play" them, fostering a news environment that approaches real-time interactivity'.
4. 'Mashing' refers to a console technique that involves pressing multiple buttons simultaneously or in rapid succession to overcome a difficult gameplay situation.
5. From the Greek word $\mu\acute{\epsilon}\theta\epsilon\xi\iota\varsigma$, meaning participation, partaking of, to take part in something.
6. Bush, quoted in BBC news report, 8 April 2003. See http://news.bbc.co.uk/2/hi/uk_news/politics/2928235.stm (accessed 11 November 2008).
7. The *Independent* put the figure sold at 'more than 30 million' in February 2007. Available at: http://news.independent.co.uk/world/science_technology/article2141636.ece (accessed 5 November 2008).
8. This statement appeared on the front cover of *Face Magazine*, June 1997 (see Figure 6.1).

9   In his famous account of the discovery of the tomb of Tutankhamen, the archaeologist Howard Carter writes of the ancient Egyptian grave-robbers he holds in contempt. Roger Atwood (2004) reiterates this distinction between archaeologists and grave-robbers, also with contempt, vis-à-vis contemporary sites, including those of post-invasion Iraq.
10 http://www.tombraider.com/legend/other/main.html, *Tomb Raider II*, in 'History', via 'Game Info' (accessed 10 April 2007). Lara also fights mercenaries, such as the group staked out in the Aleutian Islands in *Tomb Raider II Gold*; see http://au.gamespot.com/features/tombraider_hist/p4_04.html (accessed 13 September 2008).
11 In interviews released with the DVD edition of the first *Tomb Raider* film, EIDOS game developers talk of the deliberate styling of Lara as a female Indiana. For them, gender was as much a question of product differentiation (Lara had to be a new take on Indy) as it was a play for pubescent market-share (see Breger 2008).
12 In the first *Indiana Jones* film, we meet Indy in university class behaving according to the social and sexual norms of the academy. In the face of the threat that Nazism poses to 'global' Christian heritage, he is compelled to become a tomb raider himself. Similarly, throughout the *Tomb Raider* games, Lara finds herself pitted against various characters who want the objects she seeks for their own sinister purposes.
13 Lara is not a scholar in an institutional sense, but does possess extensive knowledge of ancient artefacts.
14 At http://au.gamespot.com/ps3/action/tombraider8/video/6197367/tomb-raider-underworld-official-movie-1 (accessed 14 September 2008).
15 Talk of pre-emptive action leading up to the 2003 invasion of Iraq often involved repeated use of the 'smoking gun' metaphor. While 'smoking' denotes a shot already fired, the gun's subsequent prominence in the rhetoric of the ensuing conflict arguably makes it a more dangerous weapon than any possessed by Iraq.
16 In an email to a friend sent on the day of his death, Kelly refers to 'many dark actors playing games' (BBC News, 19 July 2003). At http://news.bbc.co.uk/2/hi/uk_news/politics/3080795.stm (accessed 5 November 2008).

Chapter 7

1   'Negotiating identity and representation in the mediated armed forces', Rachel Woodward, Trish Winter and K. Neil Jenkings, 2006–7, Newcastle and Sunderland Universities, funded by the Economic and Social Research Council, grant reference RES-000-23-0992.
2   While it was not a theme of our research, it would appear that the barracks-space displays speak of other visualities (shields, crests, emblems, as well as photographs) and other geopolitical scripts (the identification of specific battles or campaigns with particular regiments).

3   'Paul was adamant he would take his camera. This was not as frivolous as it might appear. The rebels loved posing and showing off. If we were captured, it was possible that by taking photos of them and promising to send them copies, they might let us go rather than kill us. More realistically, though, a camera would be a good way of breaking the ice with anybody we met, whether friendly or not. And it did work.' (Ashby 2002: 234).
4   'Squaddie': a slang term for a British enlisted soldier. Although it can have pejorative overtones, the term is widely used within the British Army by soldiers to describe themselves.
5   'Rugsy': slang for rugged, out-doors, tough.
6   'Threaders': slang for exhausted, worn out, pissed off.
7   Bobby Sands, imprisoned in HM Prison Maze, Belfast, for firearms offences, was one of a group of Provisional IRA prisoners who extended their ongoing campaign for recognition of status as political prisoners through hunger-strike. Sands, elected during the hunger-strike as MP for Fermanagh and South Tyrone in the House of Commons, was the first hunger striker to die, in May 1981.

Chapter 8

1   Critical work on the world's fairs has examined a wide range of these events from nineteenth-century Stockholm (Pred 1985) and the Swiss tradition of the world's fair (Soderstrom 2001), via interwar Paris (Gouda 1995; Strohmayer 1996) and Johannesburg (Robinson 2002), to late twentieth-century Seville (Harvey 1996) and Lisbon (Power and Sidaway 2005). Much of this scholarship has emphasised imperial spectacles and visual displays as powerful frameworks through which the public learned to envision the colonial order.
2   There are a number of media studies that demonstrate the pervasiveness of this negative imagery and its effects on understandings of the global South. For downloadable copies of studies by the UK Department for International Development, the International Broadcasting Trust, 3WE and the VSO, see http://www.imaging-famine.org/gov_ngo.htm (accessed 4 July 2007). The figure of 80 per cent of UK respondents comes from the 2001 VSO report *The Live Aid Legacy*.
3   For the efforts of one of the authors (in conjunction with his curatorial collaborators), see the 'Africa uncovered' section of the *Imaging Famine* project at http://www.imaging-famine.org/africa/au.htm (accessed 4 July 2007).
4   The rationale for the issue is revealingly described in a multimedia interview with the editor, available at http://ngm.nationalgeographic.com/ngm/0509/editor.html (accessed 28 April 2008).
5   The live web stream had ended, but highlights are still available at 'Wild Cam Africa', http://www9.nationalgeographic.com/ngm/wildcamafrica/ (accessed 4 July 2007).

Chapter 9

1. Dickson, K. (2002a), 'The war on terror: Cities as the strategic high ground', Mimeo, p.10.
2. Iraqi foreign minister at that time, Tariq Aziz, October 2002, quoted in Bellamy, C, 'If the cities do not fall to the Allies, there may be no alternative to siege warfare', *Independent*, 28 March 2003, p.3.
3. Earlier versions of this work have been published in David Lyon (ed.) (2006), *Theorizing Surveillance* (Willan); Deborah Cowan and Emily Gilbert (eds) (2006), *War – Citizenship – Territory*, Routledge; and as a working paper by the City States Research Centre at the London School of Economics.
4. See Davis, M. (2004b), 'The Pentagon as global slum lord', *TomDispatch*, http://www.tomdispatch.com/, 19 April (accessed 10 June 2004).
5. Virilio, P. (2002), *Desert Screen: War at the Speed of Light*, London: Continuum, p.53.
6. Harris, A. (2003) 'Can new technologies transform military operations in urban terrain?', *Small Wars Journal*, available at www.smallwarsjournal.com/documents/harris.pdf, pp.38–41.
7. O'Mara, R. (2003), 'Stealth, precision, and the making of American foreign policy', *Air and Space Power Chronicles*, June, available at www.airpower.maxwell.af.mil/airchronicles/cc/omara.html (accessed February 2005).
8. Hewish and Pengelley (2001), 'Facing urban inevitabilities: Military operations in urban terrain', *Jane's International Defence Review*, August, pp.13–18.
9. Graham, 2006, op cit.
10. Misselwitz, P. and Weizman, E. (2003), 'Military operations as urban planning', in A. Franke, (ed.), *Territories*, KW Institute for Contemporary Art: Berlin, pp.272–5.
11. Peters, R. (1996), 'Our soldiers, their cities', *Parameters*, Spring, pp.1–7.
12. Taw, J. and Hoffman, B. (2000), *The Urbanization of Insurgency*, RAND: Santa Monica, CA.
13. Houlgate, K. (2004), 'Urban warfare transforms the Corps', *Naval Institute Proceedings*, November, available at http://www.military.com/NewContent/0,13190,NI_1104_Urban-P1,00.html (accessed February 2005).
14. Leonhard, R. (2003), 'Sun Tzu's bad advice: Urban warfare in the information age', *Army Magazine*, April, available at http://www.ausa.org/www/armymag.nsf/0/AA1C74DA9302525585256CEF005EED3D?OpenDocument (accessed February 2005).
15. Quoted in Sniffen, M. (2003), 'Pentagon project could keep a close eye on cities', Philly.com.
16. Huber, P and Mills, M. (2002). 'How technology will defeat terrorism', *City Journal*, 12: 24–34.
17. Defense Watch (2004), 'Combat zones that "see" everything', available at http://www.argee.net/DefenseWatch/Combat%20Zones%20that%20'See'%20Everything.htm (accessed March 2005).

Chapter 10

1. http://www.ips.gov.uk/
2. http://newsinitiative.org/story/2006/09/01/walt_disney_world_the_governments. This article also notes that several Disney executives have gone on to key advisory positions in US security and intelligence.
3. Images are available on the US Department of Defense website photo archive. See, for example, http://www.defenselink.mil/transformation/images/photos/2006-04/Hi-Res/060328-M-9174M-009.jpg.
4. A number of objections were raised regarding Accenture's contract, but for many the most problematic aspect to the selection was that Accenture is registered offshore in Bermuda, not that a private company with links to the notorious firm of Arthur Andersen would be so deeply involved in security matters.
5. See the International Biometric Group Biometric Market and Industry Report 2007–2012: http://www.biometricgroup.com/press_releases/pr_2007_BMIR2007.html.
6. National Biometric Security Project: http://www.nationalbiometric.org/02_training_education.php.

Chapter 12

1. Anon (1959a), 'Missile firing starts in Hebrides: Army's success with Corporal', *Glasgow Herald*, 24 June 1959.
2. Letter to Lt General Sir Frederick Morgan, Ministry of Supply, from Sir Richard Powell, 2 March 1955, PRO AVIA 65/1106.
3. See PRO files: AVIA 65/1108 Warhead for Corporal – VIOLET VISION correspondence; AVIA65/1106 1953–1954 Proposal to adopt weapon system Corporal; AVIA65/1107 1954–1957 Corporal VIOLET VISION warhead requirements; AVIA65/1108 1954–1957 Corporal VIOLET VISION warhead requirements; correspondence. The testing of the RED BEARD warhead at Maralinga, South Australia in 1956 went ahead with no adequate warning given to Aboriginal people in the vicinity, four of whom were immediately killed.
4. UK Aerospace and Weapons Projects, at http://www.skomer.u-net.com/projects/start.htm) (accessed 3 February 2005).
5. The following story is taken from Duncan's published account in the *Journal of the Royal Artillery*. I am grateful to Duncan for sharing his remarkable story, for many interesting exchanges about the rocketry and popular culture, and for his permission to reproduce the photographs.
6. Anon, 'Uist missile misbehaves: Failure in flight as minister watches: Mr Soames reaffirms faith in Corporal', *The Glasgow Herald*, Saturday 11 July 1959, p.1.
7. Lunan, Duncan, 'Visitor at Uist', p.41.

Index

Abraham Lincoln (aircraft carrier) 11
Abu Ghraib 11, 12, 34–7, 42, 44, 45, 48, 49, 51, 61–3, 239
Achebe, Chinua 171
Adobe Photoshop 12, 29, 35
Adorno, Theodor 60
Afghan mujahideen 23
Afghan War 26
Africa
　in cinema and photography 176–83
　in colonial photographs and contemporary cinema 167
　contemporary performances 183–90
　literary envisionings of 169–72
　museum and imperial exhibition 172–6
　scopic regimes in 168, 188
　visual practices of enacting 176
Africa (digital game) 187
Africa in Pictures (photographic exhibition) 188
An African Fairy Tale (exhibition) 175
Africa Quiz 190
Africa Speaks! (movie) 180–2
Airborne Warning and Control System (AWACS) aircraft 148
Air Force Association 71
airmail service 92, 93

airport security clearance programmes 251
Al-Jazeera 12, 31
Al Qaeda 31, 32, 34, 36, 39
　see also jihad; Laden, Osama bin
American Legion 71
American Trucking Association (ATA) 247
American WMD system 71
America's Hangar 72, 73, 75
amplification 119, 120, 126
　force of 117
　logics of 117
　process of 116
anthrax 138
anticipatory tracking systems 201
The Arcades Project (Benjamin) 28
Ashby, Phil 146
Ashcroft, John 7
ATA *see* American Trucking Association (ATA)
atomic bomb, development by USA 69
atomic bombings, of Japan 69, 70, 71
autonomous mechanized combatant 215
　see also tactical autonomous combatants
axis of evil 5, 78

Barthes, Roland 2, 27, 35
Benjamin, Walter 5, 27–9, 36
Berger, John 3, 16, 274, 287
Berlusconi, Silvio 7
Biometric Education Working Group 242
Biometric Identification System for Access (BISA) 234
biometrics 225
  geopolitical implications of 227, 232
  bodies and body politic 238–41
  techniques of observer 232–5
  time and space 235–8
  identity cards 226, 251
  identity-theft 238
  national security programmes 226
bio-surveillance 3
  see also retinal scanning
Birth of the Nation (movie) 29
BISA see Biometric Identification System for Access (BISA)
Black Hawk Down (digital game) 187
Black Hawk Down (movie) 184
Black September massacre 25
Blood Diamond (movie) 184
Bockscar (Nagasaki bomber) 74, 77
Bonanza (TV series) 36
British bomb tests, in Australia 79
B-29 Superfortresses (bomber aircraft) 69, 76
  see also *The Duke of Albuquerque* (B29 bomber)
Bumper WAC Corporal 269, 270
Bush, George W. 11, 26, 33, 37, 39, 65, 67, 68, 78, 113, 130, 275
Butler, David 82
Butler, Judith 12, 14, 41–63, 145, 148, 169, 251, 257, 264

Call of Duty 2 (digital game) 187
Campbell, David 15, 147, 167–90, 250
Camp Delta, in Guantanamo 45, 60
CCTV surveillance see closed-circuit television (CCTV)
China Clipper (M-130 airliner) 81, 92–5
Chinese weapons tests, in Lop Nur 79

cinema
  invention of 176
  and photography 176–83
  see also films; photos
cinematic images see films
civil liberties 45, 212
Clipper Flying Cloud (Boeing 307 Stratoliner) 74
closed-circuit television (CCTV) 3, 210, 233, 236, 237, 240, 254
Cold War 17, 23, 25, 27, 199
  American WMD 68
  arsenal 286
  British engagement in Germany 161
  geopolitics 271
  militarism 275
  NATO presence in Berlin 153
  nuclear arms and monuments 277
  political violence 199
  reconfiguration of geopolitical power in 270
  rocketry and 267, 270
  role of photographs during 153
  'urban warfare' doctrine during 200
  US war-fighting doctrine 26
  WMD experiments 79, 269
Cold War Aviation 72, 74
  see also World War II Aviation
Colonial Film Unit 177
Colonial Nights (exhibition) 175
'Combat Zones that See' (CTS) project 210, 211, 214, 219
'compressing the kill chain' warfare 215
Concorde, Air France 74, 75, 76
Congo (movie) 184
Connolly, William 105, 116, 117
Conrad, Joseph 170, 171, 172, 175, 184
The Constant Gardener (movie) 185
Corporal missile programme 268–71, 274–80, 283, 284, 287
counter-insurgency warfare 200
  in Global South cities 220
  see also urban warfare
Crandall, Jordan 200, 201, 219

Crary, Jonathan 227, 232, 235, 242
  analysis of alternative visual technologies 231
  epistemological model of vision 230
  examination of technical and discursive dimensions of visual technologies 228
  narrative of visual technologies 230
Crash (movie) 248–52, 257, 260, 261, 263
Criminal Investigation Command, of US Army 61
Critical Geopolitics: The politics of writing global space (Tuathail) 13, 228, 272
Croft, Lara 130–2
Croser, Caroline 219
Crown Film Unit 177
Crystal Dynamics 130
CTS project *see* 'Combat Zones that See' (CTS) project
Cuban Missile Crisis 10

Daily Mirror 35, 146
Dancing and Singing from the Colonial World (exhibition) 175
Darfur Digital Activist contest 187
Darfur is Dying (digital game) 187
dark continent *see* Africa
data-mining 34
'dataveillance' systems 254, 260
Defense Advanced Research Projects Agency (DARPA) 34, 210, 211, 212
  CTS Programme 214
Defense, Department of 42, 61, 124, 234
Defense Dictionary of Military Terms, US Department of 83
Defense Intelligence Research Center (DIRC) 205
Defense Watch (magazine) 214
Denver African Expedition 183
Derrida, Jacques 170, 261, 277, 286
Desert Storm, Operation 125
Diamond, Jared 190

digital citizen soldiers 34
digital games
  Africa 187
  Black Hawk Down 187
  Call of Duty 2 187
  Darfur is Dying 187
  EverQuest 129
  GTC Africa 187
  Metal Gear 186
  Primal 129
  as recruitment and outreach tool of US Army 124
  relationship with geopolitics 123
  Safari Adventures 186
  strategic games 126
  Tomb Raider 124, 129, 130–40
  Wild Earth Africa 186
  Wildlife Tycoon: Venture Africa 186
  worldly games 124–8
  Zoo Tycoon 2: African Adventure 186
Dillon, Michael 241
Dioptrics (Descartes) 229
DIRC *see* Defense Intelligence Research Center (DIRC)
disruptive pattern military (DPM) 156
Dole Air Race 87
Donald D. Engen Observation Tower 76
Douglas World Cruisers 86
DPM *see* disruptive pattern military (DPM)
The Duke of Albuquerque (B29 bomber) 74

Edkins, Jenny 258, 259
Electronic Privacy Information Center 235
electronic tracking 201
Empire Marketing Board (EMB) 177
Enduring Freedom, Operation 7, 78
Enola Gay (World War II bomber) 15, 66–79
Enwezor, Okwui 190
Essay on Human Understanding (Locke) 229
EverQuest (digital game) 129

facial recognition surveillance 250
Fahrenheit 9/11 (documentary) 36, 37
Falkland war 42, 152, 161–3
Farewell to the Colonies (exhibition) 175
F-105D fighter bomber 74
Feldman, Allen 168
feral cities 207
Ferguson, James 169
films
   as blocs of space-time 116
   colonial 178
   depicting after-affects of geopolitical events 116
   process of amplification 116
   relation with geopolitics 114
force de frappe tests, in Polynesia (France) 79
foreign urban battlefields 212
Foucault, Michel 239, 241, 253, 274
freedom fighters 23, 25
   see also Afghan mujahideen
French colonial films 177
French Revolution 25, 270
Frow, John 123, 128
Full Spectrum Dominance 204–5

gait-recognition surveillance 250
games *see* digital games
'gameworld geopolitics', concept of 15, 124, 127–8
Geneva Accord 46, 49, 54
Geneva Convention 45, 49, 60
Geographical Information Systems (GIS) 3, 227
geopolitics
   affectiveness of 105–6
   Cold War 271
   of curatorship 15
   differentiating affectivity through cinematic images 107–8
   events as intensities of feeling 110–11
   fields of affect 108–10
   re-scripting of emotion and intervention 112–14
   of Global South urbanisation 220

implications of biometrics 232
influence of visual demonstration on 4
and international relations 104
moving images and their affective participation in 114–18
and observant practice 272–4
power of images and image-making 14
projection of US geopolitical power across Pacific Ocean 15
relationship with
   digital games 123
   film 114
   visual culture 4, 13
representation, performance, and observant practice of 13–17
and visual grammar of persuasion 5–6
stagecraft and statecraft 10–13
veiling and unveiling 6–10
see also technogeopolitics
GIS *see* Geographical Information Systems (GIS)
The Glasgow Herald 268, 279
Global South urbanisation 202
   geopolitics of 220
Gorillas in the Mist (movie) 184
Grande Avenue des Colonies 175
The Great Artiste (B29 bomber) 77
'Green Scare' of Islam 34
Gregory, Derek 168, 218
Greystoke (movie) 184
ground-based combat systems 207
Grubbs, Major Lee 201
GTC Africa (digital game) 187
Guadalcanal 109
the *Guardian* 35, 51, 56
Guernica (Picasso) 6, 7
Gulf War 26, 27, 37, 58, 66, 67, 74, 112, 136

Hawaii 81, 85, 86, 87, 89, 91, 93, 95, 96
Heart of Darkness (movie) 170, 184
Highway Watch programme 247, 248, 251, 256, 260
   watchful politics of 262

Hiroshima 69–71, 73, 77, 79, 270
  see also Nagasaki
Hollywood cinema 183, 190
holy war see jihad
Homeland Security, Department of (DHS) 242, 247, 255, 263
'homeland security' policies 201
Honolulu Advertiser 91, 94
Honolulu Star-Bulletin 95
Hotel Rwanda (movie) 184
Hussein, Saddam 11, 27
  expulsion of IAEA officials from Iraq 68
  SCUD missile strikes 66
  use of chemical agents against Iran 66
  weaponisation of Iraq's civilian nuclear power programmes 65
  see also Iraq; weapons of mass destruction (WMD)

IAEA see International Atomic Energy Agency (IAEA)
IAFIS see Integrated Automated Fingerprint Identification System (IAFIS)
ICBM see Intercontinental Ballistic Missile (ICBM)
ICT see Institute for Creative Technologies (ICT)
Indiana Jones (movie) 129, 134
Indian nuclear warheads testing, in Pokhran Range 79
In My Country (movie) 184
Institute for Creative Technologies (ICT) 29, 30, 31
Integrated Automated Fingerprint Identification System (IAFIS) 234
intelligent munitions 216
Intercontinental Ballistic Missile (ICBM) 270
International Atomic Energy Agency (IAEA) 67
International Center for Photography 59
International Colonial Exhibition 174, 175
International Criminal Court 54

International Crisis Group 187
international law, to protect privacy of persons 60
The Interpreter (movie) 184
'inverse surveillance' activities 2
Iraq
  case of missing WMD in 69–71
  inspection of WMD sites by UNSCOM officials in 67–8
  nuclear power programme 67
  war with Iran 66
  see also Hussein, Saddam; weapons of mass destruction (WMD)
Iraqi Freedom, Operation (OIF) 65, 125
Iraq War see Gulf War
iris-recognition technologies 232, 240
Israeli warhead tests 79
Iwo Jima 11

jihad 25, 26, 32, 33, 260
  see also terrorism
Journais Das Actualidades (newsreels) 179
judgement before justice, anticipatory logic of 264

Kennedy Space Center 267
Khrushchev, Nikita 16
King Solomon's Mines (movie) 180, 184
Ku Klux Klan lynching 35

Laden, Osama bin 25–7, 29, 31–9
The Last King of Scotland (movie) 184
Lawlor, Maryann 215, 216
League of Nations 85, 88
Levinas, Emmanuel 46
Lindh, John Walker 27
Little Boy (U-238 atomic weapon) 69, 70
logistics chain management 204
Lunan, Duncan (Rocket Boy) 271, 278–88
Lyon, David 237

MacDonald, Fraser 1–17, 227, 267–88
Mackinder, Halford 13, 82, 272
Maldoror, Sarah 179
Manhattan Project 66, 69, 74, 79
The Manipulator (magazine) 23, 25

Mara, Raymond O' 204
McMahon Act 276
Metal Gear (digital game) 186
military operations on urban terrain (MOUT) 200
military photographic practice 146
Mitchell, W.J.T. 4, 16, 249, 250, 256
mobile screenic devices 253, 256, 257
monumental security 274–7
Motion Picture Association 30
movies *see* films
Multi-Purpose National Identity Card (MNIC) 226
mythoterrorism 32
    characteristics of 33

Nagasaki 69, 71, 74, 77, 270
    see also Hiroshima
National Air and Space Museum 66, 69, 70, 72, 74, 76
National Atomic Museum 74, 75
National Geographic (magazine) 178, 188
National Security Biometric Project 242
National Strategy to Secure Cyberspace 34
NATO 67, 68, 153, 268, 275, 278–85
network centric warfare 204
    principles and technologies of 205
    urban environments as physical interrupters to 205–6
    see also trench warfare
'network-centric' weapons 210
networked surveillance systems 202, 210
Newsweek 50
The New York Times 10, 12, 49, 50, 94
North Haven (freighter) 91, 92, 93
nuclear energy, weaponising of 69
nuclear explosive devices 65
nuclear strategic bombing 73
nuclear warheads 268, 275, 276, 287
nuclear weapons programme 268

On Photography (Sontag) 47
Open Door Policy 85
Osirak (Iraq) nuclear reactor 65, 67
Out of Africa (movie) 183

Pacific Cable Company 92
Pakistani bomb tests, in Ras Koh Hills 79
Pan American Airways (Pan Am Airways) 81, 87–9
    aims of survey flights of 95
    airmail service 92–4
    flying in Central Pacific route 94–5
    projection of US power 92, 96
    radio direction-finding equipment 94
    use of Navy's facilities at Alameda and Pearl Harbour 89
Paris Universal Exposition 175
'pattern recognition' software 215, 240
Pearl Harbor 81, 89, 95, 96
PEGASE programme 254
Pentagon 12, 30, 34, 38, 69
    military doctrine of 'The Long War' 220
Persian Gulf 11
Philosophical Enquiry (Burke) 267
photographic evidence 50
photographs *see* photos
photography
    abuse 49
    cinema and 176–83
    for collecting surveillance data 3
    and conventions of war photojournalism 43
    digital technology 52
    as documentation of scene 53
    explicit and tacit norms of 44
    Iwo Jima moment 11
    practice of soldier 145–50
    for recording of war crime 57
    relation between photographer and the photographed 51
    sensationalist 47
    for sexualisation of scene 59
    Shahab missile testing 12
    as tool for
        exposure of human rights abuse 55
        investigative journalism 55
photo-journalism 3, 43, 185
    see also war, photojournalism

photos
　of Abu Ghraib prisoners 63
　for digitalisation of evil 55
　functions of 53, 59
　for geopolitical exercise of military power 147
　'pornography' of 59
　for representation of reality 53
　used as evidence 52
　　for doing certain job 155–8
　　for specific military engagement 158–63
　　for visited places 150–5
planet-straddling weapons systems 202
political violence 16, 106, 186, 199
Popular Movement for the Liberation of Angola (MPLA) 179
pornography
　definition of 58
　of photo 57, 59
　torture 59
Port Stanley, liberation of 152
Portuguese colonialism 179
Powell, Colin 6–10, 31, 32, 138
power projection
　and international relations 83
　over Pacific Ocean 84
　Pan Am's trans-Pacific route 83
　technogeopolitics and 82–4
Precarious Life (Butler) 41, 42
Primal (digital games) 129
prisoners of war
　abuse in Iraq 163
　Argentinean 162
　international accords governing 45
　protocols governing fair treatment of 49
Privium Plus programme 254
'Project Alpha' 216
Project for a New American Century 204
psychological warfare 32

Rancière, Jacques 6, 14
real-time surveillance grids 216
Red Cross 49
Reebok Human Rights Foundation 187

Regarding the Pain of Others (Sontag) 42, 47, 49, 62
Regimental Sergeant Major (RSM) 279
retinal scanning 3
　see also bio-surveillance
Revolution in Military Affairs (RMA) 202–5, 208
　urban turn in
　　contestation of 219
　　criticism of 220
　　proponents of 205, 212, 217
'Road to Perdition' 262, 263
robotic killing systems, in urban warfare 212–16
robotised counter-insurgency operation 214
robo-war systems 216
Roosevelt, Teddy 78, 190
Royal Marine 143, 146, 147, 150–2, 158, 161
Rumsfeld, Donald 12, 34, 48, 106

Safari Adventures (digital game) 186
Salon 60–1
Sambazinga (movie) 179
San Francisco 81, 89, 91, 94, 96
Saturday Night Live 39
Saving Private Ryan (movie) 109
Secure Border Initiative (SBI) 263, 264
Security, Territory, Population 239
Senate Intelligence Committee 9
sensor to shooter warfare 215
'sentient' surveillance 212
Service de diffusion cinématographique (SDC) 177
Shahab missile 12
Sierra Leone 146
Sino-American trading 85
　see also Open Door policy
Skyway to Asia (Grooch) 92
social security registry 235
soldier photography, practice of 145–50, 158, 163, 164
Sontag, Susan 42, 43, 47–50, 62, 63, 147
Soviet bomb tests in Kazakhstan 79
Soviet Communist Party 16

space-based weapons systems 202
Space Shuttle Enterprise 73
Spirit of Justice (statue) 7
Stanley, Henry Morton 170
suicide bombers 25, 106
'swarming of unmanned systems' project 215

TA-7C Corsair II (fighter bomber) 74
tactical autonomous combatants 215
  see also autonomous mechanized combatant
Takhta Baig Voluntary Repatriation Centre 240
Tears of the Sun (movie) 185
Techniques of the Observer (Crary) 227, 228, 242
technogeopolitics
  and projection of power 82–4
  relationship with geopolitics 82
Telic, Operation 156
Teller, Edward 271
Territorial Army 277
terrorism 25
  'accidental' or 'collateral' victims 26
  Bin Laden's videotapes 34
  ethos of 36–8
  pathos of 29–36
  see also freedom fighters; *jihad*; mythoterrorism
terrorist attacks *see* terrorism
The Bushmen (documentary) 183
The Thin Red Line (movie) 15, 104, 109, 110
The Three Kings (movie) 15, 104, 112, 114, 118, 119
Thrift, Nigel 14, 106, 144, 158, 164, 273
Through the Dark Continent (Stanley) 170
time-critical targeting 215
Tomb Raider (game series) 124, 129
  search for WMD 130–3
    private violence 134–5
    talismanic objects 135–40
Top Gun (movie) 12
Tora Bora 26, 32

Transportation Security Administration (TSA) 247
trench warfare 32
  see also network centric warfare
Trinity test 271
Tripartite Axis Pact 78
The Truth Unveiled by Time (Tiepolo) 7
Tuathail, Gearóid Ó 13, 105, 228, 272, 287
The Twilight of the Idols 38

UN High Commission for Refugees 240
United 93 (movie) 15, 104, 110, 111, 113, 116, 117, 119
United Nations Special Commission on Iraq (UNSCOM) 67, 68, 74, 136, 137, 138
unmanned aerial vehicles 212, 216
unmanned combat air vehicles (UCAVs) 216
'Unmanned Effects' 216
Unscathed (Ashby) 146
UN Security Council (UNSC) 6, 7, 10
urban combat *see* urban warfare
urbanisation
  of battlespace 206
  global processes of 199
  of insurgency 206–7
  and revolution in military affairs 203–5
    Global South cities and verticalised military power 206–7
    signal failures and network-centric warfare 205–6
Urban Resolve (simulated urban war game) 209
urban surveillance systems 219
urban warfare
  doctrine 200
  feature of 206
  influence on geopolitics and technoscience of political violence 199
  Raytheon's vision of future 213
  robotic killing systems in 212–16
  and US military technology 199–202
  video games 209

USA (United States of America)
  engagement in Pacific 84–5
    aviation 86–7
    Washington Naval Treaty (1922) 85–6
  Full Spectrum Dominance 204–5
  geopolitical power in post-Cold War period 203
  global strategies for geopolitical dominance 205
  military doctrine of 'The Long War' 220
  military technology for urban warfare 199–202
  perception of pre-emptive war 208–10
    domination and control of Global South cities 210–12
    persistent area dominance 212–16
  social security registry 235
  urbanisation of battlespace 206
  urban operation 214
  urban warfare *see* urban warfare
  war on terror 204
US-VISIT programme 234, 236

Vietnam war 71, 150
vigilant visualities, for war on terror
  anticipatory logic 260–3
  Highway Watch programme 247–9
  representations of sight and seeing 255–9
  sight and foresight 252–5
  sight and sovereignty 249–52
VIOLET VISION 274–7, 287
'Visibuilding' programme 212, 213
visual grammar
  of display 5
  of persuasion 5–13
visual technologies 168, 230, 231, 233, 235, 241
  biometric scanning of civilians 17
  technical and discursive dimensions of 228
visual violence 259

Wainaina, Binyavanga 187, 188, 190
Wallis, Brian 62

war
  business of 54
  crimes 61
  grounds for legitimating 54
  photojournalism 43
  photos as humanitarian justifications for 58
war games, and simulated urban conflicts 209
war on terror 123, 226, 237, 241, 258
  vigilant visualities of 259
  watchful politics of 253, 263
Washington National Cathedral 33
Washington Naval Treaty (1922) 85–6, 88, 89, 136
watchful technologies, of sovereignty 250
watchful visualities, anticipatory logic of 260
weapons of mass destruction (WMD) 5, 8, 35, 65, 124
  developments in Iraq 66
  factories for biological, chemical and nuclear devices 67
  inspection by IAEA officials for evidence in Iraq 67–8
  missing cases in Iraq 69–71
  Senate Intelligence Committee's report on 9
  Tomb Raider and search for 130–3
Weems, Carrie Mae 190
White Hunter, Black Heart (movie) 184
White Sands (movie) 27
Wild Earth Africa (digital game) 186
Wildlife Tycoon: Venture Africa (digital game) 186
Wired (magazine) 29
WMD-capable delivery system 66
World Bank 188
World Court *see* International Criminal Court
World Trade Center 11, 26, 38
  bombing of 73
World War II Aviation 73, 74

Zoo Tycoon 2: African Adventure (digital game) 186